The Beginning of Boxing
in Britain, 1300–1700

ALSO BY ARLY ALLEN
AND FROM MCFARLAND

Jess Willard: Heavyweight Champion of the World (1915–1919)
(with the assistance of James Willard Mace, 2017)

The Beginning of Boxing in Britain, 1300–1700

ARLY ALLEN

McFarland & Company, Inc., Publishers
Jefferson, North Carolina

LIBRARY OF CONGRESS CATALOGUING-IN-PUBLICATION DATA

Names: Allen, Arly, author.
Title: The beginning of boxing in Britain, 1300 to 1700 / Arly Allen.
Description: Jefferson, North Carolina : McFarland & Company, Inc., Publishers, 2020. | Includes bibliographical references and index.
Identifiers: LCCN 2020025703 | ISBN 9781476681153 (paperback) ∞ | ISBN 9781476639390 (ebook)
Subjects: LCSH: Boxing—Great Britain—History.
Classification: LCC GV1123 .A55 2020 | DDC 796.830941—dc23
LC record available at https://lccn.loc.gov/2020025703

BRITISH LIBRARY CATALOGUING DATA ARE AVAILABLE

ISBN (print) 978-1-4766-8115-3
ISBN (ebook) 978-1-4766-3939-0

© 2020 Arly Allen. All rights reserved

No part of this book may be reproduced or transmitted in any form or by any means, electronic or mechanical, including photocopying or recording, or by any information storage and retrieval system, without permission in writing from the publisher.

Front cover illustration from a British 1753 newspaper depicts Jack Slack and Jack Broughton in a 1750 boxing match

Printed in the United States of America

McFarland & Company, Inc., Publishers
  Box 611, Jefferson, North Carolina 28640
     www.mcfarlandpub.com

Contents

Introduction and Acknowledgments   1

I. Wrestling and Boxing   3
II. Buffeting, Beheading and the Beginning of Boxing (c. 875–1600)   11
III. Fist-Fighting and the Earliest Rules of Boxing (617–1600)   26
IV. The First Boxers in Britain (1165–1600)   51
V. Boxing and the Duel of Honor (1570–1790)   72
VI. Boxing and the Concept of Fair Play   88
VII. The Puritans and the First Matches of Boxing   107
VIII. Gambling and Boxing   122
IX. Why Was Prizefighting Illegal?   132

Appendices

1. Bringing Back Bare-Knuckle Boxing   151
2. Was It Legal for King Richard I to Use Wax on His Fists?   151
3. Pluck Buffet   153
4. Was the *Caestus* Reintroduced into Sixteenth Century England?   155
5. Oliver Cromwell and the Squire Papers   160
6. Early English Law Cases Dealing with Boxing (1789–1882)   161

Chapter Notes   185
Bibliography   225
Index   239

To Tony Gee and his mother, Hazel Gee,
who stimulated my interest in boxing research.

Introduction and Acknowledgments

Boxing is an ancient sport, popular among the Minoans, the Egyptians, the Greeks and the Romans. It was, and remains, one of the most popular sports in the world. Yet despite this popularity, boxing disappeared as a sport in Europe with the death of the ancient world. It had to be reinvented in a new form in the modern world. We are unable to find any link between ancient and modern boxing.[1]

Many books tell the story of ancient boxing, but this is the first book to tell how the sport of boxing was rediscovered during the Middle Ages and how it was reborn in England. This book describes how and why the many rules and rituals of modern boxing developed. It also describes how modern boxing began as a crime, became the pleasure of the nobility, then became a crime again, only to redeem itself and become legal and popular once again throughout the modern world.

Boxing disappeared from European history with the repression of the Olympics by Emperor Theodosius I from 385 to 393. The last recorded ancient boxer was the youth Marcus Aurelius Zopyrus in AD 385.[2] Although Justinian's *Digest* (AD 533) speaks of public boxing matches occurring, this was in a quote from Ulpian (d. 228) and therefore is not a contemporary reference.[3]

We are unable to trace any reference to boxing in Western Europe from the fall of Rome (AD 410) until at least the beginning of fourteenth century (c. 1310–1320). Even then, we cannot find traces of boxing itself. The best we can do is to trace activities that might have influenced boxing. When boxing-like activities reappeared in England at the beginning of the fourteenth century they were primarily the outgrowth of wrestling. While wrestling is not the only source that influenced the development of boxing, it was the primary source and had the greatest impact on the creation of the new sport.

This book owes a debt to many people, first and foremost to Heather Ann Kauten, my editor, who did a masterful job of shaping my mangled notes into a readable book. It also owes much to Sara Taliaferro, a brilliant scientific illustrator, who created a number of drawings designed to make this book more useful. Without their help, this book would not be complete.

From a scholarly standpoint I owe a special debt to Tony Gee, the British prize-ring historian, author of *Up to Scratch: Bareknuckle Fighting and Heroes of the Prize-Ring* (1998), and his mother, Hazel Gee, who have guided me on the path of boxing scholarship for more than ten years. Tony is a Xen-Do black belt and the preeminent scholar of eighteenth- and nineteenth-century bare-knuckle fighting. His mother, Hazel, is his amanuensis. Together they make a great team.

Of equal value to me has been the friendship of Terry Brown, author of *English Martial Arts* (1997). Terry is a modern day descendant of the Masters of Defence, a master not only of the weapons used in England in the sixteenth century but also the oriental martial arts of Kung Fu and Singaporean Karate. He, like Tony, is a scholar of early English boxing. His gentle advice to me has been invaluable.

I need to thank as well Johanna Mae Reinhart, who has given me a fresh start after the death of my wife, Constance Huested Allen. Neither my late wife nor Johanna ever had the least interest in boxing, but both of them have been kind enough to put up with my fancy and foibles. On behalf of the history of boxing I thank them for it.

This book has been long in the making and owes much to many people. I have tried to acknowledge them in the notes and the bibliography. I feel a special debt to all who are mentioned. They are the true inspiration for this work. Needless to say, the errors to be found in the book are mine alone.

Chapter I

Wrestling and Boxing

Wrestling and War

History is the child of war. War alters nations and the behavior of peoples and gives us our common demarcation points. When we think of the medieval period we immediately think in terms of the knight on his charger. Indeed, H.W. Koch in his encyclopedic *Medieval Warfare* defined the Middle Ages as beginning in the period from AD 232 to 552 when "in military terms battles now showed the supremacy of the cavalry over the infantry."[1]

But this is an over-statement. In reality, the Middle Ages presented three very distinct schools of fighting, which existed side by side and had very little in common. The best known was that of the noble warrior who fought with weapons on horseback: the knight in shining armor. His training ground was the tournament. He epitomized the Middle Ages. The second military school was that of the common free man, the infantryman, who fought with weapons but on foot. He was not wealthy enough to have a horse although he might have had armor, a lance and a shield at his side. He made up the bulk of the armies and suffered the greatest casualties. The third school of fighting, and the least known, was that of the wrestler, who fought on foot and with no weapons at all save his own hands.[2]

Much has been written about the warrior knight; less has been written about the infantry; and still less has been written about the third school of fighting, wrestling, which existed in parallel to these other two schools.

When we think of warfare, we naturally think of weapon-fighting. Nonetheless, the most basic method of fighting was weaponless fighting, and this meant wrestling. Knowledge of wrestling underlay all military training. Wrestling was designed to protect the man who lost his weapon in battle. When that occurred, only wrestling or flight allowed the disarmed man to live and fight another day. Wrestling was initially taught as a military skill, but it soon

Fig. 1. Conventional Belt-Wrestling. The *Rutland Psalter* circa 1260, f.42r (British Library Add MS 62925).

developed into a non-military sport. In this book, I shall focus on wrestling as a sport in order to show how it became the antecedent of boxing and how these both shared features derived from their common nature of weaponless fighting.

In order to understand how boxing developed out of wrestling, let us look at a medieval English illustration from the *Rutland Psalter* from the thirteenth century (see Fig. 1 above).

Fig. 1 shows a normal wrestling match from thirteenth-century England. As can be seen in this illustration, wrestling was a close-contact sport. In conventional "West Country" or belt-wrestling (as in this example) as well as "North Country" or back-hold wrestling, the men would lean their head on their opponent's right shoulder, block their opponent's right arm with their left and grasp each other by placing their arms behind each other's back. Or, as in this picture, they might seize their opponent's belt. Their objective was to squeeze their opponent in a bear-hug, lift their opponent and toss him to the ground.

It should be noted that both men in this illustration wear clothes. They have not stripped for battle. This tells us that this is a friendly bout, played in private or in a location with only a few people present. Had it been a serious fight or one that had attracted attention, the men would have stripped so as to make better use of their limbs.

In contrast to the *Rutland Psalter* illustration (c. 1260) is Figure 2 below which dates from the fourteenth century.

An illustration from *Queen Mary's Psalter* (c. 1310–1320) shows a different type of wrestling match, in which the fighters are using unconventional holds (Fig. 2). Both fighters have stripped for combat. The man on the right is completely nude, while the man on the left wears a light robe. This signifies that they are engaged in a recognized fight, probably before a large group of people.

In Figure 2 the two men stand at an arm's length from each other, in contrast to the men in Figure 1, who fight at close quarters. The men illustrated in the psalter have no apparent interest in closing and seizing each other. The actions they display appear to be designed to attack from a distance.

Further, the way they are fighting suggests prior training. The man on the right has reached out and taken an upside-down grasp on the beard of his opponent. This is not a novice hold. It suggests the naked man has fought in this fashion before. This hold will allow him to twist the head to the right and throw his opponent off balance. His left hand is clenched into a fist and it appears that he intends to swing it up to hit his opponent in his testicles, his stomach (later known as "the mark") or his head. Swinging his fist upward

Fig. 2. Wrestling as the beginning of boxing. *Queen Mary's Psalter*, circa 1310–1320, f.168 (British Library Royal MS 2 B VII).

rather than downward is a much more sophisticated move that also suggests training.

In the illustration, the man in the robe has grasped the face of the nude man, possibly in an attempt to gouge his eye or grab his mouth. His right hand holds a small club with which he intends to hit the nude man. He is holding this club in the conventional manner of attack for a sword or a hammer. The club is above and behind his head and he is going to swing it down. This provides great strength to the blow, but it is also easy to block and if blocked, the blow cannot be redirected easily. This type of blow contrasts dramatically with the upward motion of the fist by his opponent, which is much harder to block and which can be easily redirected. Much later, in the sixteenth century, sword-fighters discovered that "a good fencer using sound technique will not raise the entire arm above the head, thus exposing himself to a quick thrust from the defender." But as illustrated in the psalter, this is exactly what the man in the robe has done. The only difference is that neither man has a sword. Instead of a sword, the nude man has a cocked fist prepared for a quick thrust to the center of his opponent's stomach or testicles. In this way, he can easily take advantage of the opening that his opponent created by his raising his arm above his head. The robed man is likely to be hit before he can hit the nude man.[3]

The man with the robe has also raised his left foot and seems to be trying to kick the left knee of his opponent to disable him. Kicking was part of early wrestling, and wrestlers were well aware that kicking the knee of an opponent could disable him.[4] However, the fact that the robed man has his foot raised also places him off balance. If the nude man uses his hold on the beard and twists his hand to the right with force, he should be able to throw the robed man to the ground. In that situation, the nude man might be able to fall on the robed man, pound him with his fists and subdue him.[5]

The fact that the robed man has a small club as a weapon is curious. Although weapons were generally outlawed in wrestling matches, it would not be uncommon for a man who was losing a fight to pick up a weapon to use against his opponent in a critical moment. In the ancient poem *Beowulf*, the hero, Beowulf, does this when wrestling with Grendel's mother. In normal wrestling matches in England, the crowd watching would have immediately reacted to the use of a weapon and might have attacked the man with the club. We cannot easily explain the appearance of this club.

The Fist as a Weapon

The use of a closed fist was something different. Fist-fighting is apparently unique to the human species. Dr. Stacy Rosenbaum, a primatologist, has recently published an article describing gorilla-on-gorilla attacks. Based upon her observation of gorilla behavior since 2004, she has written to me: "I have never seen a gorilla, nor any other non-human primate, definitively hit another animal with a closed fist, the way we would.... The manner in which they fight looks quite different than our species' fistfights, at least to someone who is not an expert on human fighting." Nor do they use weapons in their fights: "The only weapons they use when fighting are their own bodies." Although she documented fights that left the opponent battered and bleeding, she told me: "I am fairly confident that the open wounds were inflicted by teeth. That is virtually always the case when gorillas fight. Their canines are quite large and can inflict a lot of damage quickly." This analysis is echoed by Professor Brigitte Demes who also studies primate behavior: "Our closest relatives, the chimpanzees, also don't fight with their fists," says Demes. "They fight primarily with their teeth, using their hands to grab you and bite."[6]

Michael Morgan and David Carrier have recently published an article suggesting that humans are unique in their ability to use their fists for fighting.

> The shape of our hand distinguishes us from other apes. In comparison to other apes, humans have short palms and fingers (i.e., digits 2–5), but long, strong and mobile thumbs (i.e., digit 1).... These proportions, combined with the mobility and strength of the thumb, make possible two different hand grips that characterize our species: the precision grip, in which objects are held between the tips of the fingers and the tip of the thumb, and the power grip, in which the fingers and thumb are wrapped fully around the object.[7]

It is Morgan and Carrier's thesis that humans, unlike the other apes, developed evolutionarily to have the ability to fight with their fists. They also believe that fist-fighting is a learned strategy. Fist-fighting is not instinctive to humans; it takes training. As Morgan and Carrier note, not every fist design can be successfully used in a fist-fight. In a successful fist, the fingers are tucked into the palm and the thumb is tucked over the first and second digits. This protects the hand enough to avoid breaking the metacarpal bones of the hand. If the fingers are not tucked into the palm, or if they are tucked in but the thumb sticks out, one is likely to break one's fist in a fight.[8]

Captain John Godfrey (1710–1782), one of the earliest writers on boxing, was also the first to note that although strength was needed, art (by which he meant training) was more important: "Strength is certainly what the Boxer ought to set out with, but without Art he will succeed poorly. The Deficiency of Strength may be supplied by Art, but the want of Art will have but heavy and unwieldy succor from Strength." Success in fist-fighting is gained through training and practice. Godfrey was saying that unless a boxer had trained in fighting, raw strength would not easily permit him to win.[9]

E. B. Michell (1843-1926), an English barrister and sports authority, agreed with Godfrey. He pointed out that without training no fighter could triumph. He too argued that fighting with fists was not an instinctive act, even among humans:

> [I]t must be admitted that very few people resort naturally or instinctively to the use of the fist as a means of attack. Test the matter as you will, by any of the established theories for ascertaining the age of a human institution or practice, and you will inevitably arrive at the same conclusion. Children, in their earliest struggles with one another seldom or never resort to the doubled fists for disabling their infant foe. Scratching, biting and pinching are the most obvious and common methods of attack; and the victim almost invariably retaliates either with the same tactics, or by adopting some uncouth form of wrestling, or by kicking with the feet or knees.... Even if the hand is used for warlike purposes, it is in ninety-nine cases out of every hundred first used with the fingers open. In this form it presents to the uninitiated a much better prospect for damaging the foe.[10]

This view has been upheld by extensive modern research. It takes training to learn how to use your fists.[11]

The appearance of a fist in a drawing of this early era is both unusual and significant. It is the first illustration of a fist in modern fighting that I have found. The upside-down grip on the beard used by the naked man is also of interest. Finally the fact that he is bringing his fist up from underneath, rather than swinging his fist over his head and down, as his opponent is, is new. These three factors suggest training and knowledge of fighting. And the fact that the naked man, fighting without a weapon, is likely to triumph over the man with a weapon suggests the way the future will develop.

This is not a wrestling match nor is it a picture of boxing as we know it today. Rather it is an example of what I call proto-boxing. By that I mean activity that precedes and underlies the development of the sport of modern boxing. It shows that by 1300 wrestling was beginning to give birth to something new. Generally historians are not present at the birth of new events. Instead, they have to guess how things were done. But here, it would appear that we have a picture of the rebirth of boxing activity in Britain. As such it would also be the first record of a public boxing match held in Europe since the end of the ancient Olympics in AD 385, making this drawing a truly remarkable find.

Stripping for a Fight

Although the figure from *Queen Mary's Psalter* does not show a crowd surrounding this fight, it is very likely that a crowd would have been present.

Crowds were naturally drawn to fights of any kind. They also developed a proprietary interest in such events and were instrumental in developing the rules. The fact that both men are using unconventional fighting methods suggests that their fight is a special one. Further, the fact that the men have stripped shows that this is intended to be a public event. In normal matches between friends, there was no need to strip to fight. Stripping was only done when the fight was between enemies or when it was intended to be a fight of some importance.

Stripping for the fight had both a practical and a ritual purpose. The practical purpose was to allow the fighters more freedom of movement. The ritual purpose was to alert the public that a contest was about to begin; to show that the fighters had no concealed weapons, magic charms or prayers; and to show that they were fighting only with nature's own weapons. The fact that these fighters were either nude or only partially dressed was a sure sign that the crowd had formed and expressed its influence.

Nudity in athletics dated back to the ancient Greeks. The naked body was used in military training and to strike terror into an adversary. According to Larissa Bonfante, during the Classical Period of Greece (500 BC–300 BC) to strip naked meant that the athlete was ready to stand and fight. This same situation existed among the Gauls who "deliberately removed their pants and mantles and threw them aside, exposing themselves for battle." Polybius said the Celts threw off their clothing so that it would not impede their movements. Barry Cunliffe, in his analysis of the ancient Celts, also noted Polybius' comments about the Gaesatae in the battle of Telamon in 225 BC: "Very terrifying, too, were the appearance and gestures of the naked warriors in front, all in the prime of life and finely built men, and all in the leading companies richly adorned with gold torcs and armlets." Cunliffe considered Celtic nakedness a type of uniform binding these warriors together as a fighting unit. Whatever the reason for stripping for battle, this concept of naked warriors as being ready to fight lingered into the Middle Ages.[12]

The Unity of Wrestling and Boxing

Despite the fact that wrestling and boxing were two different sports, with wrestling being a full-body sport and boxing being a sport that relies upon blows of the fist, they also shared common holds. The objective of both sports was to put your opponent on the ground. In the earliest days, this allowed you to kill or capture him. In later years it was a clear sign of victory. To achieve this, both sports used the cross-buttock, in which one fighter might grab his opponent and throw him over his hip and on to the ground. In both sports, fighters also shared the desire to trip their opponents. Once the opponent was down, different strategies were used. In wrestling, the fight might continue on the ground to the point of submission or death (as in pankration or pammachon fighting), or the fall might be taken as a sign of victory by the man left standing and the match might end. In boxing, knocking your opponent to the ground was initially a sign of victory, but this was converted into merely a pause in the action, as the opponent might rise and renew the fight. In this way wrestling developed the three-fall rule, where victory was achieved after one man threw his opponent to the ground three times. In boxing the rule developed that a man might fight as long as he wished until he could no longer rise from the floor. But both rules were later developments.[13]

I believe that the illustration in *Queen Mary's Psalter* gives us security to say that wrestling was the prime influence on the beginning of boxing in Britain (Fig. 2). Until about 1550, boxing was viewed as a variation of wrestling. Only at that late date did the public give this new sport a series of new names. These new names differentiated the exercise from wrestling and set it on the path to fame. But wrestling was not the only influence on boxing; there were many other influences as well. The next chapter describes how buffeting made its own contribution.

CHAPTER II

Buffeting, Beheading and the Beginning of Boxing (c. 875–1600)

The Buffet Match

There was no history of organized fist-fighting in medieval England prior to the fourteenth century. Despite a few records of spontaneous fist-fights (to be discussed in the next chapter), the first reported example of an organized fist-fight with rules appears in the 1325 romance *Richard Coer de Lyon* (Richard the Lionheart).

In the well-known story, Richard was on his way back from the Holy Land, which he had visited as a pilgrim, when he was intercepted and thrown into prison by the King of Alemayne (Germany). The king's son, Wardrew, came to visit Richard in prison and challenged him to a match of buffets.

> Arte thou Rycharde, the stronge man, As men saye in eche londe?
> Darste thou stonde a buffet of my honde,
> And to morowe I gyve thee leve
> Suche another me to gyve? [lines 752–756].[1]

Richard quickly agreed to the buffet match. He stood unprotected as Wardrew gave him a blow on the ear (an eere cloute) that caused fire to spring from Richard's eyes and nearly knocked him off his feet. A match of buffets was more than a mere blow: it was a trial of strength between one man and another.[2]

The next day, Wardrew returned:

> The kynges sone came in than,
> To holde forwarde as a trewe man;
> And before Rycharde he stode,
> And spake to hym with irefull mode:

"Smyte," he sayd, "with all thy myght,
As thow arte a stalworthe knyghte
And yf I stope or felde,
Kepe me never to bere shelde" [lines 785–792].

There were rules to a match of buffets. After Richard had to stand unprotected and accept a blow from Wardrew's fist, Wardrew had to withstand a return blow from Richard's fist. As Wardrew stated, the objective of the game was not only to hit one's opponent as hard a blow as possible, but to knock the opponent down.

Wardrew had hit Richard with his fist as hard as he could, but Richard did not fall down. Richard was given a delay of a day, and because he had not eaten since being thrown in jail, Wardrew provided him with a good meal and promised to return the next day for his buffet. After his meal, Richard found some wax, which he used to cover his fist crossways and lengthways with a layer to the thickness of a straw. As a result, his hand was now a solid block. When he hit Wardrew on the jaw, he broke Wardrew's cheekbone in two and Wardrew fell down dead (lines 793–798).

As noted previously, this buffet match is the first example of an organized fist-fight in English history that I have found. Yet the episode with the wax, in addition to the blows on the ear and chin, demonstrates that the art of fighting with fists was already well established when this romance was written. To give one a blow on the ear or chin was to strike the most vulnerable parts of the head. Such blows could knock out one's opponent. In addition, Richard and his audience clearly understood that fighting with one's fists tended to damage one's own knuckles. By coating his hands with wax, Richard was able to protect his knuckles against damage and turn his fist into a solid block. As a result, he was able to give much greater power to his blow. By 1325, men knew how to protect their fists so as to be able to throw a killing blow.[3]

The Covenant

This challenge to suffer blows while making no attempt to defend oneself has a heroic quality to it. It was a game of honor and once agreed to neither party could easily withdraw. Indeed, entering into a match of buffets created a "covenant" between the two men, not just a simple agreement (line 865).

A covenant was a Biblical concept. It was initially an agreement between God and man. The first covenant arose after God destroyed the world with a great flood as punishment for mankind's wickedness (Genesis 6:5–7). But God considered one man, Noah, to be a righteous man who followed God's laws. Therefore He saved him with all his family. God promised Noah (Genesis 9:8–17) that there would be no further world-destroying floods, and gave the rainbow as a sign of this covenant. The Hebrew word for covenant was *berit*. "Scholars are not agreed on the etymology of the Hebrew word *berit*.... But the Akkadian root *brt* (to bind) seems to be the most probable. Hence the Hebrew word would reflect the idea of a binding tie."[4]

As A.B. Davidson wrote over a hundred years ago: "It is evident, first, that the essential thing in the covenant, distinguishing it from ordinary contracts or agreements, was the oath under the solemn and terrible rites in use.... And, secondly, as the consequence of these solemnities, that the covenant was an inviolable and immutable deed." Such a covenant was one of the most important kinds of agreement that one man could make with another in the medieval world. Not only did it rest upon a foundation of trust, but it created a religious imperative that held men accountable to God for their actions. Once entered into, the obligation to play the game was the most telling of all measures of a man's honor.[5]

A covenant then became a solemn pact, which bound both parties. This was called a "covenant of obligation." Agreeing to this covenant created an obligation on both parties involved.[6] The covenant established between Richard and Wardrew was just such a covenant of obligation. It was also a "parity covenant," that is, a covenant between equals. Once entered into, it could not be broken without serious consequences. The most obvious consequences would be gaining the title of coward and losing one's knighthood. Wardrew exemplified the role of the promiser when he stated:

"And yf I stope or felde, / Kepe me never to bere shelde" (lines 791–792).
And if I stoop or fall / Prevent me from ever bearing a shield.[7]

As we examine other types of buffet fights similar to that between Richard and Wardrew, we will find the concept of a covenant frequently used. It is either expressly mentioned, as in the Irish battles of Cuchulainn (pronounced "koo-chull-inn") and the English battles of Sir Gawain, or implied in the Scandinavian battles of the *holmganga* and later in the English duels of honor. These covenants bound each man to fight according to the rules, despite the danger such rules created. The most dangerous of these buffet fights involved the "beheading game."

Buffets as Beheadings

Reading the account of the buffet match in *Richard Coer de Lyon* immediately brings to mind a whole series of parallels from medieval literature. Although Richard and Wardrew hit each other with their fists, the earliest version of this game was played with axes and swords.[8]

The first two examples of the game appear to be in the Old Irish *Fled Bricrend* (The Feast of Bricriu, pronounced "Brick-ru") (875–1106).[9] The plot hinges on who has the right to "The Champion's Portion" of the feast. Celtic tradition dating back at least to Roman times awarded the best portion of a feast to the hero of the clan. When he was challenged for this right, it became a fighting affair.[10]

At the feast of Bricriu, three heroes, Loigaire (pronounced "loygh-i-re") the Triumphant, Conall the Victorious, and Cuchulainn contend for the prize. Initially Cuchulainn is awarded the Champion's Portion by Queen Meve and King Ailill of Connacht, but Loigaire and Conall contest this and swords begin to fly. To keep the peace, Kings Conchobar mac Nessa and Fergus mac Roig of Ulster suggest that the three champions go to Yellow, son of Fair, who will judge who gets the portion. This they do. However, Yellow refuses to judge, since they have already rejected the verdict of Meve and Ailill. Instead, he then sends them on to Terror, son of Great Fear.

Terror is a wizard and a shape-shifter. He agrees to judge, but only if Loigaire, Conall, and Cuchulainn agree to abide by his judgment:

> "I have a covenant to make with you," he quoth, "and whoever of you fulfills it with me, he is the man who wins the Champion's Portion."
> "What is the covenant?" they said.
> "I have an axe, and the man into whose hands it shall be put is to cut off my head to-day, I to cut off his to-morrow."[11]

Loigaire and Conall say that they will not agree to this arrangement. Cuchulainn, however, agrees to the covenant if he gets the Champion's Portion. Further, "Cuchulainn solemnly pledged them [Loigaire and Conall] not to contest the Champion's Portion if he made covenant with Terror. And they then pledged him to ratify it."[12] Cuchulainn then cuts off Terror's head and Terror walks off with his axe and his head on his breast.

The following day Terror returns and Cuchulainn, as a true man, stretches himself out on a stone to have his head chopped off. But Terror reverses the axe and hits Cuchulainn three times on the neck with the dull edge: "'Get up,' quoth Terror; 'the sovranty [*sic*] of the heroes of Erin to Cuchulainn, and the Champion's Portion without contest.'"[13]

Terror challenges Cuchulainn and the others to exchange reciprocal blows, as Richard and Wardrew did. He describes this challenge as a covenant, but this is not a parity covenant between equals. Instead, this is suzerain-vassal type of covenant such as that between God and Noah, in which the parties are unequal in power and status. Terror is an immortal, while the champions are all mortals. Terror cannot not be killed by the axe, but each of them can. All three mortals recognize the sacredness of this covenant and the danger, and only Cuchulainn accepts the challenge in this version. Loigaire and Conall are unwilling to accept the challenge, but also pledge not to contest the Champion's Portion if Cuchulainn keeps his bargain with Terror. Then, when they see that Terror has spared Cuchulainn, they refused to honor their pledge. Loigaire and Conall prove themselves completely untrustworthy and without honor, perhaps the worst legacy for a warrior in the medieval era.[14]

The Feast of Bricriu also has a second version of the beheading game, called "The Champion's Covenant," which dates from an earlier era. In this version Loigaire and Conall agree to accept the challenge and covenant from a bachlach, an uncouth half-giant, who has challenged them at the court of Emain Macha, the headquarters of the Ulster warriors. But after each has cut off the head of the half-giant the first day, they refuse to have their own heads cut off when the bachlach returns the following day. They break the covenant and prove themselves to be cowards and unworthy of the Champion's Portion.[15]

Another example of buffeting with weapons is given by Saxo Grammaticus (1150–1220?). This version also involves a parity covenant. Saxo tells how Agner, son of Ingel, challenges Bodvar Biarki (Little Bear) to a duel. Such a duel carries the name *holmganga*, meaning "island going" in Icelandic. By going to an island for a duel, combatants isolated themselves from interference by others. The island served the duelists in the same fashion as the boxing ring would later serve boxers: it established the ground rules for the battle by preventing others from joining.[16]

Holmganga was a type of judicial duel used when the law code did not provide a suitable result. If the challenger won, he received the prize for which both men were fighting and his opponent was considered at fault. If the man challenged won, the challenger might ransom himself, or, if he was killed, his property was forfeit to the man he had challenged, and the man challenged was not guilty of any crime. As in the case of buffets, only two fighters were allowed to participate. In addition, before the fight, the challenger had to formally recite the rules before any crowd that gathered. The fighters were bound to fight according to these rules and to stay within the closed space of the ring. There was a code of conduct that the fighters followed. Many of these features were later adopted by the English and French judicial duels. Once the two men had agreed to fight at a certain place and time, failure to appear led to public disgrace. The man who failed to turn up was rejected by society and was not allowed to swear an oath or bear witness. Originally, the duel might end in death, but in later fights it might end when the first blood was shed. This reminds us of the first wound in a duel of honor, which gave "satisfaction," and the notification of "first blood" in boxing matches.[17]

Although we do not find ritual beheadings in Scandinavia, *holmganga* duels could be exceptionally violent. Saxo describes the duel between Agner and Biarki as follows:

> At the outset there was argument for a while as to which of them should have first stroke, for in the days of old when contests were arranged they did not try to exchange a rain of blows but hit one another in a definite sequence with a gap between each turn. The strokes were infrequent but savage, with the result that it was their force rather than number which won acclaim.[18]

This precisely describes the basic rules of a buffet match.

Although Saxo does not mention a covenant it is clear that one exists. Agner is allowed the first hit, since he is senior, and Biarki has to stand defenseless while Agner strikes him a blow with his sword. Using the conventional overhead hacking motion, Agner brings his sword down on Biarki's helmet. The sword splits the helmet, but gets stuck there. Since Agner's blow has not killed Biarki, Agner then has to stand defenseless while Biarki thrusts his sword straight through Agner's stomach, killing him. Agner dies with a smile on his lips. The code that requires these two men to stand unmoved in the face of such a challenge is remarkable.[19]

In parallel with the later duels of the code of honor, there developed a strong opposition to *holmganga* and it was abolished in 1006 in Iceland and 1014 in Norway. Young men were too valuable to waste.

Sir Gawain and the Green Knight (c. 1350–1400)

The most well-known of these buffeting games was the axe duel in *Sir Gawain and the Green Knight*.[20]

King Arthur and his court are about to celebrate the New Year's Eve feast when a half-giant, the Green Knight, rides into the room. Just like the bachlach in *The Feast of Bricriu*, the Green Knight challenges one of the knights to give him a blow from his axe. Then a year and day later, the Green Knight will return the blow to the man who has given him the buffet. King Arthur takes up the axe to give the blow when Sir Gawain pleads with him for the right to chop off Green Knight's head. Arthur yields the axe to Gawain, who chops off the half-giant's head. The head rolls on the floor among the seated knights. As they recoil from the head, the Green Knight reaches in, grabs his head, hops on his horse and rides away. But before he goes he warns that if Gawain does not turn up at the Green Chapel next New Year's morn, he will be correctly called a coward (line 456).[21]

Before allowing Gawain to take up his challenge, the Green Knight has required that Gawain review the terms of the agreement in a formal fashion. This formal recitation of the terms is similar to the recitation of the terms before the beginning of the fight in a *holmganga*:

II. Buffeting, Beheading and the Beginning of Boxing (c. 875–1600)

> He calls to Gawain, that giant in green,
> "Let's repeat what we've plighted before we proceed.
> But first I would know, knight, by what name you are called.
> Tell me in truth and in terms I can trust."
> "On my word," said the other, "Gawain is my name,
> Who offers this buffet, whatever comes after.
> Twelve months from this morning you may mete me one back with what weapon you will, though I'd withstand any other on earth."
> The giant warrior spoke:
> "Gawain! Sir, by my birth,
> I'm pleased to take this stroke
> From one of such high worth" [lines 377–389].[22]

The formal recitation of terms emphasized the seriousness of the agreement. Gawain confirms that the blow he will give is to be a buffet. This exchange of buffets has now become a legal event witnessed by all of the knights of the Round Table as well as King Arthur.

The Green Knight's request to know the name of his opponent reinforces this. "For magic," as Ursula K. Le Guin (1929–2018) wrote, "consists in this, the true naming of a thing." And again, "who knows man's name, holds that man's life in his keeping." Knowing the true name of a thing allows you to understand its essence and thus gain control over it. Only by knowing the true name of an opponent can you ensure his honesty. This is why the Green Knight insists on knowing Gawain's name "in truth and in terms I can trust." It is also why the Green Knight does not give his own name, although promising to do so (lines 405–409). As we discover at the end of the poem, only when the magic spell is broken does the Green Knight give Gawain his true name (line 2445).[23]

Reinforcing this point, the Green Knight describes the agreement he has entered into with Gawain as a covenant that he made with the king (line 393).[24] And the knight insists that Gawain promise that he will carry out his part of the bargain personally (although we cannot imagine any other knight wanting to take it up).

> "Begog!" said the Green Knight, "Sir Gawain, I am glad
> I shall find at your fist the favor I've asked for. And you've rightly rehearsed, in the readiest words,
> The scope of my covenant here with the king,
> Save that you must assure me, good sir, by your truth,
> That you'll seek me yourself, where so you may guess
> I shall be found on earth, to yield you such earnings
> As you accord me in this courteous court" [lines 390–397].[25]

The knight has succeeded in placing an exceedingly heavy burden on Gawain, but Gawain does not know who he is or where he lives. This means the Green Knight can use his magic with impunity, whereas Gawain is unable to gage his strength, power and purpose. Right away, Gawain challenges him on this very point:

> "I don't know your dwelling, by Him I hold dearest.
> Nor do I know you, knight—your name or your court.
> State both of these truly; tell me your title,
> And I'll wear out my wits to wend there that day;
> I swear to it, sir, by the truth of my soul" [lines 398–404].[26]

The Green Knight has entrapped Gawain in a bout of buffets only the knight can win. This is not the case of two men equally matched, standing toe-to-toe hitting each other in sequence with the strongest man winning, as in the case of Richard and Wardrew or Agner and Bodvar Biarki. Nor is this a case, as with Cuchulainn, where one party, admittedly contesting with a wizard, gains a prize he values. There is no prize to be given to Gawain. The only reward he can look forward to is death at the hand of an immortal. And yet Gawain willingly enters into the covenant to preserve the prestige of King Arthur and the Round Table. This is an unfair fight, and because it is so manifestly unfair, it is heroic.

After traveling the length of England Gawain arrives at a remote castle on Christmas Eve. There he is welcomed by the lord of the castle, his wife and an old crone. He learns that the dwelling of the Green Knight is nearby, and on New Year's Day, wearing a protective sash of green lace given to him by the wife of the lord, along with his armor, Gawain sets forth to find the Green Chapel. After directing Gawain to the chapel, his guide refuses to go further, after warning Gawain to turn back and not continue. The chapel proves to be a hollow, over-grown hummock. This reminds us of the Sidhe, the fairy mounds of Ireland. These were enchanted spots where magic met men.[27]

Gawain calls out to the knight. The Green Knight appears with a giant axe and promises to repay Gawain the blow they agreed to in the covenant last year. As the axe descends, Gawain flinches. The knight stops his blow and reproves him: "My head fell at my feet, but I never flinched / While you, unhurt, hunker down, quailing at heart" (lines 2276–2277).[28]

Gawain admits his error and says that he will stand stoutly this time and accept the blow, even though he notes that if his head should bounce on the ground, as did the head of the Green Knight, it cannot be replaced. The Green Knight raised the axe again and this time Gawain does not flinch. But again the knight stops short of killing him, and this time praises him. This makes Gawain angry and he urges the knight to finish it. The third time, the knight raises his axe and lets it down gently, only nicking Gawain's neck before sinking it into the ground.

Seeing his blood spill on the ground, Gawain immediately jumps away, puts his helmet on and prepares to fight for his life: "I've suffered your stroke—stood still, without strife—if you offer another, I'll amply requite it" (lines 2323-2324). The knight tells him that had he wanted to deliver a powerful buffet he could have, but as Gawain has been true to him, he chose not to do so. Gawain received a nick for not telling the knight about the green lace the lady of the castle had given him as protection.

Gawain is embarrassed to have the knight discover he has been hiding the green sash and recognizes his error. He keeps the sash to remind him of his failure. He takes his leave of the knight, but before he does he again asks the true name of the knight. This time he gets a true answer: the knight's name is Bertilak de Hautdesert and he has been transformed by the old crone at the court, Morgan la Fay (Arthur's half-sister and a famous witch), into the Green Knight. He had been sent to test the quality of the knights of the Round Table.[29]

When Gawain returns to Arthur's court he shows the sash as an emblem of his shame, but Arthur requires every member of the Round Table to have a similar sash made with the words *Hony Soyt Qui Mal Pence* (shame to those who think evil) on it and to wear the sash. Thus begins the Order of the Garter.

This is a highly complicated tale, but it falls into the category we have already discovered. It parallels the earliest version of the Irish story. It begins with a challenge to fight. This challenge is accepted and becomes a covenant that is binding to death. Gawain is given a chance to strike the first buffet with the second to come a year later at a place of the knight's choosing. Unlike a buffet match between equals, this match is unequal and as a result, for dramatic effect, the immortal does not take the life of the mortal. This mimics the situation in the Irish buffet matches of Cuchulainn.

There are a series of other tales with this same strategy, although none as elaborate nor as wonderful as this one. However, it is not necessary for our purposes to discuss those in such detail.[30] Most of these tales have some but not all of the features of *Sir Gawain and the Green Knight*. Many have the challenge, many use weapons (axes, swords and spears) to attack and/or decapitate the challenger, in all Gawain (or Lancelot in one version) survivs the test and returns to King Arthur's court to the delight of his companions.

In only one version of this tale, *The Turk and Sir Gawain*, do the fighters use fists as did King Richard and Wardrew. In this tale (which dates from about 1500) the Turk also describes his challenge as a buffet: "Is there any will, as a brother, / To give a buffet and take another?" (lines 16-17).[31]

Although the manuscript is defective, it appears that Gawain has entered into a covenant with the Turk before he delivers his buffet to him. However, instead of returning a buffet to Gawain, the Turk forces him to go with him on a quest. The tale takes many strange turns before it comes to an absurd conclusion: instead of returning his buffet with his fist, the Turk demands that Gawain decapitate him with a sword. When Gawain does cut off his head, the Turk is turned into a Christian knight named Sir Gromer, whom King Arthur ultimately makes the king of the Isle of Man. But as absurd as its end is, this romance does demonstrate that knights could still buffet their opponents with their fists at the beginning of the sixteenth century.

A Diversion into Latin, French and English

The French phrase *Honi soit qui mal y pense* ("Shame on him who thinks evil of it," the motto of the Order of the Garter), reminds us that England in the late Middle Ages was a land of many languages. The Anglo-Saxons (c. 450–1066) wrote and spoke a language (which we now describe as Anglo-Saxon or Old English) that they had brought with them from northern Germany, Denmark and southern Sweden, the land of Beowulf.

The Anglo-Saxons ruled England under constant threat of repeated invasions from the Danes and the Norse. They succeeded in driving them off until the Norman invasion of 1066 brought an army of converted Vikings to England. The Normans originally spoke Old Norse, but by the time of the conquest, they spoke Old French (*Romanz*). Both groups (Anglo-Saxon and Norman) worshiped in churches where the language spoken was rusticated Latin.

The Anglo-Saxon culture was destroyed by the Norman Conquest of 1066. After that date there were three main spoken languages in England: Latin, French and English. Of the three, English was spoken by the largest number of people, yet it was the least important.

> From being a language of high status, relatively standardised in written form by scribal training, English fell into lower esteem beneath both Latin and French as written languages. Lacking any centralised authority to legislate its writing in standard form, English began to be written individually by scribes in their own local dialects, employing the skills they had learned for rendering Latin and French.[32]

French became the basic spoken language, while Latin became the language of law.[33]

Anglo-Saxon was modified into Middle English which became the language of the peasants, while Norman French and Medieval Latin became the languages of the aristocracy and the educated classes.

Once the Normans had destroyed the Anglo-Saxon culture, they had to rebuild. Unlike the Anglo-Saxons, who had an extensive written culture, the Normans had no written language of their own when they settled in England.[34] As a result, they came to rely upon the only surviving educated class, conti-

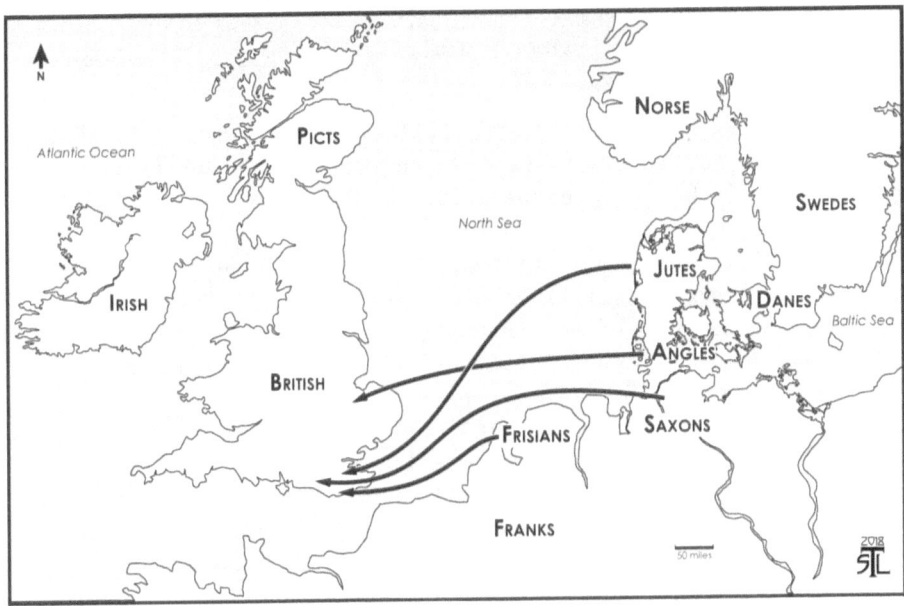

Fig. 3. The Peoples of the Anglo-Saxon Invasion of England, circa AD 450–550 (by Sara Taliaferro).

nental churchmen, who wrote and spoke Latin. This caused the Normans to adopt Latin as their literary language and, as previously noted, the language of their law. Court documents, which formerly were written in Anglo-Saxon, were now written in Latin.[35] The same was true of the first law treatises, those of Ranulf de Glanvill (1187–1189) and Henri de Bracton (c. 1260). Latin had become the language of law and education. It also became the literary language, as we can see in Geoffrey of Monmouth's *Historia regnum Britanniae* (c. 1135) and the *Gesta Herewardi* (c. 1109–1174).

This made religion, law and literature captives of the clergy. Any man who wished to aspire to power in England needed to know Latin for reading and French for speaking. But, as M.T. Clanchy tells us, "for the Norman conquerors, Latin not French was the indispensable language of lordship and management."[36]

Latin was the language of the educated. French became the spoken language of the elite, and English became the language of the conquered. As Robert of Gloucester was to write, circa 1260–1300, looking back at this period:

> Thus came, lo! England into Normandy's hand. And the Normans did not know how to speak any but their own speech and spoke French as they did at home, and also taught their children. So that high men of this land, that come from

[noble] blood, had their speech taken from them. For unless a man knows French, men esteem him little. But the low men hold to English and to their own speech yet [lines 7537–7543].[37]

Norman French became the language of the cities and the court. It became the language of the nobility, the aristocracy, and anyone who aspired to be like them. English remained the language of the countryside and the peasant.[38]

By the beginning of the fourteenth century French was displacing Latin in court, always the most conservative area of society. In 1309 "Law" French became the language of legal documents and of parliament (the word itself was French). It continued in use up to 1433, after which it was gradually replaced by English.[39]

Around 1300, English began to reassert itself. While French was replacing Latin in law, it was being replaced by Middle English in literature. In part, this change was due to the Hundred Years' War (1337–1453) between England and France. When your own language has been denied, it is hard to love the language of your enemy. The revival of English was also due in part to the fact that the Anglo-Norman nobility of England had lost their holdings in France after 1250. This forced them to live exclusively in England. As a result the aristocracy now began speaking English themselves. This is shown by the words of a romance written circa 1325 in Middle English called *Arthur and Merlin*:

> Right it is that English people, English understand,
> That was born in England.
> Some gentlemen use French
> But everyone knows English.
> Many a noble have I seen
> That could not speak French.[40]

The fourteenth century saw an efflorescence of English literature such as *Richard Coer de Lyon* (1325), *Sir Gawain and the Green Knight* (c. 1350–1400), *Piers Plowman* (1370–1390), and above all, Geoffrey Chaucer (1342–1400). Even though English-language literature was an expression of the vitality of the English society itself, it was still a literature of the aristocracy and the educated. It was only in the fifteenth century, with the Parliament of 1422 that we begin to find English used in legal documents. By 1489 French finally ceased to be used in Parliament. By 1500, English had become once more the language of most Englishmen living in England. And it was only during the sixteenth century that we first began to hear the voices of the peasants and the poor.[41]

But why does all of this matter to our investigation of boxing? There are several points to be made:

(1) Fist-fighting, in contrast to weapon-fighting, developed first among the lowest level of society and gradually spread to the aristocracy. We saw the beginnings of this in the earlier illustration from *Queen Mary's Psalter*.

(2) The peasant farmers spoke English and lived in the countryside. Although they were the first to give names to this new activity of competitive fist-fighting (which we now call "boxing"), since they could not write they were voiceless to the historian. The words they used were held in abeyance until such time as they could be recognized in literature.

(3) As fist-fighting was adopted by the aristocracy, the names that they gave this new activity were French. Since they were literate, the names they used for fist-fighting were the first recognized in written documents. This is why when King Richard and Wardrew fought with their fists circa 1325 the word they used was French: "buffeting." The names given by the common man to fist-fighting do not appear in writing until 1530 or later.

(4) The new names describing competitive fist-fighting came both from the countryside and the city. They reveal that the common English-speaking populace in the countryside and the aristocratic French-speaking populace from the city both had their part in developing the sport of boxing. To properly understand the beginning of boxing in England, we need to realize that the sport had to cross the linguistic barrier between French and English, as well as the social barrier between the common man and the aristocracy. This is why we needed to make this excursus into the languages of England.

From Buffeting to Boxing

To buffet was a French phrase used to describe an English action. But how old was the contest of buffets? The romance of *Richard Coer de Lyon* dates from 1325. Saxo Grammaticus was writing about 1200. Nonetheless, Saxo speaks of the rules of this buffeting contest being established in "the days of old." The earliest version of buffeting in the *Feast of Bricriu* seems to be that in which Loigaire and Conall agreed to the covenant with the bachlach and then broke their word when it came their turn to be beheaded. This story may date from the end of the ninth century (c. AD 875). How far back in time this strategy of exchanging reciprocal blows or buffets goes we do not know. According to Roger Sherman Loomis, the beheading game was part of an ancient vegetation myth. This takes us back to Sir James Frazer's voluminous *The Golden Bough* and the beginning of myth itself.[42]

We have also seen that buffet changed its meaning from a blow with a weapon in the ninth century to a blow with a fist in the sixteenth century. These two meanings remained in parallel use until the end of the sixteenth century. Indeed, the greatest poets of the Elizabethan Age, Edmund Spenser (1552–1599) and William Shakespeare (1564–1616), were able to use the same word in opposing ways. Spenser used buffet to mean a blow from a sword or a weapon, while Shakespeare used buffet to mean a blow from a fist.

Gradually the references to buffets with weapons faded and references to fist-fighting prevailed. As early as the beginning of the 1500s, William Horman (1440–1535), headmaster at both Eton and Winchester, was teaching his students Latin grammar by using sentences like the following: "He gave hym a scornefull buffette (*Contemtim ei colophum incussi*t)," "He gaue hym a blowe on the mouthe (*Os eius pugno perstrinxit*)," and "He came home with a face all to bounced (*Domum reuersus est facie contuse*)." For Horman and his students, a buffet now meant a blow with a fist and, by extension, a fist-fight.[43]

Still, as vigorous as Horman's students might have been, a fist-fight was not a boxing match. Fist-fighting needed to have rules to become the sport of boxing. This is what makes King Richard's buffet match so important: it had rules. But there were two things different about King Richard's bout of buffets and a boxing match. The first was that buffet matches were arranged so that, as Saxo Grammaticus put it, "they did not try to exchange a rain of blows but hit one another in a definite sequence with a gap between each turn." As a result, "the strokes were infrequent but savage, with the result that it was their force rather than number which won acclaim."[44]

Boxing, as it has come down to us, is the opposite of this. Although it had the same goal as buffets, which was to knock your opponent to the ground, in boxing it was the multiplicity of blows that typically drove one's opponent to the floor and won the match. Boxing adopted the goal of the buffet match, but it also adopted the strategy of the freelance fist-fight engaged in by William Horman's students in 1519. The measured blows of the buffets match have not survived in boxing.

The second difference was the nature and class of the buffeter. Wardrew was the son of the King of Germany, while Richard was King of England. Later, circa 1500, we encounter Sir Gawain and the Turk, whom we subsequently learn becomes the King of the Isle of Man. Around 1600, Shakespeare has King Henry V imagine that he could win his wife by buffeting for her (*Henry V*, Act V, scene ii, lines 136–142 [1599]), and he portrays Marc Antony engaging in buffet matches with "knaves that smells of sweat" in the street (*Antony and Cleopatra*, Act I, scene iv, lines 20–22 [1606–1607]).

Marc Antony is a noble, but his opponents are not. We have seen that prior to 1600, buffeting was a sport suitable to the nobility. But when Marc Antony begins to reel in the streets buffeting with knaves that smell of sweat, something new is being described. We believe that Shakespeare is describing something like the buffeting matches of William Horman's schoolboys of a century earlier. If that is so, Marc Antony is engaged a fist-fight in which there are many blows being exchanged back and forth before someone gives up. This was not a sport suitable for the nobility. By 1600, buffeting was beginning to change to boxing.

Possible Antecedents of Boxing

Although we have been able to trace buffeting back to the ninth century, we cannot do this with boxing. There is no link between ancient boxing and English boxing. Nor, as mentioned, is there any link between the boxing described in Saxo Grammaticus and English boxing.[45] It has been argued that St. Bernardine invented boxing in Siena, Italy around the year 1200 in order to reduce the number of fatal conflicts in the city. However, since St. Bernardine was not born until 1380, this attribution appears to be in error.[46] While the Chinese had a type of boxing, there was no contact between Chinese and English boxing until the late nineteenth century. Just recently it was brought to my attention that fist-fights were being carried on in Kievan Russia circa 1274. But there is no clear contact between Russian fist-fighting and English boxing prior to the twentieth century. The sport of modern boxing is, to the best of our knowledge, a purely English invention.[47]

We have indications that by 1600 the noble exercise of buffets was being converted into the peasant pleasures of boxing. As we will see in the following chapter, this exercise of fist-fighting, which was beginning to be called boxing, had been growing like a weed under the feet of the nobility unrecognized. And just when it appeared ready to burst forth to public view and be adopted by the nobility it was deflected by the duel of honor and the "Code of Courtesy." It would take another 80 years after 1600 before boxing could come out of the shadows and be seen in public.

Chapter III

Fist-Fighting and the Earliest Rules of Boxing (617–1600)

The Beginning of Fist-Fighting in England

Wrestling, both as a military exercise and as a sport, had an extensive history in medieval England. Fist-fighting did not. Organized fist-fighting with rules only began with the story of the buffet match between King Richard and Prince Wardrew in 1325. It is difficult to find examples of fists being used as weapons in England before that. This raises the question: When and how did fist-fighting begin in England?

With the fall of the Roman Empire in AD 410, the history of Britain entered a new chapter. Most of the old ways disappeared and a new civilization was born. Modern Britain was built on an Anglo-Saxon base.

The word fist *(fyst)* is Anglo-Saxon. There are only eighteen places (excluding duplicates) where *fyst* is used in Anglo-Saxon literature. And there is only one reference to the contemporary use of fists in Anglo-Saxon society. *The Laws of Aethelberht* (ante 617) decreed that if a man hit another on the nose with his fist he should pay three shillings. Although this tells us that fists were being used in fights, fist-fights were not common.[1]

We next find this type of fighting after the Norman Conquest in the *Gesta Herewardi* (c. 1109–1174). Hereward, an Anglo-Saxon freedom-fighter, disguised himself and went into the camp of the Norman, William the Conqueror, to reconnoiter. While there, one of the cooks hit Hereward a blow with his fist, then "Hereward hit him back under the ear so that he fell to the ground insensible, as if he were dead." Hereward's use of a blow to the ear is the first recorded example of an "ear cloute" in English literature. This is the only other reference to fist-fighting in England that I have found prior to the thirteenth century.[2]

Around the year 1200, fists-fights begin to reappear in the literature. In Layaman's *Brut* (1199–1225) a massive fight broke out at King Arthur's Christmas feast as men jostled for precedence. Since weapons could not be taken to the feast, first bread was thrown, then wine and finally fists were thrown. This unseemly behavior had a good outcome however. This fist-fight led to the creation of the Round Table, where all could have equal precedence in seating.[3]

In 1250 Boniface of Savoy, a new French Archbishop of Canterbury, paid a visit to St. Bartholomew's Priory outside the walls of London. He was met by the subprior as the prior was out of town. The subprior and the monks objected to his visit and said that they answered to the bishop of London. The archbishop, who was dressed in a coat of mail under his ecclesiastical garments, was greatly offended at this and hit the subprior in the face with his fist. He then hit him repeated blows, ripped off the subprior's cloak and trod it underfoot. He thrust the man up against a pillar and nearly killed him. The monks pulled the archbishop off their subprior and then attacked him. They, in turn, were attacked by the archbishop's men. The monks appealed to the bishop of London and to the king, saying that the archbishop had come to provoke a fight. Eventually the whole of London was aroused against the archbishop, and he had to flee the city.[4]

Although Boniface had come armed to St. Bartholomew's he did not use his sword or any weapon to attack the clergy. Instead, his use of his fists to assault the subprior indicates that the concept of fist-fighting had reached the highest levels of society.

It had also reached the lowest levels. In 1265–1266 the crime of battery reappeared first at the market of Westchepe in London where Adam Russel, Williams le Harpur, John le Somoter, and William [unknown] were fighting. Adam was killed and the others fled. At the same time, at the Winchester fair Amisius le Poluter (a *poulterer* was one who raised chickens) beat another chicken farmer, Bartholomew le Poluter [sic], so badly that Bartholomew died after returning to London. Again, at the fair in St. Ives in Cornwall on May 19, 1287, Henry of Longville attacked Gilbert Shearman against the peace of the lord abbot and the bailiffs, and drew blood from him. The next day, May 20, 1287, another fight occurred at the fair. This time, Hamon of Bury was accused of assaulting Bartholomew, the servant of John Waite, with a piece of turf and later striking him in the face with his fist, drawing blood. Since it was forbidden to carry weapons at fairs, these fights suggest that fist-fighting was common in fairs at least by the thirteenth century. And given the competitive nature of young men, fist-fighting may have been occurring at fairs and markets for as long as they had been in existence in Anglo-Saxon England.[5]

After 1300 it became more common to find reports of fists used as weapons. In the *Romance of Guy of Warwick* (c. 1300–1330), a duke had to be restrained from hitting Guy with his fist: "With his fest he wald have smitten Gii/Bot barouns held him owy."[6]

In the Middle English version of the *Romance of Sir Beues of Hamtoun* (c. 1327), where we first meet the word *box*, Sir Bevis escaped from jail in Damascus after killing his jailer by hitting him on the neck with his fist.[7]

In the Old French version of the story, *Boeve de Haumtone*, Sir Bevis killed his jailer with a blow from a stick. The substitution of a fist for a stick was a new invention by the English author. This shows that in England beginning circa 1300, blows with weapons were being converted into blows with fists.[8]

In *The Reeve's Tale* (c. 1390), Chaucer tells of a miller who gets into a fight with a clerk, who had seduced his daughter: "And on the nose he smoot hym with his fest, / Doun ran the blody streem, upon his brest" (lines 4275–4276). In the *Wife of Bath's Prologue* (1387–1392) Chaucer has the Wife tell of how she hit her husband, Jankyn, with her fist and knocked him into the fire. He then got up and hit her with his fist and knocked her out (lines 790–796).[9]

By 1400 fists were clearly being used in fighting and, indeed, were replacing more conventional weapons. Fists were being used by all levels in society from the Archbishop of Canterbury and Sir Bevis down to a housewife, a miller and the peasant farmer. Given this information, we must ask: If men had weapons, why did they fight with fists?

Personal Weapons in Medieval English Society

The short answer to the question of why men used fists instead of weapons is that they did so in environments where weapons were banned or were not available.

Conventionally, weapons were banned in the presence of the king or in a church. Thus, in the fight at King Arthur's Christmas feast weapons were banned, as they were when Duke Berard of Pavia wanted to fight Sir Guy of Warwick. As the duke said to Guy: "Vile traitor, / Were you not in the presence of the Emperor / I would run you through" (lines 2071–2073). Archbishop Boniface of Savoy, despite being armed and dressed in chain-mail, hit the subprior of St. Bartholomew with his fist, since he was in a church at the time. Sir Bevis hit his jailor with his fist because he was in jail and had no weapons. It is likely that fists and feet were used by the men who killed Adam Russel, as well as when the two chicken farmers had their fight at Winchester fair in 1265–66. We believe the same occurred when Henry of Longville drew blood from Gilbert Shearman at St. Ives. We suspect they used their fists since no weapons were mentioned and possibly they had no weapons at all. The same could be said when Hamon of Bury hit John Waite's servant with a piece of turf and then his fist. Finally, Chaucer's characters used their fists in domestic quarrels as fists were instantly available and weapons might have been considered too dangerous.

The longer answer to the question is that despite the fact that weapons were widely used, beginning in the twelfth century, weapon use was gradually going out of style.

Under the Anglo-Saxons, all free men were enrolled in the militia, known as the *fyrd*. The warriors fought in war bands organized by the local lord. They fought on foot, usually with lances and shields. Service in the *fyrd* was limited and military campaigns were brief and local. The only standing army was the king's personal war band.

Later kings continued this personal but limited service. In 1181, Henry II proclaimed an Assize of Arms, which was an attempt to reactivate the *fyrd*. He required all free men to maintain certain weapons at their expense. Only Jews were forbidden to have arms.[10]

Prior to the Assize of Arms, the kings only had the system of feudalism (a warrior class of knights who had been given lands to support them) for both military and police protection. But the feudal system was no longer sufficient for the needs of the country. Hence, Henry II tried to enroll free laymen and townsmen, who were outside of the feudal system, in the military to gain additional strength.

In 1242, Henry III issued a new order for keeping peace in the realm. In this order, the king required military service from all able-bodied men: "citizens, burgesses, freeholders, villeins [serfs] and others from the age of 15 to the age of 60 years." Now everyone who could fight was required to bear arms, even men who were not free (villeins). The sword and the horse were the weapons of the nobility, while farming implements and the bow and arrow were the weapons of common men.[11]

This document was reissued in 1285 by Henry's son, King Edward I, as a part of the famous Statute of Winchester. The obligations of knighthood had become a matter of money. Wealthy freemen and townsmen, who were separate from the manorial economy and were obligated only to the king, were forced to act militarily as if they were landed knights based upon the amount of income they had. There was no question of military training; all that was needed was the military equipment. If a man was wealthy enough to buy a sword, the king insisted that he do so and be prepared to use it.[12]

However, as the above documents suggest, the king was always short of knights to carry on his wars and do his bidding. According to one recent analysis there were only 4,000–5,000 armed knights in England circa 1150. During the following century, that number appears to have dropped to about 2,000. By 1308, there appear to have been only about 1,250 knights. And it has been estimated that by 1430 there were only 200 knights in the entire country. As the number of armored knights was falling, the general population was increasing. From a base of about 1,500,000 in 1000, the population of England and Wales grew to about 3,750,000 in 1300. During the same period, the number of knights had decreased from 5,000 to 1,250. Both the number of knights and the general population declined in the fourteenth century due to the advent of the Black Death (1348–1349). By 1400 the general population had dropped by one-third to 2,500,000, but the number of knights had dropped by four-fifths to 200. Now the defense of the realm lay not with the aristocratic knights and their swords, but with the English yeoman archers and their longbows.[13]

The use of the sword had been forced upon the wealthy as a type of tax, but over time, it was converted from an obligation to a privilege. The less important the sword became as a weapon, the more important it became as a status symbol. Prior to his death in 1267, Henry de Bracton, the founder of English law, codified this change when he defined the nobility in terms of the sword:

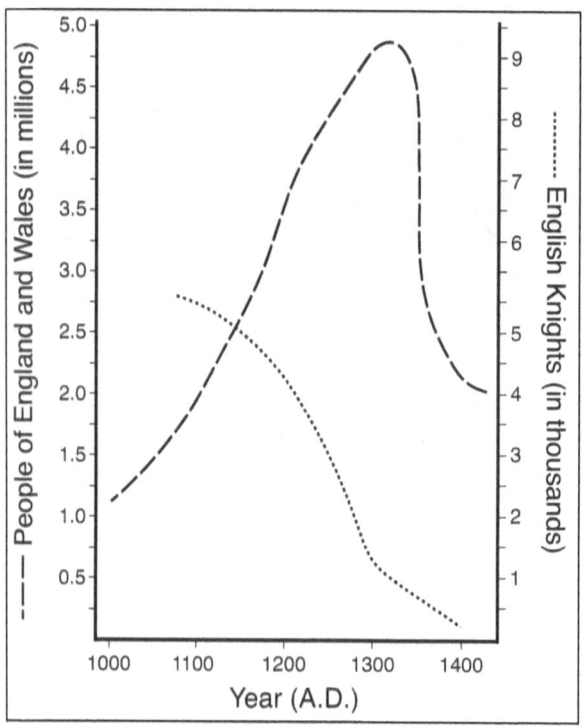

Fig. 4. The number of people (dashes) compared to the number of knights (dots) in England, AD 1000–1400. Both numbers declined after the Black Death of 1348–1349, but the class of knights nearly disappeared (by Sara Taliaferro).

God is no respecter of any men whomsoever, free or bond.... But with men, in truth, there is a difference between persons, for there are some of great eminence [who] are placed above others and rule over them....

Kings associate such persons with themselves in governing the people of God, investing them with great honour, power and name, when they gird them with swords.... [For] the sword signifies the defence of the realm and the country.[14]

In 1242 it was a crime if an aristocrat did not have a sword. Carrying a sword had become an obligation of the nobility. By 1413 it had become a crime for a man to carry a sword if he was not an aristocrat. Carrying a sword now became a sign of status and inherited wealth.[15]

The fact that by 1413 it had become a crime to wear a sword if one was not entitled to it demonstrates that England was being converted to a more peaceful society where most men did not openly carry weapons. In the "Form for keeping the peace" of 1242, despite the obligation for knights to have swords for defense, any who appeared armed contrary to the provisions of the king were to be arrested.[16] In the *Statutes of Arms* issued circa 1267, the earls and barons under Henry III sought to restrict the use of the sword at the tournament:

> And no Knight or Esquire serving at the Tournament, shall bear a Sword pointed, or Dagger pointed, or Staff or Mace, but only a broad Sword for tourneying.... And if it happen that any Earl or Baron or other knight, do go against this Statute, that such Knight, by Assent of all the Baronage, shall lose Horse and Harness [armor], and abide in prison at the pleasure of our Lord Sir Edward the King's son.[17]

In 1328 the Statute of Northampton declared that no man "great or small of what Condition soever he be," save for the king's servants, shall "ride armed by night nor day, in Fairs, Markets, or in the presence of Justices or other Ministers, nor in no part elsewhere, upon pain to forfeit their Armour to the King, and their Bodies to Prison at the King's pleasure."[18]

The objection to having men bring arms to fairs and markets was long-standing and widespread. Even before this statute went into effect, in October 1325, Meredith, son of Llowarch, was fined half a mark for carrying arms at the king's fair at Carnarvon.[19]

In the Statute of Cambridge (1388), Richard II was more practical. He forbade members of the lower sort of people from having bucklers, swords or daggers. Instead they were to practice with bows and arrows.[20]

Similar prohibitions against carrying arms appeared elsewhere. As early as 1285 the Statutes of the City of London forbade carrying arms abroad after curfew:

> For Whereas many Evils, as Murders, Robberies, and Manslaughters have been committed heretofore in the City by Night and by Day, and people have been beaten and evil intreated, and divers other Mischances have befallen against his [King Edward I's] Peace; It is enjoined that none be so hardy to be found going or wandering about the Streets of the City, after Curfew tolled at St. Martins le

Grand, with Sword or Buckler, or other Arms for doing Mischief, or whereof evil suspicion might arise; nor any in any other Manner, unless he be a great Man or other lawful Person of good repute, or their certain messenger, having Warrants to go from one to another, with Lantern in hand.[21]

These provisions were renewed periodically (1297, 1326, 1327, 1334, 1364, and 1376). A proclamation was issued circa November 1326 "that no man go armed by night or day, save officers and other good men of the City assigned by the Mayor or Aldermen in their wards." A year later a writ was issued forbidding the carrying of swords, clubs, cross-bows and bows for discharging stones and clay pellets.[22]

In 1342 innkeepers were ordered to warn their guests that carrying of arms in the City except by officers of the King and the City was forbidden. This was repeated in June 1372. Thus, when Adam Grymmesby neglected to tell his lodger to leave his knife indoors in July 1372, the knife was confiscated and Adam Grymmesby was placed in prison for contempt.[23]

Court records only list those who break the laws. Based on that, these laws appear to have had some effect. In the years between 1364 and 1381 only 35 physical assaults were reported in London court records. Of these, eight involved a sword; eight involved knives; one involved a stick and three involved arrows. A total of twenty assaults involved named weapons, while in fifteen assaults the weapons were not named. We do not know what weapons were used in these fifteen assaults, but near the end of the fourteenth century new laws appeared that ordered fines and imprisonment for those who "[struck] any one with the fist." It is possible that by 1400 fists were becoming a common weapon for Londoners, given that they were deprived of the use of knives and swords.[24]

A similar change occurred in Oxford in 1313 when the chancellor of Oxford University issued a statute against the carrying of arms within the city of Oxford. This was reissued in 1432 with heavy fines established for carrying arms. However, in the 1432 statute the university also began to outlaw hitting with fists (*percussione cum pugno*). This suggests that in Oxford as well, fist-fighting was beginning to replace sword-fighting.[25] A like situation may be found in *The Domus Day of Grippeswich*, the records of the municipal court of Ipswich circa 1436. In a statute dealing with penalties for fighting, jail terms were set for bloodshed caused by a sword, a knife or a staff. But also, penalties were set "for blood drawyn of foot or of fist or of other debaat [battery]." It seems that by this time fists as well as feet were being used in disputes in other places besides London and Oxford.[26]

From 1066 to 1550 the sword, which was the signature weapon of the conquering Norman elite, had been forced upon the wealthy non-military classes of the English countryside and town. They proved reluctant fighters, far more ready to pay for mercenaries to fight than to become knights themselves. Henry de Bracton (d. 1267) defined the sword as "the defence of the realm," while King Henry VIII in 1542 considered the longbow to be the defense of the realm, but both were wrong. With the exception of the minuscule class of the aristocracy, Englishmen were beginning to lay aside weapons to use fists. The armored knight with a sword was drowning in the rising pool of middle-class prosperity.[27]

How Violent Was Medieval England?

Johan Huizinga opens his marvelous book *The Waning of the Middle Ages* with one of the great chapters of historical literature. He describes the "violent tenor of life" lived by the continental Europeans, particularly the French and the Burgundians. He pictures the Middle Ages as a period of radical extremes:

> A present-day reader, studying the history of the Middle Ages based upon official documents, will never sufficiently realize the extreme excitability of the medieval soul. The picture drawn mainly from official records, though they may be the most reliable sources, will lack one element: that of the vehement passion possessing princes and people alike.[28]

The population flocked to see public executions. The streets of the towns were filled with processions of beggars and flagellants. The countryside was filled with poverty and danger. Instant and unexplained horror came from the Black Death (1348–1349). Nor was there sanctuary in the churches as first one, then two, then three popes fought for supremacy (1378–1417). It is no wonder that the common man might believe that no one had been able to enter paradise since the beginning of the Great Schism.

While this picture was not as grim in England, James Buchanan Given, in his study of medieval homicide, came to the conclusion that "thirteenth-century England was a violent society."[29] His view is very common, and it has precedent. Despite the laws we have just cited, in 1558, a visiting French priest, Stephen Perlin, expressed the view that "in this land everybody bears arms." Raphael Holinshead noted in 1586: "Seldom shall you see one of my countrymen above eighteen or twenty yeares old go with out [sic] a dagger at least at his backe or his side, although they are aged burgesses or magistrates of a citie, who in appearance are most exempt from babbling and contention."[30]

Nonetheless, medieval England may not have been any more violent than many other societies at many other times. The data presented by Given suggest that the frequency of murder in thirteenth-century England was not much different from that in many cities in the early twenty-first century United States, and both were far less violent than most places in modern Mexico.[31]

In modern societies the use of weapons to commit assault is reasonably frequent. Given and others felt the same was true of medieval England:

> The ubiquitous presence of weapons in medieval England possibly rendered fatal many quarrels that would otherwise have resulted only in bruises. Although medieval Englishmen did not have available such efficient means of destruction as firearms and explosives, they nevertheless habitually carried weapons.[32]

This is not entirely true, however. Given's own figures challenge this. Knives were the most common weaponm yet only 5.6 percent of the homicides he examined (136 out of 2,434) were committed with knives.[33]

By the sixteenth century there had been a significant reduction in public violence. This has been attributed to Tudor despotism. The Tudors made the use of weapons in both public and private disagreements increasingly unprofitable. Lawrence Stone felt that "the greatest triumph of the Tudors was the ultimately successful assertion of a royal monopoly of violence both public and private, an achievement which profoundly altered not only the nature of politics, but also the quality of daily life."[34] Further, even when weapons were carried, they may have been merely for show, as Raphael Holinshead suggested above.

James Given was able to find weapons used in only 18.7 percent of the recorded cases of homicide (455 out of 2,434 cases) that he investigated. This means that in 1,979 out of the 2,434 cases of homicide, or in 81.3 percent of the cases, the cause of death was unknown. To be fair, we may suspect that weapons were used in more cases and simply not reported. But Given did acknowledge that out of the 455 cases where the tools of death were known, 40 deaths, or 8.8 percent, were caused by fists or feet. We may suspect that out of the 1,979 deaths by unknown causes, a far greater number were caused by hands and feet than were reported. Given points out too that the vast majority of the homicides he investigated were committed by the poor on the poor. 77.9 percent of the people arrested for homicide had property [chattels] worth less than 5 shillings, and 60.6 percent had no chattels at all (Given, Table 7). Certainly, these people did not have wealth enough to carry swords. We may even wonder if they carried knives.[35]

As fists were becoming popular as weapons, Englishmen in London, at least, began to leave their knives at home. The authors of the most recent archaeological excavations in London, and the keepers of the largest collection of knives and scabbards of the Middle Ages, confirm this point. F.O. Grew et al. found two things. First, *there were more knives in the fourteenth century*: "Almost half the [knife] finds belong to the period of just half a century (c. 1350–1400)." Second, *men no longer carried them on their person*: "It seems that after c. 1350 fewer and fewer knives were carried in scabbards." They believed this demonstrated a social change: "These late medieval knives must have been stored where they were needed—in some cases, perhaps, specifically for use at the table—not regularly carried by their owners."[36]

This social change in leaving knives at home, rather than carrying them about, was also coupled with a change in the type of knives made:

> The increased number of longer, more elegant blades in the 14th century, coupled with extensively decorated scale-tang knife handles, may be another reflection of the emergence of the table knife. Carrying knives around in scabbards seems to have been much less common during this period and the display factor involved in laying decorated knives on the table should be considered.[37]

To sum up: Carrying weapons on one's person was going out of style in medieval England. By 1400 in London daggers were being replaced by ornate table knives, and such knives were being stored in homes and not carried about on the street. This gives us reason to believe that although there were more knives, they were not being used as weapons. Medieval London, and by extension medieval England, was neither as violent nor as full of crime as is generally assumed. After 1400, if men in London were engaged in a quarrel, they often settled it with their fists.

Naming of a New Sport

We have already seen that in London fists were replacing weapons in crimes by the end of the fourteenth century. By the fifteenth century we have found fists being used in fights in Oxford and in Ipswich as well. The use of the fist, in contrast to the use of weapons, in fights was already well advanced by the beginning of the sixteenth century.

In 1519, we find the schoolmaster, William Horman, already quite familiar with fist-fighting. On folio 132v of his Latin instruction book for students he provides the sentence: "I shall fight with the and neuer flee abacke or geue the a fote (*Dimicabo tecum pugna stataria*)." He also writes: "That stroke made hym stagre and redy to fall (*Ictus hominem genibus submitti coegit*)," and "There began a fray or they went together (*Ad manus ventum est*)." On f. 133v, he states: "He gaue hym a scornefull buffette (*Contemtim ei colophum incussit*)," and again "He gaue hym a blowe on the mouthe (*Os eius pugno perstrinxit*)." On folio 135r he writes: "They were redy to fight or lye by the earis / but if I had parted them (*Iam ad rem ventum erat nisi interuenissem*)," and finally on f. 135v: "He came home with a face all to bounced (*Domum reuersus est facie contuse*)." Clearly his students were fist-fighting.[38]

But there were two ways in which this fist-fighting differed from modern boxing. Note the comment: "I shall fight with thee and never flee back nor give thee a foot." This was the classic fighting strategy used by the buffet fighter.

Buffet fighters stood toe-to-toe. Backing up was considered cowardly. Fighting was a static activity. You stood still and upright when fighting an adversary. The strategy of the buffet match had been adopted by these boys in their proto-boxing matches.[39]

The second difference was that the buffet fighters exchanged reciprocal blows with a pause between each blow. As the Turk said to Sir Gawain: "Is there any will, as a brother, / To give a buffet and take another?" But we sense things were changing in Horman's schoolyard. The student who came home with his face "all to bounced" was probably not hit just once, as would be the case in a normal buffets match. We suspect that he had been hit by multiple buffets, that is to say, he was hit multiple times on the face by someone's fist. Despite the static strategy of standing toe-to-toe when fighting, we can imagine schoolboys being impetuous and choosing to throw many punches at one time. We also can imagine the one who was getting pelted with fists backing up and dodging to get out of range. We believe that these schoolyard battles were becoming free-flowing fist-fights. The days of reciprocal buffet blows were coming to an end. The days of multiple blows thrown at one time had begun.

While there was still the concept of static fighting, fighting in which backing up or ducking and weaving occurred had a history as well. Already in the *Gesta Herewardi (The Deeds of Hereward)* we find that Hereward defeated a much stronger enemy who was used to toe-to-toe fighting. Hereward fought in an unconventional fashion: "Continually advancing and attacking, the young man [Hereward] avoided the blows, and ducking and weaving, often inflicted blows that were unexpected and covert." Hereward's strategy was the fashion of the future. It took years before this strategy won out, but eventually boxers began to realize it was more advantageous to duck and weave than to stand still in the buffet stance and allow your opponent to hit you at will.[40]

As the use of the fist became more common, fist-fighting became recognized as an exercise distinct from wrestling and sword-fighting. It is common that whenever something new appears in society, it is described in a series of new names. So it was that as fighting with fists began to distinguish itself as a new activity, it was given new names by the public.

And yet these were perhaps not new names, but rather old names suddenly revealed. As we suggested in the previous chapter, when English replaced French as the spoken language , words that had been used to describe fist-fighting by the country folk began to be recognized in literature. It was as if a gag had been removed from the mouth of the common man and suddenly his voice began to be heard. The new words used to describe boxing were perhaps common country words dating back at least a hundred years.

Box as a Blow

The word *box*, meaning a blow, appears to have been a term invented in medieval England. Initially, *box* meant a blow from a weapon. The first recorded use of the word was in *The Romance of Sir Beues of Hamtoun* (c. 1327).[41]

Sir Bevis escaped from prison in Damascus and was pursued by King Grander and his knights. Grander caught Sir Bevis and challenged him to yield or forfeit his life. Bevis responded that with God's help, he would fight Grander and give "a lite *box* thee to paie" (line 1744). An alternative reading from another manuscript states Bevis would pay him "a stroke or two." The men fight on horseback and break their lances. Then they fight with swords and Bevis cuts off Grander's head. From this we can conclude that *box* meant a stroke with a sword.[42]

In the *Alliterative Morte Arthure* (1310–1440), King Arthur is forced into battle with the giant of St. Michael's Mount. The giant swings his club at Arthur who responds with a sword blow:

> Clenly with his clubb he crassched doune at onze
> The Kyng caste vp his schelde and couers hym faire,
> And with his burlyche brande a *box* he hym reches.[43]

> Deftly with his club he smashes down at once.
> The King throws up his shield and covers himself fully,
> And with his strong sword he strikes him a *blow*.

Clearly, the word *box* means a blow from a sword. The same meaning is found in the *Laud Troy Book* (c. 1400), where the author praises Hector for his valor:

Fig. 5. Sir Bevis boxing with King Grander, *Queen Mary's Psalter*, circa 1310–1320, f.150 (British Library Royal MS 2 B VII).

> Off alle the men that euere god wrought
> I haue most meruayle In my thought
> Off Ector certis and of his dedes:
> Ther dar non stonde of him *a box*,
> Thei fle fro him, as hen doth fro the fox.[44]

A *box* from Hector was a sword blow, but other early examples of the word are not so clear. This caused the editors of the *Middle English Dictionary* to define *box* as "a stroke delivered with a weapon; also a blow of any kind."[45]

A *box* was a blow. In *The Promptorium Parvulorum: The First English-Latin Dictionary* (c. 1440), the word box was described as a buffet. By 1440, box and buffet had become equivalents. Both of them were then defined by the Latin word *alapa, ae* f. (c.46). *Alapa* could mean a slap with the hand or a "dub" with a sword. By 1440 *box* had become a blow from the hand or a light blow with a sword.[46]

Up to the middle of the fifteenth century to strike a blow presumed the use of a weapon. But after 1440, *box*, meaning a blow, became an ambiguous act. It could involve a weapon or it could involve a fist.

This ambivalent meaning of the word *box* appears to have lasted up through the beginning of the sixteenth century. When the school teacher William Horman presented his students with his English-Latin phrasebook, it contained the line "He was *boxed out* of the place: as he had been a started hare." His use of the term *boxed out* shows that this was a colloquial phrase known to schoolboys. But if boxing no longer meant a sword blow, it still was not yet linked to a blow from a fist. Horman translated this phrase into Latin as "Explosus est non segnius ac exagitatus lepis." Horman's use of the words "explosus est" instead of the phrase "pugnatus est" shows that in the beginning of the sixteenth century, to box could mean to beat or drive out, without being a specific reference to a blow from a fist.[47]

Gradually, during the sixteenth century, *box* changed its meaning. In John Baret's dictionary (1574) we first find *boxe* defined as "To giue one a boxe or blowe with the fist (*Pugnam impingere*)." In 1581 John Studley wrote: "The naked Fist found out To scratch and cuffe, to boxe and bum." By the end of the sixteenth century, *box* definitely meant a blow from fist.[48]

By 1590 the verb *to box* had become part of a colloquial English phrase "to box one's ear." This became an archetypical English expression after William Shakespeare popularized it in a number of his plays. Shakespeare first used the phrase "a box on the ear" in *Henry VI, Part 2* (1590–91). In a discussion between Jack Cade, a rebel, and Lord Say, just before Cade's men behead the latter, Say states:

SAY: These cheeks are pale for watching for your good.

CADE: Give him a *box o'the ear* and that will make 'em red again [Act IV, scene vii, lines 84–87].⁴⁹

The same phrase is used three times in Act IV of *Henry V* (1599). It indeed becomes the focus of a sub plot. In Act IV, scene i, King Henry wanders in disguise among his troops the night before the battle of Agincourt to test their morale. He meets three soldiers, one of whom, not recognizing him, picks a quarrel with the king:

MICHAEL WILLIAMS: Let it be a quarrel between us, if you live.

KING HENRY: I embrace it.

WILLIAMS: How shall I know thee again?

KING HENRY: Give me any gage of thine, and I will wear it in my bonnet: then, if ever thou darest acknowledge it, I will make it my quarrel.

WILLIAMS: Here's my glove; give me another of thine.

KING HENRY: There.

WILLIAMS: This will I also wear in my cap. If ever thou come to me and say, after tomorrow, "This is my glove," by this hand, I will take thee *a box on the ear* [Act IV, scene i, lines 205–216].

After the battle, in Act IV, scene vii, Henry gives the glove to Captain Llewellyn to see what will happen. Thinking that Captain Llewellyn is the man with whom he has the quarrel, Williams hits him in the face. Llewellyn does not know why he was hit and immediately wants to beat Williams. When Henry acknowledges that he had met Williams before the battle, the quarrel is resolved. He then gives William the glove back filled with crowns (Act IV, scenes vii and viii). The point of this episode is to show the democratic spirit of the average Englishman, and also how Henry V, who as Prince Hal had consorted with the common man, uses that to gain advantage in the battle against the French at Agincourt. But more importantly for our purposes, it shows that armed soldiers, in the midst of a war, were willing to lay aside their weapons in private quarrels and fight with bare fists. At least among common men, fist-fighting was replacing fighting with weapons.

"To give a box on the ear" became a well-known expression in England by the 1590s. It reveals that already in this early period fist-fighters were aware that a blow to the ear or the side of the head could easily knock a man out. As all boxers now know, and as modern medicine has demonstrated, "blows on the chin or on the side of the head in the anterior temporal region seemingly produce the most knock outs."⁵⁰ Hitting a man on the ear, or the chin, with a fist might easily put him on the ground and out of the fight, as was done in the *Gesta Herewardi*. This was the goal of every fight.

Buffet: The Companion of Boxing

Box was the English word used to describe this new form of fighting; *buffet* was the French word. The *Middle English Dictionary* gives the original English meaning of *buffet* as "a blow delivered with the fist or flat of the hand, a cuff, slap."[51]

In 1530, John Palsgrave, the English grammarian, did not know the word *box*, but he did know the Old French term *buffette*, which he defined as a *buffee* or a *coup de poing* (a blow of the fist). In his "Table of Verbs," he provided the example "*I boffet*: I give one a blowe." This is amplified in two other phrases: "Gette you hence, or I shall buffet you tyll your heed shall ake" and "I gyve one a clappe on the cheke." For Palsgrave, buffet was a blow from a fist and, by extension, a fist-fight.[52]

However, in Chapter II we also found that *buffet*, like *box*, originally meant a blow with a weapon. This ancient meaning continued up through the end of the sixteenth century. Edmund Spenser (c. 1554–1599) in his epic poem *The Faerie Queen* continued to use *buffet* or *buffe* to mean a blow with a weapon.[53] William Shakespeare (1564–1616), on the other hand, used *buffet* to mean a blow with the hand or arm. By 1600 there were two meanings of the term *buffet*: the Shakespearian meaning of a blow with a fist and the Spenserian meaning of a blow with a weapon. At times it is difficult to tell which was meant, but generally speaking it appears that the Shakespearian version seems to have been the common meaning.

Cuff and *Pommel*

The first recorded use of *cuff* and *pommel* to mean "a blow" in English occurred in John Palsgrave's book on French grammar (1530): "I *cuffe* one, I *pommel* hym about the heed. *Je torche*," and "He hath all to *cuffed* aboute the eares." *Pommel* is also found as a separate entry: "*I pomell*: I beate one aboute the eares," and "He pomelled me tyll we were bothe werye [weary]." Both *cuff* and *pommel*, in this sense, were new to the English language and both meant to hit or beat with the fist. It should be noted that *cuff about the ears* and *pommel about the ears* anticipated *box about the ears* in print by nearly 70 years. Nonetheless the idiom, perhaps on the strength of Shakespeare's use, became *box about the ears*.

Pommel was a word drawn from Old French, dating from the twelfth century. It was derived from *pom*, meaning apple. *Pom* in this sense described a round ball on the hilt of a sword. The initial meaning of the phrase "to pommel one" suggests that it meant to hit with the hilt of the sword rather than the blade. But by the sixteenth century in England it meant to hit with a fist.[54]

Fig. 6. An example of sword-and-buckler fighting (note the pommels on the hilts of both swords). *The Rutland Psalter*, circa 1252–1262, f.62v (British Library MS 62925).

To pommel was used as a verb in Edward Hall's *Chronicle* (1548). The French Dauphin, hoping to embarrass the English in a tournament, brought in a giant German to meet in combat with Charles Brandon, Duke of Suffolk. The duke, being incensed against the German, grabbed him across the barrier and "by pure strength tooke hym about the necke, and *pomeled* so about the hed that the blood yssued out of his nose, & then they were departed." It seems clear that the duke grabbed the German and pulled him toward him. Then holding him around the neck (holding him "in chancery" in wrestling terms), the duke hit the German repeatedly in the face with his fist.[55]

Cuffe also occurred in Peter Levins's *Manipulus Vocabulorum* (1570). Levins defined the noun *cuffe* as a buffet. The verb *to cuff* was defined by the Latin verb *colaphizare*, meaning to give a blow with a fist, and by the French *donner de soufflets* (to give a hit or a slap). In the same dictionary, Levins also defined *to buffet* as *colophizari*.[56]

This demonstrates that by the end of the sixteenth century we have four words in use, *box, buffet, cuff* and *pommel*, all of which mean basically the same thing: a blow with a fist.

The "Sport" of Boxing

In using the word "sport" we agree with Norbert Elias:

> Every sport—whatever else it may be—is an organized group activity centered on a contest between at least two parties. It requires physical exertion of some kind. It is fought out according to known rules, including, if physical force is allowed at all, rules which define the permitted limits of violence.[57]

This is a good definition. It recognizes the critical dichotomy that creates the tension, which is so important in all sport. It talks about controlled violence, which also makes sport interesting and exciting. And it talks about the role of rules, without which sport could not be sport. But it leaves out one critical element: *play*. I would therefore simplify this definition by saying: *sport is play with rules. Play* with rules lies at the heart of *sport*. You cannot have *sport* without play and you cannot have *sport* without rules. It is the combination of rules with play that makes *sport*.

William Fitz Stephen, in his description of London (c. 1174–1183), describes the plains north of the city at Smithfield as the place where men and boys go to play at sports: "Let us consider also the sports of the City, since it is not meet that a city should only be useful and sober, unless it is also pleasant and merry." Here Fitz Stephen recognizes the play element in sport and considers

Fig. 7. The Chancery Hold as used by Charles Brandon, Duke of Suffolk, on the German champion. Once Brandon had his arm around his opponent's neck and the head locked under his arm, he was free to pommel the German's face with his fist (by Sara Taliaferro).

sport to be the activity that makes London "pleasant and merry." As part of this playing at sport, he mentions horse races and jousting in the summertime as well as wrestling matches. It was also common to see men fighting with swords and bucklers. Smithfield appears to have been the preeminent location for sport in medieval England.[58]

The wrestling schools and fencing schools held at Smithfield were so popular that they attracted a number of foreigners to London. In Edward I's proclamation of 1286 outlawing fencing schools, he complained that "most of the aforesaid villainies are committed by foreigners, who from all parts incessantly crowd thither." It appears that foreigners enjoyed learning these skills in London from 1200 on. This linking of sword-and-buckler fencing with wrestling helps us understand how the two activities could eventually merge into boxing in the sixteenth century.[59]

This hypothesis that the merging of two separate and distinct sports in the twelfth century could create a third, *boxing*, in the sixteenth, is in keeping with the suggestion of Norbert Elias that it may take many generations to create a new sport.

> Evidently this is one of those processes in the course of which specific structures of group relations and activities developed over many generations through the concourse of actions and aims of many individuals even though none of the participating people, as individuals or as groups, intended or planned the long-term outcome of their actions. Thus it is not merely a manner of speaking if one envisages the emergence of sports as a developmental and not merely as an historical problem.[60]

To apply this to boxing: the sport of boxing wasdeveloped over centuries by the common people of England. Because they lacked an efficient social communication system, their independent actions created a game that none of them planned. Nonetheless these actions solved the needs of the crowds. Boxing grew out of the need for an activity that combined vigorous action, non-fatal violence, easily understood rules, and a clear result, all within a small space and time. Boxing allowed men to determine who was the best of two bullies. If we take as our beginning the proto-boxing match of 1310–1320, the value of these efforts is proven by the fact that boxing in England has lasted 800 years.

This agrees with Elias when he argues:

> Sport is, in fact, one of the great social inventions which human beings have made without planning to make them. It offers people the liberating excitement of a struggle involving physical exertion and skill while, ideally at least, limiting to a minimum the chance that anyone will get seriously hurt in its course.[61]

Boxing grew out of wrestling, but avoided the uncertainties of wrestling in which the results were often contested, leading to riots. It competed favorably with football, which had a similar level of violence but which required more time and space. In addition, football permitted the active involvement of the crowd. A football game might take all day, cover several miles of fields and involve the participation of the citizens from two separate towns. Because of these requirements, football became restricted to feast days when both the people and the places might be available. Football was too violent to be exercised frequently during the year and too expansive to be played in a confined space. Boxing, on the other hand, could be employed at almost any time and in almost any place. It provided concentrated violence in a confined space. The crowd was critical to the success of boxing, but its members were prevented from becoming active participants by the ring. Best of all, boxing's results were clear cut. When one of the combatants cried "craven" or gave up, the match was over. The sport also provided a cathartic release for the crowd and this satisfied its goal.

We cannot be sure that the illustration from *Queen Mary's Psalter* represents a match at Smithfield, outside of London, but Smithfield would have been a convenient place to look for proto-boxers. The combination of wrestling and sword-and-buckler fighting in one place provided an ideal location for the development of the new sport of boxing, which represented a fusion of these two more ancient activities. Wrestling was a popular sport during the Middle Ages. Like football, it could involve large groups of men, but unlike football, wrestling exhibited in a series of individual matches. Wrestling drew large crowds, but the sport did not require large fields. Wrestling matches could be held in enclosed spaces. Wrestling also appealed to women. Conventional sword-and-buckler battles had the same space requirements as wrestling and boxing and also attracted crowds. Such battles were largely for show. Sir Thomas Fuller, describing the sword-and-buckler fighters at Smithfield, found men "more frightened than hurt, [and more] hurt than killed therewith." Thomas Churchyard tells us: "In the old time the fight of England was dangerous but not deadly, courageous but not cruell, valiant but not villainous, and most nobly used oftimes without any great harme."[62]

There is also another reason we might suspect that Smithfield could be the location of the first boxing matches. As previously noted, four new words described this new sport (*box, buffet, cuff* and *pommel*). *Box* and *cuff* are Middle English words, used by English speakers, while *buffet* and *pommel* are Norman French words. As we discussed in the previous chapter, Middle English was spoken in the countryside, while Norman French was spoken in the towns, most particularly in London.[63] Smithfield lay in between these two language areas. As such, it would be a natural area in which the merging of the two languages might occur in the naming of a new sport.

As this new sport developed, a social change occurred in the way in which its names were used. While *buffet* and *pommel* were applied to kings and knights, *box* and *cuff* were not. The use of Middle English suggested a rural background among the common people, while the use of Norman French suggested an urban origin and aristocratic beginnings. Kings, like Richard I and Henry V, could *buffet* while Jack Cade and Michael Williams would *box* someone's ears. Not only do we have multiple words describing this new exercise, but these words show that different social classes were involved in fist-fighting by 1600.

During the sixteenth century, the meaning of the word *box* converted to indicate fighting with fists and became common in the English language. Originally, boxing was simply a brawl. A brawl can be defined as a noisy, turbulent quarrel with no particular rules or patterns. It might be a fight between two individuals or between multiple individuals. At some point, should enough people become involved in the fight, a brawl might turn into a riot. A brawl, in short, was an expression of disorder. Sport, in contrast, was an expression of order.[64]

How do we get from a disordered brawl to the sport of boxing?

If we take the proto-boxing match of 1310–1320 to be the beginning of boxing in Britain, we must recognize that 200 years elapsed before we find the first hints of the sport of boxing in William Horman's schoolyard. How did boxing develop between 1320 and 1519? Although we will examine a second proto-boxing bout in 1458 in a subsequent chapter, we really know nothing about how or where the earliest fights were conducted.

One hypothesis is that fist-fighting was hidden in the games held at Smithfield and in wrestling matches. We suspect that wrestlers as well as individual fencing masters (*pugils*) may have used fist-fighting as part of their exercises beginning as early as the twelfth and thirteenth centuries. This approach sees fist-fighting as a supplement to other types of fighting. The many references to wrestling might have hidden the first boxing matches.

A second hypothesis is that individuals might have fought together in the streets or markets, either as buffet matches or more violent free-flowing battles. Although these fights might have been frequent and attracted crowds, they have not been recognized in literary documents, or if they were recognized, they may have been registered as some form of crime. Fist-fighting was seen originally as assault and battery or an affray, or simply a breach of the peace. Any memory preserved might appear in court records, as in the case of Hamon of Bury in Cornwall in 1287, or in the court records of Oxford in 1452 and 1456 (see note 25 in this chapter).

In truth, we do not know much about the pattern of fist-fighting until the beginning of the sixteenth century. It is only then that we can find written evidence of the beginning of boxing. And it would take another century, until about 1600, before we can attempt to define the first rules that made boxing a sport.

Establishing the Rules of Boxing (c. 1600)

In the normal course of events, if two young men met in a public street and had an argument, they might begin to fight with each other without any preliminaries. This fight might be described either as a brawl or as assault and battery. Either way it might be considered a criminal act; but it was not the sport of boxing. Boxing was not just a fist-fight; it was a fist-fight with rules.

Although I use the term "rule" here, Tony Gee, the British prize-ring historian, argues that a better term would be "procedures." In a strict sense he is correct, since "rules" suggests there was a "rule-making authority" that controlled boxing from its pre-emergent days. There was no such authority until 1743. Yet I have chosen the word "rules" to express the fact that sport requires rules to exist. In this very early period, when boxing could easily be confused with crime, I believe that certain "procedures" had to be followed in order to give the sport form and body and to distinguish it from formless brawls and crime. Without the application of these "procedures" as "rules" boxing would never have been born. Furthermore, the crowds who collected around these first-fights felt the need to have them follow certain "rules" in order to be able to bet on the outcome. Gambling required standardized "rules" to exist, and this imperative reinforced the natural demands of the crowd to find order in sport. Hence, I believe that the demand of the crowds for order in fighting led to the first "rules" of boxing, which I try to outline here.

The first rule that converted a brawl into a sport was that a challenge was issued. A challenge was typically issued by sword duelists in the *holmganga*. There were also challenges issued in wrestling matches, by the Masters of Defence and in the duel of honor. The challenge gave both parties the chance to plan for the fight. The fighters, like the two hypothetical young men mentioned above, might meet in the street and begin to fight, but because the fight was planned and announced in advance, it no longer could be considered either an ambush, assault, or an affray since the contestants agreed to come together and fight. The challenge was important since it distinguished sport from a criminal act.

The second rule was that a location for the fight was established. Unlike the rapier duel of honor, which occurred in secret, boxing occurred in public. In this it followed the pattern established in the trials by battle (judicial duels) which, as we shall see, were controlled by the courts and often overseen by public officials, including the monarch. The purpose of the public nature of a boxing match was two-fold. First, boxing was a duel with fists rather than swords. Honor was involved in placing the challenge and fighting the fight. In sport, honor could not easily be served if there were no witnesses to the event. Second, we know that in the gladiatorial (sword) prizefights, which were also public events, the crowd might contribute coins to the winner. Once boxing ceased to be a brawl and adopted rules, matches became "prizefights" fought to gain prizes for the fighters.

The third rule of boxing was that once the challenge had been accepted, the location established, and the fighters present, a "ring" was made. The "ring" was a spontaneous circle made by the individual members of the crowd grabbing hands to create an open space in which the men could fight. We will see in Chapter IV that this was done in Cornwall for wrestling matches, and it was adopted for boxing as well. Like wrestling matches, the earliest boxing matches were on the turf outside, in markets, fairs or public squares. These were unrestricted open spaces. Trials by battle, on the other hand, were much more formal and had areas (lists or "*staccati*") which were surrounded with railings to keep the populace from interfering. Boxing did not develop these until the 1700s.

Nonetheless, the "ring" was a vital and essential feature of boxing. Despite the fact that it originally consisted simply of men holding hands to create a circle, and could easily be broken, it was a major factor in creating the sport. As Johan Huizinga tells us, the space inside the "ring" was "a consecrated spot" where an "absolute and peculiar order reigns." The "ring" creates order. The "ring" becomes the "play-ground" i.e., a "forbidden spot, isolated, hedged round, hallowed, within which special rules obtain." This is a temporary world within the ordinary world, dedicated to the performance of an act apart:

> Into an imperfect world and into the confusion of life it brings a temporary, a limited perfection. Play demands order absolute and supreme. The least deviation from it "spoils the game," robs it of its character and makes it worthless.[65]

This is why the crowd instinctively creates the "ring" and why the crowd is so jealous of protecting the rules that govern the action inside the "ring." Without the "ring" boxing could not exist.

The creation of the "ring" also had an important role in law. A fist-fight in a public place such as the street or a market square, even if announced in advance, might be seen as a breach of the peace. Only the creation of a "ring" separated the public from the fight. It protected the fighters from interference by the public, but also protected the public from interference by the fighters. The "ring" was a shield that insulated the fight from the charge of breach of the peace.

The fourth rule was that the fighters stripped before the fight began. Taking off clothes or stripping before a fight had a psychological value as well as a physical value. Psychologically, stripping announced to the crowd that a serious fight was about to begin, while the act of stripping prepared the fighters for the ordeal ahead. Physically, stripping eliminated the restrictions of clothing and permitted the boxer freer use of his limbs. It also prevented the possibility that weapons would be brought to the fight. To ensure this, the fighters stripped to their doublets or shorts to demonstrate that nothing was concealed. It also prevented the fighters from hiding charms or prayers on their person. Stripping followed the pattern of wrestling in which the wrestlers stripped before the match and only one's hands, feet and head could be used to fight. While not allowed today, head-butting and kicking were used extensively in the early days of boxing and only outlawed by the *London Prize Ring Rules* of 1838.[66]

The fifth rule was that it was customary for the men to shake hands before the fight began to demonstrate that the fighters did not hold ill will (*mens rea*). Wrestlers, cudgel fighters, boxers and gladiatorial sword-fighters all did this to protect themselves against the charge of "malice aforethought." Shaking hands before the bout also showed visibly that the fighters entered the contest willingly. This was in keeping with the dictum "*volenti non fit injuria*" [the law does not recognize injury done to a willing person]. Thus, if one were hurt or killed, their opponent would be protected from a charge of assault or even murder. Such charges would arise when an unwilling person was attacked by another with malice aforethought. Shaking hands before the fight was one of the critical rules that made boxing a sport and distinguished it from an assault or other crime.

The sixth rule was that only two men could fight in the ring at one time. This rule developed out of wrestling and was fundamental to the sport. If the ring was broken by the onlookers and more than two men fought at one time, it became a brawl and not a boxing match. A brawl lacked the dynamic tension of boxing where two men were matched one against each other. Occasionally brawls were put on and were described as "battle royals." Here, multiple men might fight it out in a ring, but such events were chaotic and less interesting than a fight of two men with fists. Boxing owes its longevity and fame to the fact that two men, and only two, fight in the ring at one time.

The seventh rule was for the fighters to stand toe-to-toe and hit as frequently as they might. This rule was drawn from buffet matches in which each man stood unprotected while his opponent hit him one blow as hard as he could. To duck or flinch or step back was considered cowardly in a buffet match. In the early 1500s schoolboys changed the original rules and began to hit their opponents multiple times in succession. They still called their sport buffets, and they still believed that they should stand toe-to-toe while fighting and not give up a foot. To back up was still considered cowardly even though now boxers threw many blows at each other in rapid succession. This style of fighting made bouts bloody and brutal and led to them being abhorred by the members of the developing middle class. This perhaps explains why boxing had such a bad reputation and why we cannot find records of these early fights.

This rough and tumble style of boxing remained the fashion of fighting up until John Broughton's time (1730–1750). Broughton introduced blocking, feinting and dodging to avoid getting hit. In this, he took fist-fighting back to an earlier strategy adopted by Hereward the Wake circa 1070, and laid the foundation for modern "scientific" boxing. Broughton proved the advantage of hitting without being hit.

The eighth rule was that the goal of the match was to knock your opponent down. Originally the goal of all hand-to-hand fighting was to put your opponent on the ground where he could either be killed or captured. In early boxing, to knock down your opponent was considered a small triumph. But unlike in wrestling, to be knocked down did not end the match. Boxing allowed the man who was knocked down to get up and fight again, until such time as he no longer could get up. Initially, when one fell to the ground the man standing might hit the downed man or kick him once or twice. The fight could continue until the downed man regained his feet or cried "craven" and gave up. But eventually, boxing adopted the rule that you did not hit a man when he was down, and the fight only resumed when the downed man regained his feet. The winner of the boxing match was the one who knocked down his opponent so that he either gave up or could not continue.

It is not clear when boxing adopted the "round" system, which created a pause following each knockdown. In wrestling matches each fall naturally created a pause and then the match started again. It is likely that the same thing happened in boxing.

It is also not clear when boxing introduced the idea that a man, once knocked down, had only a short time to return to the fight. There was a natural bias on the part of the crowd to urge the knocked-down man to quickly get up and continue the fight. Eventually it was decided that there were limits to how long a man might remain down and still be able to continue. These refinements may have entered rather early, but we do not know when.

Finally, the crowd was essential to the development of boxing. The crowd helped to create the basic rules of the sport and was prepared to enforce them. Without the crowd, the sport of boxing could not have developed as it did. In addition, as we shall see, the nature of the crowd made boxing a democratic sport. As Elias Canetti notes in his work *Crowds and Power*, one of the basic attributes of a crowd is its equality: "It is of fundamental importance and one might even define a crowd as a state of absolute equality.... All demands for justice and all theories of equality ultimately derive their energy from the actual experience of equality familiar to anyone who has been a part of a crowd." The crowd of the boxing ring became one of the fundamental drivers of democracy in England and helped preserve the country from social revolution.[67]

When Did the Sport of Boxing Begin in England?

As we have seen, medieval fist-fighting began as an amateur activity. Our best analysis suggests that it began as a method of fighting that grew out of anger and reaction to a spontaneous situation. There was no public memory of the Greek or Roman *caestus* fighting. When an Anglo-Saxon male struck another on the nose with his fist, there was nothing organized about the act. There was no sport involved. Nor was there a sport contemplated when Hereward knocked out the cook. Even when we find fists being used in wrestling matches it may have been initially a spontaneous act designed to protect oneself from a fall or a loss. Only gradually did it evolve into a positive method of fighting in which the fist-fighter became the aggressor. We see the changeover from reaction to action in the illustration from the *Queen Mary's Psalter* (c. 1310–1320) (Chapter I). The nude man clearly intends to hit his opponent with his fist, but it may have taken many years for this strategy to develop.

The first clear case of fist-fighting approaching the level of a sport was when fists were used in buffeting circa 1325. Yet even then it remained (and continues to remain) an amateur exercise. But when William Horman's schoolboys carried on buffeting bouts in their schoolyards in the early 1500s, they laid the foundations for modern boxing. When these children chose to fight with their fists, they began to change the rules of buffeting from reciprocal blows to a flurry of blows without pauses in between. At this point, fist-fighting was on the way to becoming an active sport with the addition of new rules and new names.

It is clear that the modern sport of boxing began in England during the sixteenth century. The fact that it was recognized by John Baret in his dictionary in 1574 makes us think that boxing, as a sport, was in existence by the middle of the sixteenth century. On the other hand, the fact that boxing was not mentioned by the schoolmaster William Horman in 1519, nor by the grammarian John Palsgrave in 1530, despite the fact that both recognized the concept of fist-fighting, suggests that if boxing was being born at that time, it was not yet well enough known to merit a name and that the sport did not then exist. Our conclusion then is that the sport of boxing came into named existence in England circa 1550, but not before. We agree with Pierce Egan that boxing is "wholly English" since the word *box* and the concept of fist-fighting are demonstrably English and do not rely upon foreign sources. We also agree with Thomas Churchyard that the very first boxers during the 1500s may have been ruffians or rogues. In any case they were not gentlemen. But whosoever they were, they created in England a sport that has lasted 800 years and has gained worldwide acceptance.

CHAPTER IV

The First Boxers in Britain (1165–1600)

In the previous chapter we discussed how the common Englishman gradually ceased to use weapons in fighting and fought with bare hands instead. In this chapter we will discuss how sword-fighting may have influenced bare-handed fighting, and how early fencing masters may have been among the first boxers in Britain.

Boxers and Fencers: **Pugils** *and* **Ruffians**

Explaining how fist-fighters became fencers and fencers became fist-fighters is complicated. We do not have any clear example of this change as we did for wrestling converting to fist-fighting. Instead we need to explore the hidden pathways among the common folk of medieval England until we get to the end of the sixteenth century.

As we learned in Chapter III, we have very little evidence of fist-fighting during the Anglo-Saxon period (450–1066). The common man generally fought with a shield and a spear. Swords were rare and the property of only the wealthiest men. The more common weapon, carried by both men and women, was the *seax* or short knife. These were of two types, the shorter version, such as a kitchen knife, used for domestic tasks (3 inches to 13 inches), and the longer version (21 to 30 inches) used for hunting. The *seax* had a single-edged blade and, when carried about, was worn horizontally in a scabbard on the belt with the cutting edge up.[1]

After the Norman Conquest in 1066, the *seax* was joined by a center-gripped shield called a buckler. Bucklers were much smaller than the body-covering shield famous in the "shield wall" seen being used in the *Bayeux*

Tapestry. The single-bladed *seax* and the center-gripped shield gave rise to the classic sword-and-buckler style of fighting. Although some bucklers could be large, they were more effective if they did not exceed 17 inches in diameter. Often, they had a "boss" protruding out from the center of the buckler. These small bucklers had been used in Ireland circa 900 (*The Book of Kells* folio 200r) but became very popular in England in the later Middle Ages (14th to 16th centuries). They were held with one hand, and because they were small and light, these bucklers served both as defensive and offensive weapons. They could be used easily as a fist to hit the opponent. The swords were longer at this time and appear to have two edges.

Despite the fact that Norman justice had established laws that pretended to reach to the lowest levels of society, most people still had to rely upon themselves and their neighbors, not the king or his delegates, when confronted with violence or crime. An appeal to the local court system (*assize*) was uncertain and expensive. As we shall see later on, appeals to a trial by jury often were resolved in favor of the local nobility who in fact might be the culprit in the case. The trial by battle (*duello*) on the other hand could lead to outcomes that were both doubtful and dangerous.[2] This meant that most free-born youth needed to be trained in the use of the sword and buckler to provide protection for themselves and their property. This gave rise to the first regular schools of fence.

According to J.D. Aylward, the first professional fencing master on record was Wilelmus Pugilius, who failed to appear in court on the day appointed for his trial by battle in 1165.[3] We also find a Thomas Pugil (1170), Lawrence Pugil (1177) and a Bernardus Pugilis (c. 1190). All of these were professional fighters who were involved in judicial duels or trials by battle.[4]

In the thirteenth century, between 1229 and 1242, the Earl of Warwick granted land to John Archer, *pugili meo*. Later, in 1286, there is record of a certain *pugil* from Lincoln who was named Roger the Clerk ("*Cuidam pugili de partibus Lincoll' qui dicebatur Rogerus clericus*"). In the first four cases above, the name *pugil* appears as a surname, whereas in the last two cases, it appears as a trade description. John Archer was primarily a bowman before he was a fencer, while Roger the Clerk was a member of the clergy in addition to being

Fig. 8. Sword-and-buckler fighting at the beginning of the fourteenth century. *Queen Mary's Psalter*, circa 1310–1320, f.146 (British Library Royal MS 2 B VII).

a sword-fighter. Any rough-neck with a taste for violence could be a *pugil*. By the middle of thirteenth century *pugil* simply meant "hired champion."[5]

Pugils were men with a talent for fighting. They hired themselves out to fight judicial duels on behalf of others in civil property disputes. Henry C. Lea considered them to be paid gladiators: "Reckless desperados, skilled in the quarter-staff, or whose familiarity with sword and dagger, gained by a life spent in ceaseless brawls, gave them confidence in their own ability.... [I]t was an occupation which exposed them to little risk beyond that which they habitually incurred."[6]

And although these fighters were known to fight judicial duels with weapons, it is interesting that only one of them had a name that was some version of *escremir* (to fight with a sword). Rather, as we have seen, most were known as *pugils* (from which we get *pugilist* and *pugilistic*). These sword-fighters drew their names from the Latin word meaning a boxer or fist-fighter.[7]

We know that *pugils* in medieval England were fencing masters. What we have not discussed before is that they were also the first paid fist-fighters in English history. Their very names tell us that they began as fist-fighters before they picked up a sword. So far, we have not found written records demonstrating their fist-fighting roles, but their names confirm that they were the first named boxers in Britain. As late as the middle of the seventeenth century, Sir Thomas Browne (1605–1682) could still define them as such: "Pugils; that is, men fit for combat and the exercise of the fist."[8]

M.J. Russell, who examined the activities of these men, tells us: "There is no evidence of any common-form surname derived directly from *pugil*, or *campio*, or its English equivalent 'champion.'" He then corrects himself and says "except perhaps the Champenays." William the Champenays appeared as a champion in 1220. Russell also notes that a Champenays was a champion in another case of 1223, but he argues this was different man. If he was right, there were at least two men with the last name Champenays (Champion) in the 1220s. Similarly, although Russell did not know of William Pugil or Bernard Pugil, he did recognize Thomas Pugil and Lawrence Pugil, both of whom were fined for being *recreant*, or surrendering at a judicial duel. Despite Russell's comment, it is clear that *pugil* and *campio* were in fact used as surnames in the thirteenth century by those who followed these trades.[9]

Pugils were considered disreputable men and their lives were fraught with danger. They were probably young men in their late teens to early thirties. And, as Barbara Hanawalt, taking a feminist point of view, has pointed out, this "tends to be the age-group most prone to participation in crime."

> In all modern Western European and American criminal statistics, being young and being male are the most consistent conditions associated with the risk of becoming a criminal. In a society where this group is very large, there will be

more crime. This would help to explain the general lawlessness in the countryside of medieval England.¹⁰

Pugils' visible roles were to act as paid champions for the wealthy urbanites who were not skilled at fighting. As such they could be punished if they did not win their cases. In 1220, Elias Piggun, a fencing master, stood in as a warrantor for Philip King, who was accused of stealing a horse belonging to Hamo the Moor. Elias's job was to intimidate Hamo and his supporters and, if necessary, to fight a judicial duel against him. Instead, Hamo refused the judicial duel on the grounds that Elias was a hired champion. Hamo took Philip King to court for a jury trial. There Elias claimed that the horse had been given to him in Wales for teaching a certain man fencing lessons (*a quodam homine per sicut doceret ei de skermia*). He said he had sold the horse to Philip's father-in-law who then gave it to Philip. It was proven that Elias was lying. He was convicted and sentenced to have his foot cut off. The court considered this a merciful sentence, as punishment could have led to him having his hand cut off as well.¹¹

After reviewing the dangers of the profession, Henry C. Lea concluded that "with such risks to be encountered, it is no wonder that the trade of the champion offered few attractions to honest men who could keep body and soul together in any other way."¹² Fencing schools themselves, Egerton Castle informs us, were "dangerous dens, most of them, inviting attendance of the pugnacious and dissolute, and had the very worst reputation from the first time they are heard of as institutions." From the twelfth century on, fencing schools were considered schools for crime and violence.¹³

Due to their unsavory reputations, fencing schools were outlawed as early as 1180. This occurred just at the time of Henry II's Assize of Arms, which was designed to increase the number of warriors in the country. Since fencing schools were outlawed, evidently fencing masters were considered outlaws rather than warriors.¹⁴

A century later, in 1286, this ban was confirmed by Edward I when he outlawed schools of "Eskirmer au Bokeler" (sword-fighting with a buckler) in London:

> Whereas it is customary for profligates to learn the art of fencing, who are emboldened to commit the most unheard-of villainies, no such school shall be kept in the city for the future, upon penalty of forty marks for each offence. And the Aldermen shall make a thorough search in their several wards for the detecting of such offenders, in order to bring them to justice and an exemplary punishment. And, as most of the aforesaid villainies are committed by foreigners, who from all parts incessantly crowd thither, it is therefore ordered that no person whatsoever, that is not free of the City, shall be suffered to reside therein.¹⁵

Still, given the need for personal protection and thus fencing teachers, such an edict could not be easily enforced. In 1311 the Lord Mayor of London had

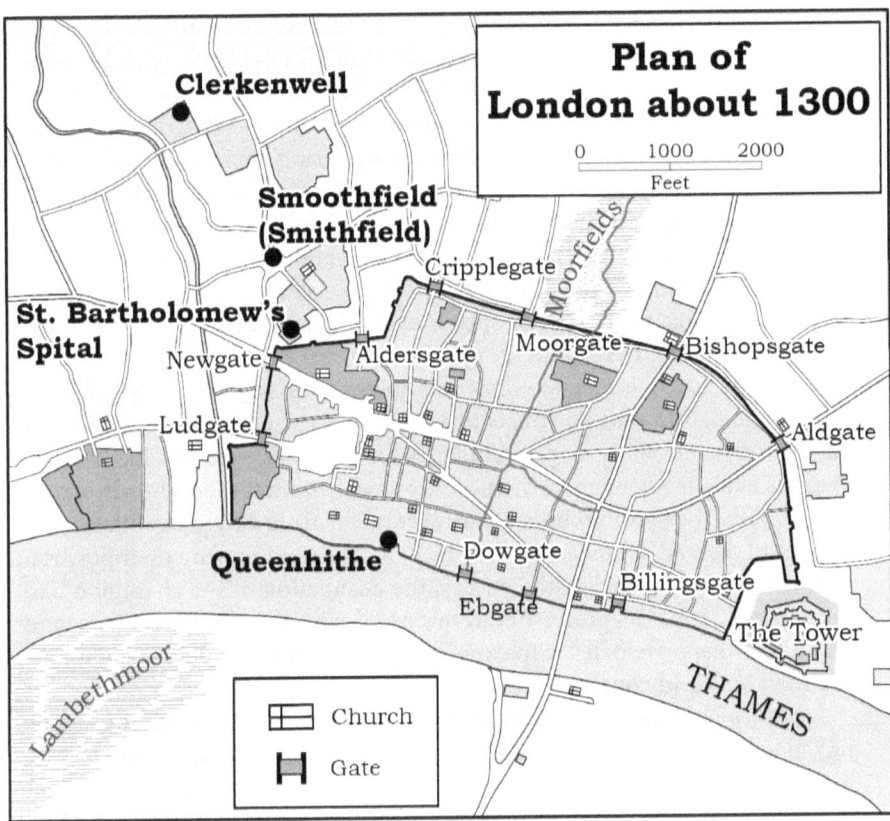

Figure 9. London about 1300. Smoothfield, now Smithfield, the center of athletic activity for London, was outside the walls, just below Clerkenwell (based upon the map originally found in *Shepherd's Historical Atlas* [Barnes and Noble, 1980] and redrawn by Sara Taliaferro for this book).

"Master Roger, le Skirmisour" arrested "for keeping fencing school for divers men, and for enticing thither the sons of respectable persons so as to waste and spend the property of their fathers and mothers upon bad practices." Roger was then thrown into jail and never heard of again. Despite this grim warning, the demand for personal protection meant that fencing schools continued in existence for centuries.[16]

These early fencing masters fought first with their fists and then with their swords. Fighting was their pastime and occupation. However, it is easier to recognize them in the records as duelists fighting with weapons than to find them fighting with bare fists in London or in markets or fairs. Nonetheless, we have already encountered Hamon of Bury fighting with his fists in the fair at St. Ives in Cornwall in 1287. Since there was no mention of any other weapons being used, presumably Amisius, the chicken farmer, mentioned in the previous chapter, was using fists and feet in his fatal battle with Bartholomew in 1265 or 1266 at the Winchester fair. In addition, we guess that when Henry of Longville attacked Gilbert Sherman on May 19, 1287, the day before Hamon's battle in St. Ives, he like Hamon was using his fists. It is clear that fighting with fists was occurring in fairs by the thirteenth century. Experience gained in such fights would explain the sophisticated holds presented in the *Queen Mary's Psalter* (Chapter I). We believe that those young men got their experience fighting with fists in fairs and markets.[17]

Despite this, *pugils* do not appear as fist-fighters in the public records. We have seen that they would set up schools to teach other young men their skills when it became apparent there was money to do so. We can also imagine that public fighting in the streets or markets was also their best method of advertising their skills to gain students for their schools. But like Master Roger le Skirmisour, many of them were probably lawless men who ultimately died in jail. They had no honor and were as far from being a gentleman as one could then be in English society. Henry C. Lea summed up their position in society: "By the thirteenth century, the occupation of the champion had become infamous. Its professors were classed with the vilest criminals, and with the unhappy females who exposed their charms for sale, as champions did their skill and courage."[18]

Still, *pugils* were not without their supporters. They were intimately linked to members of the aristocracy. As men who were willing to fight private battles, it would have been natural that they would come into the employment of the local landlord. The *pugil* John Archer was a paid retainer of the Earl of Warwick. James Buchanan Given found as well that there was a very close connection between criminals and the local aristocracy in the thirteenth century.[19] Given sums up this situation by noting: "A noble could often have use for a band of rough necks, and may have been willing to condone some unsavory activities by his retainers. Contemporaries certainly felt that some lords maintained [supported with money and protection] bands of criminals."[20]

Matthew Paris (1200–1259) gives one example of how the aristocracy became involved in criminal activities. He describes a highway robbery in the Pass of Alton near Winchester that likely occurred in 1248. According to Paris, two merchants from Brabant were robbed of 200 marks. When the merchants brought their complaint to King Henry III in the spring of 1249, they recognized some of the robbers in attendance at his court. They challenged the thieves to a trial by battle, but the thieves did not accept. The suspected people were arrested; however, they were then set free by a jury of the county. The king was forced to pay the merchants back their 200 marks and ordered a new jury to be drawn to reveal the names of the thieves. When this jury refused, the king had them thrown in jail and empaneled a third jury.

The third jury, recognizing the fate of their predecessors, immediately revealed that the entire county was full of thieves, from rich men in good standing, to royal keepers of the peace and bailiffs, to even members of the king's own household. About 30 people were hanged and a greater number were imprisoned. Although the criminals were not specifically named as *pugils* and champions in this story, it nonetheless demonstrates the collusion between criminals and the aristocracy at this time.[21]

John Bellamy confirms Matthew Paris's account and shows that such behavior continued into the fourteenth and fifteenth centuries. He finds that some local aristocrats were not only protectors but leaders of criminal gangs. He cites the case of Sir Ralph Paynel who, along with fifteen others, was indicted in 1375 for the murder of his neighbor, Sir William Cantilupe. As a testimony to Sir Ralph's influence in the neighborhood, he and all the others involved were cleared of the crime and Sir Ralph then married Maud, Sir William's wife, and took over William's lands. As Cicero might have asked of this crime: *Cui bono?* (who benefited?). In 1455 Sir Thomas Courtney, the son of the Earl of Devon, led a gang that robbed and killed a noted barrister, Nicholas Radford. The earl, Sir Thomas's father, then held an inquest and declared Radford's death a suicide. Later, in 1477, George, Duke of Clarence, who was brother to King Edward IV and who believed that justice delayed was justice denied, sent a gang of 80 men to abduct a woman whom he believed had poisoned his wife. They hauled the woman, Ankarette Twynho, across three counties, suborned a jury, then tried and executed her within three days.[22]

Lawrence Stone finds aristocrats employing such armed retainers as late as the sixteenth century. Stone cites a case in Gloucestershire in the 1570s in which Giles, Lord Chandos, used armed retainers with guns to frighten off the under-sheriff, protected servants of his who had robbed men on the highway, rigged juries, and put in place a high constable who blackmailed the local people.[23]

> Given the absence of honourable conventions in the prosecution of a quarrel, it is hardly surprising that some of the retainers of noblemen were indistinguishable from hired bullies, men who were ready to beat up or even occasionally kill at a word from their master.[24]

All of this is in keeping with our investigation that suggests *pugils* and other champions were employed as criminal "enforcers" by the local aristocracy should the need arise.

Alternatively, this type of man might join the various criminal gangs that developed during the fourteenth and fifteenth centuries. One of these criminal gangs was known to be composed of retainers of the Duke of Norfolk.[25]

In his study of crime in medieval England, John Bellamy summarizes the corrupt nature of this system:

> For the most part the leaders [of these criminal bands] were drawn from the gentry, the knights, and esquires, the very members of society on whom paradoxically the task of preserving local law and order increasingly devolved.[26]

The Church also employed *pugils* and other criminals. George Neilson mentions William Pygun who was hired as a "*magnus pugil*" by Ralph Gubiun, Prior of Tynemouth in 1214, but unfortunately lost his case. Henry of Fernbureg, known as the Marshal, became the champion of the Abbot of Glastonbury in 1258 and again in 1263. Robert Bartlett cited the case of Thomas of Bruges who was hired by the Bishop of Hereford for "so long as the said Thomas is able to perform the functions of a champion." Thomas apparently did well for he was paid 6 shillings and 8 pence every year from 1276 to 1289. And earlier we have seen that Roger the Clerk of Lincoln was a *pugil* in 1286.[27] John Bellamy agrees with Neilson: "There can be little doubt that the services of outlaws and criminals who had banded together were in considerable demand among religious houses."[28]

James Buchanan Given has a chapter in his book, *Society and Homicide in Thirteenth-Century England*, entitled "The Entrepreneurs of Violence." *Pugils*, as hired champions, could certainly be described as *entrepreneurs of violence*. Although Given focuses on the homicidal aspects of this "entrepreneurial" culture, and we have been focusing on its more benign aspects, it does not take much effort to realize that the same people could have been active in both groups. Given also finds that the homicides in his analysis "show a strong tendency to cluster near large towns and along trade routes." This is exactly the pattern we would expect from our *pugils*, who made their living teaching fencing and fighting for money in towns or markets. Such people could easily move from town to the suburbs and become robbers and thieves who might murder their victims in order to keep from being identified.[29]

By the sixteenth century the name *pugil* had disappeared and this type of fighter had been given a series of other names. Most notably, the more respectable descendants of the *pugils* were co-opted by King Henry VIII when he granted a number of them license to teach fencing under the name of the Masters of the Noble Science of Defence (1540). Still, many remained too disreputable to fit into the roles of Masters of Defence. These people were then given the generic name of "rogues" in the sixteenth century. However, Thomas Churchyard (c. 1520–1604) is more specific: "In our Elders daies fighters were called ruffians, and ruffians were so loathsome, that no honest man could abide their company."[30]

Sir Thomas Fuller (1608–1661) also says much the same in his book *The History of the Worthies of England* (1662). Speaking about the proverb "He is only fit for Ruffian's Hall," Fuller gives us a broad array of names for these fighters.[31] Fuller tells us that "*ruffians*" (men of low and brutal character, habitually given to acts of violence or crime; cut-throat villains) and "*swaggerers*" (those who quarrel and behave insolently or in a defiant manner) are similar in nature. Ruffians could be sword-and-buckler fighters, as swaggerers could be. Swaggerers were so called because they leaned forward and down in an aggressive manner when they walked as if ready to attack. There were also *"swashbucklers"* (sword-fighters who announced their presence by raking or "swashing" their sword across their bucklers and making a noise to attract attention). Due to the restrictions on teaching sword-fighting in the city, they all practiced in the fields outside London. West Smithfield was formerly called Ruffian's Hall, where such men usually met, casually or on purpose, to fight duels with a sword and buckler. From 1100 to 1500 such fighters were regularly found at Smithfield, until the appearance of Rowland Yorke, who introduced the rapier as a thrusting weapon in contrast to the usual hacking motion of the sword-and-buckler system. This proved so effective that the conventional sword-and-buckler system was rendered passé. The proverb about Ruffian Hall was then applied to quarrelsome people such as *"barraters"* (hired bullies who delighted in brawls and blows).[32]

Sword-and-buckler fighting may have stimulated the early development of fist-fighting. While the sword was the aggressive instrument, the buckler could be an offensive weapon itself. The buckler was used as a fist to hit the opponent when the sword was out of range. The sword too could be used as a fist. When the blade was blocked by the buckler, the sword might be reversed and the opponent hit with the pommel instead. This led to the concept of "pommeling," which became one of the new names given to boxing.

To sum up our discussion to this point:

(1) Our argument is that side by side with wrestlers and buffeters, the earliest fencing masters were also the first boxers in England. We note that the word *box* initially meant a sword blow and that those sword-fighters who were giving blows with their swords throughout the fourteenth century, were in fact, *boxing*. At the same time the name adopted by a group of fencing masters in the twelfth century was *pugil*, meaning boxer. *Pugil* is derived from *pugnus, i, m.*, meaning *fist* and *pugna, ae, f.*, meaning a *battle*. *Pugils* were fist-fighters before they were fencers.

(2) *Pugils* and *campios* were men who were hired champions and paid fighters during the twelfth and thirteenth centuries. They might be hired either by laymen or religious houses who "maintained" them in exchange for their services. "Maintenance" meant not only providing them shelter and food, but providing protection from punishment for their actions. When they weren't fighting these men taught fencing. Fencing was known as a disreputable trade and banned in London, but the need for training in self-protection kept the schools alive. Laws barring fencing in London may have prevented the use of swords in the city and required that these champions fight with fists instead.

(3) Sword-and-buckler fighting and wrestling were exercises held in Smithfield outside of London from the twelfth century on. Both *pugils* and wrestlers were working in the same place at the same time and sharing the same audience. The *pugils'* use of fists in fighting may have influenced the wrestlers. This made possible the merging of wrestling and sword-and-buckler fighting into boxing. This aligns with the belief of Terry Brown, the English master of early modern martial arts, who wrote to me that "the principles of boxing evolved from weapon fighting, which is why I call it the 'fencing style' of boxing."[33]

(4) The fields of Smithfield were probably the original home of boxing. It was well known as the place where athletic exercises, such as wrestling, horse-racing, archery and sword-fighting occurred. It would be natural to find boxing there as well. This suggestion is strengthened by the fact that early boxing was given a series of names, some Middle English and some Norman French. Smithfield, as the prime center for athletic exercises in England, and the meeting ground for both languages, must be considered the best location for the origin of boxing.

A Proto-Boxing Match in 1458

Still, we have not seen any boxing battles in the years prior to 1600. We have sketched an outline of the beginning of boxing in Britain around 1300. We have discovered names being given to this new exercise from 1530 to 1574. We have outlined some of the basic rules that would have converted a brawl into a sport and given it more public appeal. We have also suggested who the first boxers were and where they were to be found. Yet if the earliest matches occurred in Smithfield, we have no record of them. Instead, in order to see what one of these early fights might have looked like, we need to turn to the annals of crime. It is there where we find our closest experience to an early boxing match.

Circa 1455 a thief named Thomas Whytehorne was arrested in the New Forest near Beuley and put into prison at Winchester. In order to save himself from hanging, he appealed (accused) a number of other men for various crimes. These men were arrested, tortured and some, who had no friends or property, were hanged. Those with friends or property were allowed to pay fines and released. Whytehorne himself was kept in prison, but was paid one pence per day by the king for his room and board. In this way, Whytehorne lived in the Winchester jail for three years; being paid by the king and periodically appealing other men, who, when placed in the cells, would relate their crimes to him. At last, about 1458, he appealed a man named James Fisher, a fisherman and a tailor, who refused to admit he had committed any crime. Since Fisher had no money, he challenged Whytehorne to a judicial duel.

IV. *The First Boxers in Britain (1165–1600)* 61

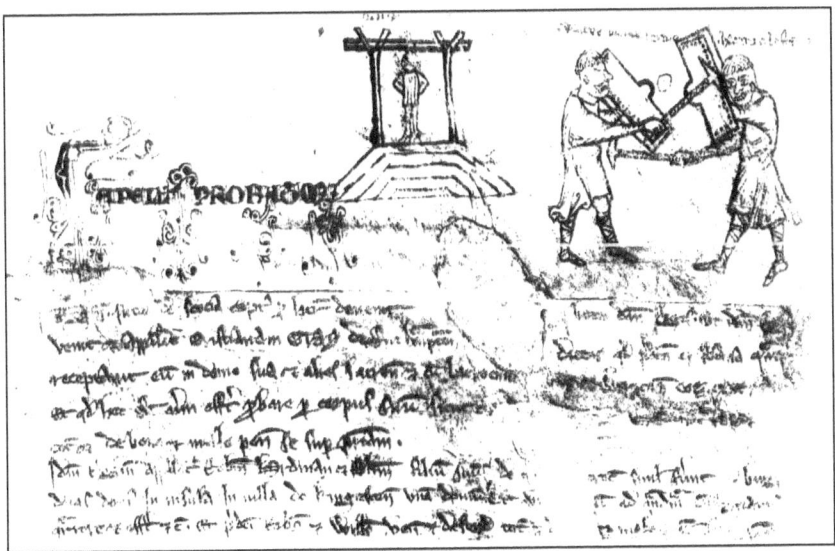

Fig. 10. Picture of trial by battle between Walter Bloweberme (left) and Hamo Stare, from F.W. Maitland, ed., *Select Pleas of the Crown*, Vol. 1, AD 1200–1225, Selden Society 192 (London: Bernard Quaritch, 1888; frontispiece). These fighters are shown with weapons looking like pick-axes and shields. Walter Bloweberme was an approver (a confessed criminal) who, to save himself, accused his colleague, Hamo Stare, of being a thief. Hamo, to save his life, denied the charges. In the background is the gallows on which Hamo was hanged after losing the trial.

The appealer (Whytehorne) and the defendant (Fisher) agreed to battle. They were dressed entirely in white sheep's leather from head to foot. They were presented with two staves of green ash about three feet long with the bark still on. On one end was a horn of iron shaped like a ram's horn with the small end as sharp as possible.[34]

The combatants were required to fast prior to the fight, and if they needed a drink "they must take their own piss." Then they were taken by the judge (Master Myhelle Skyllyng) to "the most sorry and wretched green" outside Winchester where they entered the arena for combat, the appealer (Whytehorne) entering from the East and the defendant (Fisher) entering from the Southwest.

Fisher immediately struck Whytehorne with his staff with such force that his staff broke in two. Whytehorne then struck Fisher with his staff and would have probably defeated him, but the judge's officers stepped in and stopped the fight. They took away Whytehorne's staff and ordered the two to continue the fight with bare hands:

And then they fought together with their fists a long time and then they rested. They fought again and then rested again. And then they went together by the necks. And then with their teeth, that the leather of their clothing and the flesh was all rent in many places on their bodies. And then the false appealer cast that meek innocent down to the ground and hit him in the testicles [*bote hym by the membrys*], that the silly innocent cried out. And by happenstance the innocent recovered his strength on his knees and took that false appealer by the nose with his teeth and put his thumb in his eye. And the appealer cried out and prayed mercy, for he was false unto God and unto him.[35]

The judge called an end to the bout. Whytehorne admitted that he had falsely accused Fisher and eighteen other men. He prayed for God's mercy, made his confession and was hanged. Fisher was released, became a hermit and shortly thereafter died.[36]

Once the battle was changed from one with staves to one with bare hands, it became a no-holds-barred fist-fight, with one significant difference: the fight was managed by a judge and fought according to rules. These rules were not the rules of wrestling since a throw to the ground did not end the match, nor were they the rules of any existing sport. Instead, it was a rough and tumble fist-fight to the death. The match ended only when one of the contestants cried "craven" and gave up. As such it was more like a later boxing match to the finish than a wrestling bout.

Although there were rules to this event, they did not govern the type of holds or blows that might be used. Instead the rules governed the structure of the fight: the location, how the opponents were dressed, where the crowd was placed, what weapons were used and the fact that when one's weapon was broken, the other's weapon was removed. The judge and the rules made this a different type of fight, neither a battle with weapons nor a wrestling match. Instead the two were told that "when their weapon broke they must fight with their hands, fists, nails, teeth, feet and legs." At this point, the fight was converted into a proto-boxing bout. It now resembled the Lancashire "catch-or-catch-can" wrestling, or the no-holds-barred boxing battles of early America, where both fists and teeth were used.[37]

This event occurred at least 130 years after the first proto-boxing bout shown in the illustration from *Queen Mary's Psalter* (c. 1310–1320). By 1458 some progress had been made toward modern boxing. The judge insisted on the equality of weapons. He had the power to stop the fight and determine the victor when one of the opponents gave up. Although there was no arbitrary time limit, conventionally the opponents would fight from sun-up to starlight or until one gave up. But the judge did allow the fighters to have pauses to rest and recuperate similar to pauses between rounds in later boxing. This was a trial, not a sporting event. Still, there is enough here to suggest that we are looking at a more advanced type of proto-boxing match in which fist-fighting was used in a life or death struggle. And since this was a trial, it is likely there was a fence around the list to keep the crowd from interfering. This practice became the pattern in later boxing matches on the turf.[38]

William Gregory, the man who told this story, was the Mayor of London in 1451–52. He obviously knew Master Myhelle Skyllyng, the judge in this affair, and probably had been invited by him to attend the duel. That he was an eye witness to the events seems clear. He was strongly against Thomas Whytehorne and in favor of James Fisher, establishing the pattern for later gambling on boxing matches. But his reaction to the entire event is of greater interest. For him the duel was a "foul battle." It had nothing to recommend it save the law. Despite that fact, it held his attention and led him to devote what amounted to three-and-a-half printed pages to it. Even so, he still could say "it is too shameful to rehearse all the conditions of this foul conflict." This paradoxical reaction of fascination and revulsion is perhaps one reason why it is so difficult to find examples of boxing in the early records.[39]

Thomas Whytehorne and James Fisher were unwilling fighters, but they certainly fit the description of "ruffians" given by Thomas Churchyard. What is also clear is that their fight was without honor. William Gregory, in fact, described it as a "vile and unmannerly fighting." Vincentio Saviolo, at the end of the sixteenth century, argued that sword-fighting possessed a sense of honor since it had rules that that allowed one to touch an opponent without being touched. Fist-fighting, during its first 400 years of existence, had no such rules. Its sense of honor only developed with Jack Broughton (1704–1789) who, it was said, was the first who could hit without being hit. In 1458 no techniques existed to allow Whytehorne and Fisher to fight in an honorable fashion. Pierce Egan would have called their proto-boxing match a "slaughter."[40]

Although we believe circumstances converted this duel into the equivalent of an early version of a boxing match, this does not mean that the judicial duel was the birthplace of boxing. Instead, as we are finding, many sources contributed to the development of boxing. We have already seen that wrestling, buffeting and sword-fighting each influenced boxing in some way. Now we can see that the trial by battle or the judicial duel also played a role in boxing's history by introducing an independent judge as an arbiter to the match.

The Situation at the End of the Sixteenth Century

Sword-and-buckler fighting had found refuge in the prizes of the Masters of Defence after 1540. But not everybody was welcomed in the guild. The rogues and ruffians of the past continued their unsanctioned activities as well.

This led to two types sword-fighting: sword-playing supported by the rules adopted by Masters of Defence and sword-fighting advanced by those *pugils* maintained by the aristocracy. Sword-playing describes the benign sword combat that sought to advance men to ranks in a hierarchy dedicated to civilized behavior and obedience to the monarch. Sword-fighting continued to occur among ruffians, descendants of the *pugils* of the past, who oppressed the population to benefit the wealthy. Lawrence Stone speaks of the "total lack of rules within which such violence as occurred could be confined. When personal conflict between principals took place, no holds were barred."[41] The nobility and the gentry were often the originators of this violence. They saw nothing dishonorable in attacking by surprise with superior forces, nor in hitting a man when he was down. Compared to their behavior, the behavior of the Masters of Defense was civilized and their violence was mild.

It is possible that by 1550 or shortly after, bouts in which men fought with fists in public, rather than with swords, were appearing. George Smeeton, in his book, *Doings in London* tells us (without citing his sources) that "Sir John Perrot [1528-1592] fought the first boxing-match upon record, in Southwark, where he beat two of the king's yeomen of the guards, an action which brought him into public notice at that time."[42]

During the reign of Queen Elizabeth I (1558-1603), common men developed their own sense of self-worth. They did not adopt the rapier duel as did the gentry, nor did they adopt the nobility's lack of morality. Rather, when faced by a man with a rapier they presented a unified front and responded with other types of weapons and a new morality. This new morality, which we will describe under the title of "fair play," will be discussed subsequently. Needless to say, it was reinforced by boxing. An example of this is given by George Silver (c. 1550-1620). Silver describes how an Italian, Rocco Bonetti, was first beaten in a street fight by Austen Bagger, an English swordsman, and then was beaten by a bunch of watermen.[43] After describing the battle with Bagger, Silver concludes:

> This was the first and last battle that ever Signior Rocco made, saving once at Queen Hithe, he drew his Rapier upon a waterman, when he was thoroughly beaten with Oares and Stretchers.[44]

Rocco's attack on the waterman at Queen Hythe (Queen's Harbor) might have occurred as the result of a quarrel over a fare across the river. Watermen were paid to row people up and down or across the river. Pulling a sword in a quarrel over a fare was a classic and potentially fatal mistake made by foreigners in England. To threaten an Englishman with a sword when the Englishman had none would immediately trigger an attack by any crowd present. Signor Rocco was lucky to escape with his life in this event.

Henri Misson, writing in 1697, confirmed this type of English behavior:

In *France* we punish such Rascals with our Cane, and sometimes with the flat of our Sword; but in *England* this is never practis'd; they use neither Sword nor Stick against a Man that is unarm'd; and if an unfortunate Stranger (for an *Englishman* would never take it into his Head) should draw his Sword upon one that had none, he'd have a hundred People upon him in a Moment, that would, perhaps, lay him so flat he would hardly ever get up again till the Resurrection.[45]

While the rapier had become the weapon of choice for the aristocracy during the latter part of the sixteenth century, the common Englishman did not adopt it. The sword-and-buckler techniques taught by the Masters of Defence were passing out of favor. In London, Oxford and Ipswich, knives were being left at home rather than being carried in a scabbard on one's person. Instead of knives, common men had already begun to develop skill with Nature's own weapons: the fist and the foot.

During the sixteenth century, the common Englishman had developed a sense of pride in himself and country. This led him to develop the same sense of self-worth that the nobility had embraced with their "Code of Courtesy." Instead of accepting an insult from a noble, the common man often chose to defend himself with fists rather than a sword.

George Silver gives us another glimpse of this change in attitude with his story of a second Italian, the fencing master Vincentio Saviolo (d. 1598/1599):

> Upon a time at Wels, in Somersetshire, as he [Saviolo] was in great bravierie amongst manie gentlemen of good accompt, with great boldnesse he gaue out speeches that he had bene thus manie years in England, and since the time of his first coming, there was not yet one Englishman that could touch him at the Single Rapier, or Rapier and Dagger.
>
> A valiant gentleman being there amongst the rest, his English hart did rise, to heare this proud boaster, and secretly sent a messenger to one Bartholomew Bramble, a friend of his, a very tall man of both his hand and person [a well-respected man of great courage and accomplishment], who kept a school of Defence in that town....
>
> This maister of defence presently came, and amongst all the gentlemen, with his cap off [respectfully], prayed Maister Vincentio that he would be pleased to take a quart of wine with him.
>
> Vincentio, verie scornefully looking upon him, said unto him; Wherefore shuld you give me a quart of wine? ... I haue no need of thy wine; then said the Maister of Defence: Sir, I haue a schoole of Defence in this towne, will it please you to go thither?
>
> Thy schoole, said Maister Vincentio, what shall I do at thy schoole? Play with me, (said the Maister) at the Rapier and Dagger, if it please you. Play with thee, said Maister Vincentio? If I play with thee, I will hit thee 1, 2, 3, 4 thrusts in the eie together.
>
> Then, said the Maister of Defence, if you can do so, it is better for you, and the worse for me, but surely I can hardly believe that you can hit me: but yet once againe I hartily pray you, good Sir, that you go to my Schoole and play with me.

Play with thee, said Maister Vincentio (verie scornefully) by God me scorne to play with thee.

With that word scorne, the Maister of Defence was very much moved, and up with his great English fist and stroke Maister Vincentio such a boxe on the eare that he fell over and over, his legges just against a Butterie hatch, whereon stood a great blacke Jacke [a leather pitcher lined with pitch designed to hold a large quantity of beer]: the Maister of Defence, fearing the worst against Vincentio his rising, catcht the blacke Jacke into his hand, being more than halfe full of beere. Vincentio lustily start up, laying his hand upon his dagger, and the other hand pointed with his finger, saying Verie well: I will cause thee to lie in gaile for this yeare 1, 2, 3, 4 yeares.

And well, said the Maister of Defence, since you will drinke no wine, will you pledge me in Beere? I drink to all the cowardlie knaves in England, and I thinke thee to be the veriest coward of them all; with that he cast all the Beere upon him.[46]

This instructive episode demonstrates how Bartholomew Bramble, a Master of Defence who was used to teaching weapons-fighting, instinctively reacted to an insult by hitting with his fist. Vincentio, also a teacher of fencing, chose not to respond with either the sword or the dagger he was wearing, but instead threatened a lawsuit. Here we have two sword-fighters choosing not to use their weapons. Vincentio knew the common code of the Englishman would not permit him to attack with a weapon when all Bramble had was a jug of beer in his hand. But by calling Vincentio a knave and a coward, and throwing beer on him when he chose not to fight, Bramble demonstrated that a man armed only with his fist could triumph over a man armed with a sword and a dagger. The common Englishman had developed a new sense of morality by the end of the sixteenth century. It was dangerous to threaten a man with a sword when he did not have one. As powerful as a rapier was, it now was trumped by the English attitude to bare fists.

The Proof of a New Sport

The first proof that a new sport had been born was found in the work "Plaine Percevall, The Peace-Maker of England" (1590), written by Richard Harvey (1560–1630). Harvey was a polemicist in the Martin Marprelate religious controversy (an antecedent to the later Puritan Revolution) when he spoke of a practice now well known to most boxers: "To boxe a shadowe."

> Oh so some of those companions ply the boxe, to boxe a shadowe, and beat their knuckles against a bare wall, and to get a sure card on their side, either calles for Justice, and seeks to incense our noble Queene against the other.[47]

Translation: Oh, so some of those companions (either Martin Marprelate or his opponents) are boxers. They shadow-box and beat their knuckles against a bare wall. And to get an advantage on their side, either call for Justice or seek to turn our noble Queen against their opponent.

Richard Harvey's description of "shadow-boxing" is the first solid proof we have that the sport of boxing was in existence. In and of itself, shadow-boxing could simply be an exercise to keep one fit, but a man shadow-boxing would not normally smash his fists against a bare wall. A man beating his knuckles against a bare wall was not doing it just for exercise; he was trying to strengthen his hands for a bare-knuckle match. This shows that already, by 1590, fist-fighters had recognized two important things about boxing: (1) damage to one's hands was common when bare-knuckle boxers hit one another on the head, since both the head and the fist could suffer and (2) to avoid hurting one's hands in a fight, a boxer needed to strengthen the fist before the fight. One simple way to do this was to beat one's knuckles against a hard, smooth wall.[48]

Prior to the introduction of boxing gloves (c. 1867), there was a common injury called the "boxer's fracture" that occurred when the fist hit a hard object. The force of the blow could break the metacarpal bones linking the fingers to the wrist. Street fighters had two choices: they could aim their blows at the body and try to wear down their opponent while safeguarding their hands, or they could give their opponent a box on the ear and try for a quick win. A man beating his knuckles against a bare wall was trying to toughen his hands to withstand giving blows to the ear or to the chin. By training in this fashion, the fighter demonstrated that the upcoming boxing match was important enough that he would want to gain an advantage over his opponent ("to get a sure card on their side"). Although by 1590 we have yet to see a real boxing match, Harvey's words make it clear that they were being carried on and that men trained for them in advance.[49]

In 1599, nine years after Richard Harvey mentioned shadow-boxing, William Shakespeare used the word buffet to confirm the existence of the sport. By this time, buffet was the aristocratic synonym for box. In Act V, scene ii, lines 136–142 of *Henry V*, Henry in wooing Princess Katherine says to her:

> If I could win a lady at leap-frog, or by vaulting into my saddle with my armor on my back, under the correction of bragging be it spoken, I should quickly leap into a wife. Or if I might buffet for my love, or bound my horse for her favors, I could lay on like a butcher and sit like a jack-an-apes, never off.

The phrase "Or if I might buffet for my love" shows that by the end of the sixteenth century, buffets, like boxing, had become an organized fist-fight. Henry conceives that he might win his wife by buffeting, with her being the prize. This anticipation of a prize at the completion of a fight at buffets is a very different thing from a brawl following a box on the ear. Buffeting now has rules enough to be able to determine a winner. The fact that the contestants also know in advance of the prize means that there is planning to a match of buffets. Shakespeare, like Harvey, is telling us that the first prizefights using fists, rather than weapons, had already appeared.

Shakespeare also gives us an indication as to who the boxers or buffeters were and where we might look for them in society. King Henry says that if he might buffet for his love, "I could lay on like a butcher." Butchers have long been associated with boxing. John Ford, the modern boxing historian, has noted: "One occupation above all was associated with prizefighting. A number of the greatest champions had been butchers, and butchers were numbered among the most enthusiastic followers of prizefighting and the kindred Fancy sports of bullbaiting and dogfighting."[50]

Later, in *Antony and Cleopatra* (1606–1607) (Act I, scene iv, lines 20–22), Shakespeare describes what a buffet fight might look like. Octavius Caesar speaks of Antony behaving dissolutely in Alexandria: "To reel the streets at noon, and stand the buffet with knaves that smells of sweat: say this becomes him." This confirms that buffets and boxing were contests taking place in public streets, in markets, or even in warehouses as we will see later. They were street fights between two sweaty men who were ready to stand and fight. They were also "stand-up fights" where the men might stand toe-to-toe and hit each other, not backing up or giving a foot, a rule that William Horman's students had established a century earlier. The fight might continue until one of them gave up or fell to the ground. And, if the comments in *Henry V* mean anything, the opponents fought for a prize and the fight might be scheduled in advance.[51]

Yet, we can go further. In 1602, Richard Carew of Antony (1555–1620), in his book *The Survey of Cornwall*, described a local wrestling match:

> For performing this play, the beholders cast themselves in a ring, which they call making a place, into the empty middle space whereof the two champion wrestlers step forth, stripped into their doublets and hosen, and untrussed that they may so the better command the use of their limbs, and first shaking hands in token of friendship they fall presently to the effects of anger; for each striveth how to take hold of the other with his best advantage, and to bear his adverse party down, wherein, whosoever overthoweth his mate in such sort as that either his back, or the one shoulder and contrary heel do touch the ground, is accounted to give a fall. If he be endangered, and make a narrow escape, it is called a foil. This hath also his laws, of taking hold only above the girdle, wearing a girdle to take hold by, playing three pulls for trial of mastery, the fall-giver to be exempted from playing again with the taker, and bound to answer his successor, &c.[52]

This country wrestling match shows how closely related buffets and boxing were to wrestling. The gathering of bystanders that formed a ring for wrestlers was the same as that which made the ring for boxers. The wrestlers stripped to their doublets or undershirts, just as the "sweaty knaves" might have done in a buffets match. Wrestlers began a match by shaking hands, a convention still observed in boxing. Both sports were played on the turf outdoors, and they shared some of the same rules: no weapons were used, only two men could fight at a time and, in both sports, men did not hit below the belt or girdle. In addition, both sports share many of the same holds.

These similarities confirm that boxing developed out of the English wrestling environment. Yet they became different sports. Boxing used closed fists while wrestling was fought with open hands. In early boxing when a man was thrown to the ground the round ended, but the bout might continue. In wrestling, when a man fell to the ground it might end the bout, a convention dating back to Roman times. Finally, the names given to this new sport demonstrate that boxing was recognized as different from wrestling by the public.

However, the same men often played both sports. Although Cornwall was best known as a center for wrestling, Cornishmen engaged in boxing as well. Richard Carew mentioned that "the youthlier sort of Bodmin townsmen use sometimes to sport themselves by playing the box with strangers, whom they summon to Halgavor."[53]

Halgavor, or "Goat's Moor," an area outside the town of Bodmin, was the site of a July carnival celebration dating back to Saxon times and "resorted to by thousands of people." It was also a favorite place where the youth of Bodmin used to take strangers for mock trials. "Playing the box" suggests that boxing was involved in the challenges to which strangers were subjected in the years prior to 1600. By summoning men to Halgavor the men of Bodmin were issuing a challenge that led to these country boxing matches. Similar challenges were issued in dueling matches at the same time. The existence of such challenges was considered an essential feature of the ritual of boxing and dueling. A challenge to fight was part of the rules that made boxing a sport.

Who Were the First Boxers in England?

I believe that the *pugils* were the first boxers in England. As we have seen, they first appear in the twelfth century (AD 1100–1200). Their names suggest that they began as fist-fighters first and became sword-fighters second. In either case they were boxers, since hitting a blow with a sword (prior to circa 1450) was considered "giving a box." At the same time, we cannot find any accounts of them fighting with fists in the literature. Generally, they appear as sword-fighters and participants in judicial duels. As such, theirs was not an honorable profession. Rather they were rough and tumble fighters and criminals.

By the sixteenth century, the name *pugil* had been replaced by other names: *ruffian, swaggerer, roisterer* and *vagabond*. *Roisterer* meant a swaggerer or a blustering bully while *vagabond* meant a wandering, rootless person. As we have seen, the first three of these names were used to describe fighters with a criminal background who were obnoxious and dangerous in their behavior. The last, *vagabond,* was one of the worst names that could be applied to an individual, since it meant that he had no place in settled society. By the sixteenth century, the people who merited these names most likely came from that class of "stout rogues" mentioned in the Tudor Poor Laws. They were members of an entire stratum of society that had fallen out of an ordered life into desperate poverty. Most likely they were demobbed soldiers or sailors, dismissed retainers of the nobility or agricultural workers who had been driven off the manorial lands.

We suspect that many of the sixteenth century boxers came from the vagabond class. They were converted *pugils* from the earlier eras now termed *ruffians,* augmented by wandering soldiers and other English rogues.

Viewed from the top of society, ruffians were deplorable people, but viewed from the bottom of society, they might be reasonably respectable. We have found them among the youth of Bodmin in Cornwall who boxed with strangers as described by Richard Carew. In the next chapter we will see that Richard Harvey uses the word roysterer rather than ruffian to describe this kind of man in 1590, and names Cooke and Carter as two proto-boxers willing to fight in the streets over the Martin Marprelate controversy.

By the end of the sixteenth century, there were a large number of young, strong, healthy, unemployed men who caused problems in Elizabethan society. It is from this class that we will most likely find the anonymous boxers of Britain. They might initiate their fights in the fairs and markets to gain money. They would then spend their money in the alehouses where they could meet with others of their kind.

As Edward Hext (c. 1550–1624) complained to Lord Burghley during the famine of 1596–98:

> I may justly say that the infinite numbers of the idle, wandering people and robbers of the land are the chiefest cause of the dearth [famine]: for though they labour not, and yet they spend doubly as much as the labourer doth, for they lie idly in the alehouses, day and night eating and drinking excessively.[54]

The modem scholar, Gamini Salgado, has confirmed this role of the alehouse: "For the growing number of vagabonds and for day-labourers receiving a day money wage, the alehouse was the only centre of refreshment and society." During the period 1500 to 1650, alehouses would be the most likely places to find proto-boxers and the ruffians of whom Churchyard spoke. The modern sports historian Sir Derek Birley also tells us that "Inns and Innkeepers had, of course, been a vital element in the spread of sport everywhere in Britain. Innyards were early venues for tennis, bowls and boxing matches with the innkeeper the stakeholder or matchmaker." Inn yards certainly brought together two things helpful for boxing matches—a convenient spot for sport and alcohol—while boxing brought together two things helpful to the innkeeper: crowds and entertainment.[55]

There was nothing attractive about the early boxing bouts. They were rag-tag affairs, put on to entertain the meanest sort in society. Rather than see in these fights a new type of sport, the gentry and aristocracy might have considered them simply breaches of the peace. They represented uncivilized behavior and were contrary to the efforts of the Tudors to reduce the amount of public violence. Their only significant features were their transitory nature and the violence of the fights. Like Shakespeare's Marc Antony in Alexandria, two sweaty knaves might reel the streets at noon and attract a crowd. Once the fight was over, the crowds would disperse and the fighters would return to their original occupations. A playwright, like Shakespeare, might comment on the event, but few would commend it. Given the social gap between the lower orders who engaged in fist-fighting and the gentleman littérateur, the time interval between the first appearance of these early boxing fights and their recognition in print appears to have been between 200 and 300 years.[56]

In short, ruffians were men who found violence an attractive way of life. They might have been plowmen and villeins driven off their land by the enclosures and forced into a life of crime, as Sir Thomas More suggested in his book *Utopia* (1516).[57] They might have been tradesmen such as the cooks and carters whom we will find mentioned by Richard Harvey in 1590 and the butcher mentioned by Shakespeare. They might have been young men from small towns in the country, as Richard Carew mentioned. They might have been sword-fighters at Ruffian Hall who took up the new sport of boxing as sword-and-buckler fighting gave way to rapier fighting, as Thomas Churchyard and Joseph Fuller believed. They might have been discharged soldiers or sailors such as the "rufflers" or "upright men" mentioned by Thomas Harman in his work "A Caveat or Warning for Common Cursitors Vulgarly Called Vagabonds" (1566).[58] These people traveled from fair to fair or market to market stealing, and (we believe), fighting for money. But whoever they were, and wherever they were located, those who fought for a living became the creators of a uniquely British sport that has lasted to the present day.

Chapter V

Boxing and the Duel of Honor (1570–1790)

The Rise of the Rapier

Boxing and the duel of honor were fraternal twins. Although dueling had an ancient history, the private duel of honor was born in England at the same time as boxing. Both provided solutions to the same problem: How did men prove their worth in a society undergoing rapid change? Boxing relied on fist-fighting and was a purely English solution, while the duel of honor relied upon the new rapier imported from Italy and was a Continental solution. The two grew up together in England in the second half of the 1500s.

Initially, as we have seen, the aristocracy did adopt fist-fighting as one solution to proving its worth. In 1325 King Richard I used his fist to prove his superiority over Wardrewe, the son of the king of Germany, while in 1500 the Turk challenged Sir Gawain to a buffet match. In 1600, Shakespeare imagined Henry V buffeting to win a bride, while Marc Antony fought with his fists in the streets "with knaves that smelled of sweat." But after 1570 the rapier and the new concept of "courtesy" began to capture the interest of the young members of the aristocracy. The 1600s was the century of the aristocratic duel.

The sword duel of honor became the fatal fancy of the age. When challenged, no aristocrat could refuse to fight. A duel was the only way to establish that you were truly worthy of honor, even if it resulted in your death. Gentlemen were thus caught in a dangerous trap: the slightest breach of the "Code of Courtesy" could cost a man his life.

Yeomen, however, followed a safer route. While they had the same heightened sense of honor as the aristocrats, they settled their challenges in a different manner. They adopted the fist as their weapon of choice, rather than the sword. The man who knocked his opponent down gained the honor and was the victor. The loser might be beaten, but not killed. This made rough and tumble fist-fighting an acceptable activity for the rabble. The nobility watched with envy.[1]

It should be noted that at the same time the exercise of fist-fighting was developing among the lower classes, the Tudors were working to reduce the independent power of the nobility and its predilection to violence. One method of doing this was to bring nobles to court while demanding that they leave their weapons and retainers behind. Not everybody was pleased with the results. In 1565 the Earl of Sussex complained to Queen Elizabeth that he had come to court "unarmed utterly" and without any retainers, while one of his rivals, the Earl of Leicester, had "drawnen unto him great bands of men with swordes & bucklers."[2]

As Lawrence Stone has pointed out, the success of the Tudor monarchs in reducing public violence during the sixteenth century was in part due to the conventional use of the sword-and-buckler system of fighting:

> In spite of the substantial numbers involved and the fact that all the combatants were armed, there was relatively little actual killing in the sixteenth century. If many of these great feuds turn out on close inspection to resemble the battles of Tweedledum and Tweedledee, the main reason was that the standard weapons used were the heavy sword with a single cutting edge and the buckler or shield. These weapons allowed the maximum muscular effort and the most spectacular show of violence with the minimum threat to life and limb. Fighting with them was not much more dangerous than all-in wrestling.[3]

We have already seen that Thomas Churchyard had much the same thing to say in 1593: "In the old time the fight of England was daungerous but not deadly, couragious not cruell, valiant but not villanous, and most nobly used oftimes without anye great harme."[4]

The sword and buckler had been the traditional method of swordfighting in England for centuries. The fighting strategy was to swing the sword down from above in an over-hand fashion, attacking the shield of the opponent and trying to knock it out of the way. This would allow a blow to the upper part of the torso. But the introduction of the thin rapier with its ability to thrust directly to its target made the single- or double-bladed hacking sword obsolete.

By the late sixteenth century, among the gentility, the sword and buckler were being replaced by the rapier and dagger or poniard. And by the early seventeenth century, the dagger too was eliminated and the rapier was used alone.

We have seen that beginning in the late thirteenth century a variety of forces were at work to reduce the use of the sword in society. By 1540, just about the time when we believe the sport of boxing was being born, this movement was so far advanced that King Henry VIII had become concerned that conventional military skills were falling out of fashion. Thus, reversing previous policy, Henry enrolled fencing teachers (the descendants of the *pugils* of previous chapters) into a royal guild. As mentioned in Chapter IV, he supported a new organization called the Masters of Defence. The Masters of Defence were granted a monopoly to teach martial arts in England. They were generally focused on reviving a series of obsolete weapons. The Masters ignored the guns that had recently been introduced. They ignored the joust and warfare on horseback. They also ignored archery, which every man below the level of a gentleman was required to practice. Instead, they focused on teaching gentlemen and yeomen the use of swords and other hand arms that had been used by foot-soldiers during the fifteenth century.[5]

After 1500 we no longer find *pugils* mentioned as fencing masters. Their place had been taken by the Masters of Defence. But there remained some freelance fighters who were members of the same yeoman class from which the Masters had been drawn. These freelance fighters were known as *ruffians* or *roysterers* and they continued the behavior of the *pugils*. They still fought in the streets for money and gentlemen considered them ill-mannered and beneath contempt. The creation of the guild of the Masters of Defence imposed order on this chaotic scene, and for the first time gave respectability to the teaching of fencing. The guild nature of the Masters reduced violence and introduced sword-playing in contrast to the sword-fighting of the past. Naturally, some of those whom James Buchanan Given called "entrepreneurs of violence" were displeased, as their free-flowing behavior was given check. George Silver, in his *Paradoxes of Defence*, published in 1599, echoes these sentiments. He feels that the schools of the Masters of Defence have adopted that "boyish, *Italian*, weake, imperfect fight" that limits the native abilities of the common Englishman.

> Surely, I thinke a downe right fellow, that neuer came in schoole, vsing such skill as nature yeeldeth out of his courage, strength, and agilitie, with good downe right blowes and thrusts among, as shall best frame in his hands, shold put one of these imperfect schollers greatly to his shifts. Besides, there are now in these days no gripes, closes, wrestlings, striking with the hilts, daggers, or bucklers, vsed in Fence-schools. Our ploughmen by nature wil do all these things with great strength & agility: but the Schooleman is altogether vnacquainted with these things. He being fast tyed to such schoolplay as he hath learned, hath lost thereby the benefite of nature, and the plowman is now by nature without art a farre better man than he.[6]

By signaling that "gripes, closes, wrestlings and striking with the hilts" were no longer used by the Masters of Defence, Silver is telling us that the very tactics of fencing, which had been adopted by early boxing, had been outlawed. It would appear that in regularizing weapon training during the sixteenth century, the Masters of Defence had driven out that section of fighting which was giving rise to boxing. They were leaving the new strategy of fist-fighting to the plowmen who would use this new technique of fighting "with great strength and agility" to confound the scholars of defense.

Paradoxically, by regularizing fencing and weapon training and driving out activities such as "Closes and Gripes, striking with the hilts, Daggers, Bucklers, Wrastlings, striking with the foote or knee in the Coddes," which fencing shared with boxing, the Masters of Defence may have helped boxing to become a sport. In response to this rejection by the Masters of Defence, the early boxers or ruffians may have chosen to adopt their own rules and become more respectable as well. At any rate, the appearance of boxing as a sport occurred simultaneously with the appearance of the Masters of Defence. If the behavior of Masters, to which Silver objects, led to the rise of boxing, this is a major debt that boxing owes to the Masters of Defence.

The Tudor efforts to reduce the level of violence among the aristocracy might have been even more successful had technology not intervened. Given the decline of the sword-and-buckler system of fighting and the simultaneous development of fist-fighting, we believe it is probable the aristocracy might have been converted to fist-fighting by the beginning of the seventeenth century. But this was not the case. The appearance of Italian fencing masters with their new rapier delayed the adoption of boxing by gentlemen by another two centuries.

We can compare Fig. 11 (following) with the sword-and-buckler technique seen in Chapter III (Fig. 6). The daggers have become a replacement for the buckler. Rapiers were held underhanded in a thrusting position, rather than in an over-handed hacking position. This illustration also shows a curved guard with the lower half protecting the hand and the upper half designed to catch an opponent's blade and twist it away.

As mentioned in Chapter IV, circa 1570, a Catholic soldier, Rowland Yorke, introduced the rapier into England and demonstrated its superiority over the sword and buckler. Yorke was later an officer in the Earl of Leicester's army, sent by Elizabeth to aid the Dutch in their war with Spain in 1585. While Yorke was absent in the Netherlands, a group of Italian masters, beginning with Rocco Bonetti, a man named Jeronimo (who may have been Rocco's son), and later Vincentio Saviolo began giving fencing lessons to the younger aristocracy. They popularized the rapier as a fencing weapon in England, and quickly made the sword and buckler passé. Despite the fact that the rapier was useless in war, it had a cachet as a private dueling weapon. Gentlemen deserted the schools of the Masters of Defence for the schools of the Italians.[7]

Due to the popularity of the Italian schools, by 1590 the corporation of the Masters of Defence had diminished considerably. When the corporation was reinstated by King James I in 1605, it is probable that the Masters now had to address themselves to a different type of audience: men from the lower

Fig. 11. The use of the rapier and the dagger circa 1595. Vincentio Saviolo, *Vincentio Saviolo, His Practice*, **Book 1:** *The Thyrde Dayes Discourse, of Rapier and Dagger* (London: [John Wolfe] 1595 [1594]), in *Three Elizabethan Fencing Manuals,* intro. and ed. James L. Jackson (Delmar, NY: Scholars Facsimiles & Reprints, 1972).

levels of society. These men were not gentlemen and brought with them a background in wrestling and boxing. Boxing and wrestling were not originally taught by the Masters, but wrestling at least belonged to the old school of military training.[8]

The Italian school of fencing was now the fashion. Rapier dueling captured the enthusiasm of the young gentlemen. The Masters of Defence, wrestling, and by extension, boxing, were shoved into the shadows. Wrestling and its cousin, boxing, were not considered fit sport for gentlemen.[9]

The Crisis of the Aristocracy

This change from the schools of the Masters of Defence to the schools of the Italians was due to what Lawrence Stone has called "the crisis of the aristocracy." The period from 1560 to 1641 was an age of unrivaled conspicuous consumption. Having been brought to court, the nobility had nothing but outward show to set them apart from the urban populace. An old name and title meant little or nothing amid the *nouveaux riches* of the city. As the visiting Spaniard Don Francisco de Quevedo, Jr. (1580–1645) observed, a member of the aristocracy "was Valued in the Country by those who knew where his Paternal Mannors lay, and how much he have per annum, yet in the City where they judge all things by appearance, he was like to find no more Respect than what his outside procured him."[10]

In order to compensate for this loss of status, extravagant dress and a punctilious observation of the "Code of Courtesy" was insisted upon. This new courteous behavior manifested itself in obsequiousness to superiors, gentility to equals and arrogance to inferiors. The rapier and "courteous" behavior became a deadly combination. Manners became matters of life and death: a slight given to another gentleman might result in a challenge to a duel with fatal intent. In this new world of courtesy, the only suitable response to a perceived affront was a duel of honor.

Historically, personal insults were not actionable in the royal courts. All actionable words must contain the imputation of a crime. Slander not accompanied by action did not rise to the level of a crime. It was a *damnum absque injuria*: a hurt without injury. Insults were just so much "wind."[11]

There were two reasons that personal insults to gentlemen were ignored in common law. The first and most important was the belief that private resentments were to be settled privately. A man's honor demanded that he defend himself and his family personally. In a duel of honor, it was not possible to rely upon a *pugil* or a champion to fight for you. Gentlemen must fight their own battles. To seek the help of another, and particularly a government entity like the courts, showed that the man was incompetent to protect his own. He thus proved himself the very thing against which he protested: a man without honor.

Secondly, public insults (defamation) were considered to lie within domain of the Church. Beginning in 1222 with the Council of Oxford, the English Church agreed to excommunicate those who "maliciously impute a crime to any person who is not of ill fame." While this provided punishment for the defamer, it did nothing for the man defamed. Private slander, not involving blasphemy or contempt of ecclesiastical authority, was not a subject covered by canon law. Laymen were not to invoke spiritual jurisdiction in civil matters. And yet, since there was no alternative law, and most defamation cases were civil matters, laymen were forced to plead against other laymen in church courts. This led to imperfect verdicts.[12]

Exceptions occurred when an insult was issued against a person in his capacity as a public official (contempt) or if the insult promoted discord in the realm (treason). If one gentleman accused another of treason, the state might become involved.[13]

Honesty was one of the distinguishing marks of a gentleman. Hence, when a gentleman accused a member of the commons of a crime, his accusation was assumed to be true and the member of the commons was assumed to be guilty.[14] In the early centuries after the Conquest, when one gentleman accused another of treason the same assumption of honesty applied, and the accused was compelled to declare that his accuser lied or be at mercy of the lord King for life and limb. In the absence of clear proof on either side, a judicial duel (a trial by battle) was ordered to determine the truth. The winner of the duel was judged to be the honest man, and the loser was judged to be the liar. When faced with a trial by battle, a person who refused to duel was considered convicted of the crime of which he was accused.[15]

This same theory was adopted in the sixteenth century by the duel of honor, only in this case the issue was private insult not treason. With the adoption of the new code of honor, personal insults triggered private vengeance. The code of courtesy required that any affront to a gentleman's honor demanded a response. To fail to give a suitable response (i.e., to fail to declare the person who created the affront a liar), meant that the gentleman forfeited his honor. To protect his honor, he must agree to a duel. By 1600, the motto on every gentleman's sword read "Death before dishonor." As Thomas Churchyard put it: "Now life is fought in England for an Italian lie, and nothing but blood and death can pacifie mens furies." Or, as the soldier and author Barnaby Rich put it in 1609, "Amongst persons of reputation, honour is preferred before life."[16]

The Judicial Duel

While the duel of honor drew its theory from the judicial duel, boxing may have done the same thing. The two competing strategies for solving private disputes were influenced by the same source. Boxing and the duel of honor were parallel paths to the same goal.

Despite borrowing its theory from the old judicial duel, the duel of honor was recognized by contemporaries at the end of the sixteenth century as a completely new invention. They believed it originated on the continent and was imported to England with the rapier. Thomas Churchyard considered dueling "a new deuised wilfulnesse that our old Fathers taught us not, nor scarsely was known, till our youth beganne to trauell straunge Countrys, and so brought home strange manners." King James I (1614) argued that "all men that rightly understand the nature of these Challenges, & single Fights hand to hand, or by match among Gentlemen ... must acknowledge that this bravery, was first borne and bred in Forraine parts; but after convaied over into this Island." John Cockburn, looking back in his book *The History and Examination of Duels* (1720), confirmed this: "Here in *England* there are not any instances of these *Modern Duels* before the *Reformation*." This confirms our thought that had this new import not been introduced at this time, the aristocracy might have turned toward the pleasures of fist-fighting and the sport of boxing or buffeting might well have become visible a century earlier.[17]

In both dueling and boxing, honor was at stake, and in both exercises, even the man who lost could gain honor. As one gentleman noted in 1660: "He that will Fight, though he have never so much the worse, loses no reputation."[18] Nonetheless, despite both being influenced by the judicial duel, there were significant differences between the duel of honor and boxing. Initially the duel of honor was fought in public, but by the 1590s it had become outlawed. This created a dilemma for the duelists. To protect their honor they needed to fight the duel; but if they fought a duel, they were breaking the law and betraying their duty to the king. Their solution was to fight the duel as a private event out of sight of the authorities. The duel of honor thus became a hidden event. Boxing and the trial by battle, in contrast, were public events attended by crowds of people. Since the trial by battle actually was a judicial trial, this meant that it was supported by and often attended by the monarchs. Trials by battle were serious events organized by the court, and were recorded in the letters and newspapers of the day.

Although the early boxing matches were also fought in public, they were not attended by either the monarchs or the better sort of people. Instead, they drew crowds of rabble: the ruffians and roisterers mentioned above. To attend one of the early boxing matches would have been contrary to the dignity of gentle folk. Such matches were, we imagine, similar to the "foul battle" engaged in by Thomas Whytehorne and James Fisher in 1458, but without the formalities of the trial. As a result, just like the duels of honor, early boxing matches, although they were fought in public, have been hidden from our view.[19]

One other interesting difference existed. Men fighting in duels of honor never shaved their heads. In contrast, paid champions in judicial duels from the thirteenth to the fifteenth centuries appear with shaven heads. This was a ritual passed down for centuries. We know that a shaven head designated a champion fighter, but beyond that the meaning escapes us. Still, shaving one's head before battle was adopted by the later sword gladiators who fought for money during the 1600s. It was considered a sign that they were champions as well. The shaved head was then adopted by boxers in the 1700s. And up until the 1760s both boxers and sword gladiators routinely shaved their heads before their bouts, while men fighting duels of honor did not. A shaven head was a sign of honor that did not apply to the duel.[20]

The idea of having a referee, umpires, and even surgeons in a boxing match may have also come from the judicial duel. The judicial duel was supervised by a judge and court officials who made sure that certain rules were followed. They could also stop the fight if they chose to do so. This idea was later adopted by the Masters of Defence in their prizefights and followed by the gladiator swordfights and then by boxing. Zacharias Conrad von Uffenbach described a prizefight with swords, which took place at the Bear Garden at Hockley in the Hole on July 2, 1710. One of the fighters was seriously wounded, and though he still wanted to continue, "since he had bled so profusely, neither the surgeon nor the seconds, who act as umpires, would allow this." The fact that doctors and seconds could stop the fight parallels the action of the judges in a trial by battle.[21]

The duel of honor had no judge but it did adopt the idea of seconds and surgeons. V.G. Kiernan suggests that duelists meeting in secret were wise to take a second with them to avoid ambushes and to see that there was no foul play. The concept of seconds and surgeons came from the Masters of Defence, who used them during the early sixteenth century to publicize and facilitate their prizefights. The original purpose of the second was to carry weapons, present challenges and to see that the rules were observed. Surgeons, of course, were used to treat wounds. Boxing adopted these aids as well.[22] But by the latter part of the seventeenth century, the English aristocracy took over the French custom of having seconds fight each other in duels of honor. In this, boxing and dueling once again diverged.

Initially, wrestling, boxing, and the duels of honor were all fought outside on the turf in whatever location was convenient. Wrestling and boxing matches were marked off by a "ring" of bystanders who watched the fight. The same was true of the early duels that occurred before armies. But once the duel of honor had begun to be fought in secret, it no longer attracted a ring of spectators. The absence of spectators meant that the duel had to develop its own rules. The role of the crowd in determining the rules of combat was thus taken over by the seconds in a duel of honor.

At this time the boxing "ring" underwent a significant change. Prior to this, the "ring" had been simply made by the crowd grasping hands to form a circle within which the boxers could perform. This "ring" could easily be broken by the crowd if they felt like it. As a result, early boxing matches had a riotous and confusing appearance that made them repellant to honest men and made them the refuge of ruffians. But the judicial duel was a trial and it was very important that the crowd not interfere. The trial therefore adopted a formal double-railed enclosure as the location for its duel. As mentioned in the previous chapter, the penalty for breaking through the barrier in a trial by battle could be death . The idea of a wooden barrier surrounding the trial by battle was apparently taken over from tournaments, which had created barriers to control the action. This concept of a railed enclosure was later adopted by the Masters of Defence. Their prizefights were orderly and held in public places on elevated, railed, square stages or scaffolds. This architecture kept their fights free from interference. This strategy was later applied to boxing.

This change was the creation of James Figg (1684–1734), the most famous early boxing entrepreneur. Figg was one of the last of the Masters of Defense, and the most famous sword-fighter of his day. As can be seen on his business card, Figg fought his battles on a raised and railed stage. When, in 1725 he began to present boxing matches as a supplement to his gladiatorial sword-fights, the boxing matches were held on the same stage as the sword and cudgel fights that Figg had promoted since 1719. The raised, railed stage made it much more difficult for the crowd to interfere with a boxing bout and began to reduce the riotous behavior which accompanied the early boxing matches on the turf. Figg's invention gave us the "squared circle" that we now use in modern boxing.[23]

The card shows Figg and his second standing on the raised and railed square stage or scaffold on which prizefights were held. In this case the stage was being used for sword-fighting. Figg used the same stage for boxing, which became the model for modern boxing. Note that Figg had a shaved head.

To summarize: Boxing and the duel of honor both appeared about the same time in England. Both arose in response to the new concept of personal honor which affected the upper and lower classes of Englishmen in the last half of the sixteenth century. Beginning circa 1570, the duel of honor gave new meaning to the sword-bearing

Fig. 12. The business card of James Figg designed by William Hogarth [?] circa 1733. Henry Downes Miles, *Pugilistica: The History of British Boxing*, Vol. 1 (Edinburgh: John Grant, 1906).

classes of England at a time when economics and social change were making them ever more irrelevant. The technological improvement of the sword coupled with an elitist concept of behavior drew a new line between the gentility and the common men. The sword once again became a distinguishing mark of the gentleman. The thrill of greater danger associated with the duel made it highly attractive to the young gentlemen of the era. Lawrence Stone put it very aptly: "The rapier was as dangerous a weapon as a sports car in the hands of a high-spirited young man with little sense of self-control and no rules of conduct to regulate his behaviour." The newly developing sport of boxing, coming as it did from among the pedestrian classes, could not compete. But because boxing was a non-fatal solution to the problem of personal worth, it ultimately triumphed over the duel.[24]

The Uprising of Boxing and the Downfall of the Duello

The popularity of the duel with its heightened sense of honor created obvious problems for English court society. Very few people were actually killed in these duels but the fact that all of the deaths occurred among the aristocracy captured the attention of the age. Beginning in the seventeenth century, the problem of trying to eliminate the rapier duel became a critical state issue. In 1613 and 1614, King James I issued two proclamations against dueling. Bans on issuing challenges to duels and on duels themselves were repeated throughout the remainder of the century. Both the Stuarts and the Puritans were united in this cause. This meant that the duels continued to be carried on in secret and hidden from the public.[25]

In addition to passing laws, James I also had the support of court playwrights such as Francis Beaumont and John Fletcher, who wrote a series of plays that illustrate these issues in society. The plot of *The Nice Valour, or the Passionate Mad-Man*, dated circa 1615–1616, turns on the different views of honor held by the gentleman of valor and the gentleman of wealth. The gentleman of valor (Shamont) is, like Shakespeare's Hotspur, quick to take offense. While at court, Shamont is given a light tap with a riding crop by the Duke, to gain his attention. Shamont considers this a gross insult and draws his sword only to find that he cannot challenge the Duke, his superior. Hence, to save his honor he withdraws from the court. The Duke is astonished at this delicate sense of honor: "Was ever such a touchie man heard of?"[26]

The Duke, upset with gentlemen who are so "touchie," decides to dismiss all gentlemen from his court and replace them with grooms, who are used to blows. He sends the First Gentleman (La Nove) to locate men who will willingly accept blows without being offended. A gallant appears and La Nove boxes his ear to see his reaction. When the gallant does not go for his sword, La Nove believes him to be a man for the Duke. He therefore tells the gallant to meet him later. When the gallant refuses, La Nove threatens: "And meet me, or Ile box you while I have you" (Act IV, scene i, line 188). Threatened with further "boxing" the gallant agrees to meet later. La Nove then tries the same tactic with a "plain fellow" and jostles him. The plain fellow responds by hitting La Nove with his fist, and is prepared to hit him again, when La Nove gives up. When the plain fellow leaves, La Nove is convinced that he is like Shamont and will reward insults not with a sword, but with a "cuffe" (Act IV, scene i, lines 201–213). The playwrights suggest here that for the common man, fist-fighting served the same purpose as the gentleman's duel. An insult is met with a blow of the fist (a cuffe), rather than a blow from a sword.

Earlier, La Nove had discovered a gentleman of wealth, Lapet (The Fart), who purchased his coat of arms just to make his wife happy. However Lapet perversely gets his honor from the number of blows he has taken. Lapet and his followers are the ideal courtiers for the Duke.[27] Lapet also acts as a perfect foil to Shamont. Lapet disclaims any desire to be a true gentleman since he lacks the elevated sense of honor that plagues Shamont. When Shamont meets Lapet and is distraught that the Duke has given him a "blow," Lapet replies: "Pha sir, that's nothing; I ha' tooke fourty since." Lapet then provides a catalog of blows that he has received. Lapet ends his list of blows saying: "Now we come lower, to our moderne kick, / Which has been mightily in use of late" (Act III, scene ii, lines 40–83). This refers to the fact that King James I kicked a trusted courtier after unjustly accusing him of losing some state papers. The courtier, like Shamont, could not respond so he left the court. The King called him back and apologized for kicking him. This event was adopted by the playwrights as a dramatic device to ridicule dueling. They suggest that kicking can be used in place of dueling to solve quarrels. They have Lapet write a book entitled "*The Up-rising of the Kick, and the Downfall of the Duello.*"[28]

The Nice Valour illustrates a parallel between the plain man and the gentleman of valor when insulted. The gentleman immediately draws his sword. The plain man draws his fists. At the same time the play demonstrates the difference between a gentleman of valor (Shamont) and a gentleman of wealth (Lapet). The former is driven to avenge an insult, while the latter can ignore it entirely. The play also confirms that common men did not use swords to solve their quarrels. When Lapet praises his book as being "for the common good," his servant, the Clowne, responds: "Nay sir, your Commons seldom fight at sharp [with sharp swords], / But buffet in a ware-house" (Act V, scene iii, lines 36–38). Buffeting or boxing had become an alternative to the duel for the common man. Had Lapet's book actually been written, its correct title might have been "*The Uprising of Boxing, and the Downfall of the Duello.*"

The Little French Lawyer (1619–1623), a later play by Beaumont and Fletcher, also deals with the issue of swords and fist-fighting.[29] The story is about a series of duels that go awry. The play is named for La-writ, the little French lawyer, who appears initially as a coward. But after a set of duels in which he surprisingly disarms two gallants, he conceives himself a famous duelist and challenges a judge who has thrown his cases out of court. As the judge is too old to duel, he sends his simple nephew, Sampson, to take his place. When the swordsmen meet, their seconds demand that they strip down for the duel, while the seconds hold their swords. Sampson and La-writ strip, only to find that they are freezing with cold. While they complain about the cold, the seconds leave the scene, taking the swords with them. Sampson and La-writ, standing in their underwear, discover suddenly that both their seconds and their swords are gone:

> LA-WRIT: Rogues, theeves, (boh, boh, [words signifying being cold]) run away with our Doublets? to fight at Buffets now, 't were such a May-game.
>
> SAMPSON: There were no honour in't, plague on't, 'tis scurvy.
>
> LA-WRIT: Or to revenge my wrongs at fisty-cuffes.
>
> SAMPSON: My Lord, mine Uncles cause, depend on Boxes?
>
> LA-WRIT: Let's goe in quest, if ever we recover 'em—
>
> SAMPSON: I [aye], come, our colds together, and our doublets.
>
> LA-WRIT: Give me thy hand; thou art a valiant gentleman [Act IV, scene iv, lines 115–122].

La-writ and Sampson, having convinced themselves that hitting each other with fists has no honor, now decide to kick and punch each other to keep warm:

> LA-WRIT: There's ne'r a house within this mile, beat me, kick me, and beat me as I goe, and I'le beat thee too, to keepe us warme. If ever we recover 'em—kick hard, I am frozen: so, so, now I feele it [Act IV, scene iv, lines 124–126].

In *The Noble Valour*, we learn that "plain men" are just as prone to the "touchie" sense of honor as gentlemen, but they don't duel with swords. Instead, they "buffet in ware-houses" to solve their quarrels. In *The Little French Lawyer* we are told that the duel is being outlawed in civilized countries across Europe, but as yet there is no substitute for it. The insults demand a response, and if dueling is banned, what can a gentleman do? Sampson and La-writ are presented with fist-fighting as a duel substitute. But for them it is unacceptable since it has no sense of honor. As both are reluctant duelists, they think it more honorable to resolve their quarrel rather than engage in a fist-fight. Yet ironically, after refusing to engage in boxing, they start beating and kicking each other to keep warm. *The Little French Lawyer* also confirms that the various names for boxing, "Boxes, Buffets and fisty-cuffes," all mean the same thing, and are all the common man's alternative to the duel.

These two comedies demonstrate a powerful move against dueling in society. Although dueling was outlawed, the root cause of dueling—the concept of courtesy and hair-trigger honor—remained. Without a method to restore one's honor, the thorn of anger remained to fester. This issue frustrated the best minds of England for nearly two centuries. "Every man," said the Lords of Parliament in 1668, "believes himselfe injured by those who value him lesse than he doth himselfe." For this reason "men do frequently seeke reparacion from those that doe undervalue them by sending challenges and fighting of duells."[30] As long as this elevated sense of honor remained in force, outlawing duels would have no effect. What was needed was either a change of mental attitude, or an alternative method of fighting that was not as dangerous or socially harmful as the duel. Solutions to both problems appeared in the Beaumont and Fletcher comedies of the early 1600s.

The first solution proposed was to make the aristocratic notion of duels an object of common ridicule. Nothing could defeat a duel of honor like ridicule. The figure of Lapet, admitting to being struck by a number of blows and writing a book on kicking as an alternative to duels, and the sight of Sampson and La-writ without their swords, kicking each other in their underwear, were intended to make the whole concept of dueling absurd. This strategy continued later in the century. It was to culminate in the words of a gentleman of wealth in a comedy of 1700 who responded to a challenge to a duel with the line "I can't conceive how running you through the Body shou'd contribute one jot more to my Gentility." Such words were the death sentence of the duel. They demonstrated that a challenge to a duel could now be ignored.[31]

The second solution was to propose an alternative to the duel. Any alternative had to be manly enough to merit consideration; violent enough to carry risk and reward; demanding enough that it took skill to do it well; yet benign enough to avoid fatal consequences. The exercise had to allow the contestants to punish each other to the point that one could be forced to surrender short of death. Beaumont and Fletcher suggested the possibility of having boxing become this alternative to the duel.

Despite this suggestion, La-writ's view of boxing was typical of the times. In order to replace the sword, it was necessary for any alternative to be perceived as a duel involving similar skill. Fencing had honor since it was perceived as "the art of touching without being touched." Most people felt that boxing lacked the critical value of skill and hence was without honor. It would take more than a century for boxing to develop into a skill that merited being considered a science. The first to introduce "science" into boxing was John Broughton (1703–1789), who could parry blows so well that he could not be touched by his opponent. Prior to Broughton, boxing was the domain of ruffians. It was a violent pastime that involved kicking, head-butting, biting and gouging, grappling and falling on an opponent when he was down. It appealed to the common man and repelled the gentlemen. It was not until Broughton introduced "scientific boxing" that boxing could be recognized as "the art of hitting without being hit." At that point, boxing became a sport for gentlemen.[32]

The gradual development of boxing into a sport suitable to gentlemen led to the decline in popularity of the sword. By 1727 César de Saussure, a Swiss visitor to England, spoke of the death of the duel of honor and noted that "very few [Englishmen] are partisans of dueling, so that you do not often hear of this mode of settling quarrels." Instead, de Saussure noted, the English preferred to settle their quarrels with fist-fighting. Then, in 1747, the Abbe le Blanc noted that swordfights for money were also out of favor in England: "It must be owned that these battles of the English gladiators are not so much in fashion as they have been: People of distinction have almost left frequenting them, and scarce anybody is seen at these matches but the lowest of the populace."[33]

In Virginia by 1774 fist-fights were being used at law to solve the type of insults that triggered the duels of honor in earlier times in England. By 1778, *The Malefactor's Register* could announce: "To the credit of the present age, the practice of prize-fighting is abolished." In 1784 Samuel Johnson confirmed this judgment and lamented: "I am sorry that prize-fighting is gone out of fashion.... It is absurd, that our soldiers should have swords, and not be taught the use of them."[34]

In 1789, due to the drop off in his fencing business, Harry Angelo, the last fencing master in London, was obliged to take up quarters with the boxer "Gentleman" John Jackson. As a modern writer noted: "Pugilism was replacing arms as the ruling passion of society; the younger bucks were forsaking the fencing floor for the more hectic delights of the ring."[35]

By 1790 the sword had so far given way to boxing that an anonymous "Highland Officer" found it necessary to attack boxing in order to revive interest in the sword. He published a book with the title *Anti-Pugilism, or the Science of Defence exemplified in short easy lessons, for the practice of the Broad Sword and Single Stick. Whereby Gentlemen may become Proficients in the use of these Weapons, without the help of a Master, and be enabled to Chastise the Insolence and Temerity, so frequently met with, from those fashionable Gentlemen, the Johnsonians, Big Bennians, and Mendozians* [famous boxers all] *of the present Day: a Work perhaps, better calculated to extirpate this reigning and brutal Folly* [boxing] *than a whole Volume of Sermons.*[36]

By the end of the century, the attraction of the duel of honor had faded under the dual threat of ridicule and legislation. At the same time, boxing drove out gladiatorial sword-fighting as a sport and then took over its rules, locations and even its very name: "prize-fighting." The first record we have of a boxer being described as a prizefighter was in 1789 in the trial of William Ward for murder.[37]

In an article entitled "Pugilism" in *The Sporting Magazine or Monthly Calendar* in October 1792, the mayor of Colchester issued a proclamation against public boxing matches. He announced "that the magistrates would by no means suffer any stage or prize-fighting within their jurisdiction." It is clear that by 1790 prizefighting had come to mean public boxing and no longer meant public sword-fighting.

While the duel of honor temporarily found a home in North America, "prize-fighting" became the new name for boxing in both England and the New World. During the 1700s as dueling and sword-fighting faded from the public mind, boxing became the new sport sensation. It, rather than dueling with sword or pistol, solved gentlemen's quarrels. As a ballad by John Freeth entitled "Stage Boxing" (1790) put it:

> The true art of Boxing—the old English Game,
> Of late to so fond an attention lays claim;
> John Bull seems resolv'd to throw bullets aside,
> And let by the Fist future contests be try'd.[38]

Although not entirely legal, boxing was on the verge of becoming respectable. The names of Tom Johnson, Benjamin Brain (Big Ben) and Daniel Mendoza, the great pugilists of the time, had greatly discomfited the Highland Officer cited above. Add to these the boxers "Gentleman" John Jackson (the teacher of Lord Byron) and John Gully, elected a Member of Parliament, and it was clear that boxing had become the sport of gentlemen once again.

Chapter VI

Boxing and the Concept of Fair Play

Pugnacious Presbyterians

Fist-fighting became a popular exercise beginning in fourteenth century England. But, as we have seen, it is only in the sixteenth century that we first find proof that fist-fighting has become a sport. Interestingly, some of our earliest proof is found in the pamphlets issued during the Martin Marprelate religious controversy of 1588 and 1589.

Martin Marprelate (*Mar-prelate*, meaning to harm or attack the prelates or bishops), was a pseudonym for a group of fundamentalists who opposed the Anglican Church. As the result of Henry VIII's destruction of the Catholic Church, the Anglican or Episcopal Church had become the established church in Britain. As such it was subject to many of the same strengths and weaknesses as the Catholic Church that it had replaced. Although the king had replaced the pope, the church itself remained hierarchical, ruled by bishops. Central control was exercised by the monarchy and doctrinal interpretations remained issues of law. To challenge them was equivalent to treason.

One significant change was the replacement of Latin by English in church services. Adopting English as the language of the church was a dramatic and democratic break with the past. But having gone this far, the Tudor monarchs chose to stop. They were not supporters of democracy. Both the churchmen and the monarchs feared the Anabaptists, who had turned an attack on the Church into an attack on the state during the German Peasants' War (1524–1525). The Tudor monarchs considered democracy dangerous to themselves and to the Church. King Henry VIII and his children, King Edward VI and Queens Mary and Elizabeth, all considered the Church an arm of the state. But the scent of democracy was in the air and the hierarchical system of the

Church came under attack. Martin Marprelate and his fellows were democrats who sought to have the state church ruled by representatives of the presbytery (Presbyterians). As Joseph Black, the best historian of this controversy describes it: "The primary aim of the Marprelate project was to publicize a Presbyterian system of church government." At the same time, he notes that the word "presbyterian" does not appear in the papers of the time. Instead the combatants called themselves, and were called by their opponents, "Puritans."[1]

As one modern historian notes: "While all presbyterians were puritans, not all puritans were presbyterians." The term "Puritan" was a pejorative nickname applied to the "hotter sort of Protestants." They were, wrote John Stow in 1567, people "who cawlyd themselves Puritans or Unspottyd Lambs of the Lord." The Puritans' aim was to purify the internal life of the Church and to return Christians to lives of Biblical simplicity. The Presbyterians' aim, on the other hand, was to democratize the governing structure of the Church and to return Church government to the Age of the Apostles. The Presbyterians attacked the Anglican Church for being ruled by bishops; there were no bishops in the Bible. The broader group of Puritan reformers attacked the Anglican Church for retaining Catholic customs: there were no ales, May Games and sports after church in the Bible either. Both groups believed that whatever was in the Bible was allowed; whatever was not was not. Both of these goals (eliminating bishops and eliminating Catholic customs) were combined together in the Marprelate controversy. This led to violence in the churches and the streets as the Protestant revolutionaries battled with reformers who supported the Anglican Church.[2]

But what has all this to do with boxing?

We are interested in this religious controversy since those involved in the Martin Marprelate movement were among the first to use boxing terms in print. All of them were educated men. Many of them had been scholars at Cambridge and Oxford. Thus, their battles, while vituperative, were literate and carried on in the press. It was their use of printing that reveals to us some of the earliest confirmations of boxing.

Using the new printing press to publish their articles, the Marprelates began their attack on the bishops in October of 1588, just after the defeat of the Spanish Armada. Once the Catholic threat had been eliminated, the Protestant revolutionaries felt free to speak out. These Presbyterian pamphleteers used a scholarly yet popular style, full of puns and classic references designed to appeal to the well-educated man of the middling sort. They did not intend to influence ruffians or the meaner sort of man for whom street violence and boxing were daily activities. The aim of the Marprelates was to convert other literate scholars and bishops, who defended the Episcopal Church, to the democratic ideals of Presbyterianism.

The Marprelate supporters were attacked by John Bridges, Dean of Salisbury Cathedral, and Thomas Cooper, Bishop of Winchester. Bishop Cooper worried:

> If the outrageous spirit of boldness be not stopped speedily, I feare he will prove himself to bee not onely *Mar-prelate*, but *Mar-prince, Mar-state, Mar-lawe, Mar-magistrate*, and all together, until he bring it to an Anabaptisticall equalitie and communitie.[3]

But Bridges's and Cooper's counter-attacks failed because they were too dull and pedantic. As a result, the authorities hired popular writers, themselves university men, including John Lyly (1553–1606) and Thomas Nashe (1567–1601?), to write rebuttals in the same popular style used by the Marprelate tracts.

In the process of this pamphlet war, both sides used many words drawn from boxing in their arguments. This is significant because it tells us that already by 1590 the new sport of boxing was so well established that its terms had become known to Cambridge scholars and cathedral deans. Prior to this time, we had assumed that boxing was only known to the lower orders of men, ruffians and lower tradesmen: the men of the street. These men were illiterate and certainly did not write about their own activities. However, the Marprelate debate reveals for the first time that the middling sort of people, those whom we would now consider "middle-class intellectuals" had become aware of boxing. Boxing was coming out of the shadows. It was becoming intellectually acceptable in England.[4]

The first Marprelate pamphlet was entitled *The Epistle* (October 1588) and was directed particularly at John Bridges. Almost immediately it began with an admonition that invoked boxing: "Brother Bridges, mark what Martin tells you, you will shortly I hope have twenty fists about your ears more than your own." "Fists about your ears" was sixteenth-century slang for being in an extensive fist-fight. Martin followed that up by reminding Bridges that Thomas Cartwright, an early Presbyterian and Cambridge scholar, had given Bridges so many "blows" that he was "loth to have any other so banged as he himself was to his woe." By this he did not mean actual physical blows. Rather he meant that Cartwright had beaten him badly in a series of dialectical debates about church government. Later on, Martin mentioned an odd event where physical blows were actually used: "This priest [John Aylmer, Bishop of London] went to buffets with his son-in-law, for a bloody nose." In this case we are to believe that the bishop of London actually physically engaged in a fist-fight with his son-in-law and gave him a bloody nose. Whether these incidents were real or not, the references to fists, blows and buffets show that boxing was in the author's mind as an expression of this controversy.

As a further indication of his attitude, Martin then attacked a series of bishops as "swinish rabble ... petty antichrists, petty popes, proud prelates, intolerable withstanders of reformation, enemies of the gospel, and most covetous wretched priests." This verbal attack on the bishops is what in modern boxing terminology would be considered "trash talk" designed to denigrate and anger the opponent. This was a classic tactic when preparing for a physical fight. The battle had begun.[5]

Thomas Nashe responded to *The Epistle* in an attack entitled *A Countercuffe given to Martin Junior: By the venturous, hardie, and renowned Pasquill of England, Cavaliero* (1589). Martin had initiated the battle with blows to Bridges's ear, so Nashe responded with a countercuffe. A countercuffe was a boxing blow thrown in response to an earlier blow. In modern boxing a countercuffe is called a counter punch and requires significant skill and training to be used effectively. It begins when one boxer avoids the punch of his opponent and instantly responds with a counter blow. He seeks to take advantage of an opening created by the missed punch of his opponent. A quick response in boxing can often win the match. And this was what Nashe hoped would happen in this war of words. Properly done, a counter punch can lead to a knock-out, especially if it is returned as a box on the ear. Nashe planned to knock Martin out.[6]

In the same year, 1589, John Lyly also published a tract with the unwieldy title of *Pappe [baby food] with an hatchet. Alias, A figge for my God sonne. Or Crack me this nut. Or a Countrie cuffe, that is, a sound boxe of the eare, for the idiot Martin to hold his peace, seeing the patch [fool] will take no warning.* Lyly uses many terms drawn from boxing in this work, including in the title itself, as one way to demonstrate the violent nature of the Marprelate controversy. By the use of the phrase "a country cuffe, that is, a sound box of the eare," Lyly confirms that cuffing and boxing were originally country exercises. As we have discussed in Chapter III, both *cuff* and *box* are Middle English words that originated in the countryside among the purely English-speaking population.[7]

Lyly scatters boxing references throughout his work. Speaking of Martin Marprelate and his purported son, Martin Jr., Lyly notes that "knowing your bellies full of bishops' bobs, I am sure your bones would be at rest." The editor of this work, Leah Scragg, argues that "bishops' bobs" mean verbal "taunts" thrown at the Marprelates. I would suggest instead that "bobs" mean blows of the fists directed to their stomachs (the "mark" in boxing terms) and that Lyly is saying that these blows have so damaged the two fighters and that they need to rest.[8] This theme continues a few lines down when Lyly says:

> Then I thought to touch Martin with logic, but there was a little wag in Cambridge that swore by Saint Seton he would so swinge him with syllogisms that all Martin's answers would ache. The vile boy hath many bobs, and a whole fardle of fallacies.[9]

This paragraph combines scholarly terms with boxing terms to make a disputational surprise. The word "touch" means to break through an opponent's defenses and hit the body. The "little wag in Cambridge" refers to Thomas Nashe, mentioned above, while the word "swinge" means to "beat or flog" and "bobs" means blows with the fist. While Lyly thinks to break through Martin Marprelate's defenses and hit him with his logic, Thomas Nashe joins in to beat Martin so badly with his fists in a boxing battle of syllogisms that his teeth will ache.

Still later, Lyly brings in Gabriel Harvey, an opponent of his at Cambridge, and says: "If he give you a bob, though he draw no blood yet you are sure of a rap with a bauble." Here Dr. Scragg finally admits that "bob" equals a blow that might draw blood while a "rap with a bauble" means to hit with a professional jester's bladder on a stick. This appears to me to be a double attack. Even though Gabriel Harvey's blows would draw no blood, nonetheless they could hurt Martin by making him look foolish. Alternatively, it suggests that Harvey's blows are very weak and cannot really harm Martin. And because his blows lack strength, they are no more powerful than those of a fool.[10]

On the next page, Lyly challenges Martin that if he brings 700 men to support him, "they shall be boxed with fourteen hundred boys." Dr. Scragg translates "boxed" as beaten or thrashed. I would contrast the 700 men supporting Martin with the 1,400 boxing boys opposing him. Lyly is telling us, I believe, that boxing is a popular young man's sport. Boxing was for boys and young men. No matter how many supporters Martin has, there are twice as many young men available who would box Martin out of place. Further along Lyly speaks of Martin getting "many bobs on the ear." This brings us back to the "box on the ear" used by Lyly in his title.

Finally, we find Lyly noting that "if Martin will city fight, we challenge him at all weapons.... If they buffet, we will bring fists." This confirms that buffeting, the archaic French term for fist-fighting, was a city exercise, as in the case of the bishop of London buffeting his son-in-law, while boxing was an English country exercise, again as attested to in the title.[11]

The fact that we find boxing phrases being used in this religious controversy in 1588 and 1589 shows conclusively that boxing was a popular sport well established in England a full century before we find the first notice of it in *The True Protestant Mercury* of 1681.

Richard Harvey: Boxing and Fair Play

In Chapter IV we have already met Richard Harvey (1560–1630), the younger brother of Gabriel Harvey mentioned above. He should also be added to the list of those involved in the Marprelate controversy, although he was not strictly a member of the bishops' counterattack. In his booklet *Plaine Percevall, The Peace-Maker of England* (1590), Richard Harvey tried to bridge the gap between the Presbyterians and the Episcopalians.

In *Plaine Percevall*, Harvey, like Nashe and Lyly, drew upon boxing imagery to express himself in this controversy, which foreshadowed the Puritan Revolution. Harvey begins his book with Percevall strolling through Aldersgate, from Smithfield into London, carrying a quarter-staff on his shoulder and an empty belly. He has evidently been exercising at cudgels in Smithfield. Once in London, he immediately encounters controversy in the form of quarrelsome men in the street:

> Yet I see that he that was Cooke and Carter, thought to feed Martin with these nunchions, as men feed Apes: with a bit & a boxe on the eare. Why but soft maisters, *faire plaie* and no snatching: is your feasting turned to a fray? put vp, put vp your weapons, and be some wiser then some. They were neuer tall fellows of their hands that were such hacksters in the street....[12]

Harvey is describing a street scene in which two young tradesmen, Cook and Carter, have picked an imaginary fight with Martin Marprelate. They try to feed Martin their conformist notions, as men force-feed apes, by hitting them with a box on the ear. The reference to an ape is a reference to trained monkeys, which in England were typically named Martin.[13]

In keeping with his theme of being a peace-maker, Perceval asks the fighters to put up their weapons and become wiser than roisterers who fight in the streets. The phrase "tall fellows of their hands" describes serious people worthy of respect, while "hacksters" were knife-fighters of bad repute. Hacksters were viewed by the middling sort of common folk as disgraceful ruffians or roisterers as Thomas Churchyard has described.

Although Harvey confirms the use of boxing terms in this quote, what is more significant is that this is the first use of the phrase *fair play* in the English language.

Fair play means "upright conduct in a game; equity in conditions or opportunities afforded to a player." More importantly, it means that all are treated equally, not just in a game, but in life itself. While not entirely absent from other cultures, no other culture has placed so much emphasis on fair play as the English. In England, public behavior as well as sport behavior rests on the concept of fair play.[14]

The use of the word *play* appears to reduce this subject to a frivolous level, but as Johan Huizinga has shown, play is anything but frivolous. Huizinga gives us the following definition:

> Play is a voluntary activity or occupation executed within certain fixed limits of time and place, according to rules freely accepted but absolutely binding, having its aim in itself and accompanied by a feeling of tension, joy and the consciousness that it is "different" from ordinary life.[15]

Huizinga's analysis establishes that play is not only the basis of culture but of civilization itself. Play creates its own rules and surrounds itself with a shell of protection. Play creates a special type of order that opposes and overrides the normal disorder of life. The *play-ground* is the location where the act of play occurs. The *play-ground* is a semi-sacred spot where the rules of play reign supreme. For our purposes, the boxing ring is this *play-ground*. Once the ring is created it tells us that within that space, specific rules are being followed that are different from the rules outside the ring, and these rules last as long as the bout lasts. When the ring is broken, the special order established by play disappears and the normal disorder of life returns.

While all humans (and animals too) engage in play, not all humans or animals engage in fair play. Fair play requires a type of behavior that will come to be recognized as a special quality of the English character. All play requires rules, but fair play requires unique rules, which change the behavior of anyone who adopts them. This behavior requires that equality of opportunity be granted in any contest. Two men should not gang up on one man, nor should a man with a sword hit a man who has none. *Fair play is the Golden Rule applied to sport.* That this phrase first appears in the midst of a street quarrel involving "a boxe on the eare" is dramatic proof that from a very early date, the exercise of boxing was linked to fair play. As we shall see, boxing and fair play grew up together in English society.

Although Richard Harvey was the first to use the term fair play in English, the earliest reference to it that I have found is in *The Champion's Covenant*, Chapter XVI of *The Feast of Bricriu*. This is one of the Old Irish sagas involving the hero Cuchulainn, dating from perhaps AD 875. A half-giant, a bachlach or churl, appears at the court of Emain Macha, where all of the warriors of Ulster are relaxing after their games. The bachlach challenges them to help him to fulfill his quest. Before telling them his quest, he demands fair play: "If but fairplay be vouchsafe me, I will tell it."[16]

When the warriors agree to provide him fair play, he tells them that he wishes to cut off the head of one of them that night, and then he will return the next night to have his own head cut off. The warriors reject this but agree to reverse the order; one of them will cut off the bachlach's head and then let him cut off theirs the next night. Reluctantly the bachlach agrees to this. He then hands his axe to Fat Neck, son of Short Head, who chops off the bachlach's head. The bachlach picks up his head and his axe and leaves the hall with blood streaming from his neck: "'By my people's god,' quoth Duach of the Chafer Tongue, 'if the bachlach, having been killed to-night, come back to-morrow, he will not leave a man alive in Ultonia.'"

The bachlach does indeed return the next night, but Fat Neck refused to honor his promise. The bachlach then challenges Loigaire the Triumphant and Conall the Victorious. Each agree to the covenant, but after chopping off the bachlach's head, they too refuse to have their own heads chopped off when their turn comes. The bachlach then challenges Cuchulainn, who says he does not want to enter the covenant with the bachlach. But then, shamed by the bachlach, Cuchulainn takes up the axe and cuts off the bachlach's head.

The next day Cuchulainn does show up prepared to honor the agreement. After some bantering, the bachlach brings the dull edge of the axe down on Cuchulainn's neck and awards him the champion's portion. Finally, the bachlach has found fair play.[17]

We must recognize that although this story formed the basis for *Sir Gawain and the Green Knight*, it was written in Irish, not English. It clearly influenced English literature, but we are not sure to what extent it influenced the adoption of the English concept of fair play.

In the *Battle of Maldon* (AD 991), Brithnoth, the Anglo-Saxon leader, allowed the Vikings whom he had trapped on the other side of a river to freely cross over a ford so that they could fight hand-to-hand on the land. In this he provides them fair play. But this proves to be a mistake, as Brithnoth is killed and his army routed.[18]

The earliest version of fair play in English sport was found in wrestling, which developed its rules prior to AD 1000. Wrestling required that two men meet without weapons and fight hand-to-hand. Beowulf, before his fight with Grendel, expresses this wrestling code of fair play when he puts away his armor and sword to fight Grendel hand-to-hand:

> When it comes to fighting, I count myself
> as dangerous any day as Grendel.
> So it won't be a cutting edge I'll wield
> to mow him down, easily as I might.
> He has no idea of the arts of war,
> of shield or sword-play, although he does possess
> a wild strength. No weapons, therefore,
> for either this night: unarmed he shall face me
> if face me he dares. And may the Divine Lord
> in His wisdom grant the glory of victory
> to whichever side he sees fit.[19]

Unlike Brithnoth, Beowulf wins his fight, and hangs Grendel's arm from the roof beams as a trophy while Grendel flees back to his lair.

A similar attitude toward fair play is expressed by Hereward the Wake in the *Gesta Herewardi* (c. 1100). Hereward and his men have taken refuge in the Isle of Ely and are being besieged by William the Conqueror and his men. When Richard, one of William's men, is isolated from the others and attacked by several of Hereward's men, Hereward has them separated and allows no one to do violence to Richard, "saying that it was shameful for two or three to fight against one man and [he] would in no way allow such a thing to be done by his men; and this we learnt from the mouth of Richard himself."[20]

Wrestling first developed the concept of fair play in England. It begins with Brithnoth, then Beowulf, then Hereward, and we finally see it operating in Geoffrey of Monmouth's description of the match between Corineus and Gogmagog (c. 1135). This shows us that fair play was established among the common people from as far back as memory serves.

It was then passed on in the 1500s to the Masters of Defence. A man moving to the rank of provost was to swear an oath:

> You shalbe always mercifull and whereas it maye happen you to have the vpper hande of Your enimye That is to saye vnder your feete or without Weapon or some other advantage you shall not kill him, yf he be the Queenes true subiecte savinge your selfe without Danger of Deathe or bodeley hurte according to your first othe which you Receved entringe to learne the science.[21]

This attitude is also embodied in the oath sworn by a candidate moving to the rank of Master. The Master's oath in part is as follows:

> Item you shalbe Mercifull, And Whereas you happen to have the upper hand of your enimye That is to saie Without Weapon or vnder your feete or his backe towards you, then you shall not kill him saving your selfe harmelesse without daunger of Death Except it be in the service of the prince.[22]

This admonition to not kill a person who is "Without Weapon or vnder your feete" was the difference between murder (a planned killing) and misadventure (accidental death). When two men took the field in a duel of honor, and one killed the other, the verdict would often be misadventure, which might well be pardoned because they both had weapons and were engaged in a fair fight. But when a man attacked and killed an unarmed man, or one who had not drawn his weapon, it was murder, for which the punishment was death without benefit of clergy. Thus, by 1600, fair play had become embodied in English law. Although killing a man in a duel was theoretically punishable by death, as noted in the *Edinburgh Review* of 1814: "No instance is known of the law being executed against any person for being engaged in a duel, fought in what is called a *fair* manner."[23]

On the other hand, we have already seen in Chapter IV how, when Rocco Bonetti drew his sword on an unarmed waterman, he was set upon by a crowd of watermen who beat him with oars and stretchers until he was nearly dead. To pull a sword on an unarmed man was considered foul play.

Foul Play

In contrast to this code of *fair play*, we find an example of what the English felt was *foul play* in the romance *Stanzaic of Guy of Warwick* (c. 1300).

Guy of Warwick is a knight-errant who travels across Europe and the Middle East, fighting in righteous battles. Ultimately, he returns to his home in England where he learns that King Athelstan (924–937) is being besieged at Winchester by the Danish army, headed by an African giant, Colbrond. Colbrond has challenged the English to single combat to determine who will rule England, but no one dares to face him. Ultimately Guy agrees to fight Colbrond. The giant comes equipped with a large quantity of weapons, while Guy has only a horse, spear, sword and shield.

Guy rides out to face Colbrond and promptly suffers a series of losses. First his spear breaks into five pieces, then Colbrond kills Guy's horse and finally Guy's sword breaks in two. The Danes enjoyed Guy's plight and think he is doomed. Colbrond asks him to surrender. But since Guy notes that Colbrond has a "great plenty" weapons, he asks him to lend him a battle axe. Colbrond refuses to give him one. Instead, he says that if Guy does not do his bidding, he will soon die a miserable death:

"Ac thou hast armes gret plente,
Ywis, thou most lene me
On of thine axes strong"
Colbrond swore bi Apolin, [by Apollo]
"Of al the wepen that is min
Her schaltow non afong. [You shall not have one]
Now thou wilt nought do bi mi rede [Now if you do not do my bidding]
Thou schalt dye on ivel dede [You shall die an evil death]
Er that it be ought long."[24]

Guy immediately takes offense at Colbrond's behavior and runs to where Colbrond has placed his extra weapons. Guy grabs a battle axe with a long handle and runs back to Colbrond, saying: "Traitor, you shall have an evil death now that I have a weapon with which to defend myself, in spite of your boasting." Colbrond tries to strike Guy on the helmet, but his blow misses and his sword sinks into the ground. Before Colbrond can pull it out, Guy swings the axe and cuts off Colbrond's right arm. As Colbrond attempts to pick up his sword with his left hand, Guy cuts off his head. At that the Danes flee England while the Englishmen rejoice.[25]

Colbrond's attitude may stand for the attitude of all foreigners: They do not share the British concept of fair play. Colbrond's death shows the fate that the English believed should befall anyone who did not provide fair play in a duel. As John Lydgate (c. 1370–1451) stated, in his version of Guy of Warwyk, Guy killed Colbrond "by the grace of Goddis hond."[26]

On the other hand, the Italians, the Danes, and Troilus the Trojan all believed that one should not show mercy to an opponent when they are down. The same was true of the British aristocracy prior to the seventeenth century. While the common men believed in fair play, the English aristocracy did not.

We have already seen this as typical behavior of the nobility in Chapter IV. As Lawrence Stone noted in his analysis of the behavior of the aristocracy in the sixteenth century:

> When personal conflict between principals took place, no holds were barred.... When armed retainers were employed, there were equally no conventions of fair play. Surprise ambushes, attacks from the rear, onslaughts by overwhelming numbers were all legitimate tactics in the sixteenth century, and brought no disrepute upon the organizer ... up to the end of the sixteenth century men saw nothing dishonourable in attacking by surprise with superior forces, and nothing in hitting a man when he was down. By the second decade of the seventeenth century, such behavior was becoming discreditable and is much less frequently met with.[27]

In the play *King John* (1594–96) by William Shakespeare, John is forced to give up his crown to the pope and receive it back from Cardinal Pandulph in order to preserve his kingdom. In return, Pandulph attempts to stop the French from invading England. Philip the Bastard, whom John has recognized as the son of his brother, Richard the Lion Hearted, attends John. The Bastard urges John to lead his army to defend the country rather than merely rely upon papal diplomacy:

> BASTARD: O inglorious league!
> Shall we, upon the footing of our land,
> Send *fair-play* orders and make compromise,
> Insinuation, parley and base truce
> To arms invasive? [Act V, scene i, lines 65–69, my italics].[28]

Here the Bastard treats *fair play* with scorn as less honorable than war. Eight years later, in *Troilus and Cressida* (1601–02), Shakespeare has Troilus chide Hector for his belief in *fair play* as the basis of honor:

> TROILUS: Brother, you have the vice of mercy in you,
> Which better fits a lion than a man.
>
> HECTOR: What vice is that? Good Troilus, chide me for it.
>
> TROILUS: When many times the captive Grecian falls,
> Even in the fan and wind of your fair sword,
> You bid them rise and live.
>
> HECTOR: O, 'tis *fair play*.
>
> TROILUS: Fool's play, by heaven, Hector.
>
> HECTOR: How now? how now?
>
> TROILUS: For th' love of all the gods,
> Let's leave the hermit pity with our mother,
> And when we have our armors buckled on,

>   The venom'd vengeance ride upon our swords,
>   Spur them to ruthful [woeful] work, rein them from ruth [mercy].
>   HECTOR: Fie, savage, fie! [Act V, scene iii, lines 37–49, my italics].

Troilus is expressing the Italian sense of honor, as opposed to Hector, who is expressing the common Briton's sense of honor. Vincentio Saviolo, a contemporary of Shakespeare, and the most famous Italian fencing master in England at the time (see Chapter IV), specifically warns against treating a man who challenges you with a sword as a friend:

> I will speak mine opinion of these things which concern a mans life and honour, and first I would with every one which is challenged into the feeld, to consider that he which challengeth him, dooth not require to fight him as a freend, but as an enemye, and that he is not to thinke any otherwise of his minde but as full of rancor and malice towards him.[29]

Saviolo illustrates this warning with a story of a man who was run through and killed by a person whom he thought was a friend: "Therefore when a man sees anie one with a drawen weapon, let him take care to defend himself, because it is not a matter of friendshippe." In Saviolo's world there is no such thing as a friendly bout with fair play. Any man holding a weapon is to be treated as a dangerous enemy.[30]

Boxing as a Civilizing Force in Britain

As Lawrence Stone demonstrated, the British aristocracy adopted the Italian attitude of honor along with the rapier (see Chapter V). But during the seventeenth century, as the duel began to lose favor and boxing became more popular, the aristocracy began to change its behavior. Boxing began to convert the aristocracy to the concept of fair play. As Stone noted: "By the second decade of the seventeenth century, such [Italianate] behavior was becoming discreditable and is much less frequently met with." Although boxing was not the sole reason for this change in mental attitude, it certainly helped. Boxing, not just fox-hunting as proposed by Norbert Elias, helped to civilize England and convert it into a land where fair play was taken for granted and enforced by the common man.

This attitude became fundamental to all English sports. Even a sport such as *hurling to the country*, one of the many variations of football (which generally had few rules), had by 1600 developed a sense of fair play. Richard Carew notes that those who break the rules are punished: "The lest breach of these lawes, the Hurlers take for a just cause of going together by the eares [boxing of the ears], but with their fists onely; neigther doth among them seek revenge for such wrong or hurts, but at the like play game [nor do they take revenge for such infractions or blows, save in the game itself]."[31]

Samuel Pepys (1633–1703) provided an example of this dedication to fair play when he went to the Bear Garden to see a prizefight in the tradition of the Masters of Defence (May 27, 1667):

> Then abroad by [coach?] and stopped at the Bear-garden stairs [in Southwark], there to see a Prize fought; but the house so full there was no getting in there; so forced to [go] through an alehouse into the pit where the bears are baited, and upon a stool did see them fight, which they did very furiously, a butcher and a waterman. The former had the better all along, till by and by the latter dropped his sword out of his hand, and the butcher, whether not seeing his sword dropped or I know not, but did give him a cut over the wrist, so as he was disabled to fight any longer. But Lord, to see how in a minute the whole stage was full of watermen to revenge the foul play, and the butchers to defend their fellow, though most blamed him; and there they all fell to it, to knocking down and cutting many of each side. It was pleasant to see, but that I stood in the pit and feared that in the tumult I might get some hurt.[32]

The London audience felt that it was unfair that the butcher struck his opponent when the latter's sword had fallen from his hand. To strike with a sword a man who had no weapon (even for a brief time) was considered *foul play*. This immediately brought the watermen onto the stage. The butchers were forced to respond, even though they generally agreed that their man had been wrong. This spontaneous reaction from the crowd showed that the sense of fair play was deep-seated and long standing. It was so bred in the bone of the common Englishman's version of sword-fighting that even a butcher could not take advantage of an unarmed man. Hector's sense of honor had become the sense of honor of the common man. But there were rules as to what constituted fair play: sport required fair play, but politics did not. As J. Burgh, Gentleman, was later to comment: "The London mob will not suffer in boxing the least foul play; as, for instance, two fall upon one. Yet this very mob will set upon the house, or person, of an obnoxious minister five thousand against one, and would, in their fury, tear him to pieces, without thinking of the foul play."[33]

Pepys's prizefight was a public duel with swords and bucklers according to English rules, but it is clear that we are very close to uncovering a prizefight with fists. Francis Willughby, in his uncompleted *Book of Games* (1672), provided insight into the relationship between dueling and boxing. Willughby entitled one section in his book "Duelling, Wrestling &c." In this chapter he included wrestling and fisticuffs along with fencing and cudgel-playing as a subset of dueling and subject to the same type of rules.

One of these rules dealt with the role of "seconds." Willughby reported: "Seconds either fight themselves, or onely stand by and see faire play, & are readie with salves &c. to dresse the wounds." The seconds in a duel, wrestling, or boxing match were especially appointed to ensure that *fair play* prevailed.[34]

Donna T. Andrew gives us another example of the importance of seconds and their role in ensuring fair play when she cites the duel between Captain Campbell and Captain Boyd in 1808. They fought without seconds present. Boyd was killed in the duel. As a result, Campbell was tried, convicted of murder and hanged for the act. To fight without seconds was not fair play.[35]

As we have already seen in the previous chapter, Zacharias Conrad von Uffenbach confirmed the role of seconds in a prizefight with swords in 1710: "Each of the combatants had his second by him with a large stick in his hand; they were not there to parry blows, but only to see that there was fair play on all sides."[36]

Pierce Egan, the historian of boxing, writing in 1812, also noted this aspect of the English character: "This trait cannot be more *nationally* illustrated than in the instance of the British Sailor, at the taking of Ft. Omoa [Honduras, on 20 October 1779], who, being in possession of two swords, and suddenly meeting an enemy destitute of any weapon of defence, with unparalleled manliness and generosity, *divided* the instruments of death with him, that he might have a fair chance for his life." For an Englishman, any fight must begin with an equality of arms. The hallmark of the normal Englishman always is fair play.[37]

Modern society has adopted this English attitude as the hallmark of civilized life. Even in the darkest days of conflict, *fair play*, like the blue birds over the white cliffs of Dover, has remained the standard of civilized behavior. As Johan Huizinga argued during those troubled days at the outset of the Second World War:

> Civilization will, in a sense, always be played according to certain rules, and true civilization will always demand fair play. Fair play is nothing less than good faith expressed in play terms. Hence the cheat or the spoil-sport shatters civilization itself.[38]

By 1700 the attitude of the English aristocracy, which had adopted the rapier and the duel of honor as its method of solving quarrels in 1600, was changing. We find that gentlemen were finally willing to resort to boxing in public streets instead of sword duels as a way to settle a dispute. After describing a boxing match between two boys in the street, Henri Misson states:

> These [boxing] combats are less frequent among grown men, but they are not rare. If a Coach-man has a Dispute about his Fare with a Gentleman that has hired him, and the Gentleman offers to fight him to decide the Quarrel, the Coach-man consents with all his Heart: The Gentleman pulls off his Sword, lays it in some Shop, with his Cane, Gloves, and Cravat, and boxes in the same Manner as I have described above. If the Coachman is soundly drubb'd, which happens almost always, that goes for Payment but if he [the coachman] is the Beator,

Fig. 13. Fair play as an English national trait. An English sailor at the capture of Ft. Omoa, Honduras (October 20, 1779), presenting one of the sailor's two swords to an unarmed Spanish officer, thus offering him a chance to preserve his life and freedom. Edward Barnard, *The new comprehensive, impartial and complete history of England: From the very earliest period of authentic information, to the end of the present year* (London: Printed for A. Hogg, 1783). Author's collection.

the Beatee must pay the Money about which they quarrell'd. (A Gentleman seldom exposes himself to such a Battel, without he is sure he's strongest. *Note by Misson*.)[39]

César de Saussure, confirming Misson's observation, noted that the Duke of Bolton, when challenged to a fist-fight in the street by a footman, "unaccustomed to this form of exercise and afraid of not getting the best of it, refused the offer and prudently retired."[40] Henri Misson gives us another example of a nobleman fighting a coachman with his fists: "I once saw the late Duke of *Grafton* at *Fisticuffs*, in the open Street, with such a Fellow, whom he lamb'd most horribly. (In the very widest Part of the *Strand*. The Duke of *Grafton* was big and extremely robust. He had hid his blue Ribband before he took the Coach, so that the Coachman did not know him.)"[41]

By the end of the seventeenth century gentlemen considered boxing a suitable strategy for settling private differences, particularly those involving commoners. The hints that Shakespeare had made about King Henry V and Marc Antony engaging in buffets with butchers or sweaty knaves in 1600 had become reality in 1700.

James Peller Malcolm cites a similar situation at a somewhat later date:

> The late Marshall Saxe, walking though London streets, happened to have a dispute with a scavenger, which ended in a boxing bout, wherein his dexterity received the general applause of the spectators: he let the scavenger come upon him, then seized him by the neck, and made him fly up into the air, in such a direction that he fell into the middle of his cart, which was brimful of dirt.[42]

César de Saussure cited a similar case involving the Duke of Leeds circa 1727:

> My Lord Herbert, who is a very strong and robust man, recently fought a porter, and punished him well; the man was so surprised that he exclaimed, "D—sure you are the son of a porter and not of a lord; you know how to use your fists too well."[43]

Pierce Egan also mentioned that Dr. Samuel Johnson (1709–1784) engaged in a boxing match with a brewer's assistant who had insulted him in Fleet Street, and gave him a "complete milling" in a few minutes.[44]

Indeed, even King George IV (1762–1830), when Prince of Wales (circa 1782) engaged in a fist-fight with a butcher over actions at a fox hunt:

> The scent [of the fox] was catching and uncertain, so that we could go no continuous pace at all. There was a butcher out, God damn me, ma'am, a great big fellow, fifteen stone [210 pounds], six feet two inches without his shoes and the bully of all Brighton. He over-rode my hounds several times, and I had spoken to him to hold hard in vain. At last, God damn me, ma'am, he rode slap over my favorite bitch, Ruby. I could stand it no longer but, jumping off my horse, said, "Get down, you damned rascal, pull off your coat, none shall interfere with us, but you or I shall go back to Brighton more dead than alive." God damn me, ma'am, I threw off my coat, and the big ruffian, nothing loath, did the same by

his. By God, ma'am, we fought for an hour and twenty minutes, my hunting field forming a ring around us, no one interfering; and at the end of it the big bully of Brighton was carried away senseless, while I had hardly a scratch.[45]

By 1700, the British had adopted the code of honor in which an armed man who challenged or accepted a challenge from an unarmed man was obliged to fight him with fists, not weapons. And by the end of the eighteenth century gentlemen of all ranks were quite willing to fight commoners with their fists. Boxing had become an honorable exercise.

Unlike La-writ in Beaumont and Fletcher's *The Little French Lawyer* at the beginning of the seventeenth century, in England a gentleman now had no problem laying aside his sword to use his fists: "The Gentleman pulls off his Sword, lays it in some Shop, with his Cane, Gloves, and Cravat, and boxes in the same Manner as I have described above." This is totally different from the situation on the continent. There, as we have seen, the aristocracy in France and Italy might hit an unarmed man with their sword or their cane. But this could not occur in England, Henri Misson described:

> I can't imagine what could occasion the Notion that I have observ'd in *France*, that the *English* were Treacherous. Tis strange, that they, of all Nations of the World, should lie under this Scandal, they, whose Generosity cannot so much as bear that two Men should fight without an Equality of Arms, Offensive and Defensive: He that should venture to use either a Cane or Sword against a Man that had nothing to defend himself with but his Hands, would run a Risque of being torn to Pieces by the 'Prentices of the Neighborhood, and by Mob.[46]

César de Saussure writing in 1727 confirmed this observation:

> The insolence of the populace is so great that as soon as an honest man has any disagreement with one of their kind, he is at once invited to strip and fight. It would be dangerous to retaliate with a cane or sword; the lookers-on would at once be against him and things might end badly for him. Noblemen of rank, almost beside themselves with anger at the arrogance of a carter or person of that sort, have been seen to throw off their coats, wigs, and swords, in order to use their fists.[47]

This situation arose because the English yeoman classes refused to adopt the rapier and dueling as a way of settling quarrels and instead developed boxing as their solution. Pierce Egan praises England for being

> a country where the stiletto is not known—where trifling quarrels do not produce assassination, where revenge is not finished by murder. Boxing removes these dreadful calamities; a contest is soon decided, and scarcely ever the frame sustains any material injury.[48]

Egan's testimony credits the English code of fair play as being enhanced by the sport of boxing. Once the duel of honor had been defeated by boxing, England became famous for democratic courage. Pierce Egan believed that boxing expressed the true character of the honest Englishman:

> Pugilism is in perfect unison with the feelings of Englishmen.... Distinctions of rank is of little importance when an offence has been given, and in the impulse of the moment, a PRINCE has forgot his royalty, by turning out to box, to prevent the imputation of a coward—a DUKE, his consequence in life—and a BISHOP, the sanctity of his cloth; displaying those strong and *national* traits so congenial to the soil of liberty.[49]

Unlike the French and other nationalities, the English adopted a code that demanded equality of arms. By the eighteenth century, no gentleman would think of fighting another unless both were armed in the same way. And no gentleman would dare attack an unarmed social inferior with his sword.

This explains, I believe, how the sport of boxing came to develop in England. The attitude that Misson saw in operation circa 1697 and that de Saussure saw in 1727 was not something newly born. It dated back to the times of Brithnoth, Beowulf and Hereward the Wake. It was obviously fundamental to the common Englishman. As the concept of fist-fighting developed, this idea of fair play forced the man with the weapon to lay it aside and fight with his fists. This is why we find boxing terms, not fencing terms, used in the Marprelate papers. The society in which every man went armed with a weapon was being converted, and it started at the bottom of society, not at the top. Weapons were still carried, but they were only used when the other man also carried the same weapon. And even then, as we will see, often those who carried weapons chose to lay them aside and fight with their fists. Weapon-fighting was being driven out of England and fists trumped swords.

Boxing caused this change. As it developed, boxing gained the sense of honor that was missing in 1458. It was a less dangerous and more dramatic way of settling quarrels than the secret duel. But at the same time, boxing could not have developed without this attitude, drawn from wrestling, being already present in the society. Wrestling had established the value of weaponless fighting. Boxing did its part to make this old code of honor evident. Boxing offered an alternative to the duel. By 1700, boxing had become manly enough that honor could be satisfied by fighting with fists rather than dueling with swords. Thus, English gentlemen everywhere adopted boxing as a sport in the eighteenth century. As Francis Frederick Brandt noted in his book on pugilism in 1857:

> In England, and in England alone, does the custom prevail of settling disputes by means of the weapon with which nature has provided us for the purpose. A foreigner bites, scratches, kicks, and eventually whips a knife into you. An Englishman simply knocks you down.[50]

As the visitor from Switzerland, César de Saussure, noted in England in 1727: "Very few are partisans of duelling, so that you do not often hear of this mode of settling quarrels." This is also why we see James Figg, the greatest of the Masters of Defence, promoting boxing matches at the beginning of the eighteenth century, and why by the end of the century, M. Faubert's, London's most famous fencing school, was converted to a riding academy. Boxing was replacing dueling as a much more benign method of dealing with disputes in English society.[51]

Scientific boxing became a civilizing force in England. Pierce Egan praised boxing for these reasons in 1812:

> But never let Britons be ashamed of a science;—yes, A SCIENCE that not only adds generosity to their disposition—humanity to their conduct—but courage to their national character.[52]

We find this same attitude expressed later in the nineteenth century by a member of Parliament, George Charles Grantley Fitzhardinge Berkeley (1800–1881): "In my mind, then, the prize fight and fair boxing-match are the means of teaching the people to become advocates for honest and gallant decisions in all cases of quarrel, and that the encouragement of the use of the fist is the greatest antidote that can be offered to the revengeful and dastardly resort to the assassins knife."[53]

England owes both its current low homicide rate and the ease with which it was converted to a weaponless society to the popularity of boxing. Boxing had a major role in developing a peaceful society in England. Yet oddly enough some have criticized boxing for not being civilized enough.

Modern writers such as Kenneth G. Sheard, Edith Summerskill, Thomas Myler and Jack Anderson are critical of boxing for being too brutish for their modern sensibilities. As Sheard complains, the civilizing process is not complete because boxing has not "become *less* dangerous or *less* physically injurious, or *less* violent in an absolute sense, than previously." But this criticism misses the point. It does not matter whether boxing has become less violent (although it has); what matters is that because of boxing, *the whole of English society has become less violent than in the past.* It is not just boxing, but *England itself* that has become less dangerous, less physically injurious and less violent. And this is due to the civilizing force of boxing. Due to their lack of historical perspective, Sheard and others seem to think that the very existence of boxing is an affront to modern civilization. They are unaware of the much more dangerous activities that boxing has replaced. It is ironic that boxing, which was so influential in civilizing English society, should now be attacked as a mark of incivility in this same society.[54]

While brutal, boxing was not fatal. It was designed to establish a clear winner without requiring that the battle end in the death of one of the parties. Boxing was founded on the English concept of fair play. The rule of fair play had existed for centuries as part of the English character, but became articulated during the sixteenth century, at the same time as boxing itself. Boxing and fair play were twins that grew up in the same cradle.

Chapter VII

The Puritans and the First Matches of Boxing

Robert Dover's "Olimpicks," King James I and The Book of Sports

At the end of the sixteenth century, Richard Harvey urged the enemies of Martin Marprelate to put up their weapons in their street fights. Harvey recognized that the new sport of boxing had the ability to alter opinions with violence, but that such violence needed to be tempered with obedience to the rules of fair play. The rules of boxing, which were being enforced by the crowd, even though not written down, were a powerful force for civilizing society.

Boxing could not exist without rules. The fact that boxing was well-enough known in the 1580s to figure in the Martin Marprelate controversy tells us that rules already existed to make boxing a sport acceptable to the intellectual elite. The fact that Richard Harvey could speak of men shadow-boxing and beating their fists against a wall is proof positive that some fairly advanced boxing matches were being held. These men were hoping to get an advantage over their opponents by training and attempting to strengthen their knuckles. This should not surprise us: as far back as 1320 we suspected that fighters were training for bouts.

We believe that organized boxing bouts were taking place in the period from 1550 to 1600. But by 1600 separate rules existed that not only gave the new sport form, but also allowed it to be recognized as different from wrestling and understood so by the public.

While Cornishmen were best known as wrestlers, they seem to have engaged in boxing as well. Richard Carew (1602) mentioned that "the youthlier sort of Bodmin townsmen use sometimes to sport themselves by playing the box with strangers, whom they summon to Halgavor." "Playing the box" suggests that a rural form of boxing was involved in the punishments of Halgavor court in the years prior to 1600.[1]

In the same way, it is probable that Robert Dover's games in the Cotswold Hills also had an early version of boxing. From about 1612 to 1643, Dover, a country barrister, presided over a Whitsuntide "Olympic-like" event in Gloucestershire near Oxford. Whitsuntide games had been held there since before the Norman Conquest, but Dover revitalized them as a counterbalance to the Puritan movement. Dover gained the support of Kings James I and Charles I as well as a group of playwrights and poets, who joined in a tribute to Dover in 1636. These poems celebrate Dover's games and describe their activities. One of these tributes, by William Denny, speaks of racing, wrestling and throwing the bowle and then notes:

> The warre-like Champion with his powerfull fists,
> Contended for the Prize, as in our lists,
> Rebated Edges Counter buffe at Barriers,
> An Active sport to Breathe our bravest warriors.[2]

According to Denny, a war-like champion [*pugil?*] with his powerful fists fought for the prize. Unlike in the ancient Olympic games, where men fought with leather *caesti*, he used bare fists [rebated edges], to hit back [counterbuffe] under control. Still, it was an active sport to wear out the best warriors.

This section suggests that boxing or fisticuffs (as it was then called) was occurring at the Cotswold Olympics. The reference to the "barriers" links this sport to the medieval tournament where a fence or barrier was placed between fighting warriors in the joust to prevent the horsemen from running into each other. The function of the barrier was to reduce the level of unplanned violence, and to focus the fight on the opponent. This would also have been appropriate in Dover's games, which focused on enjoyable exercise rather than violent competitions.[3]

A. R. Wright, a folklorist of the 1930s, originally suggested that boxing was one of the sports presented in the Dover Olympics, but he did not give any citations. In volume II of his work he noted that boxing was also part of the Robin Hood May games held in Nottinghamshire and elsewhere. These celebrations go back to the fifteenth and sixteenth centuries, but again there is no indication of when boxing became part of the festivities.[4]

We have said that the Cotswold Olympics were designed to be a counter to the Puritan movement. The Presbyterians (Puritans) had a reputation of being unfriendly to sports. This is not precisely accurate. They were more nuanced than is often recognized. They did not oppose sports *per se*, as can be seen from the Marprelate documents. In 1622 John Downame, a Puritan divine, in his book *Guide to Godlyness* told his readers that God approved of "the meanest duties of the basest calling, yea even our eating and drinking, lawful sports and recreations, when as wee doe them in faith." In a later book, Downame believed that participation in "allowable Sports as best fit with men's severall dispositions for their comfort and refreshing" protected people from the fatigue of constant work in one's calling. Such fatigue could lead to melancholy (depression). Rather than bringing man closer to God, melancholy drove him further away.[5]

John Winthrop, the first governor of the Massachusetts Bay Colony, admitted that he personally had fallen into such a state of melancholy, which he relieved by recreation and moderate exercise. In his sermon "A Model of Christian Charity," given in 1630 on his way to the New World, he revealed his struggles:

> When I had some tyme abstained from such worldly delights as my heart most desired, I grew melancholick and uncomfortable, for I had been more careful to refraine from an outward conversation in the world, than to keepe the love of the world out of my heart, or to uphold my conversation in heaven.... I grewe unto a great dullnesse and discontent: which being at last perceived, I examined my heart, and finding it needful to recreate my minde with some outward recreation, I yielded unto it, and by a moderate exercise herein was much refreshed.[6]

Puritans and Presbyterians understood the value of sport to a healthy life. They believed in the doctrine of *mens sana in corpore sano* (a healthy mind in a healthy body). But they also believed in the doctrine of rendering up to God the things that are God's. And this meant, above all, keeping Sunday (the Sabbath) holy. In the same year John Winthrop gave his sermon "A Model of Christian Charity" on the ship *Arbella*, the Court of Assistants in Massachusetts ordered that one John Baker "shalbe whipped for shooteing att fowle on the Sabbath day." Baker's crime was not shooting birds; his crime was doing it on the Lord's Day. Shooting was, in fact, supported by the Massachusetts Bay Colony both for food and for defense, but there was a time and place for everything and Baker had not obeyed the rules.[7]

The Presbyterians vigorously opposed substituting sport participation for church participation. They were in favor of sports to improve a man's body and military skill. They engaged in wrestling and perhaps even boxing. They were not opposed to either strenuous activity or violence. It just had to be for the right reasons. The Puritan "Roundhead" armies had no qualms about shooting or fighting the Cavaliers in the Civil War (1642–1651).

On the other hand, they particularly opposed *The Book of Sports* written by King James I to settle a dispute in Lancashire in 1617. This book had grown out of a conflict between a group of unconverted Catholics in Lancashire (who wished to continue their custom of playing sports on Sunday) versus converted Puritans (who opposed such Sunday sports). Prior to the Reformation, it was common for parishioners to engage in games, sports, and other activities both during and after church services. Since Sunday was the only day of the week in which work was not required, recreation on Sunday had a long historical precedence. But after the Henrician Reformation, the converted began to oppose the unconverted who followed the old ways and who wished to enjoy recreation both in place of and after church services. Since Lancashire had the largest population of recusant Catholics in England, Lancashire became the focal point of this conflict.

In the 1580s, under the threat of a Spanish invasion, Catholics had been persecuted as potential traitors, so their voices were silenced. By 1617 the Spanish threat had receded and the Puritans themselves were now seen as dangerous to the crown. As a result, King James I, wishing to bring peace to the area, was willing to compromise with the Catholics and reject a Presbyterian order that forbid any "profanacion upon any Saboth Day in any part of the Day or upon any festival day in tyme of Devyne service." James, who was also known as the "wisest fool in Christendom," wrote a book on sport, which he hoped would bring peace to Lancashire. He declared that "no lawful recreation shall be barred to our people." This put the emphasis on sport and ignored the key concern of the Puritans about the sanctity of the Sabbath. Thinking that he had solved the problem, in 1618 James had the book read from every Anglican pulpit in the country.[8]

According to *The Book of Sports*, James approved of "Pypinge, Dansinge either men or women, archerie for men, leaping, valtinge of anie harmles recreation & the women to have leave to Carrie rushes to the Church for the decoringre of it according to their ould Custome." In addition, he ordered that afternoon sermons should not exceed one hour so that the parishioners would have more time for play. The Presbyterians and Puritans believed these activities were Popish practices and were appalled at the restriction on the length of the sermons. As a counter-measure to the perceived Catholic bias of the book, King James forbid anyone who did not attend Sunday services (which Catholics generally did not) from enjoying and participating in the after-church recreation. This did little to appease the Puritans, and when *The Book of Sports* was reissued in 1633 under King Charles I, it became one of the contributing factors to the English Civil War. The book was ordered to be burned by the common hangman in London on May 5, 1643.[9]

Opposition to *The Book of Sports* caused the Presbyterians to be branded as opposed to sport, but as we have seen, this is only partially true. First and foremost, they opposed recreation on Sunday, the Lord's Day. They had a number of other reasons for opposing sport. They considered tennis and handball to be frivolous. They opposed sports designed to inflict injury or pain, such as cudgeling, sword-fighting and boxing. They opposed sport that involved gambling, such as bowling. They opposed sports that were boisterous,

VII. The Puritans and the First Matches of Boxing 111

Fig. 14. Frontispiece of *Annalia Dubrensia or Celebration of Captain Robert Dover's Cotswold Games,* showing the variety of activities found in Dover's Olympics. Ed. Alexander B. Grosart (Manchester, UK: Printed for the Subscribers, 1877).

particularly ball games such as football and hurling. On the other hand, they approved of hunting and fishing because these produced foods. And they also approved of wrestling because wrestling served as one of the martial arts. Lastly, they opposed activities that they believed had Popish origins, such as the theater and bear-baiting. In this, the Puritans were ridiculed by Thomas Babington Macaulay's clever, but inexact, analysis: "The Puritan hated bear-baiting, not because it gave pain to the bear, but because it gave pleasure to the spectators."[10] The long and short of the situation was that the Puritans opposed sports that, in their view, led to a disordered life and misused the Lord's Day.

Robert Dover, on the other hand, embraced sport for the sake of sport. His Cotswold "Olimpicks" drew people outside to engage in a large variety of activities. We know that he included wrestling and William Denny's lines suggest that boxing was also enjoyed.

We can see a variety of sports celebrated by Dover and others in the frontispiece from the *Annalia Dubrensia*. Among these, at the upper right, we find two men grappling in what has been described as a version of upright wrestling. This drawing suggests the opponents kicking with their feet as well as grappling with their fists. The natural assumption has been that wrestling and not boxing was intended. But it should be noted that kicking and grappling were common to both wrestling and boxing until boxing outlawed them in 1838. In either case this was a "friendly" fight since neither person had stripped to their doublet, as was suggested by Richard Carew in 1602. There seems no reason to exclude boxing from the Dover "Olimpicks," especially given William Denny's comments cited above.[11]

In his 1614 book on Roman history, Thomas Goodwin discussed the Roman games and related them to current English practice. Greek and Roman boxing made use of the *caestus*, an early version of boxing gloves. In describing this version of fist-fighting, Goodwin used the term "fisticuffs" instead of boxing or buffeting. The modification of "cuffs" to "fisticuffs" was a new word for boxing in England.[12]

Robert Armin first used the term "fisty cuffes" in his book *Foole upon Foole* (1600). Lean Leanard, a simpleton, visits a shoemaker's stall and meets several journeymen who made fun of him. A country plowman decided to join in the fun, steals some pitch from the shoemakers, and puts it on Leanard's head. Leanard attempts to pull it off, but it is stuck:

> In an envious spleane smarting ripe, [Leanard] runnes after him, falles at fisty cuffes with him, but the fellow belabored the foole cunningly and got the fooles head under his arm and bob'd [hit] his nose. The foole remembering how his head was, strikes it up, and hits the fellows mouth with the pitch place, so that the hayre [hair] of his head and the hayre of the clownes beard were glude together.

The onlookers, after laughing at the sight, separate the two. A constable arrives, puts the plowman in the stocks and takes Leanard home to his master.[13]

It is clear that "fisty cuffes" means fighting with one's fists. The plowman responds with a wrestling hold ("putting in chancery") and proceeded to hit Leanard in the face with his fists. This again suggests that "fisticuffs" were akin to wrestling and that the two were combined initially. The fact that Armin makes no attempt to define "fisty cuffes" in this first use suggests that this type of fighting with one's fists was too well known to need explanation by 1600. Although we can date "cuffs" from 1530, and the earliest date for "fisticuffs" is 1600, it seems likely that "fisticuffs" was among the very early names given to the sport of boxing by the English-speaking country folk. Such names were probably common for a century or more prior to being recognized in print.

At the same time, fisticuffs was apparently a rough and tumble country sport subject to the flaw common to all fist-fighting. As Goodwin explained in his revision of 1638, "for we must know that this kinde of fight [the adoption of leather protection for the fists] succeeded fisticuffs, and because in fisticuffs the party striking, did by the blow as well hurt his own fist, as he did him that was strucken, hereupon they invented this other kind of fight with lethern switches." In this regard, we may see fighting with the *caestus* or *whirlbats* as an early attempt at developing boxing gloves.[14]

From 1590 to 1680 the sport of boxing, including buffeting and fisticuffs, was being practiced and was well known to the English population. It is also clear that these were rural or lower-class sports and had not been adopted by the upper classes.

Dover had tried to recreate the Greek environment in the Cotswold even to the point of hiring a blind harpist to impersonate Homer. At the same time, he modified the sports to fit the tastes of the English gentry. Since both wrestling and boxing had been included in the Greek and Roman games, it was reasonable to expect to find them in the Cotswold.

The First Boxing Matches (1681–1727)

The first notice we have of an actual boxing match is the following:

Yesterday [December 30, 1681] a Match of Boxing was performed, before his Grace the Duke of *Albemarl* [sic], between the Dukes [sic] Foot-man and a Butcher, the latter won the Prize, as he hath done many before, being accounted (though but a little Man) the best at that Exercise in *England*.[15]

This news notice on page 2 in the *True Protestant Mercury* of December 31, 1681, is the first documentary proof of the existence of the sport of boxing.

Further, this is the first recorded use of the phrase "a match of boxing" in the English language. Yet brief as this notice is, it tells us an enormous amount about the beginning of boxing.

(1) We learn that by 1681 dukes no longer engaged in boxing as a sport; butchers and footmen did. Prior to 1600 we have Shakespeare's testimony that the aristocracy was willing to engage in fist-fighting. Yet, as we have seen, this did not continue. By 1681 the sport of boxing remained of interest to the nobility, but as spectators, not participants.

(2) Boxing matches were now recognized as "prizefights." Prizefights, as their name implies, were public fights being fought for a prize, not for revenge or any other motive. Already at this early date, boxing had become commercialized. There was money to be made in fighting boxing matches.

(3) The fact that the butcher won the prize shows that there were already established rules to boxing matches. There had to be accepted rules in order for a little man to defeat a big man on the big man's home ground. There had to be rules that allowed a decision to be made by the Duke of Albemarle to award the prize to the butcher and not to his own footman.

(4) Although this was the first recorded boxing match, it does not mean that boxing was a new sport. In fact, we learn that the butcher won "as he hath done many before." This confirms our belief that boxing had been occurring for many years before this notice. Already by 1681, both the butcher and boxing had an established history in England.

(5) Not only had the butcher won many previous matches, he was recognized as "the best at that Exercise in *England*." While there was no recognized ranking system at this early date, we have here what amounts to a newspaper decision that this butcher was the best at this sport. From the newspaper writer's standpoint, the butcher was the champion of England.

(6) This suggests an unexpected level of sophistication to boxing, given that this was the first mention in print of the sport.

(7) It is also clear that for this butcher to be considered the best boxer in England there had to be many other fighters and many other matches that preceded this battle. We would hope to find descriptions of these fighters and these fights somewhere in the literature, but they are difficult to find.

(8) We can conclude that by 1681 boxing had been established as a sport in England for many years. Already at this early moment it had attracted

a major following among the aristocracy. The *Domestick Intelligence* of December 31 tells us that His Grace the Duke of Albemarle had spent the day of the fight with his friends, the Duke of Grafton, the Marquess of Worcester, the Earl of Feversham and the Earl of Bridgewater, all of whom planned to dine together that night at the Inner Temple. It seems likely that these men had come to London to see the fight. In this gathering we can see the beginning of a group of aristocrats who supported boxing from its earliest days, and which we will come to call the *Fancy*.[16]

(9) We believe that as early as the Marprelate controversy of 1590 boxing existed. We have not yet discovered the boxers who fought in these earlier fights, nor, with the possible exception of the miller and the trooper (see Appendix 5), have we a record of their fights. But we are convinced that boxing had existed in England for at least a century before this first notice of 1681.

Following this first notice, there was a second boxing match held by the Duke of Albemarle in 1682. This was reported on the first page of the *Domestick Intelligence* (September 21–25, 1682):

A great Match of Boxing was performed this Week between the Duke of Albermarles [sic] Porter and a Souldier [sic] of the Foot Guards, his Majesty and his Royal Highness being present, wherein though with much difficulty the former remained Victorious.[17]

(1) From this notice we learn that both King Charles II and his brother, the Duke of York (later King James II), witnessed this fight. This means that boxing was legal and was supported by the crown.

(2) In addition, it would appear that the Duke of Albemarle was not only a supporter of boxing but perhaps had a stable of boxers working for him. This seems likely since in 1681 we encountered one of Albemarle's footmen and in 1682 we have met his porter, both as boxers in matches. This would make the second Duke of Albemarle the first known boxing promoter.

(3) The notice also suggests that already a match of boxing was a complicated affair and that victory was not easily won. As the newspaper article stated, the porter remained victorious "with much difficulty."

(4) The words "remained Victorious" also suggest that the porter had fought several other battles and had won them as well. He may have aspired to be the champion of England, if the butcher no longer held that title.

Writing a few years later, in 1697, Henri Misson gave us the first eyewitness description of a boxing match:

> Any Thing that looks like Fighting, is delicious to an *Englishman*. If two little Boys quarrel in the Street, the Passengers stop, make a Ring round them in a Moment, and set them against one another, that they may come to Fisticuffs. When 'tis come to a fight, each pulls off his Neckcloth and his Wastcoat, and give them to hold to some of the Standers-by (Some will strip themselves naked quite to their Wastes); then they will begin to brandish their Fists in the Air; the Blows are aim'd all at the Face, they kick one another's Shins, they tug one another by the Hair, etc. He that has got the other down, may give him one Blow or two before he rises, but no more; and let the boy get up ever so often, the other is oblig'd to box him again as often as he requires it.
>
> During the Fight, the Ring of By-standers encourage the Combatants with great Delight of Heart, and never part them while they fight according to the Rules. And these By-standers are not only other Boys, Porters, and Rabble, but all Sorts of Men of Fashion; some thrusting by the Mob, that they may see plain, others getting upon the Stalls; and all would hire Places, if Scaffolds could be built in a Moment.
>
> The Father and Mother of the Boys let them fight on as well as the rest, hearten him that gives Ground or has the Worst.[18]

Here, Misson clearly referred to the requirement that the boys fight "according to the Rules," and that these rules were enforced by the "by-standers." These rules permitted that the boy who got his opponent on the ground could hit him "one Blow or two before he rises, but no more." In addition, "let the boy get up ever so often, the other is oblig'd to box him again as often as he requires it." Already, 40 years before John Broughton wrote down the first rules of boxing, the crowds of "Boys, Porters, and Rabble, [and] all Sorts of Men of Fashion" knew the rules of boxing and were avid followers of the sport. Here again we see that already in the seventeenth century the group we will call the *Fancy* is present and supportive of boxing.

César de Saussure, writing in 1727, also describes one of these early boxing bouts:

> The lower populace is of a brutal and insolent nature, and is very quarrelsome. Should two men of this class have a disagreement which they cannot end up amicably, they retire into some quiet place and strip from their waists upwards. Everyone who sees them preparing for a fight surrounds them, not in order to separate them, but on the contrary to enjoy the fight, for it is a great sport to the lookers-on, and they judge the blows and also help to enforce certain rules in use for this mode of warfare.
>
> The spectators sometimes get so interested that they lay bets on the combatants and form a big circle around them. The two champions shake hands before commencing, and then they attack each other with their fists, and sometimes with their heads, which they use like rams. Should one of the men fall, his opponent may give him a blow with his fist, but those who have laid their bets on the fallen man generally encourage him to continue till one of the combatants is quite knocked up and says he has had enough.[19]

These two eyewitness descriptions of boxing matches finally give us a good picture of the nature of these early fights. This gives us a revised view of the rules of boxing in the late seventeenth and early eighteenth centuries.

The Venetian Gondolier

The fights described by Misson and de Saussure illustrate the type of informal fights that we would have expected to find flaring up among the population. They demonstrate that the concept of boxing as a method of solving quarrels was well established in England at this time. Parallel to these informal fights were the more formal bouts, initially promoted by the Duke of Albemarle and other members of the nobility, but later organized by independent entrepreneurs like James Figg and James Stokes, for entertainment and gambling. Two years before the informal fight mentioned by Caesar de Saussure, on January 20, 1725, one very remarkable example of an early entrepreneurial bout was put on by James Figg between John Whitacre and an unnamed Venetian Gondolier.[20] This may have been the first international boxing match and pitted an Italian against an Englishman. It showed that already English boxing had become so popular that it attracted foreign challengers to Britain.

Italians had engaged in pugilistic combats for centuries, but they did not have a sport that equaled British boxing.[21] Venice had established a method of mass fighting known as the Wars of the Fists, *guerre dei pugni*. These wars took place on the bridges linking the various sections of the city together. Large groups of young men would meet on the bridges and engage in *battagliole* in which the objective was to drive their neighbors off the bridge. A *battagliola* was a mass brawl or melee which differed greatly from British boxing, but occasionally there were also one-on-one battles called *mostre* [shows] which bore some resemblance to an English boxing match.

The *mostra* was a set-piece. The two champions in a *mostra* might meet at the top of the bridge. Once the preliminaries were arranged the fighters retired down to the opposite corners of the bridge. They would then rush at each other with their right arms outstretched and their left arm protecting their face, which was the main target. There were two ways to win in a *mostra*. A basic victory (*rotto*) was to bloody the opponent's face and nose and force him to retire. The second way to win was to knock one's opponent off the bridge into the water. This was a decisive win and considered by some to be a double victory. We presume the Gondolier hoped to replicate a Venetian double victory in London.[22]

The fight involving the Gondolier began with a debate between an English gentleman and an Italian gentleman:

Last Sunday Evening [January 3, 1725] a certain English Gentleman talking in Slaughter's Coffee-house in St. Martin's Lane, of the extraordinary Dexterity of the Englishman in fighting with Fists, commonly called Boxing, an Italian Gentleman in the same Coffee-house offer'd a considerable Wager on the Head of one of his own Countrymen, whereupon a written instrument for 100 guineas was immediately drawn up; which was signed by both of them, and left with the Master of the House. The Italian has already produced his Man, and we hear, the English Gentleman has pitch'd upon John Whitacre, who lately fought Baker at Hockley in the Hole. The Combat is to be at James Figg's.[23]

The story was continued by Captain John Godfrey, who was an eyewitness:

I was at Slaughter's Coffee-house when the match was made by a Gentleman of an advanced Station; he sent for Fig to procure a proper Man for him; he told him to take care of his Man, because it was for a large Sum; and the *Venetian* was a Man of extraordinary Strength, and famous for breaking the Jaw-bone in *Boxing*. Fig replied, in his rough Manner, "I do not know, Master, but he may break one of his own Countrymen's Jaw-bones with his Fist; but I will bring him a Man, and he shall not break his Jaw-bone with a Sledge Hammer in his Hand."[24]

James Figg was the most prominent prize-fighting [sword-fighting] and boxing promoter in London at this time. His place of business was the Amphitheatre in Oxford Road. It was natural that the Gentleman, seeking to find an Englishman to stand up to the Gondolier, would turn to Figg. James Figg, in turn, chose a drover, John (incorrectly called "Bob" by Pierce Egan) Whitacre (or Whitaker as he was called by Captain Godfrey), as his champion.[25]

The Battle was fought at Fig's Amphitheatre before a splendid Company, the politest House of that kind I ever saw. While the Gondelier [sic] was stripping, my Heart yearned for my Countryman. His Arm took up all Observation; it was surprisingly large, long, and muscular. He pitched himself forward with his right Leg, and his Arm full extended, and, as Whitaker approached, gave him a Blow on the Side of the Head, that knocked him quite off the Stage, which was remarkable for it's [sic] Height.

Whitaker's Misfortune in his Fall was then the Grandeur of the Company, on which account they suffered no common People in, that usually sit on the Ground and line the Stage round. It was then all clear, and Whitaker had nothing to stop him but the bottom. There was a general foreign Huzza on the Side of the *Venetian*, pronouncing our Countryman's Downfal [sic]; but Whitaker took no more Time than was required to get up again, when finding his Fault in standing out to the Length of the other's Arm, he, with a little Stoop, ran boldly in beyond the heavy Mallet, and with one *English* Peg in the Stomach (quite a new Thing to Foreigners) brought him on his Breech. The Blow carried too much of the *English* Rudeness for him to bear, and finding himself so unmannerly used, he scorned to have any more doings with his slovenly Fist.[26]

English rules allowed the downed man to get back up and fight again until he could fight no more. This was not the case in Venice, where once an opponent was knocked off the bridge into the water, the fight was generally over. The Gondolier did not expect Whitaker to get back up from his fall, nor did he expect him to dodge his arm and hit him in the stomach. This unconventional fighting strategy caused the Gondolier to retire from the battle, undoubtedly believing that the English did not play fair.

According to John Godfrey, once the Venetian was disposed of, Figg recognized the potential for another fight before such an illustrious group of supporters. Figg announced that they might think that he had picked the best man in London to defeat the Venetian. But to convince them of the contrary, if they would come back in one week he would bring a man who could beat Whitaker in ten minutes in a fair fight. This demonstrated that boxing was so popular that were many men in London who were willing to fight on a short notice. Boxing had become a popular way of making money for the lower classes.

Although the fight may have occurred a week after the fight with the Gondolier, according to Tony Gee, who has researched this fight, there is no newspaper record of a return fight taking place until perhaps May. This shows the vicissitudes of promoting boxing bouts: the most talented promoters always found holding bouts to be an uncertain affair. Still, we have Captain Godfrey's word that a fight did occur and Figg brought Nathaniel Peartree, who defeated Whitaker as Figg suggested he would. According to Godfrey's account, Peartree, knowing Whitaker's durability and courage, decided not to fight him in a conventional manner, but instead attacked his eyes.[27]

> His Judgement carried in his Arm so well, that in about six Minutes both Whitaker's [sic] Eyes were shut up; when groping about a while for his Man, and finding him not, he wisely gave out, with these odd Words—Damme—I am not beat, but what signifies my fighting when I cannot see my Man?[28]

These fights show that by the early 1700s, boxing had been adopted by all levels of English society. There were clearly many men prepared to box in public at this time. From the schoolyard to the Amphitheatre, from neighborhood quarrels to an international bout before the gentry and nobility: Boxing was displacing the rapier and the duel of honor, and was becoming the classical British method of settling quarrels. And by 1727 boxing had also become an established method of British entertainment.

I have said that boxing could not exist without rules. Even though these rules were not written down, they were recognized by the fighters themselves. The fact that the Gondolier gave up quickly in his fight with Whitacre appeared to be due to his sense that the rules of boxing as he knew them in Venice had been breached. He scorned to fight according to English rules with which he was unfamiliar. And the fact that Whitacre gave up in his fight with Peartree shows that he too was controlled by English rules. He could easily have grabbed Peartree in a wrestling hold, which might have been acceptable 100 years earlier, but this then would not have been boxing according to the current rules. Thus, although he was not beat, Whitacre gave up. Already by 1725, the rules of boxing were so well defined that they not only controlled the crowd, they controlled the fighters as well.

What then were these current rules?

The Rules of Boxing Apparently in Operation as of 1727

(1) English boxing allowed only two men to fight at one time. Unlike Italy and other countries, Englishmen would not allow crowds to fight each other in boxing matches. The crowd was important to a boxing match, but the crowd could not participate in the match. It was the function of the English boxing ring to keep the crowd from interfering in the match.

(2) When the crowd sees one or both men taking off their coats, and it appears that a fight is about to begin, the crowd spontaneously creates a ring around the fighters.

(3) The crowd does not attempt to separate the fighters, but rather urges them on.

(4) As in the case of the wrestlers in Cornwall in 1602, the fighters shake hands before commencing.

(5) Also as in the case of wrestling, the fighters strip (often until they are naked from the waist up) before they begin.

(6) If the men have any weapons, they put them aside or hand them to the bystanders to hold.

(7) Both Misson and de Saussure confirm that boxing has rules and that the crowd knows these rules. Because of the existences of these rules, the crowd begins to bet on which man will win.

(8) The fight consists of fists being brandished in the air, blows aimed at the faces and particularly the eyes, head-butting, hair-pulling and kicking of shins.

(9) It is possible that the two men try to stand toe-to-toe as they hit each other. "Giving ground" or backing up was considered cowardly.

(10) Being knocked out of the ring or the boxing scaffold did not disqualify a boxer. If he could get back in within a short amount of time, he could resume the fight.

(11) Should one fall to the ground, his opponent can hit him one or two blows while he is on the ground, but no more. Then his opponent must let him up and box him again should he desire it.

(12) When one falls to the ground, the crowd (especially those who have bet on him to win) urges him to rise and continue fighting.

(13) The fight ends when one man has knocked out the other, or when one man has decided he has had enough.

(14) The crowd comprises rabble as well as men of fashion. The mixing of classes is characteristic of English boxing and English sport in general. This mixing of classes at a sporting event will ultimately be called the *Fancy*. It is the crowd, in the form of the *Fancy*, that made prize-fighting profitable.

It is clear from these first descriptions of early boxing matches that they differ in many ways from our modern boxing bouts. Although the old matches had rules, they were not written down and they are not the same as our modern rules. Still, such descriptions for the first time allow us to visualize early boxing matches.

Boxing, by pitting one man against another, has been an ideal vehicle for gambling since its birth. Boxing's popularity has been enhanced by gambling on the outcome of the matches. This is why the first rules of boxing were established. And this is why the crowd was so important to the success of boxing. Had the crowd been opposed to boxing (as they ultimately became opposed to bear-baiting and dog-fighting), boxing would have died out long ago. The crowd created the rules of boxing and was prepared to enforce these rules.

As we will see in the next chapter, fair play and honest gambling were the two pillars of English sport. Couple them with the mixing of social classes in the *Fancy*, and English sport became the envy of other nations in the eighteenth and nineteenth centuries.

Chapter VIII

Gambling and Boxing

In the book *Disputed Pleasures: Sport and Society in Preindustrial England*, Thomas S. Henricks makes the point that "perhaps the greatest source of rule making in sport has been gambling."[1] While gambling has often been attacked as a malign influence on sport, it is perhaps more just to say without gambling, sport could never have existed.

Gambling and Play

Gambling is fundamental to the human condition. Indeed, gambling preceded the human condition. Gambling is to take a risk in hope of reward. Research has shown that a variety of animals, from rats to primates, often choose risk when presented with an opportunity for reward. In an experiment with rats it was found that a higher level of risk-taking behavior in rats correlated with social dominance. Those rats who became dominant in the group took more risks. In 2005, a Duke University study with primates showed that macaque monkeys preferred to choose a riskier target that rewarded them with variable amounts of juice over a safer target that rewarded them with the same amount of juice all of the time. Like human gamblers, they doubled down and continued to choose the riskier target even when the rewards diminished below those afforded by the safer target. The concept of risk for reward has undeniable attractions even for non-human species.[2]

Gambling is the source of one of our greatest temptations. On the good side it provides us with a reason for checking our appetites; on the bad side it tempts us to expand those appetites and lose control of them. Gambling tempts us to excess. This is why gambling has gained such a bad reputation.

When we turn to talk about sport, we find the same situation. Gambling requires established rules and without rules, sport is nothing more than random play. Hence, by insisting on rules, gambling creates sport. At the same time, it is natural for individuals involved in any sport to seek to improve their odds at winning. In the quest to maximize their rewards, gamblers are tempted to break the rules. The great weakness of gambling on sport is that it tempts us to break the very rules that create the sport. Just as gambling can create sport, it can also destroy it.

Cheating in sport stimulated by gambling introduces disorder. Disorder destroys the rules that make sport a sport. But cheating can become a self-correcting action. When the level of cheating becomes widely known, supporters, both high and low, will abandon the sport. If the supporters abandon a sport because they believe it is corrupt, the sport will die. Corrupt behavior destroys the value of rules. Destruction of rules destroys the ability of gamblers to gamble. This is why, for their own benefit, gamblers must work to keep the sport as free from the appearance of corruption as possible.

To take a recent example, during the period from the 1930s through the 1950s, when American boxing was almost completely in the hands of gangsters, it enjoyed one of its greatest periods of popularity. This was due to the fact that a murderer, Frankie Carbo, controlled nearly all of the fights and unified the forces of corruption. "Carbo was a gangster who made the rationalization of boxing his full-time job. He was the man who initiated many major bouts and whom managers and promoters had to contact to approve contests they wanted to arrange." The fact that Carbo brought the entire sport under his control created order out of chaos. Prior to his taking over, there were many crooked fights as individual managers sought to gain an advantage for their fighter. This damaged the sport as gamblers could not tell which fights were legitimate and which were not. Because of its reputation, boxing was outlawed in nearly every state in the union. A new era began when Jack Dempsey knocked out Jess Willard (1919). Both Dempsey and his manager, Jack "Doc" Kearns, were crooks with charisma. Their flair for the dramatic stimulated the sport. Under their leadership, interest in boxing revived. Frankie Carbo benefited from the revival of that interest, and because of his single-minded devotion to the sport, he gained corrupt control of American boxing.[3]

Carbo provided a broader sense of order to the sport than Dempsey and Kearns could provide. As a result, boxing was gradually legalized all across the nation, even though many of the fights were fixed. We are dealing here with what George Washington Plunkitt of Tammany Hall (1905) called "honest graft"—that is, systematic corruption, which nonetheless brought order to a disorganized system. Gambling can be a self-correcting force for order, even when it operates in an illegal fashion.[4]

Most gambling was outlawed throughout the United States in the early 1900s as immoral and destructive. One hundred years later it is being promoted as the solution to governmental fiscal problems. Far from being banned, it is being proposed that betting on sports should be made legal in the entire country. Even though betting on sports events has been illegal in every state save Nevada, over $150 billion dollars in sports bets have been placed each year. Several years ago, Pete Rose, the famous baseball player and manager, was sent to jail and permanently banned from baseball for gambling on games while he was a player and a manager. Now impecunious states wish to make sports gambling legal nationwide and tax it as a source of new revenue. The good and evil sides of gambling are ever present.[5]

Play in Sport

The impulse to gamble is innate to humans; so too is the impulse to play. Like risk-taking, play is also native to non-human species. Johan Huizinga reminds us that the play behavior of young animals is well known. Small animals play spontaneously among themselves. So too do humans. Play by its nature contrasts strongly with normality. The play moment is separate and distinct from normal life. As long as they are involved in play humans and animals behave as if they are part of a separate world. The play instinct is so fundamental to humans that Huizinga has suggested that our species should properly be named not *Homo Sapiens* (Man the Wise) but rather *Homo Ludens* (Man the Player).[6]

Huizinga argues that human civilization arises and unfolds in and as play. In fact, it is his belief that "play is older and more original than civilization." To support his view, we find that gambling (which is pure play) frequently shows up in creation myths. The story of the Garden of Eden demonstrates this; Adam and Eve gambled that by eating the apple, they could become God-like. Gambling also appears in other creation myths as well: "In Greek mythology, Poseidon, Zeus and Hades divided the world between them in a dice game.... The Ases [Gods] of Scandinavian mythology like the Hindu Siva determined the fate of mankind by throwing dice."[7] In ancient Egypt, Thoth, the god who enforced divine order, gambled with the Moon and won, increasing the length of the year by five days. His wife, Nut, then gave birth to five children, one on each of those five days, and those children populated the earth. The earth's population growth was due to Thoth's gambling. In North America, Noquilpi, the gambling god of the Navajo, supposedly won all of the people of the earth and all their possessions while gambling in Chaco Canyon, New Mexico. A reverse version of this story was told by the Jicarilla Apaches where Killer-of-Enemies (the protector of the tribe) gambled with One-Who-Wins (the gambler god). Killer-of-Enemies won back for the tribe all the things One-Who-Wins had previously gotten by gambling with the people of earth.[8] As these examples show, gambling often underlies our mythological world.

When we return to normal life, we find that gambling requires structured play. By itself, play can be random or structured. Random play may have no rules or be subject to changing rules, but the human psyche seeks to impose order on chaos. Gambling is one way to do this. Gambling sets bounds on disordered play. It converts unstructured play into play with rules. Rules provide predictability. Predictability turns play into sport. Simply put, *sport is play with rules*. The existence of rules converts play into sport and makes gambling possible. Gambling stimulates the process of rule-making and rule-making enables gambling.

Gambling and the Rules of Boxing

Boxing and gambling are linked together. Like its predecessor, wrestling, boxing pitted one man against another. As we have discussed in prior chapters, two men, and only two men, create a boxing match. To have any more participants changes the nature of the exercise from a sport to a brawl. A brawl, which we have defined as a noisy, turbulent quarrel, is an expression of disorder; the rules that create sport make sport an expression of order.[9]

When two men compete, there is a natural human inclination to favor one man over the other. Thus, the sport of boxing is ideally suited to gambling. Behavior that initially was indistinguishable from assault and battery was gradually transformed under the pressure of gambling into a predictable pattern.

The rules that governed the new sport of boxing arose from the interactions of local ruffians. When a fight between two young men occurred, the crowds, guided by their sense of fair play, began to determine on the spot what was acceptable conduct and what was not. When it was determined that, as in wrestling, the fighters could use only their own bodies, including heads, hands and feet, and no other weapons were allowed, the basic form of boxing took shape. Once these two rules (that only two men were to fight at a time, and that no artificial weapons were to be used) were established, the sport began to attract attention and was given new names.

Naturally, the rule-making did not stop there. Each fight may have resulted in new rules being devised by the onlookers. Ultimately a code of basic rules (which I have tried to outline in Chapter III and again in Chapter VII) was established. This code of rules was very rudimentary. It was held only in the minds of the onlookers and not written down. Still, it allowed boxing to gain a substantial following as a new and exciting sport. As in most human activities, new tactics and changing times meant that rules of play were continually developing. We may assume that the basic rules of boxing, which made it well known to the intellectuals in 1590, were different from the rules known to the rabble in 1727 even though we do not know what these rules were. And we may certainly assume that the rules of 1727 were different again from Broughton's Rules of 1743, as Broughton's rules were different from the rules of 1838, of 1853 and the Queensberry Rules of 1867. Had the de facto rules remained the same, there would have been no need to formally update them.

Above all, we must recognize that Broughton's written rules did not revoke the rules of the crowd. Broughton's rules of 1743 did not, for example, define legal or illegal blows. They did not say anything about wrestling holds, clinching, head-butts, gouging out eyes, biting, kicking or scratching. Nor did they say anything about how the fighters were to dress, save that they "stripped." These unstated things belonged to the rules of the crowd. Broughton's rules, on the other hand, defined how the fight should begin and how it could end. They also determined how and when the winnings were to be paid. And they established how disputes were to be settled. In short, Broughton's rules were designed for the eighteenth-century gamblers. Thus by 1743 boxing was carried on under two sets of complimentary rules: the unwritten rules of the crowd and the written rules for the gamblers. But these first written rules were equally rules of the crowd, as Broughton reminds us with his note that they were "as agreed by several Gentlemen at Broughton's Amphitheatre, Tottenham Court Road, August 16, 1743."

The Advent of Umpires

The appearance of umpires in Broughton's rules was critical:

> That to prevent Disputes, in every *main Battle* the Principals shall, on coming on the Stage, choose from among the gentlemen present two Umpires, who shall absolutely decide all Disputes that may arise about the Battle; and if the two Umpires cannot agree, the said Umpires to choose a third, who is to determine it.[10]

It is clear from this statement that the gentlemen present in the crowd knew the conventional rules of boxing at the time. Their knowledge of the rules would allow them to be the judges of the fight. We have already seen that the trials by battle had judges who had the power to manage the fight and determine the winner and the loser. This role was passed on to the Masters of Defence in 1540. There, judges evaluated the talents of the candidates and promoted them or failed them. But the duels of the Masters were not judicial trials to the death. So far as we know, no one died as a result of their duels. The power of the judges at the duels of the Masters of Defence was much more benign than that of the judges at the trials by battle, who indeed did have the power of life and death. This benign power of the Masters of Defence was passed on to Broughton's umpires, who had the power to determine the winner in these fist-fights.

The judges at the trials by battle were appointed by the court. The judges at the duels of the Masters were either the Four Ancient Masters or someone appointed by them. But in the case of boxing, the judges, or "Umpires" as Broughton calls them, were drawn from the crowd and chosen by the crowd. This shows clearly that even with written rules, the crowd was still the arbiter of the fights.

Having a mechanism to determine umpires was clearly critical to decision-making in boxing, as well as for gambling on boxing. Further, for *bye-battles* [preliminary fights, less important than the *main battle*], Broughton himself was to be in the ring with the fighters "to keep decorum" (Rule III). In this way, Broughton was taking on a role that led to our modern referee. With this structure in place, Broughton brought us into the world of modern boxing.

It is, therefore, no coincidence that the period of the greatest interest in gambling was also the period during which the first written rules of sport appeared:

> Predictably then, the gambling sports of the seventeenth and eighteenth centuries produced some of the more widely recognized sets of rules. These included the duke of Norfolk's Laws of the Leash for coursing (late sixteenth century), Kiplingcote's Rules in horse racing (1619), Cheney's Rules and Orders for Cocking (1743), Broughton's Rules in boxing (1743), and the first Laws of Cricket set forth by the London Club in 1744.[11]

Gambling gave modern sport its form and focus. By stimulating the establishment of standardized rules, gambling created national sports out of local recreations. And this, in turn, created the first sporting class, the group we call the *Fancy*, which knew the rules and supported the sport financially[12]:

> Notably such rules were not only the result, but also the source for wider participation; local rules were being replaced by more standardized forms. Rules also were useful in building an audience for sport. By the end of the preindustrial period a sporting crowd or "fancy" knowledgeable in the traditions of the game was replacing the earlier collections of curiosity seekers.[13]

The Fancy

We have encountered the organization called the *Fancy* in the previous chapter. Pierce Egan says that *Fancy* "simply means any person who is fond of a particular amusement, or closely attached to some subject."[14] But it was more than that. "The Fancy," John Ford tells us, "is usually understood as the followers of boxing, the fighters, the patrons, the trainers, the crowds and all those whose fancy was the prizering."[15] But it soon took in the enthusiasts of other sports, from dog and cock fights, to badger-, bull- and bear-baiting and finally to horse-racing. The *Fancy* was a curious amalgam of the idle rich and the idle poor, united by gambling and addiction to sport. It provided, as Washington Irving wrote, "a chain of easy communication, extending down from the peer to the pick-pocket."[16] The money provided by the *Fancy*, funded by gambling, led to a host of structural changes in English-speaking society. The first change was the creation of national organizations to govern sports:

> Gambling was, furthermore, a force for the spread of sporting organizations. Following the success of the Jockey Club in the 1750s, associations of gentlemen in cricket and boxing stepped forward to attempt regulation of their sports as well. Such clubs discouraged sharp play, in part by serving as a court of appeal of sorts for disconcerted bettors. Just as these bodies provided an aura of legitimacy to their sports, so they oiled the gambling machine. In essence, the reputation for fairness at a venue facilitated betting and furthered the popularity of a sport.[17]

The creation of national sporting organizations not only increased the popularity of each sport, but provided a focus for those interested in the sport. This made it easier for sport itself to become an integral part of British life and to remain so for centuries. This was true of boxing, horse-racing, cricket, football and other sports.

The second change was the gradual improvement in English civility. Just as these sporting clubs provided a court of appeal for the gambler, they also provided a standard of behavior for the members. Organizations created to make the sport safe for gambling also became schools for manners. The members were encouraged to wear uniforms and behave in an appropriate fashion. We have already seen an example of this when the Prince of Wales [the future George IV] had a fist-fight with a butcher because the butcher over-rode the prince's hounds in a fox hunt.

As this event shows, bad behavior, just as much as bad debts, could trigger a response by the *Fancy*. Pierce Egan gives us a brief picture of the origins of the Pugilistic Club, founded on May 22, 1814, whose object was "to keep alive the principles of courage and hardihood which distinguish the British character, and to check the progress of that effeminacy which wealth is too apt to produce." The members of the club contributed money for purses for boxing bouts and worked to expose all crooked activity in boxing. They also had a "uniform dress, consisting of blue coats and yellow waistcoats, with P.C. engraved on their buttons."[18]

A third change was the stimulation of democracy in England. The *Fancy* was a driver of democracy. The *Fancy* led to the social mixing of the upper class with the lower classes at sporting events, as in the case of the prince and the butcher. Rules of sport, enforced by gambling, and rules of behavior, enforced by proximity, created a sport-imposed sense of democracy. As the Duke of Clarence (the future King William IV) said to a nobleman who was unhappy about being placed among the rabble at a boxing match: "Be pleased to recollect, my lord, that we are all Englishmen here; and as for places we must do the best we can for ourselves."[19]

Elias Canetti in his book *Crowds and Power* supports a similar view:

> Within the crowd there is equality.... This is absolute and indisputable and never questioned by the crowd itself. It is of fundamental importance and one might even define a crowd as a state of absolute equality.... It is for the sake of this equality that people become a crowd and they tend to overlook anything which might detract from it. All demands for justice and all theories of equality ultimately derive their energy from the actual experience of equality familiar to anyone who has been a part of a crowd.[20]

Sports brought together crowds. This fundamental feature of "crowd equality" was critical to English society as sport developed under the stimulus of gambling and fair play. And because of this "crowd equality," social divisions common to other countries were less pronounced.

This led to a fourth change in English society. Nineteenth-century class warfare was muted in the English-speaking world by divisions along sport rivalries. While Marx and Engels thundered about class-solidarity, the English public was more concerned about sport-solidarity. The most important divisions for the common Englishman and his aristocratic neighbor were the divisions over sport. The enemy was not the mill owner, but the football team in the next town. The mill owner and the mill hand were united in betting on their team to win.

In the *Lives of the Gamesters* (1714), Theophilus Lucas confirms that in England gambling transcended class: "A foot-man shall play with a Marquis, or an Earl; a black-guard-boy with a Duchess; [and] barbers, pedlars, tinkers, taylors, and ostlers, with Generals, Brigadiers, and Colonels of the Army."[21] This mixing of social levels in gambling was wide and deep. Thomas Henricks points out that "in cricket matches of the 1740s we find the curious phenomenon of gentlemen performing publicly with commoners (and even servants) on a level of apparent equality." He mentions the match of Kent vs All-England of 1744 where the captain of the Kent team was Lord John Sackville's gardener, and the decisive catch was made by Lord John himself.[22] It was the opinion of Sir Derek Birley that "in cricket, as in racing gambling brought the classes together." The same could be said of boxing as well.[23] As Charles Montesquieu (1689–1755) was to say: "Being a gambler gives a man position in society; it is a title which takes the place of birth, wealth and probity. It promotes anyone who bears it into the best society without further examination."[24]

The Difference Between Violence and Death in Sport

In the previous chapters I have argued that one advantage that boxing had over sword-fighting was that boxing allowed a clear victory to be gained short of the death of one of the contestants. Deaths could occur in boxing, but they were rare and unplanned. Boxing allowed for a maximum amount of violence with a minimum amount of death.

The British were not afraid of violence in sports. Zacharias Conrad von Uffenbach found that Englishmen enjoyed betting on animal fights. Not only was the Bear Garden, where such fights often occurred, packed with paying spectators, but for Englishmen such a fight "was pleasant to see." The Englishman enjoyed controlled violence and bloodshed in moderation. He would willingly bet on a cockfight or watch a bull or a bear be killed in the ring, but the fight was the thing. When animals fought, it was not the slaughter that thrilled but the fight itself, and if the animal could be saved, so much the better.[25]

In contrast, there were no bets placed on the winner of a duel of honor. Human duels to the death were not considered sport, nor were they enjoyable. Once dueling ceased to be the result of patriotism and became the result of private pique, the duels were placed out of the public eye and became abhorrent to the normal Englishman.

Gladiatorial prizefights, where men fought with swords in the public prize ring, were popular. Up until the middle of the eighteenth century large crowds would pay to see these fights. But when men fought in the English prize ring, either with cudgels, swords or fists, it was not for their lives, but for the pleasure of fighting and the prize. They fought in theaters, bear rings, and in the open where everyone who wished to and could pay could see. Samuel Pepys, as an educated gentleman, exemplified the Englishman's love of fighting. His only concern was that by being in the middle of it, he might get hurt himself.[26]

For many men, fighting was not only an enjoyable activity, it was also a paying one. In 1661, Pepys was surprised to see the amount of money that the crowd threw on the stage for the gladiators: "Strange to see what deal of money is flung to them both upon the stage between every boute."[27]

Zacharias Conrad von Uffenbach commented on the same behavior in 1710:

> They [two fencing masters Thomas Wood and George Turner, a Moor] began the fight with broadswords. The Moor got the first wound, above the breast, which bled not a little. Then the onlookers began to cheer and call for Wood; they threw down vast quantities of shillings and crowns, which were picked up

by his second. This seemed to me quite the wrong way round, as one should have compassion on the fellow that is hit, especially since the winner receives two-thirds of the money that is taken at the gate.[28]

César de Saussure noted that the same thing occurred in boxing as well. Speaking of a bout in February 1727, he remarked: "The spectators sometimes get so interested that they bet on the combatants and form a big circle around them."[29] Gambling stimulated prizefighting and made it a paying profession.

Prizefighting, as we shall see in the next chapter, sought to entertain the public with controlled violence. It was ruined when the violence ended in death. The public was willing to pay to see controlled violence in sport. But they were repelled when death became the ultimate object. This is why the animal blood sports of dog fights, bear- or badger-baiting, and cock-fighting were ultimately discontinued in England. Violence in sport could be entertaining; death in sport was not.

To sum up: Gambling made random play into sport. It converted disorganized local games into the organized national sports that we recognize today. Boxing, cricket and horse-racing all owe their form and popularity to the control gambling imposed on their rules. Although gambling often is derided as being a corruptive influence, in a larger sense, due to its insistence on standard rules and its abhorrence of cheating, gambling created a clean and safe environment that made sport the enthusiastic fashion of society. By avoiding fights to the death, boxing helped preserve this gambling environment.

More importantly, by creating these sports and popularizing them as public favorites, gambling made Great Britain into the mother of sport. This British emphasis on sport helped insulate the common Briton from the class conflicts that led to revolutions in France and other countries in 1793 and again in 1848. Despite the deep and centuries-old class cultures that divided England, a common interest in sport united the aristocracy and the under classes. This led to a more democratic environment. We have seen this expressed in the *Fancy*, that group of aristocrats and rabble who supported the various sports through the eighteenth and nineteenth centuries, and who were a fixture at every large sport gathering. But further, the existence of the *Fancy* muted the political riots that might have occurred in England. Without the *Fancy*, other countries, which lacked the British population's interest in organized sports, took out their energies in political rebellions. England, on the other hand, may owe its prosperity and peacefulness during these years to its love for sport.

Chapter IX

Why Was Prizefighting Illegal?

The Illegality of Boxing Prizefights

As has been discussed in previous chapters, the first named "match of boxing" occurred in December 1681 when the second Duke of Albemarle pitted his footman against a butcher. The butcher won the prize as he had done "many before," making this the first recorded boxing prizefight in history. The next year, the Duke entertained King Charles II and his brother, the Duke of York, with another boxing prizefight. Since at that time anything with the king's support was lawful, boxing prizefights were clearly legal. Yet more than a century later, boxing prizefighting was on the verge of becoming the ultimate illegitimate sport. How did boxing change from being a legitimate sport supported by kings to an illegal sport banned around the world?

In 1831, Justice Sir John Patteson (1790–1861) in *Rex v. Perkins* announced: "There is no doubt that prize-fights are altogether illegal." Earlier, in 1825, in *Rex v. Billingham* Justice Sir James Burrough (1749–1837) declared: "It cannot be disputed that all these fights are *illegal*, and no consent can make them legal." Earlier still, Justice Sir John Richardson (1771–1841) in *Hunt v. Bell* (1822) had announced that "public prize fighting is unlawful." Even earlier, Sir William Blackstone (1723–1780) in Book IV of his *Commentaries on the Laws of England* in 1769 noted that a death occurring in boxing or sword-playing was a felony or manslaughter, unless the contests were sanctioned by the king. Blackstone's private judgment seems to have been that such contests were always illegal.[1]

This judgment met with favor in English jurisprudence throughout the nineteenth and into the twentieth century. In addition, statute laws were passed declaring "prizefighting" illegal in the United States and Canada. By 1910, prizefighting was illegal in every state and territory in the United States with the exception of Nevada. Even today, "prizefighting" is still illegal in Canada. Yet neither Sir William Blackstone nor Justices Richardson, Burrough and Patteson defined what was meant by "prizefights" nor did they explain why they were illegal. This chapter will try to do both.[2]

Prizefighting from the Eighth to the Sixteenth Centuries

Prizefighting is currently considered a synonym for the sport of boxing, but this was not always the case. To fight for a prize was an ancient activity, which existed centuries before the appearance of boxing. The link between boxing and prizefighting developed only during the eighteenth century. And although boxing represented a far less violent activity than the prizefights that it replaced, by becoming confused with these fights it was branded an illegal sport.

The word "prize" was derived from the late Latin *pretium, i, n.*, which meant "purchase price." After the fall of Rome, such purchase prices often embodied a sense of taking via conquest or compulsion. This sense of taking through compulsion or force was formalized in law when *pretium* came to mean the price owed for a woman taken as a bride (*pretium nuptialis* = wedding price), the price for killing a man (*pretium homicidii* = man price or *wergild*), or the price for giving up a fief (*pretium feudi*), from which latter phrase William Blackstone derived the word *felony*.[3]

As *pretium* was transformed into the Old French "*pris*" or "*prise*" in the eleventh century, the sense of "taking" was enhanced by confusion with the past participle of the verb *prendre*, to take. A *pris* could then be both the taking and the thing taken, such as a *prisoner*. Capturing prisoners brought fame and honor. Hence the word *pris* also meant fame and honor, which was later modified into *praise*, which was earned for having taken such a valuable thing. Praise and prizes were the stuff of war in the Middle Ages. Obtaining captives to ransom and other "prizes" such as lands, castles, horses and armor were often the only payment nobles and commoners received for their services. Wars were thus the original "prizefights."[4]

Tournaments, as mock wars, could also be described as "prizefights." Although tournaments were considered sport, it was not always possible to distinguish them from real war. In one of the earliest accounts of a tournament, circa 1128, Count Geoffrey of Anjou overthrew an English knight, decapitated him and then took his horse as a prize. Death in this prizefight was always a real possibility.[5]

By the beginning of the fourteenth century, the English had adopted the use of the French term *pris* to mean prize in a tournament. In the *Romance of Guy of Warwick* (c. 1300) Guy learns that the Emperor of Germany is offering his daughter as the *pris* of a tournament: "Of that tournament y schal you telle: It schal be for a maiden of pris, T'Emperors douhter sche is." Here the word *pris* had a treble meaning: "a maiden of pris" meant (1) a maiden of great beauty and social standing, who (2) naturally had, as the Emperor's daughter, a high bride price, and, in addition, she was (3) also being given as the prize to the knight who won the greatest honor in the tournament. The word *pris* had developed multiple meanings.[6]

The English also adopted *pris* to describe anything seized in war, either as booty or plunder: "Grete pris upon the werre he hadde" (1390).[7] Ships taken in war were also described as *prises*.[8] The British Admiralty still conducts a "prize court" to deal with ships and planes captured in war.[9]

However, we are concerned with the word in its meaning of a reward for winning an athletic contest.[10] During the fourteenth century, the English expanded the meaning of the French word, *pris*, to mean something taken or given as a reward in a contest other than in battle. *Queen Mary's Psalter* shows an illustration of a wrestling match in which a rooster on a pole is intended as the prize for the victor.[11] This is perhaps the first picture of an athletic "prizefight" in English history.

Later, Geoffrey Chaucer in his "General Prologue to the Canterbury Tales" and in the "Tale of Sir Thopas" (1387–1400) mentions it was then customary to give a ram instead of a cock as a prize to the winner of wrestling

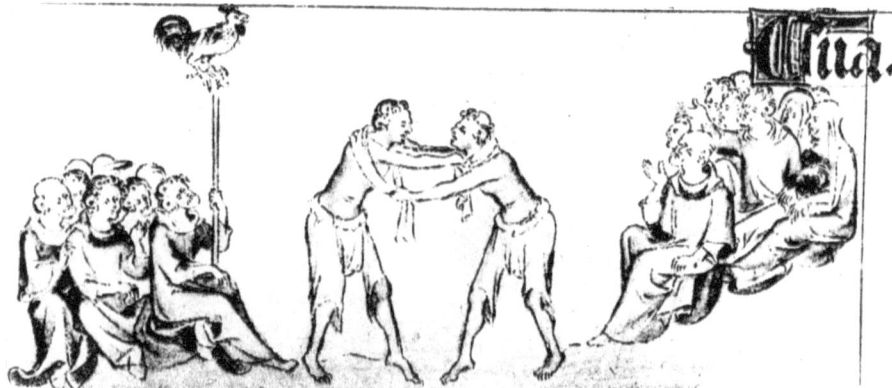

Fig. 15: The first depiction of an English athletic prizefight. Shawl-wrestling from *Queen Mary's Psalter*, circa 1310–1320, f.160v (British Library Royal MS 2 B VII). The men have stripped to demonstrate that this is a formal fight of importance. The cock on the pole is the prize for the winner of the match. (Note the two women in the audience on the right side. The one on the end appears to be holding another cock, presumably another prize.)

matches.¹² Prizes could also be won in hunting as in the case of King Houlac in *Horn Childe and Maiden Rimnild* (c. 1330–1340), where "at hunting oft he wan the priis," and in running: "Witen ye not, that thei that rennen in a furlong, alle rennen, but oon takith the prijs?"¹³ We also know from the tales of Robin Hood that prizes were awarded in archery contests.¹⁴

Despite the widespread use of *pris* as a reward for athletic contests, only wrestling could properly be described as a "prizefight." And it is in relation to a wrestling match that Shakespeare first used the modern spelling of "prize."¹⁵

By the end of the sixteenth century, prizefights were an ancient custom, with the prizes often given out by public officials. In 1598, Paul Hentzner in his *Travels in England* noted that in London it was customary for the mayor and aldermen to go by horseback on August 24 to open St. Bartholomew's Fair. There they were entertained by wrestling matches, and "the conquerors receive rewards from the Mayor." Wrestling prizefights were common, popular and supported by the government.¹⁶

Beginning in 1540 King Henry VIII provided support for the community of fencing instructors who had formerly been considered disreputable *pugils*. The creation of the Masters of Defense with their elaborate emphasis on orderly behavior converted violent sword-fighting into more regulated swordplaying. The *pugils* of the past had been indistinguishable from criminals. Considered similar to outlaws, they fought for money and to stay out of jail. The new Masters of Defence, with backing from the monarchs, taught students to advance in position as well as for fame and fortune. Although the Masters conducted schools and lived on the earnings from their students, they owed their allegiance to the king or queen of the time. The sword prize-player flourished circa 1540 to 1640. The sword prizefighter or gladiator flourished from about 1640 to 1740.

Alfred Hutton believed that "the prize-player must not be confounded with the prize-fighter. The two did not co-exist; the hundred years during which the prize-player flourished had ended before the hundred years (for they both lasted about the same time) of the prize-fighter commenced."¹⁷ Although this is not entirely true, as we shall see, it is true that the Masters of Defence did introduce order and discipline into private sword combat that had been lacking in the past.

The prize-players belonging to the Masters of Defence devoted their efforts to teaching their students the art of defense. We do not have many examples of their prizes being deadly or even bloody. The gladiators or prize-fighters who came after them lacked royal support. They were often out-of-work soldiers or sailors who fought for money and were forced to make their fights bloody in order to gain an audience. In so doing, they carried on an ancient tradition.

As we shall see in the *Commentaries* of William Blackstone, ancient Roman law protected those who killed an opponent while engaged in sport. Despite the attacks made on this concept, this law has continued into our own times. It is based upon the ancient dictum *violenti non fit injuria* (the law does not recognize an injury done to a willing person). This is called the "consent defense" or "voluntary assumption of risk" in U.S. law. Although this defense is no longer as protective as it once was, it still holds value in courts. But, as noted above, even in the fifteenth century lawyers were beginning to poke holes in this defense. While death occurring in a wrestling match was still excused, the survivor was forced to forfeit his goods and wait in prison for a pardon from the king.[18]

Despite the public having a growing dislike of a fight to the death in sport, as late as 1565 knights could still issue challenges to prizefights in which death was a real possibility. To celebrate the wedding of the Earl of Warwick to the daughter of the Earl of Bedford, four knights placed the following challenge on the court gate at Westminster:

> Yow that in warlike ways and dedes of arms delight,
> Yow that for countrys cawes or ells for ladyes love dare fight,
> Know you foure knyghts ther be that come from foren land,
> Whos hawtye herts and corage great hathe movd to take in hand,
> With sword, with speare and shild, on fote, on horse backe, to,
> To try what yow by force of fight, or otharwyse, can do.
> Prepare yowr selves ther fore this challenge to defend,
> That trompe of fame yowr prowes great abrod may sownd and send,
> And he that best can do, ye same shall have the price.
> Ye day, ye place, and forme and fight, loo here before yowr eys.[19]

We do not know the ultimate outcome of this challenge, but the wording certainly was bellicose.

Contrary to the statement of Alfred Hutton, there were two parallel types of prize combats in sixteenth-century England: sword-playing exemplified by the Masters of Defence and sword-fighting exemplified by the above challenge and the remnants of the *pugils* or ruffians who still carried on their illegal activities. The Masters brought honor to fencing, while the *pugils* continued their dishonorable fighting behavior. The Masters had two types of students: gentlemen who sought to learn the use of the sword and other weapons for their own purposes, and common men who sought to learn the use of such weapons so that they might become teachers of martial arts. This latter category of student had to progress through various levels of expertise, each level being punctuated by a formal test called a "prize." The "prize" required the candidate to demonstrate facility with a variety of weapons.

The prizes of the Masters of Defence were tame compared to the prizefights of the past, yet they were still public affairs designed to draw in crowds.

The crowd's payments might compensate the candidate for his expenses and provide him some money for his schooling. To draw a crowd, the masters typically placed advertisements, called challenges, around the town announcing the day, time and location of the fight. Then the day of the event the masters held a large parade through the town headed by trumpets and drums, with the candidate, his seconds, and the masters marching behind toward the location of the fight. Large crowds could be gathered in this fashion.[20]

J.D. Aylward provides us with an example of a challenge from the Masters circa 1605. Compare the language of this challenge to that above given at Westminster:

> BE IT KNOWN to all that profess arms that we, A.B., Master of the Noble Science of Defence, do give leave and licence to our Provost, C.D., to play his Master's Prize against all Masters in their subtile mysterie at these weapons, viz: long sword, sword and buckler, Morris pike, and rapier and dagger. These are to give notice that our said Provost will be present [with his seconds and supporters] the ... th day of the present month to perform and do his uttermost for the achievement and bearing away the prize. (God save the King.)[21]

The close relationship between the Masters of Defence and the Tudor monarchs is testified by the documents in *Sloane Ms. 2530*. Not only did the monarchs warrant the right of the Masters to teach arms, but many of the prizefights were actually fought in presence of the king or queen of the time. Although the power of the Masters declined during the last years of Queen Elizabeth I, in 1605 King James I renewed their monopoly, giving it once again the support of royal authority.[22]

With the beginning of the Civil War in 1642, the Masters of Defence deteriorated. By the second half of the seventeenth century the most common type of prizefight was that of gladiators who adopted the title, if not the ethics, of the Masters of Defence.

These gladiatorial fights differed from the earlier matches since they were not designed to test an apprentice on his skills or to advance him on the way to become a master. Nor were they, like the tournaments of old, designed to prepare men for battle. Rather they were bouts put on for pay by men who made a profession of fighting. Like their predecessors, these gladiatorial contests were held in public places, but unlike the earlier fights they became bloody affairs. Samuel Sorbiere, a Frenchman, recounted his trip of 1664 and described seeing a "prize-fight" in the Bear Garden in London. These prizefighters were usually fencing masters or their ushers (assistants) "who to gain themselves Reputation, and something else besides Blows, put out a Challenge, and lay a Wager of Twenty or Thirty Pounds against any that will fight them." These fighters fought with backsword and buckler and, although Sorbiere felt that the swords were blunt, and the fights ended with the first blood, nonetheless they still were vicious:

However, they sometimes give one another terrible Hacks and Slashes so that half a Cheek hangs down; but this is done by chance, and happens not often, tho' there is always something that is fierce in this Brutish Exercise.[23]

In 1710, the German visitor Zacharias Conrad von Uffenbach gave a very detailed description of a prizefight that he witnessed at the Bear Garden in Hockley in the Hole, at Clerkenwell (previously described in Chapter VIII)[24]:

> First a properly printed challenge was carried around and dealt out.... The place where the fight took place was fairly large. In the middle was a platform as tall as a man of middling height; it had no rail and was open all round, so that neither of the fighters could retreat. All round the upper part of the open space were wretched galleries with raised seats, like those on which the spectators sit at the play. But the common people, who do not pay much, are below on the ground.

Following the preliminaries, the main contestants (Thomas Wood and George Turner, whom von Uffenbach described as "a Moor") came on the stage:

> They had taken off their coats and tied only a handkerchief round their heads. First they bowed in every direction, and then showed their swords all round. These were very broad and long and uncommonly sharp. Each of the combatants had his second by him with a large stick in his hand; they were not there to parry blows, but only to see that there was fair play on all sides.

The gladiators began to fight with their swords and Turner was struck on the chest, which began to bleed profusely. This wound ended the first round. The second round went to Turner. The third round went to Wood, who gave Turner a nasty wound on the hand. In the fourth round Turner was so wounded that he could not continue the fight:

> He was slashed from the left eye right down his cheek to his chin and jaw with such force that one could hear the sword grating against his teeth. Straightway not only the whole of his shirt front but the platform too was covered with blood. The wound gaped open as wide as a thumb, and I cannot tell you how ghastly it looked on the black face. A barber-surgeon immediately sprang towards him and sewed up the wound, while the Moor stood there without flinching. When this had been done and a cloth bound around his head, the Moor would have liked to continue the fight, but since he had bled so profusely, neither the surgeon nor the seconds, who act as umpires, would allow this. So the combatants shook hands (as they did after each round) and prepared to get down.

After seeing this display, Von Uffenbach asked those seated next to him if any people were ever killed in the fight or died afterwards of their wounds:

> I was answered in the affirmative; they told me that four years ago the brother of this identical Moor, Turner, had lost his life. Nothing was done to the perpetrator, unless it could be proved that he had transgressed the rules of fighting and wounded his adversary with malicious intent.

In a clear case of *volenti non fit injuria*, both Turner and his brother willingly entered into a fight knowing the risks. The opponents shook hands with each other after every round to demonstrate visually to the crowd that there was no malicious intent (*mens rea*). In the case of the Moor's brother, his opponent was found innocent of murder (killing with evil intent) and manslaughter (killing without following the rules). Instead the brother's death would have been ruled an accident (*infortunium*).

Despite the enthusiasm of the crowd, after 1750, the popularity of the gladiatorial prizefights declined as they were supplanted by the rise of a new sport. Although we have the testimony of the Swiss César de Saussure that sword-fighting was being replaced by fist-fighting by 1727, Tony Gee, the British prize-ring historian, informs me that contemporary news accounts dispute this. Instead, Tony tells me that at this time "Figg's and Stokes' amphitheaters were in their heyday, and trials of skill [sword-fights] very much predominated at their establishments." He does admit, however, that James Figg began exhibiting pugilism at his booth in Southwark in 1725, and that he had a hand in training John Whitacre in his fight with the Venetian Gondolier. Still, it is Gee's belief that "there does not appear to be any definite evidence to show that Figg ever taught boxing to the public."[25]

Nonetheless, after 1725, boxing matches began to displace sword-fights. To accommodate this new sport, Figg and his successors simply adapted the locations, rules and strategies of the previous sport to the new one. This would ultimately lead to the confusion in which the name "prizefight" would come to mean public bare-knuckle boxing for money and not public sword-fights.[26]

Prizefights, be they wrestling matches, public sword-fights or boxing matches, were clearly legal in the 1690s. Despite the fact that medieval sports law was becoming obsolete, it still governed prizefights. Injury and death in such sports was an accepted risk.

Death in Sports Considered as an Accident

As early as 1227 it was recognized in England that death in a wrestling match was not a felony. Instead, it was considered a misadventure or accident and the survivor was not considered guilty of homicide or a felony.[27]

The same was true of deaths in other sports. In 1280, Henry, son of William de Ellington, received a wound while playing football with David le Ken. The inquest judged this an accident. "They were both running to the ball, and ran against each other, and the knife hanging from David's belt stuck out, so that the point, though in the sheath, stuck against Henry's belly, and the handle against David's belly. Henry was wounded right through the sheath, and died by misadventure."[28]

This medieval attitude was still prevalent in Shakespeare's time. In *As You Like It* (1599), Shakespeare has Rosalind and Celia try to persuade Orlando not to wrestle. Orlando responds with the wrestling code:

> If I be foil'd [defeated], there is but one sham'd
> that was never gracious; if kill'd, but one dead that
> is willing to be so [Act I, scene II, lines 183–189].

Death in a wrestling match was an accepted risk. In 1602 Serjeant-at-law Robert Keilwey described the rationale for the death-by-misadventure ruling:

> Note that it was held that if a man wrestle with another, and the one gave the other such a fall that he died, that is not any felony because it was the act of both of them to come together and also the intent of him that gave the fall was not to kill the said man and for that reason it is not any felony.[29]

This is a classic definition of the dictum *volenti non fit injuria*. This ancient attitude still prevailed in 1747 when Captain John Godfrey published his celebrated *Treatise upon the Useful Science of Defence*. In describing the Masters of Defence in his time, Godfrey mentioned that one of Figg's students, William Gill, fought a sword prizefight with an Irishman named Michael Butler. Gill cut Butler's leg so severely that he developed gangrene and died. Butler's death was clearly regrettable, but Godfrey's attention was focused on the admirable stroke given to Butler, not on anything wrong that Gill had done.[30]

Death in Sports Considered as a Crime

Yet at the same time we find a counter-current developing against some kinds of sports deaths. As early as 1496 sword-fights without a royal license were considered illegal. Death occurring in such illegal sports was considered a felony with the potential punishment being loss of life, although this crime was not always prosecuted:

> But if a man does an unlawful act, which he is not compelled to do by any need or for common profit—for example, where a man throws a stone over a house, or such like—and there by accident he kills another, this is manslaughter and felony and he shall lose his life. The law is the same concerning play with sword and buckler, if one man kills another. And so there is a distinction: where the act is lawful and for the common good at the beginning, and where not except in special cases.[31]

Death occurring in "lawful sports" was considered accidental, while death occurring in "unlawful sports" was considered manslaughter and a felony punishable by death.

But what made a sport lawful or unlawful? Simply put, initially this was a determination by the monarch of the time. Although we have seen that King Charles II patronized boxing in 1682, during the next century, things began to change. From 1750 to 1830 there was a major alteration in English public sentiment. The view of the monarch no longer was absolute. Instead, parliament and the middle class made decisions as to what was acceptable and what was not. The shift from a rural to an urban economy meant that many of the old sports and recreations fell out of favor. Animal sports such as bull-bating, bear-baiting and cock-throwing and human sports such as football, sword-fighting and boxing were either outlawed or heavily criticized. Responding to this new mood, in 1769 William Blackstone declared that sword-fights and boxing matches were now illegal. Writing in the fourth book of his *Commentaries*, Blackstone tells us:

> A tilt or tournament, the martial diversion of our ancestors, was, however, an unlawful act: and so are boxing and swordplaying, the succeeding amusement of their posterity; and, therefore, if a knight in the former case, or a gladiator in the latter, be killed, such killing is felony of manslaughter. But if the king command or permit such diversion, it is said to be only misadventure: for then the act is lawful. In the like manner, as by the laws both of Athens and Rome, he who killed another in the *pancratium*, or public games authorized or permitted by the state, was not held to be guilty of homicide.[32]

Blackstone served as a bridge between the medieval and the modern. He recognized the ancient rule that if the king permitted the tournament, sword prizefight or boxing match, fighters who followed the rules were protected, even if one of the participants was killed. But without the permission of the king these sports had become illegal and therefore the death was considered a felony of manslaughter. Blackstone does not tell us why this change occurred, nor do we find any written law declaring boxing illegal. Nonetheless, by 1790, Thomas Fewtrell, a boxer himself, confirmed that boxing was suffering from heavy public criticism. At some point then, between 1747 when Captain John Godfrey published his *Treatise,* which included the first modern analysis of boxing, and 1769 when Blackstone published his fourth book of *Commentaries*, boxing began to be considered an outlaw sport.[33]

When Did Boxing Become Illegal?

I believe that the critical moment when boxing began to change from a legal to an illegal sport was the day when Jack Slack defeated Jack Broughton (April 11, 1750). The bout was described in the *Gentleman's Magazine* (April 1750):

Wednesday 11. Was fought the grand boxing-match between the famous *Broughton*, master of the amphitheatre, hitherto invincible, and *Slack* the butcher of Norwich; before they began, *Broughton* gave *Slack* 10 guineas to fight him according to his promise, which Slack immediately betted against 100 guineas offer'd against him. The first 2 minutes the odds were 20 to 1 on *Broughton's* head, but *Slack* soon recovering himself beat his adversary blind, and following his blows obtain'd a complete victory in 14 minutes, to the great mortification of the knowing ones, who were finely taken in, particularly a peer of the first rank, who betting 10 to 1 lost 1000 *l*. The money received at the door was 130 *l* besides 200 tickets at a guinea, and half a guinea each, and as the battle was for the whole house, 'tis thought that the victor cleared 600*l*.[34]

The peer who lost 1000 pounds was Broughton's patron, His Royal Highness, Prince William Augustus, the Duke of Cumberland, and hero of the battle of Culloden (1746). Cumberland was 29 years old and the most distinguished patron of boxing at the time.

By the eighteenth century, violent games such as wrestling, boxing, cudgeling and sword-fighting were no longer viewed as training for war. Further, animal sports such as cock-fighting, bull and bear-baiting, horse-racing and dog-racing, were gradually falling into disrepute. Public sentiment began to turn against many of these ancient sports. Nonetheless, because of their great interest in gambling, the nobility effectively placed a shield over sports such as boxing, horse-racing and cock-fighting, even as public opinion was turning against them.

Everything changed as far as boxing was concerned when Slack hit Broughton right between the eyes, closing both of them. As Broughton stumbled around the ring unable to find his opponent, the duke cried out: "What are you about, Broughton?—you can't fight!—you're beat!" Broughton replied, "I can't see my man, your highness—I'm blind but not beat; only let me be placed before my antagonist, and he shall not gain the day yet." Unfortunately, the rules of boxing did not allow this. Jack Broughton was defeated and the duke was humiliated.[35]

The Duke of Cumberland was both a man of action and a man of spite. He did not take the loss with good grace. According to Horace Walpole, who knew him well, "His understanding was strong, judicious, and penetrating, though incapable of resisting partialities and piques. He was proud and unforgiving." Lord Waldegrave described him as a man "of strong parts, great military abilities, undoubted courage" but noted that his judgment was "too much guided by his passions, which were often violent and ungovernable."[36]

Following Broughton's defeat and Cumberland's loss of 1000 pounds, we are told that the duke

> never could speak of this transaction again with any degree of temper, declaring, that *he had been sold*, and nothing could persuade him to the contrary, being

so firmly persuaded that BROUGHTON was in every way superior to *Slack*. His Royal Highness instantly turned his back on him [Broughton], and by the interference of the Legislature, his Amphitheatre was shut up. BROUGHTON never fought again.[37]

More to the point,

> after *Broughton's* defeat—PUGILISM in the Metropolis was *done up;* and a period of upwards of four years elapsed before a battle of any consequence took place, and then it was fought in the country.[38]

Pierce Egan wrote this some 60 years after the event. He tells us that Broughton's Amphitheatre was shut down by an act of the "legislature." It is not clear exactly what this means. The duke was, of course, a distinguished member of the House of Lords and played an active role in the politics of his day. He could easily have introduced a bill banning boxing as an illegal sport and gotten it passed as statute law, but he did not do so. Rather than speak of a specific act of the legislature for which we have no proof, we suspect that the duke removed his personal protection from boxing and began to devote his time to horse-racing. In this, Cumberland perhaps allowed other public forces such as middle-class magistrates to step in and declare that boxing matches were no longer to be tolerated.

It is possible that the statute of 25 Geo II, c. 36 of 1752, which regulated the keeping of "Places of Publick Entertainment," was an outgrowth of Cumberland's unhappiness. This law may have been used to force Broughton to close down his amphitheater, but it was passed two years after the prizefight and did not directly address the issue of boxing. Nonetheless, ten years later it was used in the case of *Rex v. Higginson* (1762) to attack boxing. In that case, Thomas Higginson was indicted for keeping an "ill-governed and disorderly house" in which cock-fighting, boxing and cudgeling occurred "to the great damage and common nuisance of all the subjects of our said lord the King, his Crown and dignity." Certainly, by 1762 boxing was falling into bad repute.[39]

From Sword Prizefights to Boxing Prizefights

Boxing's great competitor was sword-fighting. The Masters of Defence, who were members of the same class of men as those who began boxing, were the descendants of the *pugils* of the past. We have met one of their members in Bartholomew Bramble during the sixteenth century. But by the eighteenth century the sword duels of the gladiators, as well as the duel of honor, were going out of fashion. As early as 1697, Henri Misson had noted: "These [gladiatorial] Fights are becoming very rare within these eight or ten Years." Although we still find gladiatorial sword-fights common until 1740 and later, the days of the sword prizefights were passing and boxing was taking over.[40]

James Figg (d. 1734) embodied this conversion. Beginning in 1714, Figg eventually enjoyed the reputation of being the most skilled swordsman of his time. He created a school to teach gentlemen fencing and the various military arts. Yet, by 1725, about the same time de Saussure described a boxing match, Figg himself was promoting boxing matches. On Saturday, September 18, 1725, Figg opened his "Great Til'd Booth" in Southwark Fair and promised that matches featuring "Buckhorse, and several other *Pugilists*, will show the Art of Boxing." Figg planned to show his own skill with the fist as well as with weapons. It had taken a long time, but a Master of Defence now openly promoted boxing. Boxing was finally recognized as one of the manly arts.[41]

The fashion of English martial arts was changing. Pugilists had now become, in the words of J.D. Aylward, "the idols of a new generation." Captain John Godfrey, a student of Figg's, was to note that "in Fig's Time, the Spirit of it [the backsword] was greatly kept up; but I have been often sorry to find it dwindle, and in a Manner, die away with him." As the English form of sword-and-buckler fighting had given way to the Italian rapier in the seventeenth century, so both the backsword and the rapier would give way to boxing in the eighteenth century. By the end of that century, gentlemen would have no problem boxing instead of dueling.[42]

Despite boxing's new found popularity, it is incorrect to claim that King George I (reigned 1714–1727) was so interested in boxing that he built a "ring" as a "recognized arena for dust-ups" in Hyde Park. Boxing was not on the king's mind when he built a large circle "two or three hundred Paces Diameter" circumscribed by a three-foot fence. Instead, it was intended as a riding ring. There are still riding trails and stables in Hyde Park to this day.[43]

By 1769 the Duke of Cumberland was dead and Blackstone had declared boxing and sword-playing illegal sports. After this we hear little about sword prizefights, for by 1770 they had nearly disappeared. Even fencing schools were going out of business. Boxing, however, was immensely popular. Although it had generally been driven underground in London, and was considered disreputable, it still was accepted as legal by the courts. This can be seen in the decision in William Ward's case in the Old Bailey (June 3, 1789), in which Ward was indicted for murder.[44]

While on his way to witness a boxing match between Richard Humphries and Daniel Mendoza (May 6, 1789) Ward, who is the first boxer we have found to be described as a "prize fighter," fell to boxing for a guinea with Edwin Swaine, a bigger man and a blacksmith, in the public street. Initially Swaine agreed to the fight, but after two rounds, in the process of which both men had been bruised and Swaine had pulled out some of Ward's hair, Swaine announced that he would not fight any more. As Swaine walked away, Ward hit him twice and Swaine fell to the ground dead. Mr. Justice William Henry Ashurst (1725–1807) summing up the case for the jury did not allow the charge of murder to stand on two counts: (1) The two men did not know each other before the fight, hence the charge of murder as homicide with malice aforethought was negated (2) nor could there be constructive malice or malice implied: "[C]onstructive malice may be where a person is acting in defiance of the law, or in opposition to the law, there the law will infer malice; but there is no pretence of any thing of the kind in the present case." Thus in Justice Ashurst's view a boxing match for a guinea was not itself "a felonious illegal act," nor were the parties operating in defiance of the law.

Instead, Mr. Justice Ashurst considered boxing the "science of fighting" and recognized that it was governed by rules. One rule was that Swaine committed a foul when he pulled Ward's hair. Such an act, Ashurst felt, "might be looked upon by the prisoner as a strong aggravation on the part of the deceased and must naturally raise his resentment." A second rule was that it was a foul for Ward to hit Swaine after the fight was over. As a result, since both men had broken the rules of boxing, the normal protection of sport law was negated and a crime had been committed. Given the circumstances, Justice Ashurst felt that the charge against Ward "can amount no higher than manslaughter, if they fight on equal terms and with equal weapons; and that is the case here." As a result the charge of murder was dropped and Ward was convicted of manslaughter, fined one shilling and given three months in jail.[45]

The Ward decision of June 1789 did two things: (1) It demonstrated that a boxing prizefight was legal at this time in London and (2) it was the first time a boxer was referred to as a prizefighter. While the first point was positive, the second point was negative as it saddled boxing with the baggage of the gladiatorial sword-fights. Since boxing had now taken over the locations of the sword prizefights, as well as their name, the two things became confused in law. In 1791, two years later, "stage fighting [sword-fighting] and Boxing matches" were outlawed in Bedfordshire, while the same year the *Northampton Mercury* held it the duty of every magistrate to repress these matches. Boxing now entered a period of uncertainty, during which it was considered neither completely legal nor illegal.[46]

From Boxing Prizefights to Prizefighting as a Crime

This period of uncertainty called forth a new view of boxing law from Sir Edward Hyde East (1764–1847), in his *Treatise of the Pleas of the Crown*

(London, 1803). In writing about the Ward case, East considered "such meetings have a strong tendency in their nature to a breach of the peace." Ward's crime was not boxing *per se*, but boxing as a cause of a breach of the peace in which a man was killed.[47]

The charge made against boxing as being a "breach of the peace" complicated things. As Francis Frederick Brandt wrote later in his book *Habet!* (1857): "Curious to relate, no law book—black-letter or otherwise—contains a definition of what constitutes a 'breach of the peace.'" After careful thought, Brandt concluded that

> any act to constitute a breach of the peace must be a public act committed in a place whither the public do resort, or whither they have a right to resort; and that if acts charged as breaches of the peace do not affect the public, they are not breaches of the peace.[48]

Ward and Swaine fought their battle in the public street, so clearly, under this interpretation, their action could be considered a breach of the peace. This would have made the fight unlawful in Brandt's view. But Brandt was writing 70 years later, and at the time Justice Ashurst did not rule this to be the case. Equally, the fight might have been ruled an affray, meaning that two or more men were found to be fighting in some public place for money or otherwise, to the terror of his majesty's subjects. Yet again, it was not so found.

Justice Ashurst's decision was in favor of boxing, which he recognized as a sport of rules. Most judicial decisions of the nineteenth century, beginning with Sir Edward Hyde East, did not favor boxing. But each decision, favorable or unfavorable, tended to rest upon a rickety framework of law. Perhaps no corner of the law has been more obscured by personal bias than boxing law.

For East lawful sports were those "manly sports and exercises which tend to give strength, activity, and skill in the use of arms." Such lawful sports were cudgels, foils and wrestling. In these cases persons playing at them "are excusable if death ensues." He did not mention boxing but he did agree that those sports "entered into merely as private recreations amongst friends, are not unlawful." Thus, a private boxing match between friends was considered lawful. He then continued:

> But the latitude given to manly exercises of the nature above described, when conducted merely as diversions among friends, must not be extended to legalize prize fightings, public boxing matches, and the like, which are exhibited for the sake of lucre, and are calculated to draw together a number of idle disorderly people.[49]

East was quoting Sir Michael Foster (1689–1763), who had already made this distinction. East, following Foster, laid the foundation for boxing law in both the nineteenth century and the twentieth century. East added another element from Foster when he linked sports conducted "for the sake of lucre" to the issue of breach of the peace. Somehow the payment of money tipped the scales of justice against the sport.

The very popularity of professional boxing also worked against it. The fact that boxing drew crowds meant, according to both Foster and East, that the ring included a number of idle disorderly people. Such crowds, by their nature, they believed, tended to a breach of the peace. East traced this concern back to restrictions placed on crowds attending jousts. Such popular diversions East felt, brought "together a great concourse of unruly spirits, not always consistent with public tranquility."

Just as jousts were deemed unlawful unless sanctioned by order of the king, so prizefights should be unlawful in the same way. Only in East's analysis, it was not the king but the newly powerful middle class that determined which sports were legal and which were not. Because the pugilistic prizefights of the time did often deteriorate into riots, it was assumed that such violence was native to boxing matches: *post hoc, ergo propter hoc* (after this, therefore because of this). In East's view, public prizefighting for money was prone to creating riots and should be considered illegal because it posed a danger to the middle-class state. This became the accepted view of English courts during the first half of the nineteenth century.[50]

The main reason that boxing matches often ended in riots at this time was that matches were now held in the open in the countryside. Boxing had been driven out of the amphitheaters following the Broughton-Slack fight of 1750. The enclosed stage fights had natural crowd constraints, which limited the opportunities for rioting and led to more placid behavior. The two-tier seating arrangement of James Figg's stage, as depicted on his card, made it much more difficult for the spectators to break into the ring and disrupt the fight. Architectural design rather than legal constraints preserved decorum in urban stage fights. When boxing matches became rural affairs with the ring pitched on the turf, crowd control became more difficult. Fans crowded the ring and there was nothing but a few ropes to hold them back. When the crowds broke the ring, riots occurred where they had not occurred before. Since East and Foster were lawyers, not architects, they put their faith in laws rather than design. Riots appeared to them to be the natural outgrowth of prizefights. Their solution was to pile law upon law with no useful result. It would take a full century to return boxing to the peaceful confines of the stage fights as managed by Figg and Broughton.

Edward East's second argument was that "prize fightings, public boxing matches, and the like" should be made illegal because the "intention of the parties is not innocent in itself, each being careless of what hurt may be given, provided the promised reward or applause be obtained." East had already drawn a distinction between the amateur version of the sport and the professional version. Such amateur activities "entered into merely as private recreations amongst friends, are not unlawful." But the professional version admitted a greater violence to please the crowd and win the prize. In making this argument, East turned attention away from the harm prizefighting offered the public (breach of the peace), to the harm prizefighting offered the fighters (assault and battery). Prizefighting posed a danger to the fighters themselves. This became the main argument against boxing in the twentieth century.[51]

This argument was carried to an extreme by Justice James Fitzjames Stephen (1829–1894) in *Regina v. Coney* (1882). Here two bare-knuckle boxers engaged in a prizefight at the Ascot races before a significant crowd of spectators. A large number of charges were brought against the fighters (Mitchell and Burke), their seconds and random members of the crowd represented by Coney. All of these charges were dismissed, save two: that Burke assaulted Mitchell and that Mitchell assaulted Burke. The counsel for the defendants argued that since Mitchell and Burke had jointly consented to the fight, no assault could have occurred. Nonetheless, these two were convicted. Justice Stephen argued on this point that

> the injuries given and received in prize-fights are injurious to the public. Both because it is against the public interest that the lives and health of the combatants should be endangered by blows, and because prize-fights are disorderedly exhibitions, mischievous on many obvious grounds. Therefore the consent of the parties to the blows which they mutually receive does not prevent these blows from being assaults.[52]

From Justice Stephen's remarks we learn that prizefighters are not merely guilty of breach of the peace, nor are they guilty of a simple assault and battery on each other as the justices believed. Rather they are guilty of a form of *lese majeste* in harming her majesty's subjects: themselves. Their consent given in joining the fight is immaterial, since by fighting they are damaging the property of the Queen. In other words, fighters participating in a bare-knuckle bout are committing treason with each blow. As the *Law Journal Reports* author said in reviewing this decision: "In fact the judgments of the court of Crown Cases are rather interesting from the insight which they give into the modes of thought of the individual judges, than useful as clear expositions of a branch of law." Yet *Regina v. Coney* remains one of the pillars of boxing law.[53]

East made another point that was lost in later law. In the above passage, East referred to both prize fightings and public boxing matches, not because they were the same, but because they were different. In this he followed William Blackstone, who recognized "boxing and sword playing" as separate activities. Even though fighting with weapons could be considered a significantly more dangerous sport than fighting with fists, Blackstone and East considered them both illegal. Yet the shift from fighting with swords to fighting with bare fists was a sign that England was becoming a more peaceful society. This change to fist-fighting rather than weapon-fighting significantly reduced the level of violence in nineteenth-century Britain. Still, boxing was given little credit for the conversion of England to a weaponless society. Instead, as public sword-fights disappeared, boxing matches became the only "prizefights" remaining. The evils of the earlier prizefights were now imputed to boxing. Once East had drawn a line between lawful amateur boxing and unlawful professional boxing, jurists ignored the old distinction between sword-fights and public boxing matches. They found it convenient to overlook amateur bouts and consider professional boxing the equivalent of sword-fighting, which had historically carried the name of prizefighting. This is why the sport still operates under two separate names: *boxing* and *prizefighting*.[54]

We can see this process in action in *Hunt v. Bell* (June 8, 1822). The case was one in which Hunt complained he was libeled by Bell. Bell had argued and Hunt had admitted that he had rented out his building called the Tennis Court for the purpose of "exhibiting from time to time therein of sportive and amicable contests, or matches, in the art of pugilism, or boxing, with padded gloves, commonly called sparring." These sparring matches had always been conducted in the most orderly manner. There was no indication of any riots on the part of the crowd. The crowd was controlled by the fact that people were admitted to see these matches upon payment of a fee: "There was no evidence that they were designed as a training or preparation for regular prize-fighting."

Bell argued however that

> the purpose to which the Plaintiff had appropriated the Tennis-court was illegal, as being, if not an absolute training for, preparatory to and promotive of, regular prize-fighting: and the preamble of the statute 25 G. 2, c.36, s.2, was referred to, as indicatory of the views entertained by the legislature on such matters.[55]

The boxing and sparring exhibitions were not shown to be harmful. Nor could this be a breach of the peace, since it occurred in a private building that required payment to obtain admission. Rather its crime was the relation to prizefighting, which was assumed to be injurious to the public. The reference to the statute 25 Geo II, c. 36, s.2 governing "Places of Publick Entertainment," which we have discussed above, was a red herring since it included nothing specifically related to prizefighting. Therefore the judge suggested to the jury that the issues were not clear and that they should find for Hunt. But instead, the original jury found for Bell.

In bringing this case for review by the Court of Common Pleas, Hunt's attorney pointed to the distinction between prizefighting and boxing or sparring. He admitted:

> Prize-fighting has always been interrupted and repressed by the magistrates but they have never interfered to prevent exhibitions of sparring, as they must have done if such exhibitions had been unlawful; and this is the first time the legality of them has been questioned.

Unfortunately, all four justices on the court ruled against Hunt. Mr. Justice Sir John Richardson summed up the court's position:

> If the question were merely, whether it is lawful or unlawful for persons to learn the art of self-defence, whether with artificial weapons or such only as nature affords, there can be no doubt that the pursuit of such an object is lawful; but public prize-fighting is unlawful, and any thing which tends to train up persons for such a practice, or promotes the pursuit of it, must also be unlawful. The jury have found that the exhibitions in question have such a tendency, and I see no reason for disturbing their verdict.

This verdict tells us that boxing matches or sparring with gloves when pursued on an amateur basis was lawful, but exhibitions put on for pay were considered training for prizefighting and "public prize-fighting is unlawful." From this point on, "prize-fighting" referred to professional public boxing matches, while "boxing [without gloves] and sparring [with gloves]" referred to the amateur version of the sport. Although in the later nineteenth century it was argued that the use of gloves in matches had created a new sport, this concept was ignored. In *Hunt v. Bell* a new definition of professional boxing as prizefighting had been established.

Appendices

1. Bringing Back Bare-Knuckle Boxing

In an article published on the BBC website on June 1, 2018, it was announced that the first bare-knuckle boxing bout sanctioned in the United States in 130 years was to be held on June 2 in Cheyenne, Wyoming (http://www.bbc.com/news/av/world-us-canada-44339038/bare-knuckle-boxing-makes-us-comeback-after-130-years). Bare-knuckle boxing matches have been held in England and Ireland for some years now, but generally out of the public arena. Most of these fights have been among the Gypsies and Irish Travelers. Last year a bare-knuckle boxing bout was held for the first time in the O2 arena in London, the second largest indoor arena in the UK (http://www.bbc.com/news/av/uk-england-berkshire-40427974/bare-knuckle-boxing-at-o2-will-be-as-popular-as-mma). While it may be a stretch to believe, as the fighter in this film clip believes, that bare-knuckle boxing will regain its popularity and rival glove boxing and MMA fighting, nonetheless, it is interesting to find boxers still pounding their fists against stone walls to toughen their knuckles, and entering the ring to engage in bare-knuckle matches once again. *Le plus ca change, le plus la meme chose.*

---

2. Was It Legal for King Richard I to Use Wax on His Fists?

In Chapter II, when discussing fist-fights with rules, Peter Larkin, the editor of *Richard Coer de Lyon,* raises the question: Was King Richard breaking the rules when he coated his hands with wax? Larkin says so in his notes to this episode: "In his use of wax, and in the lethality of his rage, Richard's response lies well outside the norms of heroic, not to mention chivalrous, behavior." I would suggest this is a misinterpretation of these events.[1]

In the legend, Richard and his friends had traveled to the Holy Land as pilgrims. In real life, they were Crusaders. Either way, they were under the protection of the Church.[2] Yet the King of Germany had accused them of being spies and had thrown them into prison. This was a crime on the part of the king. In real life, rather than legend, Pope Celestine III (1191–1198) excommunicated both Emperor Henry VI (1165–1197) and Duke Leopold V of Austria (1157–1194) for taking Richard prisoner.

Prior to the buffets match, Richard had warned the king against this illegal treatment and had predicted that misfortunes might occur as a result of his act (lines 724–733). When Wardrew challenged him, Richard saw an opportunity to punish Wardrew and, indirectly the king, whom he felt had wronged him. Richard's warning to the king of the possible consequences of his illegal act meant that Wardrew's death fell well within the rules of chivalry. Bradford B. Broughton in his book *Legends of King Richard I, Coeur de Lion*, noted that this was recognized by contemporaries in their treatment of the legends surrounding King Richard: "Thus chroniclers and other writers recorded the facts in ways which they felt would best suit their particular purposes. The writers favoring Richard placed emphasis on treachery by Leopold (who first captured Richard and then turned him over to the German king). They stressed his violation of the unwritten law of the Crusades which granted all pilgrims free entry into and departure from all countries on their crusade. The arrest and imprisonment of so highborn a crusader as Richard obviously indicated Leopold's baseness. Conversely, most of the continental writers deliberately ignore the flagrant violation of the rights of pilgrims, and chose instead to record, to the detriment of Richard's reputation, his capture in so base disguise as that of a menial kitchen helper."[3]

The second illegal act occurred when in the legend, King Henry declared Richard a traitor when he had not broken any oath of fealty to the king (lines 711–722). This declaration of treason was rejected by the king's own counselors who, after three days of debate, could not find any reason to punish Richard and his fellows (lines 970–982). But by declaring Richard a traitor when he was not one, the king gave Richard the right to defend himself. J.G. Bellamy, in examining the crime of treason, notes that "before the thirteen century many a ruler recognized a subject had the right to disobey him; tacitly this understanding was in every act of homage. It was even argued that a man wronged by his king had a duty, after offering formal defiance [*diffidatio*], to seek justice through rebellion. Who was in the right would be decided by the judgment of God as revealed by victory in a pitched battle."[4]

The third illegal act committed by the king was his attempt to kill Richard. Although this occurred after the fight with Wardrew, it confirmed Richard's heroic nature and the king's lack of chivalry. The king wanted Richard dead as revenge for killing his son and seducing his daughter, but he recognized that it was unlawful for one king to kill another save in battle:

"That he were ded I would ful fayn! [be well pleased]
But now it is ordeynyd soo [ordained so]
Men schal no kyng to deth doo!" [lines 956–958].

In order to avoid this, one councilor suggested starving the king's lion for three days and then putting him in Richard's cell: "In this manere he schal be slawe. Thenne dost thou nought agayn the lawe" (lines 1007–1008). This effort fails when Richard thrusts his fist into the lion's throat, grabs his heart, tears it out and eats it, thus earning the name "Richard the Lionheart." This was clearly a heroic act.[5]

Seen in light of these events, Richard's use of wax on his fist in the match of buffets did not break the covenant to which he had agreed. It was neither lacking in chivalry nor was it unheroic. It was covered by Richard's warning to the king of the consequences of his illegal acts, by Richard's right to rebel against the king for his attempt to brand Richard as a traitor, and by his heroic act of pulling out the lion's heart with his fist when attacked.

It was Richard who became the ideal of chivalry, not the King of Germany.

3. Pluck Buffet

As we have seen, there was a close relationship between buffeting and the later sport of boxing. Mistakenly, however, this particular account of buffets between Richard and Wardrew has been referred to as "pluck buffet," a name that has no meaning in the history of boxing.[1]

Instead, "pluck buffet" refers to an archery game described in *A Gest of Robyn Hode* (c. 1450) (line 1695; *The Eighth Fytte*, verse 424, n.1).[2]

King Edward [number unknown], disguised as an abbot, had ridden into the forest to find Robin Hood and punish him for setting free Sir Richard at the Lee, an impoverished knight, who had ignored the king's law by helping Robin Hood. Robin, not recognizing the king, intercepts him and his party, takes his money, and then offers to let him go. Edward shows Robin the king's seal and invites him to Nottingham. Robin acknowledges his love for the king and instead invites the abbot to dine with him in the forest that night. After dinner, Robin calls forth his archers and the king fears they will kill him. But

Robin sets up an archery contest with a rose-garland (a small target) hanging from a pole 50 paces away. The rules are that any archer who misses the target will lose his arrows and bow (presumably for that night). In addition, Robin proposes to give the one who missed a blow to the head ("buffet on his hede" l.1597; *The Seventh Fytte*, verse 400) with his fist. When Robin himself misses the target, he turns over his arrows to the abbot and asks him to deliver the buffet. At first the abbot demurs, but Robin gives him permission to hit him with all his strength. When the abbot does, he nearly knocks Robin down:

> And sych a buffet he gave Robyn,
> To grounde he yede full nere [he nearly fell down]:
> "I make myn avowe to God," sayd Robyn,
> "Thou arte a stalworthe frere [monk]" [lines 1629–1632; *The Seventh Fytte*, verse 408].

Robin and his men then recognize the abbot as the king in disguise and kneel down to him. The king pardons Robin and his men and again invites them to his court. The king then takes on Robin's livery by dressing in Lincoln green cloth like Robin's men. This makes him a member of Robin Hood's outlaw band and they all ride off together to Nottingham:

> Theyr bowes bente, and forth they went,
> Shotynge all in fere,
> Towarde the towne of Notyngham,
> Outlawes as they were
>
> Our kynge and Robyn rode togyder,
> For soth as I you say,
> And they shot plucke buffet,
> As they went by the way.
>
> And many a buffet our kynge wan
> Of Robyn Hode that day,
> And nothing spared good Robyn
> Our kyng in his pay.
>
> "So God me helpe," sayd our kynge,
> "Thy game is nought to lere;
> I sholde not get a shote of the,
> Though I shote all this yere" [lines 689–1704; *The Eighth Fytte*, verses 423–426].

Translation: "Robin Hood's band took their bows and rode to Nottingham, hunting along the way. The King and Robin rode together and played 'pluck buffet' as they rode. Since Robin was the better archer, the king got many buffets on his head that day, and Robin did not spare him when he lost. 'God help me,' said the king, 'This is a hard game to learn. I doubt that I could beat you if I shot all year.'"

Just as in the game of regular buffets, as proposed by Wardrew, "pluck buffets" had its own rules. But they were different rules. To begin with, the men did not enter into a covenant while engaging in "pluck buffet." While it is embarrassing to miss the target, it does not rise to the level of a test of honor as does standing unprotected and taking a blow in a buffet match. There is no religious imperative to engage in the game. "Pluck buffet" was simply an archery game wherein the man who missed his target must give his opponent an arrow and get hit on the head by his opponent's fist for every miss. The term "pluck" refers to the plucking of the bow string, while the term "buffet" refers to the blow to the head the loser receives. Unlike the true game of buffets, this game did not provide reciprocal blows one after another. Instead, one only got a buffet when one missed a shot at the target. And since these were superior archers, they did not miss often. In Robin's case, he might get a buffet very rarely. Nor is there any attempt to kill one's opponent as there was in the regular battle of the buffets. Rather the goal seems to be to shame the other archer for poor shooting and teach him to shoot better. King Edward is embarrassed, but not injured by Robin's blows, and recognizes that the purpose of the game lies in the archery, rather than in the buffeting.

Bradford B. Broughton was one of the first to note this difference: "The ballad A Gest of Robyn Hode (#117) contained the term 'Pluck buffet,' but the practice referred to differed from the practice in the Romance of Richard; there they were shooting at a mark." Roger Sherman Loomis, in his magisterial work *Celtic Myth and Arthurian Romance,* repeatedly confuses a genuine buffet match as seen in *Sir Gawain and the Green Knight* with "pluck buffet." He apparently believed that "pluck buffet" was the generic term for a buffet match, when, in fact, it had nothing to do with a real buffet match as seen in *Richard Coer de Lyon* or the beheading game in *Sir Gawain*.[3]

In summary, the term "pluck buffet" does not refer to any action that relates to the standard buffet match. Nor need we concern ourselves with "pluck buffets" in boxing. It relates simply to actions taken in an archery contest in the *Gest of Robyn Hode* and has no other meaning that I can find.

4. Was the *Caestus* Reintroduced into Sixteenth Century England?

The most popular version of Greek and Roman boxing used the *caestus.* The Greek version was a simple leather thong which originally was used only as a wrist band and then later (fourth century BC) developed into thongs that covered the fist. The Roman *caestus* was a heavy strip of leather which protected the knuckles. It has conventionally been assumed that the Romans

Fig. 16. A Greek boxer (left) and a Roman boxer each using *caestus* bindings on their hands. From Hieronymi Mercvrialis, *De Arte Gymnastica, libri sex* (Venice: Apud Ivntas, 1601), Book 2, 112. Note that both fighters hold their fists high as if they intend to strike down with a sword blow. This was the typical fist-fighting stance found in Italian cities during the Renaissance (courtesy Spencer Library in the University of Kansas Libraries).

Appendix 4. Was the Caestus Reintroduced into England?   157

studded their caesti with metal buttons or knobs as shown in the illustrations of Girolamo Mercuriale (Hieronymus Mercurialis) (1530–1606).[1]

However, Hugh M. Lee, in a recent article, has come to the conclusion that "the metal-studded *caestus* has no basis in archaeological evidence." Instead the *caesti* actually used were simply leather straps, wound around the hands as in the Mercuriale drawings but without the metal or stone studs. Lee's analysis is convincing. Despite the long history of assuming that the Roman boxers fought with metal studs we must now discard this assumption.[2]

As if in confirmation of Lee's argument, in February 2018 two examples of Roman *caesti* were excavated at Vindolandia near Hadrian's Wall in Northumberland, England. The gloves were made of leather and designed to fit snugly over the knuckles as a protective guard. The larger version was stuffed with a natural material designed to serve as a shock absorber, while the smaller version had a coil of hard twisted leather inside. Neither of the gloves had any metal in them. These *caesti* are "probably the only known surviving examples from the Roman period."[3]

Lee also presents a picture from 1502 published by Sebastian Brant (1475–1521) and printed by Johannes Gruninger [Johannis Grieninger] used to illustrate the boxing battle in the *Aeneid* (5: 362–484). The unknown illustrator shows Entellus and Dares fighting with what Lee sees as "clubs." "The clubs have a curious shape, being bent or curved. They are thickest at the end away from the hands where the club is meant to strike the opponent." Lee is apparently unaware of the medieval tradition of the substitution of "whirl bats" for the *caestus* thongs.[4]

Beginning in the fifteenth and sixteenth centuries there had been an attempt to reintroduce the *caestus* form of fighting in Europe under the name "whirl bats." Whirl bats were apparently introduced into Germany at the beginning of the fifteenth century and into England by the late sixteenth century. The fact that Denny described boxing at Dover's "Olimpicks" as similar to fencing with "rebated edges" may have been because he was comparing it with "whirl bats." Fighting with bare fists was much less violent, as Denny suggests, than fighting at whirl bats or fighting with the *caestus* (*bellare caestu*).[5]

In his 1614 book on Roman history, Thomas Goodwin noted, *a propos* of the Roman Games:

> The games and Masteries vsed in the circque were diverse; namely fisty-cuffes, fencing with swords, shaking the speare, dauncing in plaine ground, leaping, jumping, casting the dart, wrestling, running the race with chariots, which was called *certamen bigarum vel quadrigarum*; playing at whorle-bats, which was tearmed [*sic*] *bellare caestu*, casting or hurling the great stone called discus; though sometimes this discus was made of yron [iron] or brasse.[6]

Fig. 17. Entellus and Dares boxing with whirlbats before Aeneas. Sebastian Brant, *Publius Vergilius Maronis Opera cum quinque vulgatis commentariis explotissimisque figuris atque imaginibus nuper per Sebastianium Brant superadditis* (Strasbourg: Johannis Grieninger, 1502). Author's collection.

While this catalog may have been based upon the Roman Games as Goodwin states, it is also clear that it reflected the conditions in England at the time it was written. In his revision of 1638, he elaborated on the sport of "whorlebats":

> Their fighting at whorlebats they termed *bellare cestu*. The manner of the fight conceived thus the combatants had in each hand a strap of leather, with which each struck at the other (for we must know that this kinde of fight succeeded fisticuffs, and because in fisticuffs the party striking, did by the blow as well hurt his own fist, as he did him that was strucken, hereupon they invented this other kind of fight with lethern switches) these lethern switches they called Cestus, from the Greek *[kestis]*, signifying a belt or girdle: to make the fight more dangerous, they did aftertimes tye peeces of lead, or yron at the end of these

Appendix 4. Was the Caestus Reintroduced into England? 159

leatherne straps, so that they did with the force of the stroke, often dash out one anothers braines, and unlesse by the waight of the lead or yron, the strap might chance to fly out of their hands, they caused each strap to be tied fast to their armes, and shoulders: neither was this without reason, for those yron or lead pieces could not bee but very waightie, being made in the bigness, and form of Rams horns.[7]

What Lee sees as "clubs" appear to be the leather switches described by Thomas Goodwin in 1638. These leather switches may have been like padded socks, perhaps filled with sand. I do not see the lead or iron weights he mentions. The curve that Lee notes in the drawing is the result of the leather switches being swung through the air. The fact that the "clubs" are much thicker at the end then they are at the handles (something that would make

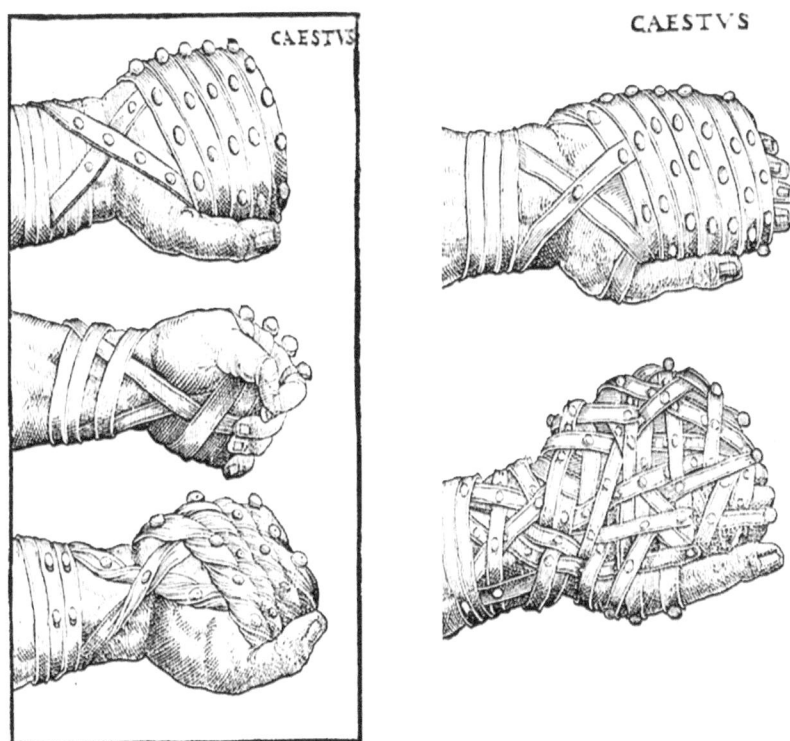

Fig. 18. The varieties of *caesti*. Hieronimus Mercurialis, *De Arte Gymnastica, libri sex* (Venice: Apud Ivntas, 1601), Book 2, 113–114. As Hugh M. Lee has recently shown, these drawings are correct in showing leather thongs, but incorrect in showing studs on the thongs. Greek and Roman *caesti* did not have metal or stones embedded in them (courtesy Spencer Library in the University of Kansas Libraries).

the clubs very unwieldy in real life) is due to the fact that the artist suffered with perspective and foreshortening in attempting to show the movement of the socks as they are being swung in combat. Brant's illustration gives us the only picture that I have found of whirl bats being used in fighting.

Whirl bats obviously did not enjoy great popularity. "Whorlebats" and "*bellare cestu*" needed explanation. They were not well known in England. On the other hand, by the beginning of the seventeenth century, fisticuffs had become a popular name for fighting with bare fists. This word and the sport were well known. Goodwin's audience knew what fisticuffs were.[8]

5. Oliver Cromwell and the Squire Papers

During the period between 1600 and 1681 it is probable that boxing matches occurred frequently and yet have not been recognized. Two uncertain boxing events have been linked to Oliver Cromwell. Mark Noble, author of the *Memoirs of the Protectorate-House of Cromwell*, mentions an early meeting between Cromwell and Charles I (then duke of York) when they were children. The royal procession stopped at the seat of Sir Oliver Cromwell, Oliver's father, and the two young men met and quarreled:

> They had not been long together before Charles and Oliver disagreed, and as the former was then as weakly as the latter was strong, it was no wonder that the royal visitant was worsted, and Oliver, even at this age, so little regarded dignity, that he made the royal blood flow in copious streams from the prince's nose.[1]

Whether, in fact, such an event actually occurred we do not know.

In 1847 Thomas Carlyle published a group of letters called *The Squire Papers*, supposedly from Oliver Cromwell, describing incidents of the English Civil War. One of these included a case of boxing. This incident occurred near Deeping. A group of Oliver's troopers encountered a miller driving a string of horses. The miller and one of the troopers got into an argument, which led to a boxing match. The trooper laid aside his weapons and the miller laid aside his coat. While they were fighting, one of the other troopers searched the miller's coat and found a number of royalist letters. The fight was stopped and the miller taken to Cromwell. After reading the letters, Cromwell said: "Truss him up." And that was the end of the miller.[2]

The Squire Papers have been challenged as forgeries, since the originals were destroyed, but Thomas Carlyle at least believed them genuine. Although a fist-fight between the young Oliver Cromwell and the young Charles I sounds apocryphal, the boxing match between the Puritan soldiers and the miller might have been real. If so, it suggests that Puritans not only knew what boxing was, but were willing to engage in the sport as the way to solve a quarrel. This also shows that a soldier was willing to lay aside his weapons when fighting an opponent who only had his fists.

6. Early English Law Cases Dealing with Boxing (1789–1882)

The Law is the true embodiment
Of everything that's excellent:
It has no kind of fault or flaw;
And I, my Lords, embody the Law.

The Lord Chancellor's song in Gilbert and Sullivan's operetta: *Iolanthe*

As discussed in the previous chapters, English law dealing with boxing and particularly boxing described as "prizefighting" was both complicated and inconsistent. As shown earlier, the term "prizefighting" had referred to several other activities before it came to be applied to boxing in the eighteenth century. These activities included war and tournaments and sword-fighting, in which the death of the contestants was a normal occurrence. And although death did occur in boxing matches, boxing proved to be a much less dangerous sport than those that it replaced.

Nonetheless, due to the imperfect memories of those tasked with establishing the laws in England, boxing's more benign character was overlooked, and by the nineteenth century it was viewed as a uniquely dangerous and violent sport.

This then led to a strange structure of laws designed to deal with this new threat to civilized society. What follows below are key court cases dealing with boxing which have been quoted verbatim with only a short commentary added by me to each case. Hopefully this will be useful as a summary to this history of the beginning of boxing in Britain.

The first law case to attract our attention is the William Ward case at the Old Bailey "William Ward, Killing: Murder, 3rd June, 1789," *The Proceedings of the Old Bailey*, Ref. t17890603-17, https://www.oldbaileyonline.org/browse.jsp?id=t17890603-17-off79&div=t17890603-17case number 17

(1) WILLIAM WARD.

https://www.oldbaileyonline.org/static/Crimes.jsp#killing;
https://www. oldbaileyonline.org/static/Crimes.jsp#murder.
3rd June 1789

REFERENCE NUMBER: t17890603-17

VERDICT: https://www.oldbaileyonline.org/static/Verdicts.jsp#guilty > https://www.oldbaileyonline.org/static/Verdicts.jsp#partialmanslaughter

SENTENCE: https://www.oldbaileyonline.org/static/Punishment.jsp#miscellaneous punishments > https://www.oldbaileyonline.org/static/Punishment.jsp#misc-fines; https://www.oldbaileyonline.org/static/Punishment.jsp#imprisonment

442. WILLIAM WARD was indicted, for that he, not having the fear of God before his eyes, but being moved and seduced by the instigation of the devil, on the 5th of May last, at the parish of Enfield, in and upon Edwin Swaine, in the peace of God and our Lord the King then and there being, feloniously, wilfully, and of his malice aforethought did make an assault, and him the said Edwin Swaine, with both his fists, in and upon the head, face, breast, and stomach, divers times did violently strike and beat, giving him by such striking and beating divers mortal blows, strikes and bruises, in and upon his head, face, breast, and stomach, of which he instantly died; and so the indictment charges that he, the said William Ward, feloniously, wilfully, and of his malice aforethought, him, the said Edwin Swaine, did kill and murder. He was also charged on the Coroner's inquisition, with feloniously killing and slaying the said Edwin Swaine.

The indictment opened by Mr. Leach: and the case by Mr. Knowlys, as follows,

May it please your Lordship.—Gentlemen of the Jury: you have heard the indictment opened by my learned friend, which contains the charge of murder, and when I am addressing myself to a Jury, who have discharged their duty so well this sessions, I need say nothing to you to call your attention to so important a charge; you well know what is due to publick justice upon a satisfactory conviction of such a crime; you likewise well know how immense a stake a prisoner has who stands under such accusation: gentlemen, I will state the case to you, as shortly as I can. It happened on the 6th of May, a famous battle was expected to take place at Stilton, between two men, of the name of Humphries and Mendoza, it was a matter of much public conversation, and on the day preceding, the Lincoln coach was passing through Enfield to this place; on the outside was the prisoner at the bar, when the coach stopped, the prisoner cried out what odds? not addressing himself to any person particular; the deceased happened to stand near the coach; he immediately said I will take thirty-five shillings to a guinea; meaning on the event of this battle, upon which the prisoner looked at him, and said to him, what are you a fighter? the deceased immediately said yes, I think I am able to fight you; upon this, Ward came from the box, and there was an offer at that time to fight for a guinea; it seems that the deceased was after this informed, that the man who offered to fight him, was a man known as a fighter, and more experienced than himself; upon this occasion the deceased rather failed in point of courage; then the prisoner finding him reluctant, offered to change that bet for a half crown bowl of punch; the deceased declined the fight; the prisoner went up and used several aggravating words, and put his fist in his face; a person of the name of Badder endeavoured to prevent it, but the deceased turned round to a man of the name of Peacock, and said this is too much; they had two rounds; they fell twice; on the second fall the deceased was accused of pulling the hair of the prisoner; when they got up, the deceased said I will fight no more; he left the prisoner, and moved round a cart, saying he had enough and would fight no more; the prisoner went round on the other side, met him; and I understand some attempts were made to prevent his striking him, but he almost at the same instant hit the deceased, who was not then in the attitude of fighting, with his left hand in the stomach, and with his right almost in the same instant a blow on the temple; upon that the deceased fell, and in almost an instant appeared dead, and never shewed the least signs of life afterwards.

Gentlemen, these are the circumstances attending this business; the deceased declined to fight, he was provoked to it, and at one time had given up the battle. If it appears to you that at the time the deceased declined to fight any more, and had left the prisoner; the prisoner had sufficient time to cool from the heat of the engagement, and went round the cart purposely to meet him, that he went to give him some very violent injury, even though he did not mean death, that he went deliberately to do an injury; even though he might think it short of death; then, under my Lord's direction, I shall hold it was murder; but if you think he did not go round purposely and deliberately, but that having once set his fighting talents at defiance, the prisoner acted under the impression of the rage which that occasioned, then I think you cannot carry it any further than manslaughter.

Gentlemen, I shall call all the witnesses; you will hear the whole of the case fairly and impartially, and I am sure the decision that you will give under the direction of the Court, will satisfy all the world.

MICHAEL BADDER sworn.
Examined by Mr. LEACH.

Where did you happen to be on the evening of the 5th of May last?—I was at Enfield highway when the Lincon coach stopped.

Do you remember seeing the prisoner at the bar there?—I remember seeing a man of the name of Ward there; that may be the man, but I am not sure: the passengers asked what was the odds on the battle depending at Stilton to morrow ; with that Mr. Swain said he would take thirty-five shillings to a guinea, but of which party I am not sure; and I believe one of the passengers, I cannot tell which, asked him if he could fight; he said he would fight him for a guinea; upon that, the gentleman came from the coach, and went to him, and I put my stick to him, and said Swain shall not fight; then Swain asked the other if he would take the law of him, and he said he would not; then some person asked me what I had to do with it; then Mr. Ward I believe hit Swain on the head, whether he fell to the ground I am not sure; people came in between him and me, and they set to it to fight, and they had a round together, and fell side by side as nearly as possible, and in the rising, some man, but who it was I cannot say, went to the assistance of Swain, and he got up with his hand in Ward's hair, and when he was got up, he said he would fight no more, and Ward held his hair towards the passengers in the coach, and said it was not fair; with that one of the passengers said Swain ought to have his liver cut out, or something of that nature, for fighting unfair; Swain went round the cart and stood there, and Mr. Ward met him, and he drew back and said he would not fight any more; Mr. Ward then hit him twice, and he fell and never got up any more.

Mr. Leach. Was Swain in a fighting posture when Ward gave the two last blows?—Not that I know of.

You did not see that he was?—No.

Did Swain after he received these blows and had fallen in consequence of them, shew any signs of life?—No, I never saw him stir afterwards.

Prisoner's Counsel. Blows were given on both sides?—Certainly.

Then they fell down both together?—Yes.

Then Swain the deceased, with one hand had hold of Ward by the hair?—Yes.

And with the other hand he was pegging him?—I did not see him strike, he had hold of him, but I did not see him strike.

Ward was pretty much beat?—I do not know, I did not take any notice of him; I did not see him; but as he came to the coach with a handkerchief up; my attention was about Swain.

These men did not know each other?—No Sir, not to my knowledge.

They offered to try their manhood for love, I believe at one time?—I believe they did, I never saw the prisoner before; nor Swain never saw him before; Swain was an intimate acquaintance of mine.

Swain was a pretty goodish man in your part of the country?—I never saw him strike any person in my life; I looked upon him to be a strong lusty hale man.

Did not you hear him, when this coach came up, talking very largely how he had challenged a man of the name of Johnson?—Yes Sir, I have often heard him say that; he was often romancing that way, but I never knew him to fight anybody in that way.

Did you see him pull off his apron, and swear he would whip Ward; did you hear him say he would smack his backside?—He might say so, but I did not pay any attention to it.

He was a blacksmith?—He was so; I remember something of his pulling off his apron.

He was a stouter man than Ward?—Much so.

JOSEPH ROWE sworn.

I was at the Black Horse, at Enfield Highway, when this matter took place; the first that I saw was; I was going there to give a horse a mouthful of hay; when the coach stopped, Ward the prisoner sat on the right hand side on the roof, the blacksmith stood by; they were talking about Mendoza, and mentioned immediately a guinea; the blacksmith mentioned about a guinea, and he offered to fight that man for a guinea, with that Ward got off of the roof and went to him; the coachman got hold of the blacksmith's coat and he gave him a pull, and he said for God's sake do not fight that man, for that is Ward the prize fighter; upon that, Swaine changed very white, and he said he would not fight; with that Ward said thus? says he, what will you not fight, you country hawbuck, and with that he tapped him, and said, I could have you here, and I could have you there, and slapped him over the face; with that he says no I shall not fight you now; but another time I will fight you for twenty pound; but now I will not; with that he said, what you will not fight me now? no, says he I will not; with that he kept tapping him; I could have you here, I could have you there; the blacksmith said I cannot put up with this any longer, and with that the blacksmith told him that he would knock him down if he could; with that they had a little bit of a hold, then they had a bit of a skirmish, and the little cart stood, and the blacksmith got hold of Ward's head of hair, he pulled some hair off his head; they were down both together, and the young man that is along with me now, he parted them, like one parted on one side the cart, and one on the other; different parties parted them and lifted them up; when they came up, the blacksmith walked up to the Black Horse bar window, and going in this man says will not you stand another round? they went one on the one side of the cart, and one on the other; the horse and cart stood facing the door way; with that, when they were going up there, he said, you blackguard I never had my hair pulled before in my life, will not you stand another round?

Did Swain make any answer to what was said by Ward?—He said he would fight no more; and as he was going up he hit him over the shoulder, and Swaine the blacksmith made to go into the house, and Ward hit him with his right hand in the belly, and with his left hand on the side of the head, and down the poor man dropped.

At the time he received these two blows, one of which you say was on the head and the other in the belly, was Swaine in a fighting posture?—No, he was not.

How did he appear after he fell, with these two blows he received from Ward?—never saw him take no breath at all; he died on the instant; I said doctor lay still, do not get up again till the coach is gone, do not stand to be paid about so; I little thought the man was dead; then Ward went into the coach.

Mr. Garrow, another of Prisoner's Counsel. This was the Lincoln coach, and he went into the coach he came in?—Yes.

You thought the doctor had the worst of it, and had better not fight any more?—Really I did so.

Did you know the doctor much?—Yes.

He was a swaggering man I believe, he thought himself a good man?—I believe he was; I never heard he offered to fight Johnson.

Did you see him take off his leather apron?—Yes, I did.

What did he say, now, when he took the apron off?—Why he flung it down when he gave Ward the challenge.

What did he say that he would do with his apron?—That I cannot say.

You did not hear him say that he would slap his backside with it; did you? recollect yourself now, and remember you are sworn to tell the whole truth?—I would tell the truth; I cannot recollect he did.

They had two pretty good rounds?—No, Sir, not pretty good rounds.

You are not fond of fighting; you do not like it?—I have seen a little of it.

Except the hair it was all fair?—No, asking your pardon, it was not two fair rounds.

I confess I am not much of a fighter, and if any shame belongs to that confession, I must take it; all the rest was fair except his getting his hands into his hair; that is not fair?—No, I do not think it is.

It is still less fair to tear off a man's hair?—No, it is not; to be sure he did pull some of his hair off.

These two men were strangers; this prisoner was a passenger on the coach?—Yes.

You had so little supicion that he was dead, that you advised the doctor to lay snug?—I did.

DANIEL NORRIS sworn.

I drove the Lincoln coach, I was at the Black Horse, Enfield Highway, I stopped my horses to water, which I always do; the blacksmith was standing

Appendix 6. Early Law Cases Dealing with Boxing (1789–1882)

at the door, or near the door, and Ward was at the top of the coach; somebody in the coach, or on the coach, offered to lay a bet of twenty pounds to ten pounds on the fight at Stilton; the blacksmith made answer immediately, and said, he would lay a guinea to thirty-five shillings; Ward says to him, what do you know about fighting? if you do, you have not a guinea to lay; I then took the blacksmith by the coat, and said to him, my friend do not you meddle with people you have nothing to do with, for it is Ward the fighter, and you will get licked, and lose your money; the blacksmith said again, if you will get off the coach, I will lick you, be you whom you will; I then pulled him by the coat again a second time, and desired him to be quiet; and he says to Ward; if you will get off the coach, I will whip your a—e with my apron; he got down, and they soon after fell to fighting; they fought away from me, I staid by my horses; they fought to the back part of the coach; I saw no more of it.

PHILIP SCOLEY sworn.

I was present when this matter took place; when we stopped at the Black Horse to water the horses, Ward sat at the back part of the roof of the coach with me; this blacksmith was standing down against the window, and he offered to lay a guinea to thirty-five shillings on the fight at Stilton, that was Swaine, I never saw him before; Ward upon the coach asked him what he knew about laying at fighting, and told him he had not a guinea to lay; and Swaine said he would fight Ward for a guinea, and make it up the twenty; Ward got off the coach, and they had some words between them after he got down, and Swaine pulled off his apron, and threatened to whip him with it; in a little time they fell to fighting, the blacksmith catched Ward by the hair, and bent him back a great way, and they both fell down together; and after they got up again they set to fighting again, and I did not see any more; I did not see the blow struck, when the accident happened.

MR. KNOWLYS. Then you say, that from the time of Ward's getting down from the coach, and the time of their beginning to fight, there were some words past?—Yes, there was, but I do not know exactly what it was.

MR. GARROW. He had offered to fight Ward for a guinea before Ward got down?—He had a guinea in his fingers; Ward was very much beat, he had a cut across his temples, he had a deal the worst of the beating; the blacksmith was stouter a great deal than Ward.

ROBERT WATSON sworn.

I was in the Lincoln coach on the 5th of May, going to Stilton, I saw the fight there; they stopped at the Black-horse Enfield Highway, the coachman stopped to water the horses, and this man Swaine stood at the door drinking along with some more, and he said I will lay a guinea to thirty-five shillings on the fight, which was to be the next day, and some gentlemen said they would lay two to one on the fight; and Ward asked him, what do you know about fighting? Swaine said, d—n me, I will fight you for a guinea or twenty; he took the guinea out in his hand, and held it in his hand, and threw it on the ground; Ward got down off the coach, and Swaine took his apron off, and said he would whip his a—e with it; a few words passed between them, and they went to fighting; Swaine had him held by his hair, and he hit him while he had hold of his hair, and the gentlemen that were there, cried out foul! foul! and they both fell down together; Swaine got up, and Ward got up, and Swaine stooped a little bit back, and they got fighting again, and fought till the very last moment; they stood up hitting at one another till the last moment the accident happened.

MR. LEACH. You know you are sworn to tell the whole truth?—Yes.

Did you or did you not see the deceased desist from fighting, and hear him say he would fight no more; and in order to avoid fighting, did you see him go round the cart?—No, Sir, I did not, I think I was near enough to hear.

Might he have gone round the cart and you not see him?—Yes he might.

PRISONER'S COUNSEL. Upon your oath did you hear him give out at all?—No, and I think I was close enough.

This poor fellow was beat about the head pretty well?—Yes, he had two black eyes, and desperate blows on the temples, the temple was all green and yellow, I do not know whether it was cut.

I believe a man who is beat about the head pretty handsomely, cannot hear so well as those that are not?—No, Sir, they can not.

JOHN PEACOCK sworn.

MR. KNOWLYS. Tell us as strictly as you can, what you saw pass on this occasion?—I was at the Black Horse at Enfield Highway when it happened; the Lincoln coach came up to the door, and Swaine was standing drinking a pint of beer, and some of the people upon the roof of the coach called out, what is the best odds for tomorrow? I do not know who it was that said so; and Swaine said he would take thirty-five shillings against a guinea; with that there were some words between the parties, and Ward got down from the coach; there were a good many words passed between them both, but I do not know what it was, Ward came up and held his fist in his face, and asked him if he was a fighting man, or would he fight; and Swaine said no, he did not want to fight, but he did not think Ward was much of a fighter; Ward said he would fight him for a guinea, or a bowl of punch, if he chose it.

COURT. Did Ward say that to Swaine, or Swaine to Ward?—Ward said so to

Swaine; there were many words passed after that, and then Ward struck him, and Swaine had his apron in his hand, and a guinea, and he flung his apron down, and gave the guinea to me; I was standing close by, I did not hear him say any thing at all about his apron, any more than flinging it down; then they went to fighting; after some blows they got hold of one another some way, and both fell down to the ground; when they got up again, Swaine said he would fight no more; there stood a cart in the road, and Swaine went round the cart one way, and Mr. Ward came round the cart the other.

COURT. Did any thing happen about Ward's hair?—I cannot say that he hung in his hair, I heard people say so, but I did not see him; Ward met him at the head of the horses again, and struck him again; I saw him strike one blow on the head, and he fell to the ground; Swaine was standing by the cart, going with his hands in this form (folded).

Was he at all in an attitude of defence?—No, he was not, he never stirred hand nor foot after.

MR. GARROW. They went round the cart, and as soon as they met he struck him a blow?—Yes.

Upon your oath, did not you hear the people call foul, foul?—I heard some of the people call foul, but I do not know what they meant by it.

Was not it explained at the time to mean that Swaine had fastened in his hair?—I do not know, I heard people say it was foul play; hit him again, I heard several people say that.

Upon which the smith went round one way, and Ward went the other, and instantly he struck him, and down he fell?—Yes.

You saw him take off his apron?—Yes.

Upon your oath did not you hear him say that he would whip this man with it?—I did not; I was within three yards of him.

Other people might not hear that which you heard?—No, they might not.

You will not swear that he did not say, when he took off the apron, I will slap your backside with this?—No, I will not swear it, he was no particular friend of mine.

A good strong man, was not he?—A strongish man, I do not know the strength of the man, I never tried his strength.

Was not he a very strong labouring blacksmith?—He was a stout built man.

Was not he a remarkable stout man?—No, I do not think he was, he was a stouter man than the prisoner, and taller.

THOMAS BALL sworn.

I was going by the door of the Black Horse on the 5th of May last, I saw the Lincoln coach stand, and there were some men making words; I went up to the door, and there was Ward and Swaine, and Ward offered to fight him for a guinea; and if he would not fight with two hands, Ward said he would fight him with one; or for a bottle of wine, which he liked; and he stood squaring his fist close in his face; he said here I could have you, and there I could have you, slashing at him; and at last they went to fighting, and they fought, and they tumbled down in the path-way, and they got up again; and the blacksmith Swaine said, he would not fight any more, and he was going up towards the bar of the house, and Ward went round and met him, and he struck him, and he tumbled down; I saw nothing more of it.

PRISONERS COUNSEL. Mr. Ball then you was there at the beginning?—No, I was not there at the beginning, Mr. Ward was on the ground when I went round.

JOHN FOWLER COLLUP sworn.

I am a surgeon, I saw the deceased, I believe it was the 5th of May, he was dead; I examined the body, I was informed what happened, but not particularly.

In your judgment was the death owing to blows?—That is beyond a doubt, that his death arose from the blows he received.

PRISONER'S COUNSEL. You opened the body, I take it of course?—I did not, I was once reprimanded by Mr. Philips the late coroner, for opening a body before he had seen him.

What external appearance would there be on a body, to convince you from the inspection of the body, that there was any blow to occasion his death?—A blow he received on the temple.

That is not always the occasion of death?—Not always, it very frequently is.

A person falling down may occasion a concussion of the brain?—It certainly may.

But you never opened the head to see?—I did not.

Then there was no concussion of the brain, no fracture of the scull?—No.

Suppose a man had been fighting, got a black eye; would you tell from that what was the cause of his death?—No further than from the bruises.

But bruises are not mortal in general; some subjects turn black much sooner than others?—Yes.

Men who live hard, do not turn black so soon as you or I would?—No.

You was not examined before the coroner?—No, I was not.

Mr. SHERWIN sworn.

I am a surgeon, I saw the body the day after the accident.
Did you examine it?—Yes.
What do you think was the occasion of the death?—I do not know, I cannot tell.
Were there any external marks of injury?—There was a bruise on the left cheek bone, the only external mark of injury; I saw none else.
Did you examine the body throughout?—I examined it externally as well as I could, I did not open it, I did not think it of consequence.

MR. GARROW. Did you observe any thing externally, that could distinguish it from a death by apoplexy?—Certainly not.
You have been long in the business?—Yes, more than twenty years.

PRISONER'S COUNSEL. My Lord, we make no defence.

The learned Judge summed up the evidence to the Jury, and then added: Gentlemen; this is the evidence against the prisoner; the crime charged is murder; as to that, there does not appear from the evidence, to have been any circumstances from which you will be at liberty to infer that he has been guilty of that crime; for in order to constitute the crime of murder, it must be done with malice aforethought, either expressed or implied; express malice is, where there has been any previous enmity between the parties, where there has been threats made use of, tending to shew a malicious intention in the mind, and some bad feeling of resentment which induced him to take vengeance for a supposed injury; malice implied, or constructive malice, is where the party is either in the prosecution of a felonious illegal act, and murder ensues; the law in that case, will impute malice though perhaps he had no actual antecedent malice against the party; so again, constructive malice may be where a person is acting in defiance of the law, or in opposition to the law, there the law will infer malice; but there is no pretence of any thing of the kind in the present case; neither is there any evidence from whence you can infer actual malice; for they were utter strangers, and this happened in course of words that fell between them, upon which they fell to fighting; therefore the utmost that this crime can amount to in point of law, is the crime of manslaughter; but there is another consideration which you must take into your minds, whether the death of the party happened from the blow that was given; or whether from any extraordinary exertion he might have died of an apoplexy or in a fit, or by breaking a blood vessel; so that if it is not imputable to any blow given from Ward, then you will find him not guilty; but if you think that death was owing to the blow he received, then you are to consider whether or no you will, or will not, find the prisoner guilty of manslaughter: as to that, where people happen to have words, and any sudden quarrel ensues, and death takes place from the blows; yet it can amount no higher than manslaughter, if they fight on equal terms and with equal weapons; and that was the case here; you find from some of the witnesses that the deceased was the aggressor, and first all challenged the prisoner to fight for a guinea; but whether one way or whether the other way, does not make any material difference in the consideration of the law, for it can amount no higher than manslaughter in this case: most of the witnesses seem to say that the first challenge came on the part of the deceased, and not originally by Ward; in that case Swaine was most to blame; you find they fought perfectly on equal terms, and if you believe the witnesses, the deceased was the stronger man of the two, therefore they fought on equal terms; one or two of the witnesses have said, that before he hit him the last blow that he declined fighting any longer, and that he was not on the defensive; now whenever there has been time to cool, it has been said by the counsel, that in that case it shews malevolence by the party continuing to shew his resentment, when the other had declined the combat; but I do not think much about that, for you find the interval was exceedingly short indeed between their actual fighting and Swaine declining the combat; one of the witnesses has said that they fought to the last, there was no interval, but that of of merely going round the cart; another matter is the aggravation on the part of the deceased, by catching hold of Ward by the hair; now that in this science, which I am very sorry prevails so much in this kingdom as it does at present, it is not any honour at all to the civilisation of this country, and I wish it was laid aside; but if in the science of fighting, it is looked upon as unfair, it might be looked on by the prisoner as a strong aggravation on the part of the deceased, and must naturally raise his resentment; now supposing that to be the case, the interval was so very short; it is not such an interval as the law will consider sufficient for a man's warmth of temper to cool: the law makes that allowance for human frailty; (though to be sure every man ought to keep a guard over his passions) that when a thing is done in heat, and before a man has had time to cool, if death happens, the law will not impute it to any higher crime than manslaughter; therefore there does not seem to be any ground to infer upon that very short interval, if any there was; that he had sufficient time to cool; especially after receiving that fresh provocation of taking hold of him by the hair, which was almost the last thing that was done previous to giving him that blow; therefore at all events this crime cannot amount to more than manslaughter: Gentlemen, if on the other hand, you are of opinion the death was not owing to the blows and bruises he received; you will find the prisoner not guilty.

GUILTY, of Manslaughter.

GUILTY, on the Coroner's Inquisition.

To be fined one shilling, and imprisoned three months.

Tried by the first Middlesex Jury before Mr. Justice ASHURST.

Appendix 6. Early Law Cases Dealing with Boxing (1789–1882)

COMMENTARY: The occasion was May 5, the day before the prizefight between Richard Humphries and Daniel Mendoza which was to be held May 6, 1789. At that time prizefighting had regained its popularity with the aristocracy. A previous fight between Humphries and Mendoza (January 9, 1788, won by Humphries) had been attended by HRH the Prince of Wales, the dukes of York, Clarence and Hamilton as well as Lord Baltimore and others. Their support made prizefighting legal at that time.

William Ward was on his way to the fight. The coach in which he was riding stopped at the Enfield Coach House to water the horses. Ward, who himself was a prizefighter of some reputation, asked the crowd what odds they were giving on the fight. He was answered by Edward Swaine, a blacksmith and a heavyset man, that he would give thirty-five shillings to a guinea (21 shillings) on the match. This intrigued Ward who got down from the coach and asked Swaine if he was a fighter. Swaine said that he was and offered Ward a guinea to fight. He said that he thought he could beat Ward, who was a little man.

Several men then urged Swaine to not fight Ward, telling Swaine that Ward was himself a prizefighter. Swaine then decided not to fight Ward. Ward provoked Swaine to fight by slapping him several times in the face. After first refusing to fight, Swaine took off his leather apron and said he would whip Ward's backside with it. They began to fight and after beating each other they both fell to the ground to end round one. Round two began and Swaine grabbed Ward's hair and pulled him backward tearing out some hair as he did so. Members of the crowd cried foul at this and the men fell again, ending round two.

At this point Swaine said he would not fight anymore and went around the coach while Ward followed him around the coach on the other side to continue the fight. People tried to separate the two, but before they could do so, Ward hit Swaine with a left to the stomach and a right to the temple and he fell dead. Ward was arrested and charged by the coroner with murder.

In trying the case, Justice Ashurst, in contrast to later justices, acknowledged that even though this was a spontaneous and unplanned fight they were engaging in a science which was governed by rules. It had been entered into as a result of Swaine's bet of one guinea and his challenge to Ward. Justice Ashhurst discounted the charge of murder on the grounds that neither man knew the other (hence there could be no malice aforethought), nor could there be any constructive malice since prizefighting was legal and they were fighting on equal terms with equal weapons. On the other hand both men had broken the unwritten rules of prizefighting: Swaine had grabbed Ward's hair in the fight and pulled it out, at which the spectators cried "foul," while Ward had hit the final blows when Swaine was walking away, had said he was not going to fight any more, and was not in a defensive posture. Because both had broken the rules, an assault had been committed. Ashurst suggested that the charge of manslaughter was the highest crime allowed. The jury agreed and found Ward guilty of manslaughter.

(2) *Hunt v. Bell*, June 8, 1822, 130 *English Reports*, 1–3
[1] Cases Argued and Determined in the Court of Common Pleas, and Other
   Courts, in Trinity Term, in the Third Year of the Reign of George IV.
Hunt v. Bell June 8, 1822
[S.C. 7 Moore, 212. Referred to, *Foulger v. Newcomb*, 1867, L.R. 2 Ex. 330]

1. In an action for libeling the Plaintiff in his vocation as an exhibitor of sparring matches, the jury were directed to consider whether the Plaintiff's exhibitions were not illegal, as tending to form prize-fighters, the Judge declaring such to be his opinion, but recommending the jury to find a verdict for the Plaintiff, in order that the question might be fully discussed on a motion to set aside such verdict: a verdict having been found for the Defendant, the Court refused to grant a new trial.—2. Semble, that public exhibitions of sparring matches are illegal.—3. A party who pursues an illegal vocation has no remedy by action for libel regarding his conduct in such vocation.

This was an action on the case for a libel against the Plaintiff, in regard to his conduct as a proprietor of a building called the Tennis-court, which, the declaration stated, he had himself appropriated, and had permitted others (for money therefore paid to him) to appropriate for, (amongst other lawful purposes) the [2] exhibiting from time to time therein of sportive and amicable contests, or matches, in the art of pugilism or boxing, with padded gloves, commonly called sparring, by and between persons skilled in such art, for the amusement of any persons desirous of being spectators thereof, and paying for their admission into such building a certain sum of money per head.

The general issue was pleaded. At the trial before Dallas C. J., Middlesex sittings after Easter term last, the above statement as to the nature of the exhibitions at the Tennis-court was fully made out, and also that those exhibitions consisting of sparring, chiefly by professors of pugilistic sciences, had always been conducted in the most orderly manner. There was no evidence that they were designed as a training or preparation for regular prizefighting. The publication of the matter complained of was admitted by the Defendant, and it appeared to be clearly libellous; but the defence was, that the purpose to which the Plaintiff had appropriated the Tennis-court was illegal, as being, if not an absolute training for, and preparatory to and promotive of, regular prize-fighting; and the preamble of the statute 23 G. 2, c. 36, s. 2, was referred to, as indicatory of the views entertained by the legislature on such matters.

DALLAS, C.J. first put it to the jury to consider, whether the Plaintiff's exhibitions were not illegal, as tending to form prize-fighters, declaring such to be his opinion at the moment, although he was unwilling to decide the point without further time for deliberation, and he then recommended the jury to find a verdict for the Plaintiff, which the Defendant might afterwards move to set aside, and so fully discuss the question: but the jury found a verdict for the Defendant. Whereupon

[3] Bosanquet Serjt. now moved for a new trial, on the following grounds: The verdict was given under the supposition that the Plaintiff's vocation was illegal; but there is no evidence that his exhibitions were designed as a training or preparation for regular prize-fighting; and a mere exercise of pugilistic skill, divested of violence by the use of padded gloves, is not illegal, such exercise being not only unaccompanied with a breach of the peace or danger, but being highly beneficial as promotive of bodily strength and agility, and as furnishing means of defence against unprovoked attacks. Prize-fighting has always been interrupted and repressed by the magistrates, but they have never interfered to prevent exhibitions of sparring, as they must have done if such exhibitions had been unlawful; and this is the first time the legality of them has been questioned. If it be unlawful in the way of exhibition, or otherwise, to give and receive instruction in the art of pugilistic attack and defence, those instructions being unaccompanied with violence or danger, except from accident, which might equally occur in tennis, cricket, or other games, a fortiori must all instruction or practice in fencing, broad-sword exercise, or archery, be illegal; yet exhibitions of, and practice in the two former, have never been interrupted, though publicly carried on. There are numerous enactments for the encouragement of archery; and in *Rex* v. *Handy* (6 T. R. 286), Lord Kenyon must be taken to have spoken of fencing as not illegal. The price demanded for admission would prevent exhibitions of this kind from occasioning idleness in the poorer classes of society; though if it were otherwise, Lord Coke says (11 Rep. 87, case of *Monpolies*), "When King Edw. 3, in the 39th year of his reign, commanded the exercise of archery and artillery, and prohibited the exercise of casting stones and bars, and [4] the hand and foot-balls, cock-fighting, et alios vanos ludos, yet no effect followed till divers of them were prohibited upon a penalty by divers acts of parliament." But there is no act of parliament which forbids sparring exhibitions, and they do not even fall within the preamble of 25 G. 2, c.36, s.2. Stage representations they cannot be called, with more propriety than the feats of tumblers, which latter have been holden not to be stage representations within that act. *Rex* v. *Handy*.

DALLAS, C.J. When this cause was tried, I certainly delivered an opinion, such as I could form at the moment, and under some difficulty; for I think there may be difficulty in this question, and I have wished for further time to consider it. Without going into matters foreign to the point under discussion, we know that, in the early periods of their history, it has been the practice of all civilized nations to train up their population to exercises of activity and courage; and, with a view to national defence to promote emulation in amicable contests of strength. I stated to the jury the difficulty of distinguishing between fencing and boxing. Many persons, now present, can recollect the exhibitions of skill by Angelo, Roland, St. George, and others; and yet, is not fencing the art of attack as well as defence, and is it not more dangerous that boxing? But is fencing illegal? or is it illegal to attend a fencing-school? is it illegal to practice the bow and arrow? are archery meetings illegal? On all these views of the subject, I felt considerable difficulty. But, on the whole, when I consider that these sparring exhibitions are conducted by professors of pugilism; that they are meeting which may tend to encourage an illegal vocation, and to form prize-fighters, I see no reason for disturbing the present verdict.

[5] PARK J. If it were necessary for us to decide, whether exhibitions, such as those in which the Plaintiff was engaged are illegal, I should wish for more time before I came to a conclusion, because exercises of such a kind have long existed. The argument drawn from the supposed legality of fencing exhibitions, would be stronger in favor of sparring exhibitions, if persons who learned fencing were trained to prize-fighting, as pugilists notoriously are; but such is not the case: and it having been put to the jury, whether the Plaintiff's exhibitions did not tend to form prize-fighters, I see no reason for disturbing the verdict.

BURROUGH J. I am of the opinion that the practice in question is illegal. The chief object for which persons attend these exhibitions is to see and judge the comparative strength and skill of the parties, who may be afterwards matched as prize-fighters, and that, frequently, to the loss of life; for there can be no doubt that the skill acquired in these schools enables the combatants to destroy life, in some instances, by a single blow; and it is notorious that persons assembled at these exhibitions engage in illegal bets on the issue of such encounters.

RICHARDSON J. If the question were merely, whether it is lawful or unlawful for persons to learn the art of self-defence, whether with artificial weapons or such only as nature affords, there can be no doubt that the pursuit of such an object is lawful; but prize-fighting is unlawful and any thing which tends to train up persons for such practice, or to promote the pursuit of it, must also be unlawful. The jury have found that the exhibitions in question have such a tendency, and I see no reason for disturbing their verdict.

Rule refused.

COMMENTARY: Thirty-three years following the Ward decision a new view of prizefighting prevailed. The setting in this case was inside a private building devoted to sport: The Tennis Court. The environment was out of the public way and the activities were carried on in an orderly fashion. The public was admitted but only upon the payment of a fee. As a result, it could not be argued that Hunt had created a breach of the peace. The combatants did not fight with bare fists but wore padded gloves which were assumed to reduce the level of violence. This was considered sparring, not prizefighting. During the 1780s royalty had revived their interest in boxing prizefighting, but after 1800 middle-class morality overwhelmed the aristocracies' interest and as a result, prizefighting was no longer considered legal. Fighting with bare knuckles (which was considered prizefighting) had now become illegal, but fighting with padded gloves (called sparring) was not. There was no evidence that the activities in the Tennis Court were designed as training or preparation for regular prizefighting. Nonetheless, Hunt was accused of running a school for prizefighters, which was held to be illegal.

Chief Justice Robert Dallas confessed that he was not clear on how much training in boxing differed from fencing or archery, and argued that if training for those activities was legitimate could not training for boxing be also? Justice Park said that he would have been more impressed with this argument "if persons who learned fencing were trained to prize-fighting, as pugilists notoriously are; but such is not the case." This demonstrates that by 1822, the memory of sword prizefights, which were common in the 1700s, had completely vanished from the minds of the public. As a result, as Justice Burrough argued: "The chief object for which persons attend these exhibitions is to see and judge the comparative strength and skill of the parties, who may be afterwards matched as prize-fighters" and since prizefighting was illegal, sparring contests must be illegal as well.

(3) *Rex v. Billingham*, 172 *English Reports*, 106
July 19th, 1825
Rex v. Billingham, Savage, and Skinner.
(All persons present countenancing a prize-fight, are guilty of an offence.
  When a prize fight is expected, the magistrates ought to cause the intended combatants to be brought before them, and compel them to enter into securities to keep the peace till the assizes or sessions, and if they refuse to enter into securities, to commit them.)
[Explained, *R. v. Coney*, 1882, 8 Q. B. D. 534]

The prisoners were indicted for a riot, and for assaulting Daniel Rogers, Esquire, a magistrate, in the execution of his office.

It appeared, that Billingham and Savage had agreed to fight a pitched battle; and for that purpose they met at a place near Hagley, and about one thousand persons were assembled to witness the fight. Mr. Rogers was applied to to prevent it, and for that purpose went (with others) to the place, and told them that they should not fight. The defendant Skinner said that they should, and a scuffle ensued between him and Mr. Rogers, who endeavoured to apprehend him, which ended in a general tumult on the part of the mob, and the rescue of Skinner.

BURROUGH, J.—By law, whatever is done in such an assembly by one, all present are equally liable for; which ought to make persons very careful. It cannot be disputed that all these fights are illegal, and no consent can make them legal, and all the country being present would not make them less an offence. They are unlawful assemblies, and every one going to them is guilty of an offence. The inconvenience in the country is not so great, but nearer London the quantity of crime that these fights lead to, is immense. My advice to magistrates and constables is, in cases where they have information of a fight, to secure the combatants before hand, and take them to a magistrate, who ought to compel them to enter into securities to keep the peace till the next assizes or sessions; and if they will not enter into such security, to [235] commit them to prison. In this way the mischief would be prevented, and the fights put a stop to.

Verdict—Guilty.

Russel and Ryan, for the prosecution.

[Attornies—Hill, and —].

COMMENTARY: Justice Sir James Burrough (1769-1837) argued that prize-fighting was clearly illegal and not only the individual combatants, but all those who witnessed the fight were equally guilty. "It cannot be disputed that all these fights are illegal, and no consent can make them legal, and all the country being present would not make them less an offence. They are unlawful assemblies, and every one going to them is guilty of an offence." This proved to be neither sound law nor sound policy. It was not sound law because as late as 1789, when Burrough was 20 years old, Justice Ashurst had found boxing prize-fights legal. Neither was it sound public policy since it was impossible to convict all those who witnessed a prizefight. Recognizing that this view of the law could not be enforced, Justice Burrough compounded his mistake by urging magistrates to arrest the combatants before they committed the crime and put them in prison unless they promise not to engage in a prizefight. "In this way the mischief would be prevented, and the fights put a stop to."

This case, in which those arrested were found guilty, demonstrated the absurd nature of prizefight law.

(4) *Rex* v. *Perkins*, 172 *English Reports*, 814
[537] Before Mr. Justice Patteson

March 3rd, 1831

Rex v. Perkins and Others.

(Persons who are present at a prize-fight, and who have gone thither with the purpose of seeing the persons strike each other, are all principals in the breach of the peace, and indictable for assault, as well as the actual combatants; and it is not at all material which of the combatants struck the first blow.)

[S.C. 2 Man. & Ry. M.C. 306. Considered, *R.* v. *Coney,* 1882, 8 Q.B.D. 534. Referred to *R.* v. *Clarkson,* 1892, 66 L.T. 297]

Indictment for a riot and an assault on Robert Coates.

It appeared that a prize-fight was fought between the defendant Perkins and Robert Coates, and another of the defendants, named Weekly, acted as a second of the defendant Perkins, and that the two other defendants were present, the one collecting money for the combatants, and the other walking round the ring and keeping the people back. It appeared that many hundred persons were assembled, and that the defendant Perkins struck the first blow.

Mr. Justice Patteson (in summing up).—It appears, in this case, that a great number of persons were assembled together on this occasion, and that there was a breach of the peace. It is clear, that the parties went there intending that a breach of the peace should be committed. There is no doubt that prize-fights are altogether illegal; indeed, just as much so, as that persons should go out to fight with deadly weapons; and it is not at all material which party struck the first blow. It is proved that all the defendants were assisting in this breach of the peace; and there is no doubt that persons who were present on such an occasion, and taking any part in the matter, are all equally guilty as principals.

The foreman of the Jury said, that they doubted whether they could find all the defendants guilty of an assault.

Mr. Justice Patteson.—If all these persons went out [538] to see these men strike each other, and were present when they did so, they are all, in point of law, guilty of an assault. There is no distinction between those who concur in the act and those who fight.

Verdict—Guilty of the riot, but not guilty of the assault.

Cooper, for the prosecution.

Ludlow, Serjt. for the defence.

[Attornies—B. Alpin, and ——.]

Commentary: In arguing the same points of law as in the *Billingham* case, Justice Sir John Patteson (1790–1861) found that the jury would not support a verdict of assault on all of those who witnessed the prizefight. The jury would admit that the attempt to arrest the principals had led to a riot, but refused to support Justice Patteson in declaring anybody guilty of assault. Regardless of the view of the judge that all those attending were guilty, the jury would not agree that mere presence at a prizefight was a crime, even if it led to a riot. The jury was bringing a level of sanity back into boxing law.

(5) *Regina* v. *Coney*, Queen's Bench Division for the High Court 1882, 534
Coram: Cave J., Stephen J, Hawkins J, Lord Coleridge CJ, Lopes J, Huddleston B

A public prize-fight was unlawful. Spectators were tried at Berkshire County Quarter Sessions with common assault. The Chairman of the Quarter Sessions directed the jury to convict the spectators of common assault on the basis that having stayed to watch the fight, they encouraged it by their presence.

HELD: Each protagonist was guilty of assaulting the other and a number of bystanders were held to have encouraged, and thus to have been guilty of aiding and abetting, the assaults of both. However, mere voluntary presence at a fight did not as a matter of law necessarily render those present guilty of assault. The court was not saying that the jury could not have convicted the spectators on the basis merely of their presence. The objection of the majority was that the case had been withdrawn from the consideration of the jury.

CAVE J said: "The true view is, I think, that a blow struck in anger, or which is likely or is intended to do bodily corporal hurt, is an assault, but that a blow struck in sport, and not likely, nor intended to cause bodily harm, is not an assault, and that an assault being a breach of the peace and unlawful, the consent of the person struck is immaterial."

HAWKINS J said: "The cases in which it has been held that persons may lawfully engage in friendly encounters not calculated to produce real injury to or to rouse angry passions in either, do not in the least militate against the view I have expressed; for such encounters are neither breaches of the peace nor are they calculated to be productive thereof, but if, under colour of a friendly encounter, the parties enter upon it with, or in the course of it form, the intention to conquer each other by violence calculated to produce mischief, regardless whether hurt may be occasioned or not, as, for instance, if two men, pretending to engage in an amicable spar with gloves, really have for their object the intention to beat each other until one of them be exhausted and subdued by force, and so engage in a conflict likely to end in a breach of the peace, each is liable to be prosecuted for assault." And

"Whatever may be the effect of a consent in a suit between party and party, it is not in the power of any man to give an effectual consent to that which amounts to, or has a direct tendency to create, a breach of the peace; so as to bar a criminal prosecution, in other words, though a man may by consent debar himself from his right to maintain a civil action, he cannot thereby defeat proceedings instituted by the Crown in the interests of the public for the maintenance of good order; ... He may compromise his own civil rights, but he cannot compromise the public interests."

LORD COLERIDGE CJ: "I conceive it to be established, beyond the power of any argument however ingenious to raise a doubt, that as the combatants in a duel cannot give consent to one another to take away life, so neither can the combatants in a prize-fight give consent to one another to commit that which the law has repeatedly held to be a breach of the peace. An individual cannot by such consent destroy the right of the Crown to protect the public and keep the peace."

STEPHEN J said: "The principle as to consent seems to me to be this: When one person is indicted for inflicting personal injury upon another, the consent of the person who sustains the injury is no defense to the person who inflicts the injury, if the injury is of such a nature, or is inflicted under such circumstances, that its infliction is injurious to the public as well as to the person injured. But the injuries given and received in prize-fights are injurious to the public, both because it is against the public interest that the lives and the health of the combatants should be endangered by blows, and because prize-fights are disorderly exhibitions, mischievous on many obvious grounds. Therefore the consent of the parties to blows which they mutually receive does not prevent those blows from being assaults.

In cases where life and limb are exposed to no serious danger in the common course of things, I think that consent is a defence to a charge of assault, even when considerable force is used, as, for instance, in cases of wrestling, single-stick, sparring with gloves, football, and the like; but in all cases the question whether consent does or does not take from the application of force to another its illegal character, is a question of degree depending upon circumstances."

LOPES J said: "I understand the ruling of the Chairman to amount to this, that mere presence at a prize fight, unexplained, is conclusive proof of aiding and abetting, even if there had been no evidence that the person or persons so present encouraged or intended to encourage the fight by his or their presence. I cannot hold, as a proposition of law, that the mere looking on is ipso facto a participation in or encouragement of a prize fight. I think there must be more than that to justify conviction for an assault. If, for instance, it was proved that a person went to a prize fight knowing it was to take place, and remain there for some time looking on, I think that would be evidence from which a jury might infer that such a person encouraged and intended to encourage the fight by his presence. In the present case three prisoners were merely seen in the crowd, were not seen to do anything, and there was no evidence why or how they came there, or how long they stayed."

HUDDLESTON B commented on the direction of the Chairman of Quarter Sessions: "If he had told the jury that going to a prize fight to see the combatant strike each other, and be present when they did so, was evidence from which they might find that the defendants countenanced what was going on, and that therefore they might find them guilty, I should have been disposed to support the ruling. But that is not the effect of his summing up."

COMMENTARY: Justice Cave's view that a blow struck in anger is an assault while a blow struck in sport is not an assault was valuable. Ultimately, but not immediately, it was adopted as the fundamental basis of sport law and was supported by the public. Justice Stephen, on the other hand, held the extreme view that prizefighting was injurious to the public, not merely through a breach of the peace, but because it was damaging to public welfare: "But the injuries given and received in prize-fights are injurious to the public, both because it is against the public interest that the lives and the health of the combatants should be endangered by blows, and because prize-fights are disorderly exhibitions, mischievous on many obvious grounds. Therefore the consent of the parties to blows which they mutually receive does not prevent those blows from being assaults." Virtually all of the justices denied the validity of the doctrine of consent as a protection against the charge of assault. As Lord Coleridge, CJ, put it: "An individual cannot by such consent destroy the right of the Crown to protect the public and keep the peace."

But eventually, despite these views, the doctrine of consent in sport once again became established law. Even Justice Stephen was willing to admit that the doctrine of consent was a defense against a charge of assault "even when considerable force is used, as, for instance, in cases of wrestling, single-stick, sparring with gloves, football, and the like." This begins to take the law back to the question raised by Chief Justice Dallas in *Hunt v. Bell*: "I stated to the jury the difficulty of distinguishing between fencing and boxing. Many persons, now present, can recollect the exhibitions of skill by Angelo, Roland, St. George, and others; and yet, is not fencing the art of attack as well as defence, and is it not more dangerous that boxing? But is fencing illegal? or is it illegal to attend a fencing-school? is it illegal to practice the bow and arrow? are archery meetings illegal? On all these views of the subject, I felt considerable difficulty."

Justice Lopes began to perceive that it was impossible to hold the spectators guilty of assault for merely being at the prizefight. This point had been made by the jury in Rex v. Perkins (1831) and would become settled law during

Appendix 6. Early Law Cases Dealing with Boxing (1789–1882)

the twentieth century. No matter how the justices fulminated, the public would not agree that presence at a boxing match constituted a crime.

Distilling these points down, I would argue that there was a strong bias against boxing *per se*. I would argue further that the law dealing with boxing was tortured out of logic compared to the law dealing with other sports. Why this was the case, I cannot say. It may have something to do with the fact that boxing began as a rough and tumble sport developed among the common people in contrast to fencing which was an aristocratic sport. Or it may be that boxing did not develop out of the military as did wrestling, which is why wrestling was never outlawed and boxing was.

In looking back into history, we find that many arguments made in favor of other sports and against boxing were simply not true. In the twelfth and thirteenth centuries fencing was outlawed in England, although Chief Justice Dallas was not aware of this in 1822. We know that sword gladiators routinely engaged in prizefights as did boxers in the early 1700s, even though Justice Park was not aware of this in 1822. We know that beginning in 1725 when James Figg and later John Broughton began holding boxing matches on elevated stages the concept of boxing as a breach of the peace virtually disappeared. We do not know in what way the payment of a fee to watch a boxing match rendered that fight illegal. Nor do we know how boxing came to be illegal when there was no law written against it in England.

Whatever the reason, it is clear that boxing law was biased law. Most law cases dealing with boxing were built on scaffolds without rails from which the eminent jurists were like to fall and break their necks, if they extended themselves too far in their arguments.

Chapter Notes

Introduction and Acknowledgments

1. Saxo Grammaticus (d. circa 1220) spoke of Danes who were famous boxers, but a recent editor of his work disputes this: "Boxing was not known in the early Middle Ages in northern Europe and the nearest equivalent would be wrestling. Pugilism was practiced among the Greeks and Romans, and Saxo may have been influenced here by the detailed account of the contest in Book V of the *Aeneid*." Saxo Grammaticus, *The History of The Danes*, Books 1-9, ed. and commentary Hilda Ellis Davidson, trans. Peter Fisher (Cambridge: D.S. Brewer, 2008 [1979-1980]), Vol. 1, sect. 63, 69; Vol. 2, 51, n. 2.

2. Roger Pearce, "When Were the Olympic Games Abolished?" http://www.roger-pearce.com/weblog/2012/08/04/when-were-the-olympic-games-abolished. See also Panos Valavanis, *Great Moments in Greek Archaeology* (Los Angeles: J. Paul Getty Museum, 2007), 115; For "Aurelius Zopyrus, Marcus" see Mark Golden, *Sport in the Ancient World from A to Z* (New York: Routledge, 2004), 24, where Golden says Zopyrus won "the boy's boxing event in 385 CE to become our latest datable Olympic Victor."

3. *The Digest of Justinian*, Vol. 1, trans. Alan Watson (Philadelphia: University of Pennsylvania, 1998 [1985]), Book 9 *Lex Aquilia*, sect. 7, 4.

Chapter I

1. H.W. Koch, *Medieval Warfare* (New York: Crescent, 1983 [1978]), 15.

2. Egerton Castle, *Schools and Masters of Fencing from the Middle Ages to the Eighteenth Century* (Mineola, New York: Dover, 2003 [1885]), 13-14.

3. Craig Turner and Tony Soper, *Methods and Practice of Elizabethan Swordplay* (Carbondale: Southern Illinois University Press, 1990), 32. They discuss the teaching of Giacomo Di Grassi, *His True Arte of Defence* (1594). See also Di Grassi's dictum: "Without all doubt, the thrust is to be preferred before the edge-blow, as well because it strikes in less time, as also for that in the said time, it doth more hurt" (Turner and Soper, *Methods and Practice of Elizabethan Swordplay*, 37). To translate this into boxing terms, we might say that the straight jab is to be preferred to the roundhouse right because it strikes in less time and does more hurt. Boxing learned a good deal from fencing, as we will discover.

4. Sidney Anglo, *The Martial Arts of Renaissance Europe* (New Haven and London: Yale University Press, 2000), 277, fig. 183 shows a duelist kicking an opponent's knee in similar fashion. Terry Brown, *English Martial Arts* (Hockwold-cum-Wilton, UK: Anglo-Saxon, 1997), 190 figs. c and d, shows a similar strategy with the follow-through.

5. In Giacomo Di Grassi's work on fencing of 1594, he argues that proper footwork

is critical to success in fighting: "Leg movement should match body and hand movement. For instance, when thrusting or parrying with the sword in the right hand, the right foot position is critical: when thrusting the foot and leg give drive to the motion of the sword; when defending, foot and leg provide a solid base for parrying." This doctrine was new in the sixteenth century, and was clearly unknown to the man with the robe in this fourteenth-century illustration. His opponent, the nude man, seems more knowledgeable. He has already moved his left leg forward in preparation to hitting with his left fist. As he shifts his weight to this leg it will give him power to swing his fist to whatever spot he wishes to hit. Turner and Soper, *Elizabethan Swordplay*, 34.

6. Stacy Rosenbaum et al., "Observations of Severe and Lethal Coalitionary Attacks in Wild Mountain Gorillas," *Scientific Reports* 6, 37018 (2016), 1–8, doi:10.1038/srep 37018; Stacy Rosenbaum, personal correspondence, June 25, 2018; Brigitte Demes quote in Ed Yong, "Scientific Punch Up over Idea That Our Hands Evolved to Fight," *National Geographic*, December 19, 2012.

7. Michael H. Morgan and David R. Carrier, "Protective Buttressing of the Human Fist and the Evolution of Hominin Hands," *Journal of Experimental Biology* 215 (2013): 236–244. For a criticism of Morgan and Carrier, see John Rennie, "Evolved Fists or the Best Weapons at Hand," http://blogs.plos.org/retort/2013/02/26/evolved-fists-or-the-best-weapons-at-hand/. Historically, boxers have found the fist a delicate fighting instrument and, unless properly bandaged, prone to breakage, such as the boxer's fracture. See "Boxer's Fracture," *WebMD*, https://www.webmd.com/a-to-z-guides/boxers-fracture#1-1. This would be a significant reason why humans, unlike the other apes, typically fight with weapons. Tool use was once thought of as the distinct domain of humans, but recent research has shown that many animals use tools as well. However, only chimpanzees, in addition to humans, appear to use tools in fighting and hunting. See J.D. Pruetz et al., "New Evidence on the Tool-Assisted Hunting Exhibited by Chimpanzees (*Pan troglodytes verus*) in a Savannah Habitat at Fongoli, Senegal," *Royal Society Open Science* (2015): 2, http://dx.doi.org/10.1098/ rsos. 140507. Pruetz argues that "Savannah chimpanzees (P.t.verus) at Fongoli, Senegal are the only known non-human population that systematically hunts vertebrate prey with tools" (1).

8. Morgan and Carrier, "Protective Buttressing," 238 fig. 2, 239 figs. 3 and 4.

9. John Godfrey, *A Treatise upon the Useful Science of Defence* (repr. N.p.: Andesite Press, 2017 [London, 1747]), 46. Following Captain Godfrey's advice, a whole industry has been created to teach men the skills of boxing. Very few men have the natural ability, without training, to fight well with their fists. To help train them, there is a vast literature on how to box. Jack Dempsey, the heavyweight boxing champion of the 1920s, agreed with Captain Godfrey. He summed up his teaching in his book *Championship Fighting: Explosive Punching and Aggressive Defence* (New York: Simon and Schuster, 1978 [1950]) with the simple statement: "Punchers are made; not born" (14).

10. E.B. Michell "Boxing and Sparring," in Walter H. Pollock et al., *Fencing, Boxing and Wrestling*, Badminton Library of Sports and Pastimes (London: Longmans, Green, 1902), 117. Contrary to Michell, V.G. Dowling, the author of *Fistiana or the Oracle of the Ring* (London: Wm. Clement, Jr., 1841), 21, believed that boxing was "coeval with the existence of man himself."

11. Modern child research supports Michell's view. See, for example, Anthony D. Pellegrini, "Rough and Tumble Play from Childhood through Adolescence: Development and Possible Functions," in *Blackwell Handbook of Childhood Social Development*, ed. Peter K. Smith and Craig H. Hart (Oxford: Blackwell, 2002), 438–453; Marion K. Underwood, "Sticks and Stones and Social Exclusion: Aggression among Girls and Boys," *Blackwood Handbook*, 533–548; and Eric Scott and Jaak Penksepp, "Rough-and-Tumble Play in Human Children," *Aggressive Behavior* 29 (2003), 539–551. See also Peter K. Smith, Rebecca Smees and Anthony D. Pellegrini, "Play Fighting and Real Fighting: Using Video Playback Methodology with Young Children," *Aggressive Behavior* 30 (2004): 164–173.

12. See John Mouratidis, "The Origin of Nudity in Greek Athletics," *Journal of Sport History* 12, no. 3 (Winter 1985): 213–232;

Larissa Bonfante, "Nudity as a Costume in Classical Art," *American Journal of Archaeology* 93 (1989): 543–570; Paul Christesen, "On the Meaning of *gymnazo*," *Nikephoros* 15 (2002): 7–37; Jean-Paul Thuillier, "La nudite athletique, le pagne et les Etrusques," *Nikephoros* 17 (2004): 171–180; Polybius quoted in Barry Cunliffe, *The Ancient Celts* (London: Penguin, 1999 [1997]), 99. It should be noted that as late as 1185 the Irish were still charging naked and unarmed into battle. See Gerald of Wales, *The History and Topography of Ireland*, trans. John J. O'Meara (London: Penguin, 1982 [1951]), c. 93, 101.

13. I have been reminded by Tony Gee, the British prize-ring historian, that Sir Thomas Parkyns of Bunny (1663–1741) wrote several paragraphs on boxing at the end of his famous book *The Inn-Play or Cornish-Hugg Wrestler* (1727). Parkyns's comments confirm both that boxing required training and that boxing owed much to wrestling. On the other hand, Parkyns's statements are not easily recognized as applying to modern boxing. Still, as the first written comments on boxing, they are worth printing.

"Boxing"

1. By all means have the first blow with your head of fist at his breast, rather than at his face; which is half the battle, by reason it strikes the wind out of his body.

2. If you have long hair, soap it: The best holds are the pinnion [to disable or restrain by binding the arms] with your arms at his shoulders, and your head in his face, or get your right arm under his chin, and your left behind his neck, and let your arms close his neck strait, by holding each elbow with the contrary hand, and crush his neck, your fingers in his eyes, and your fingers of your right hand under his chin, and your left hand under the hinder part of his head; or twist his head round by putting your hand to the side of his face, and the other behind his head.

But if your adversary taketh fast hold with each of his hands of each side of the collar, and thrusteth his thumbs against your throat and windpipe, speedily that you may not want wind, with your right hand hold his fast there by the wrist, and with the left fort elbow, press on the top of his arm upon his feeble, betwixt your right hand and his elbow, or quick over his wrist for the gripes.

Or proceed for the pinion as in Pag. 43 [of Parkyns's book *The Inn-Play*], or if he hath his hands in your hair, and he thrusted his thumbs in your eyes, you preceed after the foregoing method.

With the exception of the first item, which could be considered boxing, the rest of this discussion deals with wrestling strategy. Item no. 2 is clearly a statement of how great a debt boxing owed to wrestling. See Parkyns, Thomas of Bunny, *The Inn-Play or Cornish-Hugg*, transcribed by Ken Pfrenger and Shannon Pfrenger (1727), http://neohemas.wordpress.com/library/The-Inn-Play-or-Cornish-Hugg-Wrestler-by-Sir-Thomas-Parkyns-of-Bunny-Baronet/. Seen October 10, 2017.

Chapter II

1. Peter Larkin, ed., *Richard Coer de Lyon*, TEAMS: Middle English Texts Series, University of Rochester (Kalamazoo: Medieval Institute Publications, Western Michigan University, 2015). References in the text are cited by lines. Peter Larkin criticizes King Richard for his action in hitting Wardrew with his wax-coated fist. I consider this action in Appendix 2 of this work.

2. "Buffet" was an Old French word meaning to give a blow. It could mean both a blow with a fist and a blow with a weapon. J.A. Simpson and E.S.C. Weiner, eds., *The Oxford English Dictionary*, 2nd ed. (Oxford: Clarendon, 1989) "buffet, sbl"; and Hans Kurath and Sherman M. Kuhn, eds., *Middle English Dictionary* (Ann Arbor: University of Michigan Press, 1957), "buffet, n. 2." See also Frederic Godefroy, *Dictionnaire de l'Ancienne Langue Francais et de touts ses Dialectes du IXe au XVe Siecle*, Vol. 1 (repr. Vaduz: Kraus Reprint, 1965 [Paris, 1880]), "buffe, 2." See also "buffet, buf- s." and "buffeter, -ater, buffeter v. a." to strike, buffet, in Louise W. Stone and William Rothwell, *Anglo-Norman Dictionary* (London: Modern Humanities Research Association, 1977), fascicle 1. The concept of having two men standing toe to toe hitting each other with reciprocal blows, as demonstrated by King Richard and Prince Wardrew, is common to many cultures. Although the Eskimos can-

not have either influenced or been influenced by English behavior, they did have a sport called *ungatanguarneg* in which two men stood face to face and took turns slugging each other with their fists until one man succumbed or relented. Stephen Craig, *Sports and Games of the Ancients* (Westport, CT: Greenwood, 2002), 203. The sport still exists and was also found in the United States in the 1970s under the name "Kansas Thump-thump." See Robert Day, *The Last Cattle Drive* (Lawrence: University of Kansas Press, 1987 [1977]), 167–168. Finally, the fact that Wardrew gave Richard an "ear cloute" shows that blows to the ear were part of the earliest strategy of fist-fighting. This parallels the ear clout given by Hereward the Wake to the cook mentioned above.

3. The topos of killing a man with a single blow of one's fist dates back at least to 1135 in French literature. See Sally North, "The Ideal Knight as Presented in Some French Narrative Poems, c. 1090–c. 1240: An Outline Sketch," in *The Ideals and Practice of Medieval Knighthood*, ed. Christopher Harper-Bill and Ruth Harvey (Dover, NH: Boydell, 1986), 111–114. It should be noted that the first French literary works were written in England, not in France, and that they began to appear circa 1135. Thus the topos of killing a man with the blow of one's fist may actually belong to England. See below, note 34. In *The Romance of Sir Beues of Hamtoun* (c. 1327), Sir Beves escapes from prison in Damascus by hitting his jailor on the neck (presumably just below the ear) with his fist and killing him. Eugen Kolbing, ed., *The Romance of Sir Beues of Hamtoun*, Early English Texts Society (EETS), Extra Series (ES), Vol. 46 (London, 1885–1894), part 1, 84, lines 1615–1616; Ronald B. Herzman, Graham Drake and Eve Salisbury, eds., *Four Romances of England: King Horn, Havelok the Dane, Bevis of Hampton, Athelston*, The Consortium for the Teaching of the Middle Ages (TEAMS) Middle English Texts Series (Kalamazoo: Western Michigan University, 1999), 244, lines 1615–1616. The use of beeswax as an adhesive has an ancient history. A recent article, Michael Baales, Susanne Birker and Frank Mucha, "Hafting with Beeswax in the Final Palaeolithic: A Barbed Point from Bergkemen," *Antiquity* 91, no. 359 (October 2017), 1155–1170, notes that beeswax was used to attach a point to a fish spear as far back as circa 11,000 BC in Germany. Richard's use of beeswax to coat his hands and bind his fingers into a fist would have been well understood by AD 1325. See Appendix 2.

4. A. Yonick, "Covenant (in the Bible)," in *The New Catholic Encyclopedia*, Vol. 4, 2nd ed. (Detroit: Thomson Gale, 2003), 324–328.

5. A.B. Davidson, "Covenant," in *A Dictionary of the Bible*, ed. James Hastings, Vol. 1 (Peabody, MA: Hendrickson, 1988 [1898–1904]), 509.

6. Delbert R. Hillers, "Covenant," in *The Encyclopedia of Religion*, ed. Mircea Eliade, Vol. 12 (New York and London: Macmillan, 1987), 133–137.

7. Larkin, *Richard Coer de Lyon*, 40.

8. See George Lyman Kittredge, *A Study of Gawain and the Green Knight* (Gloucester, MA: Peter Smith, 1960 [1916]), where he analyses the many parallel stories.

9. [Moelmuiri mac Mic Cuinn Na M-Bocht], *Fled Bricrend: The Feast of Bricriu*, ed. George Henderson, Vol. 2 (London: Irish Texts Society, 1899).

10. Athenaeus, *The Deipnosophysts*, trans. Charles Burton Gulick, Loeb Library, Vol. 2 (London and New York: William Heinemann and G.P. Putnam's Sons, 1927), b. 4, s. 154, 201, quoting Poseidonius.

11. [Moelmuiri mac Mic Cuinn Na M-Bocht], *Fled Bricrend*, chapter 14, sect. 76, 99.

12. [Moelmuiri mac Mic Cuinn Na M-Bocht], *Fled Bricrend*, chapter 14, sect. 77, 99.

13. [Moelmuiri mac Mic Cuinn Na M-Bocht], *Fled Bricrend*, chapter 14, sect. 78, 101.

14. [Moelmuiri mac Mic Cuinn Na M-Bocht], *Fled Bricrend*, chapter 15, sect. 79–90, 101–115.

15. [Moelmuiri mac Mic Cuinn Na M-Bocht], *Fled Bricrend*, chapter 16, sect. 91–102, 116–120. For a further discussion of this section, see Chapter VII.

16. Saxo Grammaticus, *The History of the Danes*, Vol. 1, Book 2, sect. 51, 54. Latin original in Saxonis Grammatici [Saxo Grammaticus], *Gesta Danorvm*, ed. Alfred Holder (Strassburg, France: Verlag von Karl J. Trubner, 1886), Book 2, 56, lines 13–19. Hilda

Ellis Davidson, *The Sword in Anglo-Saxon England* (Woodbridge, UK: Boydell, 1994), 204–210 also discusses the *holmganga*.

17. For a recent analysis of the history of judicial duels see Ariella Elema, *Trial by Battle in France and England* (Ph.D. diss., University of Toronto, 2012), https://tspace.library.utoronto.ca/handle/1807/67806. The classic work is George Neilson, *Trial by Combat* (Clark, NJ: Lawbook Exchange, 2009 [1890]). Parallels with *holmganga* are many: the trial by battle might be fought on an island; the public could watch but not interfere; there was a recitation of the terms of the fight before the event for the benefit of the audience; the weapons were to be equivalent; the contestants were to foreswear magic; the fighters not only used weapons but could also wrestle, bite and gouge out their opponents' eyes; a loser might lose his property and be no longer allowed to swear an oath or to participate in a lawsuit. There are many examples of *holmganga* in Scandinavian Literature. See Jesse Byock, "Holmganga," in *Medieval Scandinavia: An Encyclopedia*, ed. Philip Pulsiano (New York and London, 1993), 289–290; Marlene Ciklamini, "The Old Icelandic Duel," *Scandinavian Studies* 35, no. 3 (August 1963): 175–194.

18. Saxo Grammaticus, *The History of the Danes*, Vol. 1, Book 2, sect. 51, 54.

19. Agner used the conventional sword strike by raising his sword above his head and hacking down. This gave great force to his blow, but when his blade became trapped in Biarki's helmet, he could not recover. Biarki used a sword thrust that allowed him to direct his blade to do the most damage. The sword thrust became the most popular method of fighting in the late sixteenth century. Biarki was before his time.

20. J.R.R. Tolkien and E.V. Gordon, eds., *Sir Gawain and the Green Knight*, 2nd ed., revised by Norman Davis (Oxford: Clarendon, 1967); see also Joseph Glaser, trans. and notes, *Sir Gawain and the Green Knight* (Indianapolis and Cambridge: Hackett, 2011). The Middle English text (Tolkien and Gordon) is cited in the paper by lines, while the Modern English translation (Glaser) is cited by page numbers.

21. The challenge in *Sir Gawain and the Green Knight* is described as a buffet at lines 382, 1754, 2343. There are many parallels between Sir Gawain and the Irish myth of the bachlach described above. Both the Green Knight and the bachlach are half-giants who suddenly appear at the royal court when the warriors are assembled. Both the Green Knight and the bachlach are immortals who challenge the assembled warriors to exchange buffets with an axe. Each proposes a covenant in which a member of the warrior group chops off the visitor's head, and later the visitor will return to chop off the warrior's head. In both cases the immortals spare the hero (Cuchulainn or Gawain) who agreed to play the game. And at the end they reveal that the purpose of the beheading game was to test the bravery of the warrior group. Based upon these parallels, Roger Sherman Loomis considered the Green Knight and the bachlach the same person. See comment by Loomis at note 29, below.

22. Glaser, *Sir Gawain and the Green Knight*, 15.

23. Ursula K. Le Guin, *A Wizard of Earthsea* (Berkeley, CA: Parnassus, 1968), 59, 84. Jacob, when wrestling with God, asked, "Tell me, I pray thee, thy name" (*Genesis* 32:29), just as Gawain did of the Green Knight. "A name was much more than a label of identification; it belonged to the essence of a personality. Know a name and you have a way open to the secret of the person. You could use the name not only for invocation but as a spell of incantation." "The Names of God," in George Arthur Buttrick, ed., *The Interpreter's Bible* [...] *in Twelve Volumes*, Vol. 1 (New York and Nashville: Abingdon, 1952), 726. See also James George Frazer, *The Golden Bough: A Study in Magic and Religion*, abridged ed. (New York: Macmillan, 1956), 284–308. "Many savages at the present day regard their names as vital parts of themselves, and therefore take great pains to conceal their real names, lest these should give to evil-disposed persons a handle by which to injure their owners" (284–285).

24. The agreement is called a covenant repeatedly throughout the text (lines 393, 2242, 2238, 2340), although at one point it is called a "statute" between Sir Gawain and the Green Knight (line 1060). A statute carried the same value as a covenant but without the religious implications.

25. Glaser, *Sir Gawain and the Green Knight*, 15–16.

26. Glaser, *Sir Gawain and the Green Knight*, 167.

27. W.Y. Evans-Wentz, *The Fairy-Faith in Celtic Countries* (No Location: University Books, 1966 [1911]), 283–307. The Sidhe, pronounced Shee, is a fairy mound where the spirit people live who originally populated Ireland under the name of *Tuatha De Danann* (The Tribe of the Goddess Danu). They were driven underground by the Milesians (Soldiers of Spain: Mil Espaine = Miles Hispaniae = Milesians) who came from Spain to conquer Ireland. The *Tuatha De Danann* populate a magic world and occasionally take humans into their mounds as husbands or wives. The fact that the Green Knight associated himself with a Sidhe-like mound shows the link between the English story and Irish myth and deepens the magical nature of the story.

28. Glaser, *Sir Gawain and the Green Knight*, 73.

29. As Roger Loomis noted: "I have proved that bachlach [the Irish word for churl] was transformed into a proper name and appears in *Sir Gawain and the Green Knight* as Bertilak." Bertilak and the bachlach are the same magical being. Roger Sherman Loomis, *Celtic Myth and Arthurian Romance* (New York: Columbia University Press, 1927), 16. For a discussion of the meaning of Hautdesert, see the article by Noel C. Brindley, *Sir Gawain and the Green Knight: A Study of Hautdesert, Wilderness and Purlieus*, http://hautdesertpurlieu.wordpress.com. Seen March 27, 2017.

30. For a discussion of each of these tales, see Kittredge, *A Study of Gawain and the Green Knight*.

31. Thomas Hahn, "The Turk and Sir Gawain," in *Sir Gawain: Eleven Romances and Tales* (Kalamazoo, MI: Medieval Institute Publications, 1995), 337–358. For more on "The Turk and Sir Gawain" see Loomis, *Celtic Myth and Arthurian Romance*, 100–104.

32. David Burnley, *The History of the English Language: A Source Book*, 2nd ed. (Harlow: Pearson Education, 2000 [1992]), 67.

33. John H. Fisher, *The Emergence of Standard English* (Lexington: University Press of Kentucky, 1996), 44.

34. M.T. Clanchy argues that the Normans had no written language prior to the Conquest. The task of governing, and the fact that they had conquered a people more literate than themselves, forced them to create a written language. M.T. Clanchy, *From Memory to Written Record: England 1066-1307* (Oxford: Blackwell, 1993 [1979]), 215–220. In her beautifully written work, Charity Urbanski, *Writing History for the King: Henry II and the Politics of Vernacular Historiography* (Ithaca and London: Cornell University Press, 2013), 26 shows that the first Old French texts began to appear in 1135, and they first appeared in England, not France.

35. "From their first attestation, Anglo-Saxon laws were written in the Old English vernacular, distinguishing them from contemporary Latin counterparts on the European continent." Lisi Oliver, "Legal Documentation and the Practice of English Law," in Clare A. Lees, ed., *The Cambridge History of Early Medieval English Literature* (Cambridge: Cambridge University Press, 2013), 499–500.

36. Clanchy, *From Memory to Written Record*, 214.

37. William Aldis Wright, ed., *The Metrical Chronicle of Robert of Gloucester* (London: Eyre and Spottiswoode, 1887), 543–544; and Albert C. Baugh and Thomas Cable, *A History of the English Language*, 5th ed. (Upper Saddle River, NJ: Prentice-Hall, 2002 [1935]), 115.

38. Baugh and Cable, *A History of the English Language*, 114. Baugh and Cable point to modern-day Belgium where a similar situation exists: the upper classes speak French and the lower classes speak Flemish (Dutch) (115).

39. The *Stamford Articles* of 1309 were basically a translation into French of the Latin, *Articuli super Cartas* of 1300. S.B. Chrimes and A.L. Brown, eds., *Select Documents of English Constitutional History, 1307-1485* (London: Adam and Charles Black, 1961), 6–8. See also 266–271, statutes nos. 240–243.

40. Baugh and Cable, *A History of the English Language*, 145–146.

41. See cc: 28–32 in document 228 in Chrimes and Brown, *Select Documents of English Constitutional History, 1307-1485*, 251–252. See also document 230 Parliament of 1423, on pages 253–254. For the literature of the poor, see two books by Gamini Sal-

gado, *Cony-Catchers and Bawdy Baskets: An Anthology of Elizabethan Low Life* (Hammondsworth, UK: Penguin, 1972); and Gamini Salgado, *The Elizabethan Underworld* (Phoenix Mill, UK: Sutton, 2005 [1977]).

42. Loomis, *Celtic Myth and Arthurian Romance*, 77–83; Davidson, *The Sword in Anglo-Saxon England*, 207. The sword duel was an established practice in Germanic law and common to all of the German tribes. It is possible that "buffeting" with swords could date back to the ancient pre-migration Germans. Robert W. Henderson, *Ball, Bat and Bishop* (Urbana and Chicago: University of Illinois Press, 2001 [1947]) argues that sport contests often are relics of religious rites.

43. William Horman, *Vulgaria* (London: [Richard Pynson,] 1519), ff. 132v–135v.

44. Saxo Grammaticus *The History of the Danes*, Vol. 1, Book 2, sect. 51, p. 54.

45. See Chapter I. Saxo Grammaticus, *The History of the Danes*, Vol. 1, Book 3, 69, describes Hother, son of Hothbrod, as being distinguished in "swimming, archery and boxing." But Hilda Ellis Davidson notes that "boxing was not known in the early Middle Ages in northern Europe." Instead, she believes that Saxo is being anachronistic by conflating events in Virgil's *Aeneid* with his own time (Davidson, *The Sword in Anglo-Saxon England*Vol. 2, Book 3, 51, n. 2).

46. Joseph Forsyth, *Remarks on Antiquities, Arts, and Letters during an Excursion in Italy in the Years 1802 and 1803* (Newark: University of Delaware Press, 2001), 63–64; and Pierce Egan, *Boxiana* (Vol. 2), *or Sketches of Modern Pugilism from the Championship of Cribb to the Present* Time (London: Sherwood Jones, 1824), part 2, 738–739. But see "Bernardine of Siena, St.," in *New Catholic Encyclopedia*, 2nd ed., Vol. 2 (Detroit: Thomson Gale, 2002), 320–321. Siena, like many of the Italian city-states, had intramural battles (called games) between various sections of the city. In Siena one of these games was called the Game of the Fist *(Gioco della Pugna)*. This is probably the boxing game that Joseph Forsyth had in mind in his story about St. Bernardine. This game began shortly after 1291when a previous game, the *Gioco dell'Elmora* or the Game of the Helmet, left ten dead. To play the *Gioco della Pugna* the city was divided into sections and all who wished might participate. In 1324 nearly 1,200 men fought in a city-wide Game of the Fist. Rather than fight a series of individual matches, crowds of young men came together in one continuous battle. Similar melees occurred in Florence in the game of *Calcio*, in Pisa in the Game of the Bridges *(Gioco del Ponte)* and in Venice in the Wars of the Fists *(Guerre dei pugni)*. All of these consisted of melees *(battagliaccia)* in which many men fought at the same time. These games were nothing like English boxing with its emphasis on two, and only two men fighting at one time. See Raymond E. Role, "The War Games of Central Italy," *History Today*, June 6, 1999, historytoday.com/raymond-e-role/war-games-central-italy/. Seen December 3, 2017.

47. For Chinese boxing see Wu Bin, Li Xingdong and Yu Gongbao, *Essentials of Chinese Wushu* (Beijing: Foreign Languages Press, 1992). Zach Gaskell has suggested to me that boxing survived the breakdown of the Roman Empire and persisted among the Kiev Rus as a holdover sport from the Byzantine Empire. It does appear that a type of fist-fighting was singled out by Metropolitan Kirill III (1250–1281) of the Orthodox Church for condemnation in the Council at Vladimir of 1274. See Daniel H. Shubin, *A History of Russian Christianity*, Vol. 1 (New York: Algora, 2004), 92. According to Shubin, "Metr. Kirill disclosed to the council the incidence of fighting between drunken men, even to their death, and the crowds of people who watched such fights. The council issued a decree prohibiting fist-fighting, and forbidding priests from performing a memorial mass or requiem on behalf of any who died in such fights." If the fist-fighting condemned by Metropolitan Kirill was based upon Greek boxing and was drawn from the Olympics, this would be a clear indication that ancient boxing survived into the medieval era. However, I have not been able to confirm that boxing existed in Russia at this time. Nor have I been able to find that the variety of fist-fighting found in Medieval Russia had any influence on the development of boxing in Britain. The same was true of later Russian fist-fighting. According to Robert Nisbet Bain, Peter the Great (1672–1725) sought to restrict Russian boxing (*kulachny boi*): "Thus a Ukaz was issued to put

a stop to the brutality of the *kulachny boi,* or fist-fight. This popular game was not abolished, but those who chose to amuse themselves thereby, were to do so, in future, under police supervision, and were forbidden to use sticks, stones, knives and bullets, as supplementary weapons, or to throw sand in each other's eyes." Robert Nisbet Bain, *The Pupils of Peter the Great: A History of the Russian Court and Empire from 1697 to 1740* (Westminster, UK: A. Constable, 1897), 89. Bain's comments suggest that Russian boxing was significantly different from English boxing. Again there is no indication that *kulachny boi* had any influence on British boxing.

Chapter III

1. Joseph Bosworth and T. Northcote Toller, eds., *An Anglo-Saxon Dictionary* (Oxford: Oxford University Press, 1964 [1898]), 355; and T. Northcote Toller, ed., *An Anglo-Saxon Dictionary Supplement* (London: Oxford University Press, 1966 [1921]), 277. The Laws of Aethelberht (ante 617) are found in F.L. Attenborough, ed. and trans., *The Laws of the Earliest English Kings* (Clark, NJ: Lawbook Exchange, 2006 [Cambridge, 1922]), 11, c. 57. The laws then talk about penalties for bruises made by fists (cs. 58, 59, 60).

2. For Hereward giving a "box on the ear" to the cook, see Michael Swanton, trans., "Gesta Herewardi (The Deeds of Hereward)," in *Medieval Outlaws: Ten Tales in Modern English,* ed. Thomas H. Ohlgren (Phoenix Mills, UK: Sutton, 1998), 49. Hugh M. Thomas argues for a date of composition between 1109 and 1174 for the *Gesta.* Hugh M. Thomas, "The *Gesta Herwardi,* the English, and their Conquerors," *Anglo-Norman Studies* 21, ed. Christopher Harper-Bill (1998): 213–232.

This is the first example of a "box on the ear" in English literature. A box on the ear was recognized as one of the most powerful of all blows a boxer could give. Such a blow could easily disrupt the blood flow to and from the brain and lead to instant loss of consciousness with blood running from the ears, mouth and nose. It was a dramatic blow and one that would be long remembered by those witnessing it. This apparently was what happened to the cook when Hereward hit him. See Godfrey, *A Treatise upon the Useful Science of Defence,* 51.

3. G.L. Brook and R.F. Leslie, eds., *Layamon: Brut,* EETS 2, Original Series, no. 250 (London, 1978), 594–595, line 11370.

4. Matthew Paris, *The Illustrated Chronicles of Matthew Paris: Observations of Thirteenth-Century Life,* trans. and ed. Richard Vaughn (Corpus Christi College, Cambridge: Alan Sutton, 1993), 146–151; John Stow, *A Survey of London (1603),* Vol. 2 (Oxford: Clarendon, 1908 [1603]), 25–26; "Boniface of Savoy (Bishop)," *Wikipedia.* Seen September 18, 2017.

5. Martin Weinbaum, ed., *The London Eyre of 1276* (London: London Record Society, 1976), 49n179–180; Charles Gross, ed., *Select Cases Concerning the Law Merchant (AD 1270–1638),* Vol. 1, *Local Courts,* Selden Society 23 (London: Bernard Quaritch, 1908), 29–30. Fists are not specifically mentioned in either the deaths of Adam Russel and Bartholomew le Poluter or the beating of Gilbert Shearman, but it seems likely that fists were the instruments of battery since men were forbidden to carry weapons in fairs and since no other weapons were mentioned.

6. Julius Zupitza, ed., *The Romance of Guy of Warwick,* EETS, ES, Vol. 59 (London, 1891), part 3, 528 (Auchinleck MS), c. 9197, lines 4–5; Alison Wiggins, ed., *Stanzaic Guy of Warwick,* TEAMS Middle English Text Series (Kalamazoo, MI: Medieval Institute Publications, 2004), lines 2068–2069.

7. Eugen Kolbing, ed., *The Romance of Sir Beues of Hamtoun,* EETS, ES, Vol. 46 (London, 1885–1894), part 1, p. 84, lines 1615–1616. Herzman, Drake and Salisbury, *Four Romances of England,* 244, lines 1615–1616. We suspect that Sir Bevis's blow was to the side of the neck under the ear, as this would have been both convenient and fatal. We find the same situation in *The Tale of Gamelyn* (c. 1350–1370) where Gamelyn, coming home from a wrestling match where he defeated the champion, finds that a porter tried to keep him out of the castle: "He struck the gate with his foot and broke away the bolt. The porter saw then that it might be no better, and he set his foot on earth and began to flee. 'By my faith,' said Gamelyn, 'that effort is lost, because I am as light of foot as thou even if you swore to the contrary.' He

overtook the porter and avenged his anger, and struck him on the neck, breaking the bone. He took him by one arm and threw him in a well that was seven fathoms deep as I heard tell." Stephen Knight, "The Tale of Gamelyn," in Thomas H. Ohlgren, *Medieval Outlaws: Ten Tales in Modern English* (Phoenix Mills, UK: Sutton Publishing, 1998), part 3, p. 177. Later, Gamelyn hit a crooked justice with his fist and broke his cheekbone. Then throwing him over the bar of the court, broke his arm (part 4, p. 185).

8. A. Stimming, ed., *Der Anglonormannische Boeve de Haumtone*, in *Bibliotheca Normannica*, Vol. 7 (Halle, Germany: Niemeyer, 1899), 42, lines 1065–1066. Killing an opponent with a single blow from a fist was a well-known motif as early as 1135–1160. North, "The Ideal Knight," 111–132.

9. Geoffrey Chaucer, *The Canterbury Tales*, in *The Works of Geoffrey Chaucer*, ed. F.N. Robinson, 2nd ed. (Boston: Houghton-Mifflin, 1957), I (A), 59, lines 4275–76, III (D), 83, lines 790–796.

10. David C. Douglas and George W. Greenway, eds., "The Assize of Arms, 1181," in *English Historical Documents, 1042–1189*, 2nd ed., Vol. 2 (London: Eyre Methuen, 1981), 449–451.

11. "Form for Keeping the Peace, 1242," in Harry Rothwell, ed., *English Historical Documents, 1189–1327*, Vol. 3 (1975) no. 33, 357–359.

12. "Statute of Winchester (1285)," *English Historical Documents, 1189–1327*, ed. Harry Rothwell, Vol. 3 (1975), n. 59, 460–462; William Stubbs, ed., *Select Charters and Other Illustrations of English Constitutional History*, 8th ed. (Oxford: Clarendon, 1905), 456–457. As late as 1503, Henry VII was still forcing people to become knights whether they wished to or no: "All those with L 40 or more per year in land or revenue, in hand or to their use in fee, and not yet knighted, will prepare themselves to assume the order of knighthood." Paul L. Hughes and James F. Larkin, eds., *Tudor Royal Proclamations*, Vol. 1: *Early Tudors (1485–1553)* (New Haven and London: Yale University Press, 1964), n. 53, 59. In 1192, Nigel de Longchamp of Canterbury could complain: "There are many knights without skill and practice in arms, who for that reason are called 'Holy Mary's knights' by the others." Quoted in Peter Coss, *The Knight in Medieval England, 1000–1400* (Phoenix Mill, UK: Alan Sutton, 1993), 44.

13. For the numbers of knights in England, see Coss, *The Knight in Medieval England, 1000–1400*, 27, 70, 82, 134. See also Peter Coss, *The Origins of the English Gentry* (Cambridge: Cambridge University Press, 2003), 69–108, where he modifies in some respects his arguments of 1993. The population estimates were taken from Colin McEvedy and Richard Jones, *Atlas of World Population History* (Hammondsworth, UK: Penguin, 1978), 41–44.

14. George E. Woodbine, ed., *Bracton, De legibus et consuetudinibus Angliae*, trans. Samuel E. Thorne, Vol. 2 (Cambridge, MA: Belknap Press of Harvard University Press, 1968), 32. For examples of the king investing nobles with the sword, see Joel T. Rosenthal, *Nobles and the Noble Life: 1295–1500* (London: George Allen & Unwin, 1976), n. 2 (1337), 105–106.

15. As early as 1381, Richard II issued a proclamation for keeping the peace in London which began with the following admonition: "Be it proclaimed on behalf of our Lord the King, for the safekeeping of the peace, that no one repairing unto the City [of London], after he shall have taken up his lodging there, shall go armed, or shall carry upon him, or have carried after him, a sword, unless he be a knight. And that no one shall go with armour for the body, save only the peers of the realm, and a knight or esquire of the household and retinue of our Lord the King; on pain of forfeiture of such armour, and of imprisonment." Henry Thomas Riley, ed. and trans., *Memorials of London and London Life in the XIIIth, XIVth, and XVth Centuries, being a series of extracts [...] from the Early Archives of the City of London* (London: Longmans, Green, 1868), 453. On November 17, 1413, Nicholas Holand, marshal of the King's Bench, sought to arrest Edmund Stoke for wearing a sword in court. Holand had been instructed by the aforesaid court "to arrest men bearing arms" contrary to the terms of the king's proclamation. This proclamation (1 Henry V) restricted arms to "a lord or a knight [who may have] a sword only in accordance with the degree and estate of each of them." Thus, when Nicholas "found a certain man whom he did not know, wearing a sword, he wished to have

arrested him there." Edmund's servants then assaulted Nicholas and prevented him from arresting Edmund. Gaining reinforcements, Nicholas then arrested Edmund and his servants. Stoke sued Holand for trespass for assaulting and arresting him. It took several years before the issue was finally tried before a jury in Easter 1416, at which time Nicholas defaulted and Edmund was awarded 10 pounds damages. Despite the outcome, the case showed that wearing a sword was forbidden to all but the privileged few by 1413. G.O. Sayles, ed., *Select Cases in the Court of the King's Bench under Richard II, Henry IV and Henry V*, Vol. 7, Selden Society, Vol. 88 (London: Bernard Quaritch, 1971), 229–230. Also, in 1413 Parliament recognized the "gentleman" as a social class with the right to wear the sword. Those below the rank of gentleman were forbidden to carry a sword. See Maurice Keen, *The Origins of the English Gentleman: Heraldry, Chivalry and Gentility in Medieval England (c. 1300–c. 1500)* (Stroud, UK: Tempus, 2002), chapters 6–8.

16. "Form for Keeping the Peace, 1242."

17. "*Statuta Armorum* (The Statutes of Arms)," *Statutes of the Realm*, Vol. 1, (London: Printed by command of His Majesty King George the Third, 1810–1824), 230–231. For dating, see N. Denholm-Young, "The Tournament in the Thirteenth Century," in *Studies in Medieval History Presented to Frederick Maurice Powicke* (Oxford: Clarendon, 1948), 257–263.

18. "Statutes of Northampton (1328)," in *Statutes of the Realm*, Vol. 1, 258. Henry VII issued a proclamation in 1487 prohibiting the carrying of weapons in any town or city of the realm. See "Prohibiting weapons in frays, punishing vagabonds," *3 Henry VII (1487)*, in Hughes and Larkin, *Tudor Royal Proclamations*, Vol. 1, 17.

19. Gross, *Select Cases Concerning the Law Merchant (A.D. 1270–1638)*, Vol. 1, 108.

20. "Statute of Cambridge," c. VI in *Statutes of the Realm*, Vol. 2, 57.

21. "Statutes of the City of London," in *Statutes of the Realm*, Vol. 1, 102. A different version, without a date, is published in Henry Thomas Riley, ed., *Munimenta Gildhalle Londoniensis; Liber Albus, Liber Custumarum, et Liber Horn*, Vol. 1: *Liber Albus*, [Roll Series] *Rerum Britannicarum Medii Aevi Scriptores* (London: Longman, Brown, Green, Longmans, and Roberts, 1859), Vol. 12, n. 1, 275–276 (Norman French); and Vol. 3, *Liber Albus* (London: Longman, Green, Longman, and Roberts, 1862), Vol. 12, n. 3, 93 (English translation). Beginning in 1215, the government of London was placed in the hands of the members of the merchants' guilds. The Guildhall was thus the Town Hall and all local government records were stored in the Guildhall.

22. Riley, *Memorials of London and London Life*, 34–35, 192–193. The Proclamation of 1334 adds "that no person, denizen or stranger, other than officers of the City, and those who have to keep the peace, shall go armed, or shall carry arms, by night or day, within the franchise of the said city, on pain of imprisonment, and of losing arms. Also, it is agreed that whosoever shall draw sword, or knife, or other arm, in affray of the people, shall be forthwith attached [arrested], and shall have imprisonment, without being left to find surety, according to the discretion of the Mayor and of the Aldermen of the City." A.H. Thomas, ed., *Calendar of Plea and Memoranda Rolls ... of the Corporation of the City of London at the Guildhall, Rolls A1a–A9, 1323–1364* (Cambridge: Cambridge University Press, 1926), roll, A1b, 14–17 (Circa November 1326), 18–19 (January 2, 1327), 45 (November 8, 1327); Riley, *Liber Albus*, Vol. 3, 156. This was dated 1364 by H.T. Riley in his introduction to *Liber Albus*, Vol. 1, xlvi. It was reissued May 3, 1376. See Thomas, *Calendar of Plea and Memorandum Rolls of the Corporation of the City of London at the Guildhall, 1364–1381* (Cambridge: Cambridge University Press, 1929), roll A21, 218–219.

23. For the warning to the hostelers, see Thomas, *Calendar of Plea and Memoranda Rolls, 1323–1364*, roll, A4, 154 (August 27, 1342), 163–164 (August 10, 1343) and 156 (December 1343). It was repeated again in 1353. Riley, *Memorials of London and London Life*, 272–273. For the reissued version of 1372, see Riley, *Liber Albus*, Vol. 3, 137. For the case of Adam Grymmesby, see Thomas, *Calendar of Plea and Memorandum Rolls, 1364–1381*, roll A17, 146. Records of other such cases can be found. From this it would appear that by the end of the fourteenth century a ban against the carrying of swords and knives was being enforced in

London against all but the highest nobility and officers of the government.

24. Thomas, *Calendar of Plea and Memorandum Rolls, 1364–1381*, passim. This seems to be confirmed by the *Liber Albus*, in an undated ordinance of the late fourteenth century, which stated that if a man "strike any one with the fist, but have not drawn blood, he is to pay unto the City three shillings, or be imprisoned eight days. And if he draw blood with the fist, he is to pay unto the City forty pence, or be imprisoned for twelve days." A later version amended this to add "and if he strike with the palm, and does not draw blood, two shillings or imprisonment for eight days." Riley, *Liber Albus*, Vol. 3, 157–158, 193, 239.

25. Henry Anstey, ed., *Munimenta Academica, or Documents Illustrative of Academical Life and Studies at Oxford*, part 1, *Libri cancellarii et procuratorum*. Roll Series. *Rerum Britannicarum Medii Aevi Scriptores*, Vol. 50 (London: Longmans, Green, Reader, and Dyer, 1868), 91–92, 304–306. The court of the Chancellor shows two cases of people being fined for fist-fights: part 2 *Acta curiae cancellarii et memoranda ex registris nonnulla*, (1452), 635, (1456), 665.

26. Travers Twiss, ed., *Monumenta Juridica. The Black Book of the Admiralty*. Appendix, Part 2, Roll Series. *Rerum Britannicarum Medii Aevi Scriptores*, Vol. 55 (London: Kraus Reprint, 1965), no. 2, 95.

27. "An Acte for the Mayntenace of Artyllarie and debarring of unlawful Games" (1541–42), *Statutes of the Realm*, Vol. 3, 837–838.

28. Johan Huizinga, *The Waning of the Middle Ages* (Mineola, NY: Dover, 1999 [1924]), 11.

29. James Buchanan Given, *Society and Homicide in Thirteenth-Century England* (Stanford, CA: University Press, 1977), 188–189.

30. "The husbandman, when they till the ground, leave their bucklers and swords, or sometimes their bows, in the corner of the field, so that in this land everybody bears arms." Stephen Perlin, *A Description of England and Scotland* (1558), in James Beeverell, *The Pleasures of London*, trans. and ed. W.H. Quarrell (London: Witherby, 1940), 70. Raphael Holinshed (1586) quoted in J.D. Aylward, *The English Master of Arms from the Twelfth to the Twentieth Century* (London: Routledge & Kegan Paul, 1956), 17.

31. Given, *Society and Homicide in Thirteenth-Century England*, 33–41. Given estimates the murder rate in London during the thirteenth century at 12 per 100,000 persons. He cites statistics of cities in Mexico where the homicide rate from 1928 to 1965 was as high as 300 per 100,000. In 2015 the official Mexican homicide rate was 16.35 per 100,000, but this rate was severely under reported. See Christopher Woody, *Business Insider*, November 1, 2016, http://www.ieyenews.com/wordpress/killings-in-mexico-climbed-to-new-highs-in-2016-and-the-violent-rhythm-may-only-intensify/. The overall homicide rate in 2018 in the United States was about 5.35, while that for England and Wales was 1.22. See United Nations Office on Drugs and Crime, *Global Study on Homicide Report* (Vienna: United Nations Office on Drugs and Crime), https://www.en.wikipedia.org/wiki/List_of_countries_by_intentional_homicide_rate. Seen April 6, 2019. Individual city homicide rates per 100,000 residents from the United States in 2015: New York, 4.1; Los Angeles, 7.1; Dallas 13.0; Houston 13.3; Chicago, 18.1; Washington, D.C., 24.1; Detroit, 42.5; Baltimore, 55.2. See Matthew Friedman, Ames C. Grawert, James Cullen, "Crime in 2016: A Preliminary Analysis" (New York: Brennan Center for Justice, New York University School of Law, 2016), Table 2, 6.

32. Given, *Society and Homicide in Thirteenth-Century England*, 188.

33. Given, *Society and Homicide in Thirteenth-Century England*, 188. Catherine Kappauf, *The Early Development of the Petty Jury* (Ph.D. diss., University of Illinois, 1973) demonstrated statistically that medieval English society was far less violent than many modern industrial societies. Warren C. Brown, *Violence in Medieval Europe* (Harlow, UK: Pearson Education, 2011) follows Johan Huizinga (*Waning of the Middle Ages*) and focuses on northern Europe in the fourteenth century. He believes that Europe was not that much different in the amount of violence from modern western society, but that the type of violence was different.

34. Lawrence Stone, *The Crisis of the Aristocracy, 1558–1641* (OE) original edition (Oxford: Clarendon, 1965), 200 and (AE)

abridged edition (London: Oxford University Press, 1967), 97. This opinion is shared by J.A. Sharpe: "Violence and lawlessness were probably high by modern English standards, but not sufficiently so to constitute a society that was quantitatively different. Certainly the portrayal of early modern society (and, in all probability, late medieval) England as a brutal society, where life was cheap and might be easily taken, is vastly overdrawn." J.A. Sharpe, *Crime in Early Modern England 1550–1750* (London and New York: Longman, 1984), 175.

35. The poverty of the murderers suggests that knives may not have been available and the weapons used may have been very primitive. In only 455 cases (18.7%) were any weapons described. Of these 40 cases (8.8%) death was caused by the use of bare hands. Of the rest, 136 people (29.9%) died of knife wounds, 100 by blows from sticks, 64 by axe blows, 15 were hit by stones, 7 by forks, 4 by scythes, 2 by spades, one by a mattock, one by a trivet, one by a stool and one by a piece of firewood. For comparison, the FBI reports in the United States for 2003 show that out of a total of 14,408 homicides, 946 (6.6%) were the result of beatings with hands, fists or feet while 12,105 (84%) were committed with weapons of some kind: guns, knives or blunt objects. The fact that in 40 cases (8.8%) death was caused by the use of bare hands shows that fists were already being used in place of other weapons in the thirteenth century. Given does not mention swords, but in my own review of 156 cases (n. 37 to n. 193) of the London Eyre of 1244, I found swords used in only three deaths. See Helen Chew and Martin Weinbaum, eds., *The London Eyre of 1244* (London: London Record Society, 1970), nos. 83, 108,156. Given believed that one reason swords do not appear frequently in these records is that the wealthy, who owned swords, tended to avoid non-institutionalized violence. Given, *Society and Homicide in Thirteenth-Century England*, 189. However, Gregory Durston, *Crime and Justice in Early Modern England: 1500–1750* (Chichester, UK: Barry Rose Law Publishers, 2004), 54–61, pointed out that the upper classes who used swords were routinely given immunity from prosecution, and this is why they did not often appear in the court records.

36. F.O. Grew et al., "Introduction," *Medieval Finds from Excavations in London*, 1: *Knives and Scabbards*, ed. J. Cowgill, M. de Neergaard and N. Griffiths (Rochester, NY: Boydell, 2011 [1987]), xi–xiii. Grew et al. reject the idea that the scabbards were not found simply due to their deterioration: "This change is not related to poorer preservation of leather in the later deposits."

37. Margrethe de Neergaard, "The Use of Knives, Shears, Scissors and Scabbards," in *Medieval Finds from Excavations in London*, 1: *Knives and Scabbards*, ed. J. Cowgill, M. de Neergaard and N. Griffiths (Rochester, NY: Boydell, 2011 [1987]), 51–61, quote on 51.

38. Horman, *Vulgaria*, ff. 132r–138r.

39. Backing up was still considered cowardly by sword-fighters in 1599. In his first book of his practice, Vincentio Saviolo has his student Luke announce: "In deede, it is accounted disgracefull to giue ground, because therein a man seemeth to feare his enemie." Vincentio Saviolo, *Vincentio Saviolo, His Practice. In Two Bookes* (London, 1595), in *Three Elizabethan Fencing Manuals*, intro. and ed. James L. Jackson (Delmar, NY: Scholars Facsimiles & Reprints, 1972), Book 1, 254. This belief had a strong influence on fist-fighting at the time. See also George Silver, "A Briefe Note of Three Italian Teachers of Offence," in Jackson, *Three Elizabethan Fencing Manuals* (Delmar, NY: Scholars Facsimiles & Reprints, 1972), 562–570.

40. Swanton, "*Gesta Herewardi* (The Deeds of Hereward)," 23.

41. Simpson and Weiner, *The Oxford English Dictionary*, Vol. 2, 464, "box, sb 3."

42. Kolbing, *The Romance of Sir Beues of Hamtoun*, parts. 1–3, Vols. 46, 48, 65, part 1, pp. 88–90, lines 1721–1784; Herzman, Drake and Salisbury, *Four Romances of England*, 246–248, lines 1740–1780.

43. Valerie Krishna, ed., *The Alliterative Morte Arthure: A Critical Edition* (New York: Burt Franklin, 1976), 71, lines 1109–1111. I am indebted to Terry Brown, Master of Defence and scholar of English martial arts, for this citation.

44. J. Ernst Wulfing, ed., *The Laud Troy Book* (London: Early English Text Society [EETS], Kegan Paul, Trench, Tubner & Co. Ltd., 1902 [c. 1400]), part 1, lines 6715–6720.

45. Kurath and Kuhn, *Middle English*

Dictionary, 1102, "box n. (3)."

46. A.L. Mayhew, ed., *The Promptorium Parvulorum. The First English-Latin Dictionary, c A.D. 1440.*, EETS, ES (London, 1908), n. 102.

47. Horman, *Vulgaria*, 137, para 17. Erasmus says that boys knew about boxing as early as his colloquy on Sport (March 1522), but their knowledge came from Vergil's *Aeneid*, and not necessarily from their own practice. Horman tells us that his boys were actually fist-fighting, not just reading about it. Desiderius Erasmus, *The Colloquies of Erasmus*, trans. Craig R. Thompson (Chicago and London: University of Chicago Press, 1965), 29. We can't be sure that fist-fighting had been recognized as boxing in England until at least 1550.

48. John Baret, *An Alvearie or Triple Dictionarie* (London: Henry Denham, 1574), B ante O, between 993 and 994. Under B ante U at 1374, Baret also gives "to boxe or buffet." John Studley, *The fourth and most ruthful tragedy of L. Annaeus Seneca entituled Hyppolytus* (London: Thomas Marsh, 1581), Act II, scene i, 64 b.

49. G. Blakemore Evans and J.J.M. Tobin, eds., *The Riverside Shakespeare*, 2nd ed. (Boston and New York: Houghton-Mifflin, 1997). Shakespeare used the phrase again in the *Merchant of Venice* (1596–1597) (Act I, scene ii, lines 79–81); in *Henry IV*, part 2 (1598) (Act I, scene ii, lines 194–197); and in *Measure for Measure* (1604) (Act II, scene i, lines 180–181).

50. Godfrey, *A Treatise upon the Useful Science of Defence*, 51, was well aware of the power of a boxing blow under the ear: "I look upon the Blow under the Ear to be as dangerous as any, that is, if it light between the Angle of the lower Jaw and the Neck; because in this Part there are two Kinds of Blood Vessels considerably large; the one brings the Blood immediately from the Heart to the Head, whilst the other carries it immediately back. If a Man receive a Blow upon these Vessels, the Blood proceeding from the Heart to the Head, is partly forced back, whilst the other Part is pushed forward vehemently to the Head: The same happens in the Blood returning from the Head to the Heart, for the part of it is precipitately forced into the latter, whilst the other Part tumultuously rushes to the head: whereby the Blood Vessels are immediately overcharged, and the Sinuses of the Brain so overloaded and compressed, that the Man at once loses all Sensation, and the Blood often runs from his Ears, Mouth, and Nose, altogether owing its Quantity forced with such Impetuosity into the smaller Vessels, the Coats whereof being too tender to resist so great a Charge, instantly break, and cause the Effusion of blood through these different parts." See also Kaplan and Browder, *J. Am. Med. Ass.* (1954) 156:1139–1144, quoted in Friedrich Unterharnscheidt and Julia Taylor-Unterharnscheidt, *Boxing: Medical Aspects* (Amsterdam: Academic Press, 2003), 62. See also the discussion of the effect of blows to the Carotid Sinus, which lies just under the ear. A solid blow to that area can easily lead to knock outs (242–249).

51. Kurath and Kuhn, *Middle English Dictionary*, "buffet n. 2"; Mayhew, *The Promptorium Parvulorum*, n. 102.

52. John Palsgrave, *Lesclarcissment de la langue francoyse par Jean Palsgrave, suivi de la grammaire de Giles du Guez, publies pour la premiere fois en France*, ed. F. Genin in *Collection de documents inedits sur l'histoire de France, Deuxieme serie. Histoire des lettres et des sciences* (Paris: Imprimerie nationale, 1852). *The Thirde Boke* "The Table of Substantives." 201, col. 2; 205, col. 2; B before O, 459, col. 2. Note that Palsgrave's tables or glossaries have been excluded from the most recent edition John Palsgrave, *L'eclarissement de la langue francaise (1530)*, ed. Susan Baddeley, *Textes de la Renaissance: Serie Traites sur la langue francaise*, no. 69 (Paris: Honore Champion, 2003).

53. Edmund Spenser, *The Fairie Queen*, Book 1, ed. George Armstrong Wauchope (New York: Macmillan, 1922), 37.

54. For cuff and pommel, see Palsgrave, *Lesclarcissment de la langue*, 502, col.2, 662, col.1. For pommel, see A.J. Greimas, *Dictionnaire de l'ancien francais jusqu'au milieu du XIVe siecle* (Paris: Librarie Larousse, 1968), "pom"; Alain Rey, *Dictionnaire historique de la langue francaise* (Paris: Dictionnaire Le Robert, 1993), "pommeau"; A. Hindley, F.W. Langley, B. Levy, *Old French–English Dictionary* (Cambridge: Cambridge University Press, 2000), "pom" and "pomel." On June 5, 1233 Roger de Rysingges, a clerk, and Moses, his servant, invaded the home of Gilbert the

Marshall. Roger struck Maud, Gilbert's wife, with a hammer and his servant Moses struck her in the face with the hilt of his sword (*Moyses eam helta gladii sui in facie sua*). Chew and Weinbaum, *The London Eyre of 1244*, no. 83, 34–35. Terry Brown informs me that this strategy of hitting one's opponent with the pommel of the sword was well-known and used in early modern fighting. See the examples in Brown, *English Martial Arts*, 129, fig. d, 136, fig. d. However, I have not found the verb *to pommel*, meaning to hit with a pommel or a fist, used in France at this time. The verb, if not the technique, may be an English invention.

55. Edward Hall "The Triumphant Reigne of Kyng Henry the VIII," in [Edward Hall], *The Vnion of the Two Noble and Illustre Famelies of Lancastre & Yorke* [...] *Beginning at the Tyme of Kyng Henry the Fowerth, the first aucthor of this deuision, and so successiuely proceadyng to the reigne of the high and prudent prince Kyng Henry the Eight, the vndubiate flower and very heire of both the said linages* (London, 1548). Otherwise known as *Hall's Chronicle* (London: Printed for J. Johnson et alia, 1809), 572.

56. Peter Levin, *Manipulus Vocabulorum: A Rhyming Dictionary of the English Language*, ed. Henry B. Wheatley (London: Early English Text Society, 1867 [1570]), Vol. 27, 264; col. 93, line 35.

57. Norbert Elias, "An Essay on Sport and Violence," in Norbert Elias and Eric Dunning, *The Collected Works of Norbert Elias*, Vol 7: *Quest for Excitement: Sport and Leisure in the Civilizing Process*, ed. Eric Dunning (Dublin: University College Dublin Press, 2008 [Oxford: Basil Blackwell, 1986]), 154–155.

58. William Fitz Stephen, *Norman London* (New York: Italica Press, 1990), 56.

59. For the discussion of wrestling around Smithfield and the Priory of Clerkenwell from 1300 on, see W.O. Hassall, "Plays at Clerkenwell," *Modern Language Review* 33, no. 4 (October 1938): 564–567. R.A. Donkin, "Changes in the Early Middle Ages," in *A New Historical Geography of England*, ed. H.C. Darby (Cambridge: Cambridge University Press, 1973), 75–135. London drew a large number of immigrants from all parts of England as well as other countries. Donkin cites E. Ekwall, *Studies on the Population of Medieval London* (Stockholm, 1956) as finding 7,000 people living in London with place names from outside the city during the period 1270–1350. This confirms the concern of Edward I about the influx of foreigners.

60. Elias, "An Essay on Sport and Violence," 155. Charles Homer Haskins, *The Renaissance of the Twelfth Century* (Cleveland and New York: World Publishing Company, 1967 [1927]), lays the foundation for Elias's comments when he notes that in the twelfth century (when Fitz Stephen was writing) the centers of cultural activity were isolated: "Men of education were concentrated in certain definite groups separated one from another by wide stretches of rural ignorance" (32). A center for sport like Smithfield was both unique and isolated. As such it was likely to draw interested people from many distant lands.

61. Elias, "An Essay on Sport and Violence," 164.

62. Thomas Fuller, *The History of the Worthies of England*, new ed. by P. Austin Nuttall, Vol. 2 (London: Thomas Tegg, 1840 [1662]), 347; Thomas Churchyard, *Churchyards Challenge: A Discourse of True Manhood* (London: John Wolfe, 1593), 60.

63. "Outside the professions, French seems to have been generally known to governmental officials and the more substantial burgesses in the towns. It was the language of parliament and local administration. The business of town councils and the guilds seems to have been ordinarily transacted in French, although there are scattered instances of the intrusion of English ... [but] French can have had little currency among the middle classes outside of the towns." Baugh and Cable, *A History of the English Language*, 147.

64. "A brawl: A noisy, turbulent quarrel, a row, a squabble." See Simpson and Weiner, *The Oxford English Dictionary*, Vol. 2, 498.

65. Johan Huizinga, *Homo Ludens* (New York: Roy, 1950), 10. Modern boxers feel very protective about the ring. As one boxer notes: "Right now, the ring is what make Willie M-be Willie M-. I feel at home in the ring. I feel like this is *my* environment, this is where it's me." After reporting this, the analyst notes: "Boxers feel that, by stepping into the squared circle, they can achieve

something inaccessible or forbidden to them outside." Loic J.D. Wacquant, "The Pugilistic Point of View: How Boxers Think and Feel about Their Trade," *Theory and Society* 24, no. 4 (August 1995), 489–535, on 510.

66. For the London Prize Ring Rules of 1838 see Dowling, *Fistiana*, 63–66. Alternatively, see http://boxrec.com/media/index.php/London_Prize_Ring_Rules.

67. Elias Canetti, *Crowds and Power* (New York: Viking, 1966 [1960]), 29.

Chapter IV

1. Richard Underwood, *Anglo-Saxon Weapons and Warfare* (Stroud, UK: Tempus, 1999); Davidson, *The Sword in Anglo-Saxon England*, 36–42. See also Herbert Schmidt, *The Book of the Buckler* ([Derby?], UK: Wyvern Media, 2015), for an analysis of the science of the buckler.

2. Ranulf Glanvill (c. 1130–1190) preferred the trial by jury to the trial by battle, which he considered time consuming, dangerous and doubtful: "Fewer essoins [delays for cause] are allowed in the assize [the trial by jury] than in battle, as will appear below, and so people generally are saved trouble and the poor are saved money." G.D.G. Hall, ed., *The Treatise on the Laws and Customs of the Realm of England Commonly Called Glanvill* (Holmes Beach, FL: Wm. W. Gaunt and Sons, 1983 [1965]), II, 7, 28.

3. Aylward, *The English Master of Arms*, 10, citing *Pipe Roll of 11 Henry II* = 1165. I consulted the *The Great Roll of the Pipe for the Eleventh Year of the Reign of King Henry the Second (A.D. 1164–1165)* (London: Publications of the Pipe Roll Society, 1887), for Norfolk and Suffolk, and was not able to discover Wilelmus Pugilius.

4. For Thomas and Lawrence Pugil see M.J. Russell, "Hired Champions," *American Journal of Legal History* 3, no. 3 (July 1959): 242–259, on 253; For the seal of a miller known as Bernardus Pugilis (c. 1190) see the article by William Brown, "Trial by Combat," *Yorkshire Archaeological Journal* 23 (1914): 300–307. A brief search of the records in the archives of Warwickshire reveals the names of Hugh "Pugil," Gilbert "Pugillatore," three gifts with warranty by John, son of Robert "pugillis" of Turlast to Adam Wagestaft, a Simon "pugillo," and a Richard "pugillo," all in the thirteenth century. John, son of Robert pugillis, was clearly a wealthy man, showing that not all pugils met an unpleasant end. The fact that all of these pugils appeared in land deeds shows that they had not been barred from legal status. See http://archivesunlocked.warwickshire.gov.uk.

5. See V.H. Galbraith, "The Death of a Champion (1287)," in *Studies in Medieval History Presented to Frederick Maurice Powicke* (Oxford: Clarendon, 1948), 286n2, 293, Appendix I.

6. Henry C. Lea, *Superstition and Force* (New York: Greenwood, 1968 [1892]), 142. See also Henry C. Lea, *The Duel and the Oath* (Philadelphia: University of Pennsylvania Press, 1974 [1866]), 186. Although we have not found any *pugil* actually boxing during this early era, we do have the picture of an English fencer (Versez) wrestling in a French tavern in the period 1214–1215. See Madelyn Timmel Mihm, ed., *The Songe d'Enfer of Raoul de Houdenc: An Edition Based on all the Extant Manuscripts* (Tübingen, Germany: Max Niemeyer, 1984). This gives support to our belief that the same people could be both wrestlers and fencers in the period from 1100 to 1400. And if both wrestlers and fencers, we can assume they also could be boxers and fencers.

7. Charlton T. Lewis and Charles Short, *A Latin Dictionary* (Oxford: Clarendon, 1962 [1879]), "pugil, pugilis m."; P.G.W. Glare, ed., *Oxford Latin Dictionary*, (Oxford: Clarendon, 1982), "pugil, pugilis m."; *Dictionary of Medieval Latin from British Sources*, Vol. 13 (Oxford: Oxford University Press, 2010), "pugil."

8. Thomas Browne, "Enquiries into Vulgar and Common Errors," *Pseudodoxia Epidemica*, ed. Geoffrey Keynes (Chicago: University of Chicago Press, 1964), Book 4, c. II, 305. For an illustration of a *pugil* actually fist-fighting, see Appendix IV, fig. 1, from Hieronymi Mercvrialis, *De Arte Gymnastica, Libri Sex* (Venice: Apud Ivntas, 1601), Book 2, 112.

9. Russell, "Hired Champions," 253. Neilson, *Trial by Combat*, 69 notes as well that "'Champion' was now [last half of the 1200s] becoming, indeed had already become, a well-known surname."

10. Barbara A. Hanawalt, *Crime and Con-

flict in English Communities, 1300–1348 (Cambridge, MA: Harvard University Press, 1979), 127. This feminist viewpoint ignores other aspects that may have led to crime such as lack of gainful employment, local warfare and other social conditions that deprived young men of a place in society. But ignoring the deeper issues, it is true that having a large number of idle people, men or women, in a society can indeed lead to more crime.

11. Frederic W. Maitland, ed., *Select Pleas of the Crown*, Vol. 1: *AD 1200–1225*, Selden Society 192 (London: Bernard Quaritch, 1888), 123–127. Neilson, *Trial by Combat*, 52 mentions another Pigun, William Pygun in 1237, who is described as a "magnus pugil." From this we can deduce that Pigun was a corruption of Pugil. Neilson then notes: "The Piguns were a large and fighting family." Russell, "Hired Champions," 253, suggests that "piggun" was derived from "pigo" meaning fierce. He lists John Piggun (1205), Ralph Piggun (1207), Hugh Piggun (1219) and Elias Piggun (1220), all champions in disputes.

12. Lea, *Superstition and Force*, 141; Lea, *The Duel and the Oath*, 185.

13. Castle, *Schools and Masters of Fencing*, 16. The same view was held by Craig Turner and Tony Soper, *Method and Practice of Elizabethan Swordplay* (Carbondale: Southern Illinois University Press, 1990), 3.

14. Aylward, *The English Master of Arms*, 254.

15. Castle, *Schools and Masters of Fencing*, 16–17.

16. Castle, *Schools and Masters of Fencing*, 17. Aylward, *The English Master of Arms*, 9. According to Aylward, Master Roger was well known to the Lord Mayor. He had been involved in a brawl in 1300 in which another devotee of fencing, Walter le Chapelain, was killed. Roger had fled from punishment at that time but had later returned to London. Thus, when he was arrested in 1311, he was summarily put into jail and was lost to history.

17. For an overall view of medieval fairs and the role the criminal classes played in them, see Salgado, *The Elizabethan Underworld*, 55–72. See also Henry Morley, *Memoirs of Bartholomew's Fair* (Detroit, Michigan: Singing Tree, 1968 [London: Chatto and Windus, 1880]).

18. Lea, *The Duel and the Oath*, 187.

19. Given, *Society and Homicide in Thirteenth-Century England*, 122–124.

20. Given, *Society and Homicide in Thirteenth-Century England*, 125.

21. M.T. Clanchy, "Highway Robbery and Trial by Battle in the Hampshire Eyre of 1249," *Medieval Legal Records edited in Memory of C.A.F. Meekings* (London: Her Majesty's Stationery Office, 1978), 26–61.

22. John Bellamy, *Crime and Public Order in England in the Later Middle Ages* (London: Routledge & Kegan Paul, 1973), 54–58.

23. Stone, *The Crisis of the Aristocracy* OE, 229–230, AE, 111.

24. Stone, *The Crisis of the Aristocracy*, OE, 227, AE 109.

25. Bellamy, *Crime and Public Order in England*, 69–73.

26. Bellamy, *Crime and Public Order in England*, 72.

27. Neilson, *Trial by Combat*, 52–54; Robert Bartlett, *Trial by Fire and Water: The Medieval Judicial Ordeal* (Oxford: Clarendon, 1986), 112. Neilson, *Trial by Combat*, 51, gives this man's name as Thomas of Brydges.

28. Bellamy, *Crime and Public Order in England*, 74.

29. Given, *Society and Homicide in Thirteenth-Century England*, 106–133, quote on 111.

30. "A Ruffian is the same as a swaggerer, so called because endeavouring to make that side to swag or weigh down whereupon he engageth. The same with swash-buckler, from swashing, or making a noise on bucklers. West Smithfield (now the horse-market) was formerly called Ruffian's-hall, where such men met casually and otherwise, to try masteries with sword and buckler. More frightened than hurt, hurt than killed, therewith, it being accounted unmanly to strike beneath the knee, because in effect it was one armed against a naked man. But since that desperate traitor Rowland Yorke first used thrusting with rapiers, swords and bucklers are disused and the proverb only applicable to quarrelsome people (not tame but wild barreters) who delight in brawls and blows."

31. Fuller, *The History of the Worthies of England*, Vol. 2, 347.

32. For Yorke, see Sarah Clayton, "Yorke, Rowland (d. 1588)," *Oxford Dictionary of*

National Biography, Vol. 60 (Oxford: Oxford University Press, 2004), 855–856.

In contrast to Fuller's explanation, Herbert Schmidt suggests that the term "swashbuckler" arises from the fact that the buckler was carried by a loop of leather so that it hung in front of the scabbard slightly below the hilt of the sword. As a result, it swung back and forth when the swordsman was walking and knocked against the scabbard creating a noise, making a sound which reminded people of running water (swash), thus giving rise to the term "swashbuckler." Schmidt, *The Book of the Buckler*, 80.

33. Terry Brown, personal correspondence, October 14, 2018. See also Turner and Soper, *Method and Practice of Elizabethan Swordplay*, 45–46; Giacomo Di Grassi, *Art of Defence*, trans. L.G. Gentleman (London: Temple Barre at the Signe of the Hand and Starre, 1594 [1570]), 82–90.

34. "William Gregory's Chronicle of London," in James Gairdner, ed., *The Historical Collections of a Citizen of London in the Fifteenth Century* (London: Camden Society, 1876), s.2, Vol. 17, 199–202. See also Neilson, *Trial by Combat*, 154–158. Maitland and Montague suggest that the ram's horn staves and the pick axes of the earlier fight represent a sacral holdover "ever since an age which knew not iron." Such a suggestion takes us back into truly ancient history. Frederic W. Maitland and Francis C. Montague, *A Sketch of English Legal History*, ed. with notes by James F. Colby (New York and London: G.P. Putnam's and Sons, 1915), 50.

35. Equality of weapons was common to judicial duels throughout Europe. Lea, *The Duel and the Oath*, 176–177.

36. "William Gregory's Chronicle of London," 199–202.

37. For Lancashire wrestling, see "Wrestling," *The Victoria History of the Countries of England: Lancashire*, Vol. 2 (London: Institute of Historical Research, University of London, 1966 [1908]), 499–500. See also Walter Armstrong, "The Lancashire Style (Catch as Catch Can)," in *The Encyclopedia of Sport*, Vol. 2, ed. Earl of Suffolk and Berkshire, Hedley Peek, and F.G. Aflalo (London: Lawrence and Bullen, 1898), 548. For the United States see Elliott J. Gorn, "'Gouge and Bite, Pull Hair and Scratch': The Social Significance of Fighting in the Southern Backcountry," *American Historical Review* 90, no.1 (February 1985): 18–43. Gorn notes that the governor of North Carolina referred to these battles as "boxing" when seeking to outlaw them in 1746.

38. The term "lists" describes an encircling palisade or a railed enclosure. This had been handed down from the joust and was adopted by the trial by battle, then by wrestling matches and finally by boxing matches. This was critical to prevent interference by the crowd. See Simpson and Weiner, *The Oxford English Dictionary*, "List II, Boundary, 9a, b and 10a." Breaching the lists could be punished by death. Neilson, *Trial by Combat*, 296, describes a judicial duel in 1548 in which the combatants fought in a market place in a list 40 feet long and 30 feet wide. After they had taken an oath that their cause was just, a proclamation was made prohibiting "under pain of death, all persons from entering within the rails surrounding the place of battle." See also "On pain of death, no person be so bold/ Or daring-hardy as to touch the lists/ Except the marshal and such officers/ Appointed to direct these fair designs." William Shakespeare, *Richard II*, Act I, scene iii.

39. Joseph Strutt, who compiled the encyclopedic *The Sports and Pastimes of the English People*, ed. and enlarged by J. Charles Cox (London: Methuen, 1903 [1801]), did not mention boxing at all in his book. Boxing was clearly a popular sport at the time he wrote, yet it did not achieve a single reference. Strutt's reluctance to include boxing is curious but it may illustrate the middle-class abhorrence of the sport.

40. Captain Godfrey, who knew John Broughton (1704–1789) personally, describes how Broughton was able to win his fights by guarding himself from blows while defeating his opponents. Godfrey described how a right-handed man turned his left side to his adversary and used his left arm as kind of a buckler to ward off blows. This was the key to Broughton's strategy. See Godfrey, *A Treatise upon the Useful Science of Defence*, 48. He then describes how "Broughton steps bold and firmly in, bids a Welcome to the coming blow; receives it with his guarding arm; then with a general Summons of his swelling Muscles, and his firm Body, seconding his Arm, and supplying it with all

its Weight, pours the Pile-driving Force upon his Man" (56). Pierce Egan, who did not know John Broughton and was writing in 1811, analyzed the changes Broughton brought to boxing: "Previous to the days of Broughton it [boxing] was downright *slaughtering*—or, in the modern acceptation, either *gluttony* [willingness to accept massive punishment], *strength*, or *bottom* [courage], decided almost every contest. But after Broughton appeared as a professor of the gymnastic art, he drew crowds after him to witness his exhibitions; there was a *neatness* about his method completely new and unknown to his auditors— he stopped the blows aimed at any part of him by his antagonist with so much skill, and *hit* his man away with so much ease, that he astonished and terrified his opponents beyond measure; and those persons who had the temerity to enter the lists with Broughton were soon convinced of his superior knowledge and athletic prowess: and most of his competitors[,] who were compelled to *give in*, from their exhausted and beaten state, had the mortification to behold Broughton scarcely touched, and to appear with such cheerfulness and indifference as if he had never been engaged in a *set-to*." Pierce Egan, *Boxiana* (Vol. 1), *or Sketches of Ancient and Modern Pugilism, from the Days of the Renowned Broughton and Slack to the Championship of Cribb* (Brighton, MA: Elibron Classics, 2006 [1811–1830]), 16–17.

41. Stone, *The Crisis of the Aristocracy*, OE, 225, AE, 109.

42. Sir John was reputed to be the illegitimate son of Henry VIII. According to Smeeton "in stature and high spirit he bore a strong resemblance to that monarch." He was knighted in 1547 and appointed by Queen Elizabeth I, Lord Deputy of Ireland (1584–1588). According to Alfred Webb, writing in the *Compendium of Irish Biography* (1878) "Sir John Perrot was a man in stature very tall and big ... almost equal to the mightiest men that lived in his time.... He was by nature very cholorcke, and could not brook any crosses or dissemble the least injuries." This attitude would be consistent with that of a *pugil* and might easily have led to the first boxing match. Perrot would have been 23 in 1550, about the time we believe that boxing made its first named public appearance. Although we do not know where Smeeton got this information, nonetheless, John Perrot might indeed have been the first named boxer in England.

43. George Silver, *Paradoxes of Defence* (London: Edward Blount, 1599). Reprinted in *Three Elizabethan Fencing Manuals*, ed. and intro James J. Jackson (Delmar, NY: Scholars Facsimiles and Reprints, 1972); Silver, "A Briefe Note," 64, reprinted in *Three Elizabethan Fencing Manuals*, ed. and intro James J. Jackson (Delmar, NY: Scholars Facsimiles and Reprints, 1972), 562.

44. Silver, "A Briefe Note," 66 (Jackson edition, 564).

45. M. [Henri] Misson, *Memoirs and Observations in his Travels over England with some account of Scotland and Ireland*, trans. Mr. Ozell (London: D. Brown, etc., 1719), 306.

46. Silver, "A Briefe Note," 68–69 (Jackson edition, 566–567).

47. [Richard Harvey], *Plaine Percevall the Peace-Maker of England, Sweetly Indevoring with his blunt persuasions to botch vp a Reconciliation between Mar-Ton and Mar-tother* ([London]: Printed in Broad-Streete at the signe of the Pack-staffe, [1590]), 12.

48. [Harvey], *Plaine Percevall*, 12. Tim Ruzicki, a practitioner of bare-knuckle boxing and trainer of bare-knuckle boxers, tells me that modern bare-knuckle fighters still hit walls to build up bone density in their fists before bouts. Tim Ruzicki, "From Bare-Knuckles to Modern Boxing: How Gloves Have Changed the Art of Pugilism," https://www.bullshido.net/forums/showthread.php?t=49452&s=479e3d718cef8b9993e93669fb86b7c9. See also Tim Ruzicki, personal correspondence, December 20, 2006. Monte Cox, the boxing historian, has drawn my attention to "Wolff's Law," https://www.en.wikipedia.org/wiki/Wolff%27s_law, which states that bone density increases when it is regularly stressed. Monte Cox, personal correspondence, February 2, 2015. Jack Dempsey notes there are no referees in fist-fights: "You don't win a fist-fight on points." He concludes with the critical advice: "You've got to knock 'em out in fist-fights." Dempsey, *Championship Fighting*, 20–23.

49. Just recently (February 2018) a pair of boxing gloves dating from Roman times was uncovered at Vindolandia at Hadrian's Wall in England. These apparently were designed as practice gloves for *caestus* fighting.

"Roman Boxing Gloves," http://archaeology.org/news/6389-180220-roman-boxing-gloves. The first modern boxing gloves (mufflers) were introduced by Jack Broughton in 1743, but they too were only designed for training exercises. They began to be required in boxing matches by the Marquess of Queensberry rules of 1867. For the boxer's fracture, see Linda Altizer, "Boxer's Fracture," *Orthopedic Nursing* 25, no. 4 (July–August 2006): 271–273, and Manuel Hernandez et al., "Boxer's Fracture," http://www.emedicinehealth.com/boxers_fracture/page2_em.htm. Seen 1/26/2017. The adoption of gloves was designed to protect the boxer's hands, not to lessen the impact of his blows. Unterharnscheidt and TaylorUnterharnscheidt, *Boxing*, 206–211. Another way to protect one's hands when fighting bareknuckle was to turn the fist so it hit on the diagonal. In this way, the knuckles were aligned and hit with force. If one hits with the fist vertically aligned or horizontally aligned to the target, the weakest knuckles tend to take the hardest blow and perhaps break.

50. John Ford, *Prizefighting: The Age of Regency Boximania* (Newton Abbot, UK: David and Charles, 1971), 46; Tony Gee, *Up to Scratch: Bareknuckle Fighting and Heroes of the Prize-Ring* (Mackerye End, UK: Queen Anne, 2001 [1998]) 45–46. See also the *London Journal*, January 16, 1725 (4) where "a great body of Butchers" wished to bet on a boxing match.

51. Two men standing toe-to-toe to fight without backing up was a classic strategy. See Spenser, *The Fairie Queen*, Book 1, canto 2, stanza 17, 37.

52. Richard Carew of Antony, *The Survey of Cornwall*, ed. F.E. Halliday (London: Andrew Melrose, 1953 [1602]), 150. Michael Drayton, the poet of "The Poly-Olbion" (1613) said similar things about Cornish wrestling:

Or by the girdles grasp'd, they practice with the hip
The forward, backward, falx, the mare, the turn, the trip,
When stript into their shirts, each other they invade
Within a spacious ring by the beholders made,
According to the law [quoted in *The Survey of Cornwall*, 44].

53. Carew, *The Survey of Cornwall*, 197.

Joseph Strutt quotes Robert Heath, *A Natural and Historical Account of the Islands of Scilly* [...] *and a General Account of Cornwall* (London: R. Manby and H.S. Cox, 1750), as describing a carnival held every July on Halgavor Moor "resorted to by thousands of people." Strutt, *The Sports and Pastimes of the English People*, 22.

54. "Crime and Disorder in the Localities, Edward Hext to Lord Burghley, Reporting on Somerset, 25 September 1596," in *English Historical Documents (1558–1603)*, ed. Ian W. Archer and F. Douglas Price, Vol. 5A (London and New York: Routledge, 2011), 1125.

55. Gamini Salgado, *The Elizabethan Underworld* (London: J.M. Dent & Sons, 1977), 134. Salgado goes on to say that by the time of Edward VI (1547–1553) there were 20,000 alehouses in England and by 1625 there were 33,000. Mark Hailwood, *Alehouses and Good Fellowship in Early Modern England* (Woodbridge, UK: Boydell, 2014), 3–4, believes there were around 24,000 alehouses in 1577, or 1 alehouse for every 142 inhabitants in England, and by 1630 there were around 50,000. By 1700 the ratio was closer to 1 alehouse to 87 people. Alehouses also had a reputation of being the deposit banks of the criminal class and equally the home of those who sold stolen property. Inns catered to a higher class of clientele than alehouses. Nonetheless, an innkeeper might find the excitement generated by a boxing match helpful to business. However, I have not been able to find any example of boxing at an inn yard in my research, despite the suggestion of Derek Birley, *Sport and the Making of Britain* (Manchester and New York: Manchester University Press, 1993), 117.

56. There can be a considerable gap of time between the beginning of an activity and its recognition in print. Recent attempts to trace the origins of the Robin Hood myth now suggest it began with a fugitive "Robert Hod" who appeared in the pipe rolls of York between 1225 and 1234 as an "outlaw and evildoer of our land." If this link is accurate, it took nearly 140 years before the myth was first recognized as the "rymes of Robyn hood" in *Piers Plowman* circa 1370. And it took an additional 150 years before we actually find the "rymes" themselves in written form. This means that nearly 300 years separated the

historical figure from the literary legend. R.B. Dobson and J. Taylor speculate that this was due to the fact that although the Robin Hood myth was widely known in oral form, it was associated with the lower classes and thus not fit for literary presentation. It seems possible that a similar period of time may have elapsed between the beginning of boxing and its first recognition in literary sources, and for the same reasons. See the comments of R.B. Dobson and J. Taylor, *Rymes of Robyn Hood: An Introduction to the English Outlaw*, rev. ed. (Phoenix Mill, UK: Alan Sutton, 1997), xxxii–xxxvi, 1–36. In another case, Kenneth H. Jackson, *The Oldest Irish Tradition: A Window on the Iron Age* (Cambridge: Cambridge University Press, 1964), 53–54 argued that the Ulster sagas of Cuchulainn took about 300 years to transition from oral to written form. Finally, Norbert Elias suggests that, with the unique exception of basketball, it takes many generations between the time a pastime is begun and a sport is born. Elias, "An Essay on Sport and Violence," 155.

57. Thomas More, *Utopia*, trans. and ed. H.V.S. Ogden (New York: Appleton-Century-Crofts, 1949 [1516]), Book 1, 7–9. See also Frank Aydelotte, *Elizabethan Rogues and Vagabonds*, Oxford Historical and Literary Studies, Vol. 1 (Oxford: Clarendon, 1913); A.V. Judges, *The Elizabethan Underworld* (New York: E.P. Dutton, 1930); and Salgado, *Cony-Catchers and Bawdy Baskets*.

58. Thomas Harman, *A Caveat or Warning for Common Cursitors Vulgarly Called Vagabonds* (1566), reprinted in Salgado, *Cony-Catchers and Bawdy Baskets*, 89–95. Harman notes only one fist-fight in which an Upright Man (an aristocrat of the vagabonds) beats an Ostler (a man who takes care of horses and mules) who insulted his doxie (female companion), 125.

Chapter V

1. As we shall see in chapter VI the aristocracy never did personally take up boxing in a professional manner. Yet by the end of the seventeenth century they did willingly adopt Marc Antony's strategy of fighting rogues in the street to settle a quarrel.

2. Stone, *The Crisis of the Aristocracy*, OE, 232. This quotation was deleted from the abridged edition.

3. Stone, *The Crisis of the Aristocracy*, OE, 242, AE, 118. John G. Bellamy, *Criminal Law and Society in Late Medieval and Tudor England* (Gloucester and New York: Alan Sutton, 1984), 67–71 suggests that most of these battles were formulaic and were designed to win through intimidation rather than by killing their opponents. In this they followed the pattern of animal fights in which bluster and bravado, rather than actual combat, win the day.

4. Churchyard, *Churchyards Challenge*, 60.

5. Brown, *English Martial Arts*, gives excellent illustrations of how these weapons were used (106–220).

For the history of the Masters of Defence see Aylward, *The English Master of Arms*; and Herbert Berry, *The Noble Science: A Study and Transcription of Sloane Ms. 2530. Papers of the Masters of Defence of London, Temp. Henry VIII to 1590* (Newark: University of Delaware Press, 1991). Jay P. Anglin, "The Schools of Defense in Elizabethan London," *Renaissance Quarterly* 37, no. 3 (Autumn 1984): 393–410, suggests that the Masters of Defence only taught the lower classes. However, it seems more likely that they originally taught gentlemen the use of arms prior to the arrival of the Italians and the rapier. Once Rocco Bonetti arrived on the scene, the Masters lost the patronage of the gentlemen of the court and had to rely upon the yeoman class for their patrons. See, for example, the "Ruills and Constitutions of the Schole" dating from Queen Elizabeth's reign (1558–1603), which declares that the Masters may "teache in their scholes all manner of estates gentilmen or yomen of what estate so ever he or they be" (Berry, *The Noble Science*, 111).

6. Silver, *Paradoxes of Defence*, 522–523.

7. Rocco Bonetti is generally considered to have introduced the rapier to England. However, Fuller, *The History of the Worthies of England*, Vol. 2, 347 credited Rowland Yorke with this honor. "But since that desperate traitor Rowland Yorke first used thrusting rapiers, swords and bucklers are disused [in Smithfield outside of London]." Rowland Yorke fought against the Spanish and for the Dutch in Holland between 1572 and 1578 and probably learned to handle a rapier there. He was accused of treason and

imprisoned in Brussels in 1584. He was released and fought with the Earl of Leicester against the Spanish in 1585 but handed over to the Spanish the Fort of Zutphen, and transferred his allegiance to the Spanish. Hence he was considered a traitor by Fuller. The Spanish distrusted him as well and poisoned him in 1588. His nephew and heir, Edmund Yorke, was executed at Tyburn in 1595 for attempting to assassinate Queen Elizabeth. Just when Rowland Yorke introduced the rapier to England we do not know, but presumably in the 1570s. See Linda McCollum, "Rocco Bonetti," *The Fight Master: The Journal of the Society of American Fight Directors* 9 (May 1986): 13–17, on 14; Clayton, "Yorke, Rowland (d. 1588)," 855–856. Silver, "A Briefe Note," 562–570, and most others give credit to Rocco Bonetti (d. 1587) for teaching Englishmen the use of the rapier. He notes that Bonetti came to England some thirty years earlier (c. 1570) and "taught the Noblemen & Gentlemen of the Court" (562). Silver describes "Jeronimo that was Signior Rocko his boy." Silver was a supporter of the old school and had nothing but contempt for the rapier. Silver, *Paradoxes of Defence*, 496. In contrast to Silver, Vincentio Saviolo saw the rapier as the sign of gentility in 1595. Saviolo, *Vincentio Saviolo, His Practice*, 209. Egerton Castle gives the classic definition of the rapier in England: "The word has always meant, since its introduction into the language, a sword especially convenient for thrusting, and adorned with a more or less elaborate guard." Egerton Castle, *Schools and Masters of Fencing from the Middle Ages to the Eighteenth Century* (Mineola, NY: Ringgold, 2003 [London, 1885]), 21. Anglo, *The Martial Arts of Renaissance Europe*, 99–112 argues that this description of the rapier needs to be re-examined. The rapier was not, however, well designed for hacking as was the style with the sword and buckler.

8. For James I's charter to the Masters of Defence see Aylward, *The English Master of Arms*, Appendix F, 258–260. During the sixteenth century wrestling matches were still being held in Clerkenwell at the time of St. Bartholomew's Fair (August 24). Charles Wriothesley, *A Chronicle of England during the Reigns of the Tudors, from AD 1485 to 1559*, ed. William Douglas Hamilton, Camden Society, s. 2, Vol. 20 (Westminster, 1877), Vol. 2, 21, 42, 54, 101, 139. However, wrestling matches had lost their favor among the upper classes. Richard Mulcaster (1581), an educator who favored the use of physical exercise for children, felt wrestling was fit only for the meanest level of the populace. Richard Mulcaster, *Positions Concerning the Training Up of Children*, ed. William Barker (Toronto: University of Toronto Press, 1994 [1581]), chapter 17, 83. Shakespeare, in *As You Like It* (1603), Act I, scenes i–ii casts a wrestler as a villain and makes him a lower-class professional, not a gentleman. John Stow (1603) noted wrestling had gone out of fashion, "that of olde time the exercising of wrestling, and such like hath beene much more vsed then of later years." John Stow, *A Survey of London*, ed. Charles Lethbridge Kingsford, Vol. 1 (Oxford: Clarendon, 1971), 95. And Henry Peacham (1622) considered wrestling suitable only for soldiers in camp or the prince's guard. Henry Peacham, *The Complete Gentleman, The Truth of Our Times and The Art of Living in London*, ed. Virgil B. Heltzel (Ithaca, NY: Published for the Folger Shakespearian Library by the Cornell University Press, 1962 [1622]), 137.

9. The term "gentleman" was a recognized social grade of the aristocracy in medieval and renaissance England. At the time of Henry VII (1457–1509) there were four categories of noble degree: lords, knights, esquires and gentlemen. A gentleman ranked above a yeoman and below an esquire. Maurice Keen, *The Origins of the English Gentleman: Heraldry, Chivalry and Gentility in Medieval England (c. 1300–c. 1500)* (Gloucestershire: Stroud, NPI Media Group, 2002), 102. Originally these classifications reflected military service: lords, knights and esquires were military ranks. A gentleman held property and did not work with his hands. It was not a military rank. Despite the belief of John Ferne that "if riches suffice to make men noble, then Pyrats and Theeues, bankers, and brothels, with the lyke, shall challenge nobility," by the sixteenth century the increasing wealth of merchants made the class of gentlemen highly porous. John Ferne, *The Blazon of Gentrie* (London: J. Windet for T. Cook, 1586), 14. This porosity made insistence on proper manners and civility to other gentlemen become especially important. It also led to a new emphasis

being placed upon the wearing and use of the sword. See above all the excellent work by Ruth Kelso, *The Doctrine of the English Gentleman in the Sixteenth Century* (Urbana: University of Illinois Press, 1929). See also Markku Peltonen, *The Duel in Early Modern England: Civility, Politeness and Honour* (Cambridge: Cambridge University Press, 2003); and Coss, *The Origins of the English Gentry*.

10. Francisco de Quevedo, Jr., *The town adventurer. A discourse of masquerades, playes, &c.* (London, 1675), quoted in Peltonen, *The Duel in Early Modern England*, 68. César de Saussure, a Swiss writing in 1727, found this still true. Speaking of English women he noted: "A sign that they are very fond of wealth is that as soon as you mention anyone to them that they do not know, their first inquiry will be, 'Is he rich?' In this country one is esteemed for one's wealth more than for anything else." César de Saussure, *A Foreign View of England in the Reigns of George I & George II: The Letters of Monsieur César de Saussure to his Family*, trans. and ed. Madame Van Muyden (London: J. Murray, 1902), 207–208. The Code of Courtesy was derived from Baldassare Castiglione's work *The Book of the Courtier* (1528). The anonymous Italian author of *A Relation, or Rather a True Account, of the Island of England [...] about the Year 1500*, trans. Charlotte Augusta Sneyd, Camden Society no. 37 (London, 1847), 43 ascribed the wealth of London to the *nouveaux riches*: "These great riches of London are not occasioned by its inhabitants being noblemen or gentlemen; being all, on the contrary, persons of low degree, and artificers who have congregated there from all parts of the island, and from Flanders, and from every other place." Frances Baldwin noted that by the reign of Elizabeth I (1558–1603), responding to this pressure: "The nobility and gentry displayed magnificence in their mansions, dress, and entertainments surpassing all that had yet been known in England." Frances Elizabeth Baldwin, *Sumptuary Legislation and Personal Regulation in England* (Baltimore: Johns Hopkins University Press, 1926), 194.

11. "Ferur v. Ralph Leech (1287)," and "Chaplain v. Shepherd (1315)," in *Select Cases on Defamation to 1600*, ed. R.H. Helmholz, Selden Society 101 (London, 1985), introduction and n. 36, 29 and n. 46, 33. See also Morris S. Arnold, ed., *Select Cases of Trespass from the King's Courts (1309–1399)*, Selden Society, Vol. 100 (London, 1985), Vol. 1, xxxii–xxxiv. John Baker, *The Oxford History of the Laws of England, Vol. 6 (1483–1558)* (Oxford, 2003), 781–799. See also J.H. Baker, *An Introduction to English Legal History* (London: Butterworths, 1990), 495–508, on 496. But note the difference in the Law Merchant where "assault with vile words" (*insultavit verbis turpissimus*) could be punished with fines. Gross, *Select Cases Concerning the Law Merchant (A.D. 1270–1638)*, Vol. 1, 17, 30, 33, 57, 71, 84–85.

12. Helmholz, *Select Cases on Defamation to 1600*, xiv–xviii.

13. Ranulf Glanvill, *The Treatise on the Laws and Customs of the Realm of England Commonly called Glanvill (c. 1187–1189)*, ed. and trans. G.D.G. Hall (London: Thomas Nelson and Sons, 1965), XIV, c. 1, 171–173.

"The Statute of Westminster" (3 Edward I, 1275, c. 34) stated "that henceforth none be so hardy to tell or publish any false News or Tales, whereby discord, or [occasion] of discord or slander may grow between the King and his People, or the Great Men of the Realm," on penalty of prison. *Statutes of the Realm*, Vol. 1, 35. This was reissued in "Statute of Gloucester" (2 Richard II, 1378–79, c. 5) and in the "Statute of Cambridge" (12 Richard II, 1388, c. 11). See *Statutes of the Realm*, Vol. 2, 9, 59.

14. "There ought more credence to be giuen by the Iudge to the oth of two Gentlemen produced, as witnesses, then to a multitude of vngentle persons.... Persons of base and vngentle estate, are no competent witnesses against a Gentleman of bloud, and coate-armor perfect." Ferne, *The Blazon of Gentrie*, 81. See also Marjorie Dunlavy Lewis, "Shakespeare's Uses of the Duelling Code for Comic and Satiric Effect" (Ph.D. diss., University of Kansas, 1967), 67–120. By 1250 trial by battle was generally being superseded by the trial by jury. Nonetheless, the precedent remained active and trial by battle was not outlawed in England until 1819. See Clanchy, "Highway Robbery and Trial by Battle in the Hampshire Eyre of 1249"; Maitland and Montague, *A Sketch of English Legal History*, 49–50, 62–63.

15. The judicial duel or the trial by battle

was introduced into England by William the Conqueror after 1066. Cases of treason were generally overseen by the Court of the King's Bench (*Coram Regis*). Beginning in 1348 the new High Court of Chivalry began to take over cases of treason and issues dealing with the laws of arms. See G.D. Squibb, *The High Court of Chivalry: A Study in the Civil Law of England* (Oxford: Clarendon, 1959), 22–28. Preparations for a trial by battle on an accusation of treason occurred at Smithfield on February 18, 1444 between Thomas Fitz Gerot, Prior of the Knights of St. John of Jerusalem, and James, the Earl of Ormond. Scaffolds were built for seating and a "grete nombr of peple gadered as ever was seyn afore in such caas." At the last minute the king declared that the battle would not take place. Ralph Flenley, ed., *Six Town Chronicles of England* (Oxford: Clarendon, 1911), 118–119, 120–121 (1446). Cases involving property might come under the jurisdiction of the Court of Common Pleas. The judicial duel was outlawed in London in 1131. Judicial duels were more common in the countryside than the cities, which is why the judicial duel may have been adopted as a model for boxing matches. Out of 1,241 judicial duels mentioned in English sources between 1066 and 1650, only 363 actually went to battle. Elema, *Trial by Battle in France and England*.

16. Churchyard, *Churchyards Challenge*, 60. Quote by Barnaby Rich in Peltonen, *The Duel in Early Modern England*, 43.

17. Churchyard, *Churchyards Challenge*, 59; "By the King: A Proclamation against Private Challenges and Combats" (Westminster, 4 February 1614), James F. Larkin and Paul L. Hughes, eds., *Stuart Royal Proclamations*, Vol. 1: *Royal Proclamations of King James I, 1603-1625* (Oxford: Clarendon, 1973), 307; John Cockburn, *The History and Examination of Duels* (London: G. Straken etc., 1720), 349.

18. Peltonen, *The Duel in Early Modern England*, 2. V.G. Kiernan, *The Duel in European History: Honour and the Reign of Aristocracy* (Oxford: Oxford University Press, 1988), 46 quotes Pierre de Bourdeille Brantome (d. 1614) saying much the same thing: "In our encounters either a man settles a difference at once in a blaze of glory, or he dies leaving a fine reputation, because he had the courage and resolution to venture on a fight; and if the fortune of the sword did not smile on him, it is still a great thing to have made the attempt. As they say in Latin, *In rebus ardus tentare satis est* [when attempting great deeds, it is enough to try]." A contrary view was held by the Italian Annibale Romei (1597), who defined a "Combate" as "a battaile between two of equal interest, in some point of honour, in the end whereof the vanquished incurreth infamy, and the victor remaineth possessed of honour." Quoted by Jeremy Horder, "The Duel and the English Law of Homicide," *Oxford Journal of Legal Studies* 12, no. 3 (Autumn 1992): 419–430, quote on 422.

19. Both boxing and the judicial duel were public events. As we have seen, there were two types of judicial duels. The first and most important dealt with treason or capital crimes and pitted the contesting individuals against each other. The second type was generated by property disputes which pitted individuals against each other by proxy. In the first type of combat, death of one of the parties was often the outcome. In the second type, where the actual combatants were hired champions who stood in for the individual parties, loss of the case and property was often the outcome. John Stow describes the elaborate preparations for one judicial duel (Lowe and Kyme v. Paramore) from 1571 where the principles both hired champions: Henry Naylor for Lowe and Kyme and George Thorne for Paramore. Queen Elizabeth and her court went to Tuthill fields "where was prepared one plot of ground one and twentie yards square, double railed for the combate, without the west [side of the] square, a stage being set up for the Judges, representing the court of common pleas. All the compasse without the listes was set with scaffolds one above another, for people to stand and behold. There were behind the square where the Judges sate, two tents, the one for Naylor, the other for Thorne." Ultimately, at the last moment, Simon Lowe, one of the plaintiffs, did not appear. His case was declared forfeit and Paramore won without a battle. John Stow, *The Annales of England [...] from the first inhabitation vntil this present yeere 1592* (London, [1592]), 1141–1144. See also the account as given in Berry, *The Noble Science*, 9–11.

20. Neilson, *Trial by Combat*, 53. Champions shaved their heads, but approvers did not. This explains why the fighters in Fig. 3 in chapter V did not have shaved heads; neither of them was a champion. For a case of a champion shaving his head, see Henry of Fernbureg, the Marshall (c. 1258) (Neilson, *Trial by Combat*, 53). Henry was to be paid ten marks at the agreement to duel, five marks on being shaven (*in tonsione mea quinque marcas*) and the rest on the day of the duel. The fact that the document quoted uses the word "tonsure" for the shaving seems to link this to the religious practice of monastic tonsure. Neilson suggests that this custom had some religious or ceremonial origin and that "the idea that it was simply to hinder the hair from being grasped in the combat is simply inadequate" (57). Maitland and Montague agree: "We also know that the champion's head was shaved, but are left to guess why this was done." Maitland and Montague, *A Sketch of English Legal History*, 59. In contrast to the above, C.H. Williams, *Yearbooks of Henry VI: 1 Henry VI (AD 1422)*, Selden Society 50 (London: Quaritch, 1933), xxx says the following: "When an approver did battle his head was shaven, but in an action on a writ of right the head of the champion was not shaven. The court was not certain about all the details." Clearly the details of this ritual need clarification. Head shaving was carried over into gladiatorial sword-fighting. This can be seen in the picture of James Figg (Fig. 3 below). See also the other pictures of Figg in *Midnight Modern Conversation* (1732–33) and *Southwark Fair* (1733–34), both by William Hogarth. Following Figg, many of the early boxers also shaved their heads, such as John Broughton and Jack Slack. See Nat Fleischer and Sam Andre, *An Illustrated History of Boxing*, 6th rev. updated ed. (New York: Citadel, 2001 [1959]), 12, as well as the two boxers in Hogarth's picture *The March to Finchley* (December 1750). See also two pictures of the boxer Thomas Smallwood (1751–1758) by George Townshend, 1st Marquess Townshend, one in which he is dressed with a wig, and the other in which he is stripped as a boxer with his head shaven. National Portrait Gallery, London. Bill Stevens, "The Nailer" and George Meggs, "The Collier," both champions in the 1760s, had shaved heads, but few fighters after their era did so. See pictures in Fleischer and Andre, *An Illustrated History of Boxing*, 13. The fact that this tradition of shaving the heads of champion fighters continued in England for at least five centuries (1250–1760 AD) tells us that it was a significant act. It is a pity that we don't know its meaning.

21. Zacharias Conrad von Uffenbach, *London in 1710: From the Travels of Zacharias Conrad von Uffenbach*, ed. W.H. Quarrell and Margaret Mare (London: Faber & Faber, 1934), 88–91. The four Ancient Masters of Defence exercised similar control over their prizefights. On May 10, 1578, Isake Kennard failed his master's title since he "was stroken downe at the backe sworde by Willyam Muckelowe and so was dismiste for that tyme." See Berry, *The Noble Science*, 47. Modern boxing still has judges who determine the winner of the fight, a referee who supervises decorum in the ring and who can stop the fight, and seconds and doctors attending the fighters who also can stop the fight.

22. "The primary duty of seconds was to guarantee fair play, an equal chance for both men by agreeing on time, place, weapons, and procedure, and seeing to it that no illicit advantage was taken." Kiernan, *The Duel in European History*, 138. According to von Uffenbach describing the prizefight on July 2, 1710, "Each of the combatants had his second by him with a large stick in his hand; they were not there to parry blows, but only to see that there was fair play on all sides." Von Uffenbach, *London in 1710*, 89. Such a person is seen standing with James Figg in Fig. 2. It is still commonplace for umpires at rural wrestling matches in England to carry sticks. For this reason they are called "sticklers," leading to our modern meaning of a stickler as one concerned with rules.

23. As mentioned above (note 19) the preparations for the trial by battle in 1571 involved creating a double-railed square in which the champions were to fight. This was adopted as well by the Masters of Defence for their prizefights and later (c. 1725) by James Figg for his gladiator sword-fights and boxing prizefights. This became the standard for boxing until 1750 when, as a result of the Broughton-Slack fight, boxing was driven out of London. At that time, boxing returned to its origins on the turf.

24. Stone, *The Crisis of the Aristocracy*, OE, 243, AE, 118–19. There were several distinguishing marks that separated a gentleman from a yeoman. Of these the right to carry a sword, and, by 1600, particularly the rapier, was the most visible outward sign. See Keen, *The Origins of the English Gentleman*, 105.

25. Larkin and Hughes, *Stuart Royal Proclamations*, Vol. 1, no. 132, 295–297, no. 136, 302–308. See also *An Ordinance against Challenges, Duells, and all Provocations thereunto*. Ordered by his Highness the Lord Protector and His Council (London, June 29, 1654); and *By the King. A Proclamation against Fighting of Duells*. Charles R. (London: Printed by John Bill and Christopher Baker, 1660). Lawrence Stone, *The Crisis of the Aristocracy*, OE, Appendix XV, 770 points out that during the sixty years between 1580 and 1639 there were only forty-seven recorded challenges and duels involving the nobility and forty-nine other acts of unregulated violence affecting the peers. This was about 1.5 incidents a year. Since there were only between 60 and 120 peers at the time, this represented a relatively high percentage of duels per members of the peerage. Given a general population of around 6,250,000 in 1600 the number of duels was ridiculously small. "Nonetheless, the actual number of duels was relatively unimportant. What was much more significant was the widespread public interest in the news about duels. Even a combat between two completely obscure gentlemen was thought to be worth reporting in both newsletters and private correspondence. This suggests that, whilst duels were far from daily incidents, they attracted rapt attention." Peltonen, *The Duel in Early Modern England*, 205.

26. Fredson Bowers, ed., *The Dramatic Works in the Beaumont and Fletcher Canon*, Vol. 7 (Cambridge: Cambridge University Press, 1989), Act II, scene i, line 270.

27. Stone, *The Crisis of the Aristocracy*, OE, 65–128, AE, 37–61, discusses selling of honors by the monarchy of James I. He shows that James I created 906 new knights in the first four months of his reign after March 1603 and 1,161 new knights by December 1604, OE, 74–75, AE, 41. He mentions how Henry Gawdy heard of an attorney nicknamed "nimblechappes" who purchased a knighthood for 7 pounds, 10 shillings during that time. "Nimblechappes" may have been the model for Lapet.

28. Baldwin Maxwell, *Studies in Beaumont, Fletcher, and Massinger* (Chapel Hill: University of North Carolina Press, 1939), 130–131. Kicking was a part of both wrestling and boxing at this time. Kicking was not outlawed in boxing until 1838. See "New Rules of Prize-Fighting," in Dowling, *Fistiana*, 63–66, rule 17, www.cyberboxingzone.com/boxing/london-rules-1838.htm.

29. Fredson Bowers, ed., *The Dramatic Works in the Beaumont and Fletcher Canon*, Vol. 9 (Cambridge: Cambridge University Press, 1994).

30. Peltonen, *The Duel in Early Modern England*, 221. The issue might have been solved by laws dealing with slander, but this section of the law was undeveloped at the time. Common Law in the royal courts held no actionable cause for private insults. As Kelso, *The Doctrine of the English Gentleman in the Sixteenth Century*, p. 103 was to note: "The laws take care of public injuries but not of private; knightly dignity will not allow carrying a quarrel to the magistrate and asking for vindication. Lost honor cannot be regained by the law, or by the force or value of another, but by a man's own valor and virtue." King James I himself was forced to admit "how cunningly some argue for excuse of Challenges, by imputing weakenesse (as they would have us apprehend) to the Lawes and Statutes of the Realme, in that they forbeare either out of insensibilitie or neglect, to give satisfaction to some certaine termes and reproches, As for example to that of the Lye." As a result, men "follow their old Paradox, supposing no satisfaction to be sufficient, besides that which the partie that hath bene offended, taketh with his owne hand, and by the sword." *By the King. A Proclamation against Private Challenges and Combats* (February 4, 1614), published in Larkin and Hughes, *Stuart Royal Proclamations*, Vol. 1, n. 136, 303–305.

31. George Farquhar, *The Constant Couple (or a Trip to the Jubilee)*, ed. Simon Trussler (London: Methuen, 1988), Act 4, scene i, 30. Equally telling was the case circa 1763 noted by J.D. Aylward of two fencing masters, an Italian and an Irishman, who met

on a London street and fell to fisticuffs. Following the altercation, the Italian challenged the Irishman to a duel. The Irishman refused and instead sent the matter to his lawyer. By the middle of the eighteenth century even fencing masters were abandoning the use of the sword to settle private disputes. Aylward, *The English Master of Arms*, 199–200.

32. Pierce Egan credits John Broughton (1704–1789) with being the first man to introduce science into boxing. Broughton was able to parry blows, yet hit his man so easily that he could defeat an opponent and appear to be untouched himself (Egan, *Boxiana*, Vol. 1, 16–17). Egan justly praises boxing for being a "science" which adds generosity to the Englishman's disposition, humanity to their conduct and courage to their national character. See also "Boxing," *Encyclopedia Britannica*, 11th ed., Vol. 6 (1910–1911), 350, where boxing is reckoned "the art of hitting without being hit."

33. de Saussure, *A Foreign View of England*, 179–181; L'Abbe [Jean Bernard] le Blanc, "Letter to the Chevalier de B [...]," in *Letters on the English and French Nations*, Vol. 2 (London: J. Brindley, 1747), 137.

34. Gorn "Gouge and Bite, Pull Hair and Scratch," 19; *The Malefactor's Register, or, the Newgate and Tyburn Calendar* (London: Alexander Hogg, [1778]), 75; *Dr. Johnson's Table Talk: or, Conversations of the late Samuel Johnson, L.L.D.* (London: G.G.J. and J. Robinson, 1785), 157.

35. Information about Harry Angelo and quote about pugilism from Aylward, *The English Master of Arms*, 212.

36. A Highland Officer, *Anti-Pugilism...* (London: J. Autkin, 1790) is listed in Paul Magriel, *A Bibliography of Boxing: A Chronological Check List of Books in English Printed before 1900* (Mansfield Center, CT: Martino Publishing, 2002), 267. Donna T. Andrew, "The Code of Honour and Its Critics: The Opposition to Duelling in England, 1700–1850," *Social History* 5, no. 3 (October 1980): 409–434 chronicled the criticism of dueling in the eighteenth century. She was puzzled as to why dueling disappeared. She noted that dueling was a private law solution to the preservation of honor and could not be easily abolished unless there was some "alternative policing method to replace it" (414). Andrew overlooked the fact that boxing served the same function. As the duel disappeared, boxing filled the gap.

37. For William Ward see "William Ward, Killing: Murder, 3rd June, 1789," *The Proceedings of the Old Bailey, 1674–1913*, Ref. t17890603-17, oldbaileyonline.org. For his history as a boxer, see Egan, *Boxiana*, Vol. 1, 117–119.

38. John Freeth, *The political songster, or a touch on the times, on various subjects and adapted to common tunes, the sixth edition, with additions* (Birmingham, 1790), 161; For the background of sword and boxing prizefights in the United States during the nineteenth century, see Arly Allen, "The Boxer and the Duelist: The Origins of the Missouri Prizefight Law of 1874," *Missouri Historical Review* 104, no. 4 (July 2010): 213–232.

Chapter VI

1. Joseph Black, ed., *The Martin Marprelate Tracts: A Modernized and Annotated Edition* (Cambridge: Cambridge University Press, 2008), xviii.

2. Peter Lake, *Anglicans and Puritans? Presbyterianism and English Conformist Thought from Whitgift to Hooker* (London: Unwin Hyman, 1988), 7, 81–85; for John Stow's comments see Patrick Collinson, "Antipuritanism," in *The Cambridge Companion to Puritanism*, ed. John Coffey and Paul C.H. Lim (Cambridge: Cambridge University Press, 2008), 19–20.

3. Thomas Cooper, *Admonition to the People of England* (1589) quoted in Joseph Black, "The Rhetoric of Reaction: The Martin Marprelate Tracts (1588–1589), Anti-Martinism, and the Uses of Print in Early Modern England," *Sixteenth Century Journal* 28, no. 3 (1997): 707–725, quote on 710. For the Anabaptists, who so terrified the Anglican Church leaders, see Norman Cohn, *The Pursuit of the Millennium: Revolutionary Messianism in Medieval and Reformation Europe and Its Bearing on Modern Totalitarian Movements* (New York: Harper and Brothers, 1961 [1957]), 272–306.

4. For the type of people initially drawn to boxing, see the discussion in chapter V. For a description of the "middling sort" now being drawn into boxing's orbit, see the article by Peter Earle, "The Middling Sort in

London," in *The Middling Sort of People: Culture, Society and Politics in England, 1550–1800*, ed. Jonathan Barry and Christopher Brooks (New York: St. Martin's, 1994), 141–158.

5. Black, *The Martin Marprelate Tracts*, 3–45. The quotations are on 7, section 2; 7–8, section 2; 33, section 37; 10, section 5. Martin Marprelate's vituperate attack on the bishops had a long and contentious history. Johan Huizinga *Homo Ludens: A Study of the Play-Element in Culture* (Boston, MA: Beacon Press, 1955 [1950]), 65–71 points out that "slanging-matches" in which competitors boast about their abilities and verbally besmirch those of their opponents before physically attacking one another, are common in many cultures throughout history: "It is remarkable how large a place these bragging and scoffing matches occupy in the most diverse civilizations" (65). Thorstein Veblen too draws attention to the role of slang in athletic fights. "The slang of athletics, by the way, is in a great part made up of extremely sanguinary locutions borrowed from the terminology of warfare. Except where it is adopted as a necessary means of secret communication, the use of a special slang in any employment is probably to be accepted as evidence that the occupation in question is substantially make-believe." Thorstein Veblen, *The Theory of the Leisure Class: An Economic Study of Institutions* (New York: Mentor, 1953 [1899]), 171.

6. Thomas Nashe [?], *A Countercuffe given to Martin Junior:Bby the venturous, hardie, and renowned Pasquill of England, Cavaliero*, in *The Works of Thomas Nashe*, ed. Ronald B. McKerrow, Vol. 1 (Oxford: Basil Blackwell, 1966), 57 sgg. The name Pasquill Cavaliero refers to a gladiator statue discovered in Rome in 1501 and placed in the Piazza Navona. It became the custom to clothe this statue and address satirical commentaries to it. The name Pasquill was borrowed from a local wit who lived in the area and who may have been a barber. See Thomas Nashe, "Pasqvils Retvrne to England," in McKerrow, *The Works of Thomas Nashe*, Vol. 1, 72, lines 3–5; Vol. 4, 42, 4.

7. John Lyly, *Pap with an Hatchet: An Annotated Modern-Spelling Edition*, ed. Leah Scragg (Manchester, UK: Manchester University Press, 2015). This is an outstanding edition, despite the fact that Dr. Scragg is not familiar with boxing terminology and ignores the numerous references included in the work by Lyly. *The Oxford English Dictionary* considers "pap with a hatchet" as an ironical phrase suggesting doing a kind thing in an unkind manner. In this instance Lyly seems to have considered the Marprelates as children who deserved punishment for their ideas.

8. Lyly, *Pap with an Hatchet*, 50, line 16. *Oxford English Dictionary*, "bob," "to strike with the fist, to pommel, buffet." The phrase "knowing your bellies full of bishops' bobs, I am sure your bones would be at rest" seems odd to the modern ear but comfortable to the old boxers. Daniel Mendoza, in his autobiography (1826), says, after thrashing a man who insulted his ability to ride a horse, "I have no doubt that he was too much in need of ease and rest himself to molest anyone else that evening." W.C. Heinz and Nathan Ward, *The Book of Boxing* (Kingston, NY: Total Sports Illustrated Classics, 1999), 239.

9. Lyly, *Pap with an Hatchet*, 51–52, lines 28–31.

10. Lyly, *Pap with an Hatchet*, 59–60, lines 127–128. For Gabriel Harvey, see *Oxford Dictionary of National Biography*, Vol. 25 (Oxford: Oxford University Press, 2004), 655–658. Thorstein Veblen expresses the Victorian middle-class contempt for non-utilitarian activity when he notes that "the temperament which inclines men to them [sports] is essentially a boyish temperament. The addiction to sports, therefore in a peculiar degree marks an arrested development of man's moral nature. This peculiar boyishness of temperament in sporting men immediately becomes apparent when attention is directed to the large element of make-believe that is present in all sporting activity." Veblen, *The Theory of the Leisure Class*, 170. We can substitute Huizinga's concept of "play" for Veblen's term "make-believe."

11. Lyly, *Pap with an Hatchet*, 61, line 139; 67, line 231; 78, lines 390–395.

12. [Harvey], *Plaine Percevall*, A, 3 and 4.

13. "Who knoweth not, that Apes men Martin call…[?]" John Lyly, "A Whip for an Ape," in *The Complete Works of John Lyly*, ed. R. Warwick Bond, Vol. 3 (Oxford: Clarendon, 1902), 418, l.7.

14. *Oxford English Dictionary*, "Fair, III, 10c fair play."
15. Huizinga, *Homo Ludens*, 28.
16. [Moelmuiri mac Mic Cuinn Na M-Bocht], *Fled Bricrend*, 117–129, quote on 119 c.94.
17. [Moelmuiri mac Mic Cuinn Na M-Bocht], *Fled Bricrend*, 121, c.95; 123, c. 96; 129, c. 102. The concept of fair play is also found in the old Irish saga, *The Destruction of Da Derga's Hostel*. Here Ingcel, the One-eyed, challenges those who would attack him, saying: "Do not violate fair play with us, for ye are more in number than we." Tom Peete Cross and Clark Harris Slover, *Ancient Irish Tales* (New York: Henry Holt and Co., 1936), 104. Fair play was also discussed in *The Death of Finn* (c. 1200). Finn is attacked by Fer-li, his hereditary enemy: "It suits my honor that Fer-li should importune me tonight nor grant me fair play. A time will come," he said, "when no one will grant fair play to another" (Cross and Slover, *Ancient Irish Tales*, 427). From this it appears that the ancient Irish had a concept of fair play before the English, but, as Finn's comment suggests, they may have lost this sense early on, while it matured among the English.
18. D.G. Scragg, ed., *The Battle of Maldon* (Manchester, UK: Manchester University Press, 1981), https://www.lightspill.com/poetry/oe/maldon.html#note.
19. Seamus Heaney, *Beowulf: A New Verse Translation* (New York and London: W.W. Norton, 2000), 47, lines 677–687.
20. Swanton, "*Gesta Herewardi* (The Deeds of Hereward)," 46.
21. Berry, *The Noble Science*, 99.
22. Berry, *The Noble Science*, 89.
23. *Statute of Gloucester* comments by Serjeant Robert Keilway in Samuel E. Thorne and J.H. Baker, eds., *Readings and Moots at the Inns of Court in the Fifteenth Century*, Vol. 2: *Moots and Readers' Cases* (London: Selden Society, 1990), Vol. 105, 74, no. 27. See also Andrew, "The Code of Honour and Its Critics," 412. Quote from the *Edinburgh Review* (1814), 74.
24. Wiggins, *Stanzaic Guy of Warwick*, 113, lines 3184–3192.
25. Wiggins, *Stanzaic Guy of Warwick*, 114–115, lines 3193–3230.
26. John Lydgate, *Fabula duorum mercantorum and Guy of Warwyk*, ed. Pamela Farvolden, TEAMS Middle English Texts Series (Kalamazoo, MI: Medieval Institute Publications, 2016), 118, line 417.
27. Stone, *The Crisis of the Aristocracy*, OE, 225–226, AE, 109.
28. The quotations of William Shakespeare are taken from Evans and Tobin, *The Riverside Shakespeare*.
29. Saviolo, *Vincentio Saviolo, His Practice*, 217–218.
30. Saviolo, *Vincentio Saviolo, His Practice*, 221.
31. Carew, *The Survey of Cornwall*, 148. Carew notes as well: "I cannot well resolve whether I should more commend this game for the manhood and exercise, or condemn it for the boisterousness and harms which it begetteth; for as on one side it makes their bodies strong, hard and nimble, and puts courage into their hearts to meet an enemy in the face, so on the other part it is accompanied with many dangers, some of which do ever fall to the players' share. For proof whereof, when the hurling is ended, you shall see them retiring home as from a pitched battle, with bloody pates, bones broken and out of joint, and such bruises as serve to shorten their days; yet all is good play, and never attorney nor coroner troubled for the matter" (149–150).
32. Samuel Pepys, *The Diary of Samuel Pepys*, ed. Robert Latham and William Matthews, Vol. 8 (London: G. Bell and Sons, 1970–1983), 239.
33. J. Burgh, *Political Disquisitions*, Vol.1 (Philadelphia: Robert Bell and William Woodhouse, 1775), 211.
34. David Cram, Jeffrey L. Forgeng and Dorothy Johnston, eds., *Francis Willughby's Book of Games: A Seventeenth-Century Treatise on Sports, Games and Pastimes* (Aldershot, UK and Burlington, VT: Ashgate, 2003), 226.
35. Andrew, "The Code of Honour and Its Critics," 412–413.
36. von Uffenbach, *London in 1710*, 89.
37. Egan, *Boxiana*, Vol. 1, v–vi.
38. Huizinga, *Homo Ludens*, 211.
39. Misson, *Memoirs and Observations*, 305–306.
40. de Saussure, *A Foreign View of England*, 113–114.
41. Misson, *Memoirs and Observations*, 306. Note by Misson. Italics by Misson. The

first Duke of Grafton was Henry Fitzroy (1663-1690), the illegitimate son of Charles II and Barbara Villiers. He died fighting in Ireland for King William. The blue ribbon referred to by Misson was the insignia of the Order of the Garter which, following an ordinance of November 19, 1682, "should be worn over the upper habit beltways over the left shoulder and under the right arm in such a manner as that it might be best seen." William A. Shaw, *The Knights of England*, Vol. 1 (Baltimore: Genealogical Publishing Company, 1971), iii.

42. James Peller Malcolm, *Anecdotes of the Manners and Customs of London during the Eighteenth Century*, Vol. 1 (London: Longman, Hurst, Rees and Orme, 1810), 384. Maurice de Saxe (1696-1750) was the illegitimate son of Augustus II, "The Strong," King of Poland. He was an adventurer who fought in many wars, finally earning the title of Marshal of the French Armies. The incident probably happened after the War of the Spanish Succession (1701-1712) when, as a young man, Saxe fought on the side of the British with John Churchill, Duke of Marlborough.

43. de Saussure, *A Foreign View of England*., 180-181. Although de Saussure says this incident involved the Duke of Leeds, there is some confusion. Thomas Osborne, the first Duke of Leeds, died in 1712. His son, Peregrine Osborne (1659-1729), the second Duke of Leeds, would have been about 68 in 1727. His son, Peregrine Hyde Osborne (1691-1731), may have been the proper age to fight, but he was not yet the Duke of Leeds, and had the wrong name for this description. That "my Lord Herbert" fought such a fight is probable, but that Herbert was the Duke of Leeds seems less probable. L.S., "Osborne, Sir Thomas, Duke of Leeds (1631-1712)," *The Dictionary of National Biography*, Vol. 14 (Oxford: Oxford University Press, 1964), 1189-1197; J.K.L., "Osborne, Peregrine 2nd Duke of Leeds (1658-1729)," *The Dictionary of National Biography*, Vol. 14, 1185-1186.

44. Egan, *Boxiana*, Vol. 1, 19. Samuel Johnson came from a pugnacious family. His uncle, Andrew Johnson, was a well-known sword gladiator who fought out of James Figg's Amphitheatre and reputedly taught young Sam how to box. Richard B. Schwartz, *Daily Life in Johnson's London* (Madison: University of Wisconsin Press, 1983), 70.

45. Quoted in Charles Chenevix Trench, *The Poacher and the Squire: A History of Poaching and Game Preservation in England* (London: Longman and Green, 1967), 132-133.

46. Misson, *Memoirs and Observations*, 73. Italics by Misson.

47. de Saussure, *A Foreign View of England*, 181.

48. Egan, *Boxiana*, Vol. 1, 2-3.

49. Egan, *Boxiana*, Vol. 1, 3.

50. Francis Frederick Brandt, *Habet! A Short Treatise on the Law of the Land as It Affects Pugilism* (London: Robert Hardwicke, 1857), 8-9.

51. de Saussure, *A Foreign View of England*, 179; Aylward, *The English Master of Arms*, 92-107, 212.

52. Egan, *Boxiana*, Vol. 1, 2-3. For boxing as a civilizing force see also Randy Roberts, "Eighteenth Century Boxing," *Journal of Sport History* 4, no. 3 (Fall 1977): 246-259. Norbert Elias could have supported his contention about the civilizing process more completely, and in fewer words, by comparing boxing with sword-fighting as a civilizing force. See Norbert Elias and Eric Dunning, "An Essay on Sport and Violence," in *Quest for Excitement: Sport and Leisure in the Civilizing Process*, ed. Elias and Dunning (Oxford: Basil Blackwell, 1986), 150-174. For a similar view see Ruud Stokvis, "Sports and Civilization: Is Violence the Central Problem?" in *Sport and Leisure in the Civilizing Process: Critique and Counter-Critique*, ed. Eric Dunning and Chris Rojek (Toronto and Buffalo: University of Toronto Press, 1992), 123-136. Stokvis suggests that boxing and football are better examples of civilizing sports than fox hunting.

53. Quoted in Henry Downes Miles, *Pugilistica: The History of British Boxing*, Vol. 1 (Edinburgh: John Grant, 1906), 5 note.

54. Kenneth G. Sheard, "Aspects of Boxing in the Western 'Civilizing Process,'" *International Review of Sociology of Sport* 32 (March 1997): 31-57, quote on 48. See Edith Summerskill, *The Ignoble Art* (London: William Heinemann, 1956); Thomas Myler, *Boxing's Hall of Shame: The Fight Game's Darkest Days* (Edinburgh and London: Mainstream Publishing, 2006); and Jack Ander-

son, *The Legality of Boxing: A Punch Drunk Love?* (Abingdon, UK: Birkbeck Law, 2007).

Chapter VII

1. Carew, *The Survey of Cornwall*, 197.
2. William Denny, "Encomiastick To His worthy Friend Mr. Robert Dover, on his Famous Annual Assemblies at Cotswold," in *Annalia Dvbrensia: Vpon the yeerely celebration of Mr. Robert Dovers Olimpick Games vpon Cotswold-Hills* (London: Robert Raworth, for Mathewe Walbancke, 1636), 12. The best book on the history of the Dover Olympics is Christopher Whitfield, ed., *Robert Dover and the Cotswold Games: Annalia Dubrensia* (London: Henry Sotheran, 1962). Celia Haddon, *The First Ever English Olimpick Games* (London: Hodder & Stoughton, 2004), 73–74 notes Denny's poem, but thinks that if boxing was included in Dover's games, it was dropped later when support was sought from King James. This is possible, as the poems were apparently collected by Dover over a period of years until he had enough to make a volume. Alexander B. Grosart, *Annalia Dubrensia, Or celebration of Captain Robert Dover's Cotswold Games* (Manchester, UK: Printed for the Subscribers, 1877), xx. But see the other reference to boxing with the *caestus* in note 11 below. With reference to the line "an Active sport to Breathe our bravest warriers," Lord Byron, an aficionado of boxing, noted that "at any rate exercise is good, and this is the severest of all: fencing and broadsword never fatigued me half so much." *Diary*, March 17, 1814.
3. The poems in the *Annalia Dubrensia* emphasize the joy of young men and women enjoying outdoor sport on the Cotswold fields. This is in keeping with Sydney Anglo's view of the use of barriers, which had reduced the joust by the sixteenth and seventeenth centuries to "merely an effete and pointless show." Anglo, *The Martial Arts of Renaissance Europe*, 169.
4. A.R. Wright, *British Calendar Customs. England*, Vol. 1: *Movable Festivals* (London: Folk-Lore Society, 1936), 164–165; A.R. Wright, *British Calendar Customs. England*, Vol. 2: *Fixed Festivals: January–May, Inclusive* (London: Folk-Lore Society, 1938), 231.
5. Nancy Struna, "Puritans and Sport: The Irretrievable Tide of Change," *Journal of Sport History* 4, no.1 (Spring 1977): 1–21, quotes on page 3.
6. Struna, "Puritans and Sport," quote on 3.
7. Struna, "Puritans and Sport," quote on 4.
8. Alistair Dougall, *The Devil's Book: Charles I, The Book of Sports and Puritanism in Tudor and Early Stuart England* (Exeter, UK: University of Exeter Press, 2011), 72–86; See also Bruce C. Daniels, *Puritans at Play: Leisure and Recreation in Colonial New England* (New York: St. Martin's, 1996 [1995]), 165–166.
9. Dougall, *The Devil's Book*, 150. Rocky Marciano (1923–1969) was asked to box on Sunday when he was heavyweight champion. He refused, saying: "No. I'm a Roman Catholic and I go to church on Sunday." Times change things. See Rocky Marciano, "How It Feels to Be Champ," in Heinz and Ward, *The Book of Boxing*, 218–225, on 222.
10. Daniels, *Puritans at Play*, 166; Thomas Babington Macaulay, *Macaulay's History of England*, Vol. 1, Everyman's Library (London: J.M. Dent and Sons, 1957 [1848]), c.2, 121.
11. See also the poem by John Stratford "To my kind Cosen and Noble Friend, Mr. Robert Dover, on his sports upon Cotswold." Here Stratford praises "Eutellus, hee at Cestus had the best, / In mighty strength surpassing all the rest. / Such were the old Worlds sports; now transferr'd over/ Into our Cotswold, by thee, Worthy *DOVER*." Grosart, *Annalia Dubrensia*, 49. For Eutellus and Dares fighting with the Cestus, see Appendix 4. For a modern recreation of the drawing in the *Annalia*, see the pictures of bare-fist-fighting in Brown, *English Martial Arts*, especially 193a, b, c.
12. Thomas Goodwin, *Romanae historiae anthologia* (Oxford: Printed by Joseph Barnes, 1614), Lib. 2, Sect. 3, 68.
13. [Robert Armin], *Foole vpon Foole or Six Sortes of Sottes* (London: Printed for William Ferbrand, 1600): "How this leane foole Leanard eating his belly full, was revenged of one that clapt corziars wax to his head."
14. Thomas Goodwin, *Romanae historiae anthologia* (Oxford: Printed by Leonard

Lichfield for Henry Crypps, 1638), Lib. 2, Sect. 3, 92.

15. *True Protestant Mercury: or Occurrences Foreign and Domestick*, no. 103, December 28–December 31, 1681, 2.

16. *Domestick Intelligence: Or News both from City and Country impartially related.* numb. 64, December 29, [1681] to January 2 [1682], 1.

17. *Domestick Intelligence: Or News both from City and Country impartially related.* numb. 140, September 1 to September 25, 1682, 1. I owe the reference to the match of 1682 to the admirable biography by Estelle Frances Ward, *Christopher Monck, Duke of Albermarle* (London: John Murray, 1915), 147–148.

18. Misson, *Memoirs and Observations*, 304–305.

19. de Saussure, *A Foreign View of England*, 180.

20. There are a number of problems with the history of this bout. The wrong date has been given for the bout as well as the wrong name of the contestants. Tony Gee, the British prize-ring historian, has done exhaustive research in the contemporary English records of the time and will be publishing the results in his forthcoming book on John Broughton. In a large part, I follow his work. Although the Venetian Gondolier was sometimes named Tito Alberto de Carni, that name only appears in records dating from the late nineteenth century, and was not given in contemporary English sources. Thus, along with Tony, I consider him unnamed. (Tony Gee, personal correspondence, December 12, 2019). It should be noted that I have not examined Italian sources on this fight.

21. See my Chapter II, note 46.

22) Robert C. Davis, *The War of the Fists: Popular Culture and Public Violence in Late Renaissance Venice* (New York and Oxford: Oxford University Press, 1994).

23. *Weekly Journal: or, British Gazetteer* (9 January 1725). Reference courtesy of Tony Gee, personal correspondence December 28, 2019.

24. Captain John Godfrey, *A Treatise upon the useful science of defence...* (London: Printed for the author, by T. Gardner 1747), 58–59.

25. See Tony Gee's brief article in the *International Boxing Research Organization Journal*, issue 144 (December 2019), 16. Gee will have more to say in his forthcoming book on John Broughton. The newspapers of the time give the preferred spelling of *Whitacre*, but since Godfrey spells his name *Whitaker*, to avoid confusion, I will follow Godfrey's lead.

26. Godfrey, *A Treatise upon the useful science of defence...*, 59–60. Tony Gee notes (in personal correspondence of December 18, 2019) that the attending crowd included "Count Staremberg and other Foreign Ministers being present, together with several of the English Nobility and Members of Parliament."

27. Personal correspondence with Tony Gee, December 17, 2019 and *Daily Post*, May 11, 1725.

28. Godfrey, *A Treatise upon the useful science of defence...*, 61. Similar words have been attributed to John Broughton after his fight with Jack Slack in 1750. However, after many years of research in contemporary sources, Tony Gee was not able to confirm Broughton ever uttered these words, or anything like them. It seems likely then that these words belong to John Whitaker [Whitacre] as reported by John Godfrey. Personal correspondence with Tony Gee, December 18, 2019.

Chapter VIII

1. Thomas S. Henricks, *Disputed Pleasures: Sport and Society in Preindustrial England* (New York: Greenwood, 1991), 175. See also Ford, *Prizefighting*, 89–90: "All the sports we have discussed [horse-racing, cricket, prizefighting, cock-fighting, dog-fighting, bull-baiting] were promoted primarily for the purpose of gambling by the promoters.... The sports would not have developed in this organised fashion had not the passion for gambling been widespread."

2. Cited in David G. Schwartz, *Roll the Bones: The History of Gambling* (New York: Gotham, 2006), 5. This is the finest book on the history and culture of gambling I have ever seen. The study on rats is J.F. Davis and E.G. Kraus, "Dominant Rats are Natural Risk-Takers and Display Increased Motivation for Food Reward," *Neuroscience* 162, no. 1 (August 4, 2009): 23–30. The study on

macaques is Allison N. McCoy and Michael L. Platt, "Risk-Sensitive Neurons in Macaque Posterior Cingulated Cortex," *Nature Neuroscience* 8 (2005): 1220–1227.

3. Steven A. Riess, "Only the Ring was Square: Frankie Carbo and the Underworld Control of American Boxing," *International Journal of the History of Sport* 5, no. 1 (1988): 29–52; https://www.hannibalboxing.com/omerta-man-when-frankie-carbo-ruled-boxing/; Myler, *Boxing's Hall of Shame*.

4. George Washington Plunkitt, "Honest Graft and Dishonest Graft" (1905), https://www.panarchy.org/plunkitt/graft.1905.html. In Europe, legal bookmaking has helped keep sports honest. Reuven Brenner, "Legal Gambling Can Be Good for Sports—and Even for Opera," *Wall Street Journal*, August 4–5, 2018, A11.

5. "States Eager to Bank on Sports Betting," *Wall Street Journal*, April 9, 2018, A3; "High Court Voids Ban on Sports Gambling," *Wall Street Journal*, May 15, 2018, A1; "Sports," *Wall Street Journal*, May 15, 2018, A12.

6. Johan Huizinga, *Homo Ludens: A Study of the Play-Element in Culture* (Boston: Beacon Press, 1953 [1950]), 75.

7. Gerda Reith, *The Age of Chance: Gambling in Western Culture* (London and New York: Routledge, 1999), 14.

8. Schwartz, *Roll the Bones*, 20–21, 136; Morris Edward Opler, *Myths and Tales of the Jicarilla Apache Indians*, Memoirs of the American Folklore Society, Vol. 31 (1938) (New York: American Folk-Lore Society, G.E. Stechert and Co., 1938), 128–136.

9. "Brawl," *Oxford English Dictionary*, Vol. 2, 498.

10. *Broughton's Rules* (1743), http://www.cyberboxingzone.com/boxing/1743.htm. Rule VI, my italics.

11. Henricks, *Disputed Pleasures*, 175.

12. For a description of the *Fancy*, see Ford, *Prizefighting*, 147–165.

13. Henricks, *Disputed Pleasures*, 175. Reith, *The Age of Chance*, 58–73 argues that the expansion of gambling in the seventeenth and eighteenth centuries was due to the rise of the mercantile economy. Commercial activities were fraught with both risk and reward. The growth of the money economy created a new standardized, universal measure of value. Combined with the inherent risks in commercial entrepreneurship, this new measure of value naturally led to the rise in gambling, both in business and in leisure. Great fortunes were made in business and lost in gambling.

14. Egan, *Boxiana*, Vol. 1, 1n1.

15. Ford, *Prizefighting*, 147.

16. Ford, *Prizefighting*, 163.

17. Henricks, *Disputed Pleasures*, 175. Gambling was critical to the creation of most popular sports. As Henricks points out, the first public announcement of a cricket match (1697) proclaimed that it was "eleven a side for fifty guineas" (142).

18. Egan, *Boxiana*, Vol. 2, 24–28; Dowling, *Fistiana*, 44–45, 55. The Pugilistic Club was succeeded by the Fair Play Club.

19. Ford, *Prizefighting*, 149.

20. Canetti, *Crowds and Power*, 29.

21. Theophilus Lucas, *Memoirs of the Lives, Intrigues, and Comical Adventures of the most Famous Gamesters and Celebrated Shapers in the Reigns of Charles II, James II, William III and Queen Anne, wherein is Contained the Secret History of Gaming* [...] (London: James Brown and Ferdinando Burleigh, 1714), 177.

22. Henricks, *Disputed Pleasures*, 142–143.

23. Birley, *Sport and the Making of Britain*, 147.

24. Quoted in Reith, *The Age of Chance*, p. 65. But as a counter-argument to this statement, in 1674 a tailor was punished for racing his horse against that of a planter "it being contrary to Law for a Labourer to make a race, being a sport only for Gentlemen" (73).

25. See von Uffenbach, *London in 1710*, 48 (for cockfighting), 59 (animal-baiting).

26. Samuel Pepys, *The Diary of Samuel Pepys*, ed. Robert Latham and William Matthews, Vol. 7 (Berkeley and Los Angeles: University of California Press, 1974), (27 May 1667), 239.

27. Samuel Pepys, *The Diary of Samuel Pepys*, ed. Robert Latham and William Matthews, Vol. 4 (Berkeley and Los Angeles: University of California Press, 1971), (1 June 1663), 168.

28. von Uffenbach, *London in 1710*, 89.

29. de Saussure, *A Foreign View of England*, 18.

Chapter IX

1. The citations are as follows: *Rex v. Perkins and Others, The English Reports* 172 (Nisi Prius) Vol. 3 ([Edinburgh]: Carswell, 1928), 814–815; *Rex v. Billingham, Savage, and Skinner, The English Reports* 172 (Nisi Prius) Vol. 3 ([Edinburgh]: Carswell, 1928) 106; "*Hunt v. Bell*," in *The English Reports* 130, Common Pleas, Vol. 8, (Edinburgh: William Green & Sons, 1912), 1–3. William Blackstone, *Commentaries on the Laws of England in Four Books, Book 4: Of Public Wrongs*, ed. Ruth Paley (Oxford: Oxford Edition of Blackstone, 2016), chapter 14, s II (Excusable Homicide) s.1, # 183, 120–121. For U.S. secondary sources, see Jack Anderson, "Brief Legal History of Prize Fighting in Nineteenth Century America," *Sport in History* 24, no. 1 (Summer 2004): 32–62; and Elmer Million, "The Enforceability of Prize Fight Statutes," *Kentucky Law Journal* 27, no. 2 (January 1939): 152–168. For primary sources on Canada, see *Revised Statutes of Canada*, 1985, Vol. 3, Criminal Code, part 2, C-46, sect. 83 (1) *Prize Fights*: "Every one who (a) engages as a principal in a prize fight (b) advises, encourages or promotes a prize fight, or (c) is present at a prize fight as an aid, second, surgeon, umpire, backer or reporter, is guilty of an offence punishable on summary conviction." For secondary sources, see Erik Magraken, "Prize Fighting Prosecutions and Combat Sports in Canada," *Combat Sports Law*, https://combatsportslaw.com/2013/07/29/combat-sports-in-canada-and-prize-fighting-criminal-code-prosecutions/. Despite the existence of statute law in Canada and the United States, there was no statute against prizefighting in England. The only statements outlawing prizefighting in England were either jurisprudence or personal pronouncements such as those of Blackstone. This was confirmed by an analysis of 1976 when Justice Murray V. McInerney could say in the Australian case *Pallante v. Stadiums Pty Ltd (No.1), Victorian Reports* 331 at 337 that "it has never been the case that there has been an offence designated as 'prize fighting' recognized at common law."

2. The best book on the early legal status of boxing (when described as prizefighting) is Anderson, *The Legality of Boxing*. Also valuable are his excellent articles "Pugilistic Prosecutions: Prizefighting and the Court in Nineteenth Century Britain," *Sports Historian* (now *Sport in History*), 21, no. 2 (November 2001): 37–57; and "The Legal Response to Prize Fighting in Nineteenth Century England and America," *Northern Ireland Legal Quarterly* 57, no. 2 (2006): 265–287. In addition there is also the article by Elmer Million, "History of the Texas Prize Fight Statute," *Texas Law Journal* 17, no. 2 (February 1939): 152–159. See also Neil Parpworth, "Boxing and Prize Fighting: The Indistinguishable Distinguished," *Sport and Law Journal* 2 (Spring 1994): 5–8; and Michael Gunn and David Ormerod, "Despite the Law: Prize-Fighting and Professional Boxing," in *Law and Sport in Contemporary Society*, ed. Steve Greenfield and Guy Osborn (London: Frank Cass, 2000), 21–50.

3. "Conquiset [i.e.: conquisivit] ibi terra vinea cum praetio suo [724 AD]; Accepi ego necessitate compulsis in precio ... sol. 3. lb. [786 AD]." J.R. Niermeyer, *Mediae Latinitatis Lexicon Minus* (Leiden, The Netherlands: E.J. Brill, 1984), "pretium," 845. Blackstone, *Commentaries on the Laws of England*, Book 4, chapter 7, # 96, 63.

4. "Prison" and "prisoner" were drawn from OF *prise* meaning a prize or captive taken in war. Simpson and Weiner, *The Oxford English Dictionary*, "prison, sb." For the many meanings of the Old French word, *pris*, see A.J. Holden, ed., *History of William Marshal* (c. 1219–1226), Occasional Publication Series 1, no. 4 (London: Anglo-Norman Text Society, 2002), lines 680–681, 999, 2187, 2584, 3022, 3028, 8369, 8895 where *pris* means capture; lines 682, 754, 1102, 1172, 1384, 1517, 1952, 3042, 7189, 8370, 8896 where it means honor or fame; lines 2622, 3192, 3196 where it means a feat of arms or combat.

5. David Crouch, *Tournament* (London and New York: Hambledon and London, 2006), 164–166. Crouch notes that death and injury were common to the tournament (98–102), but doubts that Geoffrey actually killed the English knight, since it would have been considered murder. This was not the view of the monastic writer of the time, John of Marmoutier, who clearly believed killing the knight added glory to Geoffrey's name. For the comparison of the tournament with war, see Juliet R.V. Baker, *The*

Tournament in England, 1100–1400 (Bury St. Edmunds, UK: Boydell, 1986), 17–44.

6. Julius Zupitza, ed., *The Romance of Guy of Warwick*, part 1, EETS, ES, n. xlii (London, 1883), Auchinleck Ms., c. 511, lines 802–804. See also Caius Ms., lines 801–804, 48–49. Johan Huizinga, *Homo Ludens* (Boston, MA: Beacon Press, 1955 [1950]), discusses the Latin word *pretium*: "It is very curious how the words 'prize,' 'price' and 'praise' all derive more or less directly from the Latin *pretium* but develop in different directions" (51). "Prize" is a word pregnant with meaning.

7. G.C. Macaulay, ed., *The English Works of John Gower*, Vol. 1, *Confessio Amantis*, EETS, ES, n. lxxxi (London, 1900), 200, line 2595 (P.i. 246).

8. "One Shippe Royall being of the Portage of Two Hundred Tonnes or above, with Ordinance and Apparell of every such Prise that shall fortune to theym in the said werre." 3 Henry VIII (1512), in Thomas Rymer, *Foedera*, 2nd ed., Vol. 13 (London: J. Tonson, 1727), 328 c. 2. See also "Ordering Release of French Prisoners and Prizes," 1 Edward VI (1547), in Hughes and Larkin, *Tudor Royal Proclamations*, Vol. 1, no. 291, 405–406.

9. See "Prize," in *Halsbury's Statutes of England and Wales*, Vol. 34, 4th ed. (London: LexisNexis UK, 2004), 1125–1157.

10. Prizes given as rewards for athletic contests are as ancient as the contests themselves. The Greek word for prize, *athlon*, is the root of the English word *athlete*. Nigel B. Crowther, *Sports in Ancient Times* (Westport, CT: Praeger, 2007), 41.

11. George Warner, ed., *Queen Mary's Psalter: Miniatures and Drawings by an English Artist of the 14th Century, Reproduced from Royal MS. 2 B.VII in the British Museum* (London: British Museum, 1912), plate 193, c, ff. 159v–161. See also note on 41.

12. Chaucer, *The Canterbury Tales*, in *The Works of Geoffrey Chaucer*, I (A), lines 545–548, VII, lines 736–741; B2, lines 1930–1931.

13. Maldwyn Mills, ed., *Horn Childe and Maiden Rimnild* (Heidelberg, Germany: Carl Winter, Universitätsverlag, 1988), stanza 24, line. 284; Josiah Forshall and Frederic Madden, eds., *The New Testament in English According to the Version of John Wycliffe about A.D. 1380 and Revised by John Purvey about A.D. 1388* (Oxford: Clarendon, 1879), 1 Cor. 9:24, 345.

14. "A Gest of Robyn Hode: The Fifth Fytte," cited in in Dobson and Taylor, *Rymes of Robyn Hood*, 99–100.

15. *As You Like It*, in Blakemore and Tobin, *The Riverside Shakespeare*, Act I, scene i, lines 161–162.

16. Paul Hentzner, *Travels in England during the Reign of Queen Elizabeth*, ed. and trans. Horace, late Earl of Oxford (London: Edward Jeffrey, 1797), 118. Reprinted in William B. Rye, *England as Seen by Foreigners in the Days of Elizabeth and James the First* (New York: Benjamin Blom, 1967 [1865]), 107–108.

17. J.H. Baker, ed., *The Reports of Sir John Spelman*, Vol. 2 (London: Selden Society, 1978), Vol. 94, Introduction, 312–314.

18. Thorne and Baker, *Readings and Moots at the Inns of Court in the Fifteenth Century*, Vol. 2, Vol. 105, 74.

19. John Stowe, *Historical Memoranda*, in James Gairdner, ed., *Three Fifteenth-Century Chronicles, with Historical Memoranda by John Stowe, the Antiquary*, Vol. 28 (London: Camden Society, 1880), 134.

20. Parades before prizefights were a long-standing tradition. Jorevin de Rochefort writing in 1670 explained how "when any fencing masters are desirous of shewing their courage and their great skill, they issue mutual challenges, and before they engage, parade the town with drums and trumpets sounding, to inform the public there is a challenge between two brave masters of the science of defence, and that the battle will be fought on such a day." "Visit of Jorevin de Rochefort," in James Beeverell, *The Pleasures of London*, trans. and ed. W.H. Quarrell (London: Witherby, 1940), 155–156. By 1701 the Grand Jury of Middlesex had enough of this and protested against "the late boldness of a sort of men that stile themselves Masters of the Noble Science of Defence, passing thorough the City with beat of drum, colours display'd, and swords drawn." Aylward, *The English Master at Arms*, 124.

21. Adapted by Aylward, *The English Master at Arms*, 33, from Ben Jonson, *Cynthia's Revels* (1600), Act V, scene iii, as published in G.A. Wilkes, ed., *The Complete Plays of Ben Jonson*, Vol. 2 (Oxford: Claren-

don, 1981), 78. For the discussion of prize-playing, see "Prize Playing," *Wikipedia*, https://www.en.wikipedia.org/wiki/Prize_Playing; Aylward, *The English Master of Arms*, 30–38. See Strutt, *The Sports and Pastimes of the People of England*, 319–323, on sword-play and sword-dance. See particularly Brown, *English Martial Arts*, 106–220 for pictures of those weapons in use by the Masters of Defence.

22. For the series of prize-playing combats held in the presence of the various Tudor monarchs, see Berry, *The Noble Science*, 37–38. For the warrant of James I renewing the monopoly of the Masters of Defence in 1605, see Aylward, *The English Master of Arms*, Appendix F, 258–260.

23. [Samuel] Sorbiere, *A Voyage to England Containing many Things relating to the State of Learning, Religion, and other Curiosities of that Kingdom* (London: J. Woodward, 1709 [1664]), 71–72.

24. "Whenever we hear of fencing-masters in the seventeenth century, they are also spoken of as prize fighters who made of their stage fights an advertisement of their trade as well as a profitable occupation, even as the pugilists of the next century depended chiefly on the success in the prize ring for a livelihood." Castle, *Schools and Masters of Fencing*, 187–188; Von Uffenbach, *London in 1710*, 88–91.

25. Tony Gee, personal correspondence, May 25, 2019. Tony does not believe that Figg himself ever taught or demonstrated boxing techniques. Nonetheless, Figg clearly had an interest in advancing boxing, as he showed in the episode with the Venetian Gondolier, where he not only provided John Whitacre to defeat the Venetian, but also Nathaniel Peartree to defeat Whitacre. Godfrey, *A Treatise upon the Useful Science of Defence*, 58–61. Pierce Egan, writing a century after Figg, considered him the father of pugilism. Egan, *Boxiana*, Vol. 1, 20. While I defer to the expertise of Tony with regard to Figg, it does seem to me that it is possible that Figg did exhibit his knowledge of physical boxing. See for example the advertisement for his Great Til'd Booth at Southwark, Saturday, September 18 (1725 OS), where the activity would conclude "with a grand parade by the Valiant Fig [sic], who will exhibit his knowledge in various Combats—with the Foil, Backsword, Cudgel, and Fist." Egan, *Boxiana*, Vol. 1, 44. The fact that Figg would exhibit his knowledge of combat with the fist makes me suspect that he did indeed demonstrate (if not perhaps "teach") boxing to the public.

26. The fact that Figg promoted boxing as well as sword-fighting in his booth at Southwark shows, I believe, that boxing could occur in the same locations as gladiatorial prizefighting. Boxing adopted a number of features of the gladiatorial prizefights such as the raised square stage in place of the original circular ring, the concept of seconds, the concept of rounds and the idea of sparring and the fighting for a prize. By 1800 it would appear that professional boxing had taken over the very name of prizefighting.

27. Naomi Hurnard, *The King's Pardon for Homicide before 1307* (Oxford: Clarendon, 1969), 137n2. In 1279 Richard de Horeslay and John Molendinario of Tutlington in Northumberland were playing and wrestling when by accident Richard's knife fell out of his scabbard and wounded John so that he died. Richard was not suspected of being responsible for the death, but since he fled from the scene, his property was confiscated. William Page, ed., *Three Early Assize Rolls for the County of Northumberland*, Saec. XIII, Publications of the Surtees Society, Vol. 88 (Durham, UK: Andrews, 1891), "Assize Roll, Northumberland, 7 Edw. I (1279)," 323. Prior to 1828 the defendant was "blameable to some extent" in cases of misadventure (*per infortunium*) and self-defense (*se defendendo*) in which a man was killed. Although his life was spared, he nonetheless had to pay for a pardon, forfeited his goods to the crown and might be imprisoned prior to trial. After 1828 (9 Geo. 4, c.31, s. 10), no punishment or forfeiture was required of one who killed another by misadventure or in self-defense. James Fitzjames Stephen, *A History of the Criminal Law of England*, Vol. 3 (London: Macmillan, 1883), 40–77.

28. Morris Marples, *A History of Football* (London: Secker & Warburg, 1954), 26.

29. Thorne and Baker, *Readings and Moots at the Inns of Court in the Fifteenth Century*, Vol. 2, Vol. 105, 74. See also J.M. Kaye, "The Early History of Murder and Manslaughter," *Law Quarterly Review* 83, no. 43 (October 1967): 571n43.

30. Godfrey, *A Treatise upon the Useful Science of Defence*, 41–42.

31. Baker, *The Reports of Sir John Spelman*, Vol. 2, Vol. 94, Introduction, 314.

32. Blackstone, *Commentaries on the Laws of England in Four Books*, Book 4, chapter 14, s. ii, n. 1, # 183, 120–121. Note that Blackstone in 1762 and Sir John Spelman (d.1546) both consider deaths in sword-play to be possible felonies. Stephen, *A History of the Criminal Law of England*, Vol. 3, 58 notes that according to the *Yearbook of 11 Henry 7* (1495–1496), 23a: "If two men fight with sword and buckler by consent and one kills the other it is felony, unless they fight by the king's command."

33. Thomas Fewtrell, *Boxing Reviewed: Or the Science of Manual Defence* (London, 1790), vi: "This Volume was written for the purpose of vindicating Pugilism from the unjustifiable censures of illiterate and weak minds, and proving its utility on rational principles." Sir Michael Foster (1689–1763) provided the basis of Edward Hyde East's argument that "friendly exertion of strength" is not unlawful: "I therefore cannot call these exercises [persons playing at cudgels, or foils, or wrestling by consent] unlawful; they are manly diversions, they tend to give strength, skill and activity and make fit people for defence, publick as well as personal, in time of need." Then he went on: "I would not be understood to speak of prize-fighting and public boxing-matches or any other exertions of courage ... of the like kind which are exhibited for lucre, and can serve no valuable purpose, but on the contrary encourage a spirit of idleness and debauchery." Sir Michael Foster, *A Report of some of the Proceedings on the Commission for the Trial of the Rebels in the year 1746,* [...] *and other Crown Cases to which are added Discourses upon a few branches of the Crown Law*, 3rd ed. (London: E. and R. Brooke, 1792), *Discourse II of Homicide*, c. I, sect. 2, 259–260. See also Richard L. Binder, "The Consent Defense: Sports, Violence, and Criminal Law" *American Criminal Law Review* 13 (1975): 239.

34. *Gentleman's Magazine*, April 1750, 184.

35. Egan, *Boxiana*, 58–59; Tony Gee, the British prize ring historian, disputes this anecdote: "I have never been able to find the anecdote (despite years of looking)" in contemporary newspapers. Tony Gee, personal correspondence, May 25, 2019; Miles, *Pugilistica*, Vol. 1, 27–29.

36. W.A. Speck, "William Augustus, Prince, Duke of Cumberland (1721–1765)," *Oxford Dictionary of National Biography*, Vol. 59 (Oxford: Oxford University Press, 2004), 105–113. Interestingly, while Cumberland may have been responsible for boxing becoming illegal, he was also given credit for driving out gladiatorial prizefights. An anonymous author in 1792 wrote as follows: "About fifty years ago, prince William Augustus duke of Cumberland, countenanced the pugilists, which brought on the decline of what was called the noble science of defence, with the broad sword; for it was at that time customary for prize-fighters, as they were termed, to entertain the public with exhibitions of their art; the heroes paraded the market-places on horseback in their shirts with their heads bare, ornamented with scars; on the sword arm was tied a ribbon, which might be fancied the favor of some fair one, and at the same time swelled the muscles of the arm, and gave it a more vigorous appearance; a slight cut or two, that the spectators might have some blood for their money, decided the combat." *Farrago. Containing essays, moral, philosophical, political, and historical: On Shakespeare, truth, boxing, kings* [...], Vol. 1 (Twekesbury: Dyde and Son, 1792), 11. This description of the prizefighter matches exactly the picture of James Figg in William Hogarth's print of Southwark Fair (1733).

37. Egan, *Boxiana*, Vol. 1, 58–59; Miles, *Pugilistica*, Vol. 1, 27–29. Tony Gee notes that "there is no contemporary evidence of Cumberland declaring that he had been sold out (and there are newspaper comments which definitely appear to cast doubts on this); and there were indubitably at least several battles of consequence in the period after the event (mainly involving Slack)." Personal correspondence, May 25, 2019. On the other hand, the phrase in the *Gentleman's Magazine* (April 1750) quoted above, citing "the great mortification of the knowing ones, who were finely taken in, particularly a peer of the first rank, who betting 10 to 1 lost 1000 *l*" suggests that Cumberland might well have considered himself "sold out." I can certainly believe he was angry

over this affair. Therefore, I do not feel comfortable denying the value of Egan's comments. It should be noted that Tony is currently in preparation of a biography of Jack Broughton that will provide more documentation on these events.

38. Egan, *Boxiana*, Vol. 1, 61. Tony Gee, in a book on Jack Broughton yet to be published, has a number of descriptions of boxing bouts which were held in London during this period. He argues that boxing was not driven out of London, but merely driven underground. Personal correspondence May 27, 2019. Egan, *Boxiana*, Vol. 1, 19 gives us another possible reason for the demise of boxing in London: "Boxing and cudgeling, it appeared, degenerated into downright ferocity and barbarity at this [Southwark] Fair, from the drunkenness and inequality of the combatants, and the various artifices adopted to get money, which at last became so disgusting, that it was declared a public nuisance, and, in 1749, Southwark Fair was suppressed."

39. *Rex v. Higginson* (1762), *The English Reports* 92 (King's Bench Division) Vol. 26 (Edinburgh and London: Wm. Green and Sons, 1909), 806; "An Act for the better preventing Thefts and Robberies, and for regulating Places of Publick Entertainment, and punishing persons keeping disorderly Houses," 25 George II (AD 1752), c. 36, in *Statutes at Large, from the Magna Charta to the end of the tenth year of George III inclusive*, Vol. 7 (London: Mark Baskett, 1769–1771), 438–440. Although 25 Geo. II, c. 36 was not specifically cited in this case, it was cited in the case of *Hunt v. Bell* of 1822 (see below) as a reason to close Hunt's boxing establishment.

40. Tony Gee notes that "trials of skill" (gladiatorial sword-fights) still remained popular with the public in the first half of the century: "Figg, for instance, was stated in a 'Daily Post' report (15 Oct. 1730) to have been fighting his 271st trial of skill, whilst Sutton, in a 'Daily Advertiser' advert (25 June 1735) was said to have had 354 such contests" (Tony Gee, personal correspondence, May 25, 2019).

41. See the fair bill printed by Egan, *Boxiana*, Vol. 1, 44; and in Miles, *Pugilistica*, Vol. 1, 10. For James Figg, see, Miles, *Pugilistica*, Vol. 1, 8–12; and Tony Gee, "Figg, James," *Oxford Dictionary of National Biography*, Vol. 19 (Oxford: Oxford University Press, 2004), 534–536. "There is no doubt that his [Figg's] establishment was a showcase for some of the best early exponents of regular boxing and, as such, a strong case can be made for considering him England's first pugilistic promoter" (Gee, *Up to Scratch*, 13). Tony Gee has also informed me that James Stokes and his wife Elizabeth had opened a new amphitheater in Islington Road near Sadler's Wells in London in 1726. This was designed to compete with James Figg's establishment by offering both sword-fights and boxing matches. See Tony Gee, "Stokes, Elizabeth," *Oxford Dictionary of National Biography*, Vol. 52 (Oxford: Oxford University Press, 2004), 857–858.

42. Aylward, *The English Master of Arms*, 142–143; Godfrey, *A Treatise upon the Useful Science of Defence*, 39.

43. Bob Mee, *Bare Fists: A History of Bare-Knuckle Prize-Fighting* (Woodstock and New York: Overlook, 2001), 4: "By 1723 boxing was so popular that on the orders of George I a ring, a circular piece of ground encircled by railings, was erected in Hyde Park about 300 yards from Grosvenor Gate for the use of the public." But see H. Misson's description of this ring: "Here the People of Fashion take Diversion of the Ring ... and the Coaches drive round and round this. When they have turn'd for some Time round one Way, they face about and turn t'other: So rowls the World." It is clear that far from being a permanent boxing ring, this was a driving ring designed for horses and carriages. Misson, *Memoirs and Observations*, 126. Mee and others have been ensnared by the word "ring," which, in this case, had nothing to do with boxing.

44. "William Ward, Killing: Murder, 3rd June, 1789."

45. Justice Ashurst noted that Swaine grabbed Ward's hair and this constituted a foul and possible provocation. However, six years later, in the championship bout between John Jackson and Daniel Mendoza (1795), Jackson grabbed Mendoza by the hair and smashed his face. This was not considered a foul at that time. See Egan, *Boxiana*, Vol. 1, 293.

46. Robert W. Malcolmson, *Popular Recreations in English Society, 1700–1850*

(Cambridge: Cambridge University Press, 1973), 145.

47. Edward Hyde East, *A Treatise of the Pleas of the Crown*, Vol. 1 (Clark, NJ: Lawbook Exchange, 2004 [1803]), 270. The idea that crowds drawn together by sporting events would turn to riot had long been a political concern. As early as 1373 the Sheriff of London arrested Adam de Kent and seven others on the basis "that they and others with force and arms, to wit, swords and knives, made an assembly, under colour of playing football, in order to assault others, occasion disputes, and perpetuate other evil deeds against the peace." Thomas, *Calendar of Plea and Memoranda Rolls, 1364-1381*, roll A18, 152. In 1589 the Privy Council was willing to allow sports as long as they were not of the "disordered and riotuos sorte." Oliver Cromwell banned cockfights and horse races in 1654-1655, not because he was opposed to the sports, but because of the concern that the crowds would riot. See Gregory M. Colón Semenza, *Sport, Politics, and Literature in the English Renaissance* (Newark: University of Delaware Press, 2003), 65, 142.

48. Brandt, *Habet!*, 5, 12.

49. East, *A Treatise*, Vol. 1, 268, 270.

50. Anderson, "Pugilistic Prosecutions," 37-57.

51. Prior to 1861 prizefighting was illegal because it was dangerous to public peace. After 1861 it was illegal because it was dangerous to the boxers themselves. According to Gunn and Ormerod, "Despite the Law," 21-50, this change occurred as a result of the Offences against the Person act of 1861, but East's work clearly foreshadowed this. In support of East's contention see Misson, *Memoirs and Observations*, 308. Speaking of the sword prizefights, he said, "The edge of the sword was a little blunted, and the Care of the Prizefighters was not so much to avoid wounding one another, as it was to avoid doing it dangerously: Nevertheless, as they were oblig'd to fight 'till some Blood was shed, without which no Body would give a Farthing for the Show, they were sometimes forc'd to play a little ruffly."

52. *Regina v. Coney*, 8 Queen's Bench Division for the High Court, (1882), 534.

53. Quoted in the "*Regina v. Coney*," *Ohio Law Journal* 3 (1882): 100.

54. American English considers prizefighting to be a synonym for professional boxing. *Merriam-Webster Collegiate Dictionary*, 10th ed. (Springfield, MA: Merriam-Webster, 1994). British English considers prizefighting to mean bare-knuckle fighting. This difference is only one of the many the historian encounters.

55. *The English Reports*, Vol. 130 (Common Pleas), Vol. 8 (Edinburgh: William Green & Sons, 1912), n. 1, 1-3.

Appendix II

1. Larkin, *Richard Coer de Lyon*, lines 740-98 (page 195).

2. James A. Brundage, *Medieval Canon Law and the Crusader* (Madison, Milwaukee and London: University of Wisconsin, 1969), 12-14, 160-165.

3. Bradford B. Broughton, *The Legends of King Richard I Coeur de Lion: A Study of Sources and Variations to the year 1600* (The Hague and Paris: Mouton, 1966), 115.

4. J.G. Bellamy, *The Law of Treason in England in the Late Middle Ages* (Cambridge: Cambridge University Press, 1970), 10.

5. Larkin, *Richard Coer de Lyon*, notes lines 740-98 (p. 195). See also Broughton, *The Legends of King Richard I Coeur de Lion*, 120-123.

Appendix III

1. *Robin Hood and Other Outlaw Tales*, ed. Stephen Knight and Thomas Ohlgren, TEAMS Middle English Texts Series (Kalamazoo: Western Michigan University, 1997), 80-168, cited by lines; Dobson and Taylor, *Rymes of Robyn Hood*, 109-110, cited by *Fyttes* and verses.

2. Broughton, *The Legends of King Richard I Coeur de Lion*, 122.

3. Roger Sherman Loomis, *Celtic Myth and Arthurian Romance* (Chicago: Academy Chicago Publishers, 1997 [1967]), 61, 76, 91, etc.

Appendix IV

1. Michael B. Poliakoff, *Combat Sports in the Ancient World: Competition, Violence and Culture* (New Haven and London: Yale University Press, 1987). See also Miles, *Pugilistica*, Vol. 1, xiii-xiv.

2. Hugh M. Lee, "The *caestus* in the Sixteenth Century: Brant, Raphael, Mercuriale, and Ligorio," *Nikephoros* 18 (2005): 207–217.

3. "Roman Boxing Gloves Unearthed by Vindolandia Dig," *BBC News*, February 20 2018, bbc.com/news/uk-england-*tyne*-43120 942; Rogers, James, "Ancient Roman Boxing Gloves Discovered near Hadrian's Wall," *Fox News*, February 21, 2018, foxnews.com/science/2018/02/21/ancient-roman-boxing-gloves-discovered-near-hadrians-wall.html.

4. *Oxford English Dictionary*, "whirlbat"; *Middle English Dictionary*, "hurlebat."

5. John Stratford, a relative of Dover, also suggests that a modified version of *caestus* boxing was brought to the Cotswold. He compares the sports at the Cotswold Olimpicks with those of ancient Greece. After noting that "Wrastling, Running, Leaping, were games of Prize" he remembers "Eutelleus, hee at Caestus, had the best/ In mighty strength surpassing all the rest. / Such were the old World's sports; now transferred over/ Into our Cotswold, by thee, Worthy Dover." "To My Kind Cosen, and Noble Friend, Mr. Robert Dover, on his Sports upon Cotswold," in Whitfield, *Robert Dover and the Cotswold Games*, 180. See also A.B. Grosart ed., *Annalia Dubrensia* (No location: Nabu Public Domain Reprints, 2010), 47–49.

6. Thomas Goodwin, *Romanae historiae anthologia* (Oxford: Printed by Joseph Barnes, 1614), Lib. 2, Sect. 3, 68.

7. Thomas Goodwin, *Romanae historiae anthologia* (Oxford: Printed by Leonard Lichfield for Henry Crypps, 1638), Lib. 2, Sect. 3, 92.

8. Goodwin's description of the *caestus* appears to be a leather lash rather than the leather wrapped fists generally associated with Roman boxing. This adds confusion to the meaning of the term "whorlebat" in Tudor England. Levin, *Manipulus Vocabulorum*, col. 37, line 33, defined "an Hurlebatte" as an adides or dart, and linked it to Hurle, to throw, 294. The *Oxford English Dictionary* notes that Hurlbat "is used to render two quite different words, aclys [a small javelin], or caestus." The illustration by Sebastian Brant (Fig. 2 above) is the only one that seems to match Goodwin's description. Still, it is not clear what type of sport "whorlebats" really was, or how the word was spelled.

Appendix V

1. Mark Noble, *Memoirs of the Protectorate-House of Cromwell*, Vol. 1 (Birmingham: Pearson and Rollason, 1784), 110–111.

2. W. Aldis Wright, "The Squire Papers," *English Historical Review* 1 (1886): 311–348, on 336, https://archive.org/details/squirepapersletOOsquigoog.

Bibliography

Allen, Arly. "The Boxer and the Duelist: The Origins of the Missouri Prizefight Law of 1874." *Missouri Historical Review* 104, no. 4 (July 2010): 213–232.

Altizer, Linda. "Boxer's Fracture." *Orthopedic Nursing* 25, no. 4 (July–August 2006): 271–273.

Anderson, Jack. "Brief Legal History of Prize Fighting in Nineteenth Century America." *Sport in History* 24, no.1 (Summer 2004): 32–62.

Anderson, Jack. "The Legal Response to Prize Fighting in Nineteenth Century England and America." *Northern Ireland Legal Quarterly* 57, no. 2 (2006): 265–287.

Anderson, Jack. *The Legality of Boxing: A Punch Drunk Love?* (Abingdon, UK: Birkbeck Law, 2007).

Anderson, Jack. "Pugilistic Prosecutions: Prizefighting and the Court in Nineteenth Century Britain." *Sports Historian* (now *Sport in History*), 21, no. 2 (November 2001): 37–57.

Andrew, Donna T. "The Code of Honour and Its Critics: The Opposition to Dueling in England, 1700–1850." *Social History* 5, no. 3 (October 1980): 409–434.

Anglin, Jay P. "The Schools of Defense in Elizabethan London." *Renaissance Quarterly* 37, no. 3 (Autumn 1984): 393–410.

Anglo, Sidney. *The Martial Arts of Renaissance Europe* (New Haven and London: Yale University Press, 2000).

Anonymous. *A Relation, or Rather a True Account, of the Island of England ... about the Year 1500*. trans. Charlotte Augusta Sneyd, Camden Society no. 37 (London, 1847).

Anstey, Henry, ed. *Munimenta Academica, or Documents Illustrative of Academical Life and Studies at Oxford*. part 1, *Libri cancellarii et procuratorum*. Roll Series. *Rerum Britannicarum Medii Aevi Scriptores*. Vol. 50 (London: Longmans, Green, Reader, and Dyer, 1868).

Armin, Robert. *Foole vpon Foole or Six Sortes of Sottes* (London: Printed for William Ferbrand, 1600).

Armstrong, Walter. "The Lancashire Style (Catch as Catch Can)." *The Encyclopedia of Sport*. Vol. 2, ed. Earl of Suffolk and Berkshire, Hedley Peek, and F.G. Aflalo (London: Lawrence and Bullen, 1898), 548.

Arnold, Morris S., ed. *Select Cases of Trespass from the King's Courts (1309–1399)*. Selden Society 100 (London, 1985).

Athenaeus. *The Deipnosophysts*. trans. Charles Burton Gulick, Loeb Library, Vol. 2 (London and New York: William Heinemann and G.P. Putnam's Sons, 1927).

Attenborough, F.L., ed. and trans. *The Laws of the Earliest English Kings* (Clark, NJ: Lawbook Exchange, 2006 [Cambridge, 1922]).

Aydelotte, Frank, *Elizabethan Rogues and Vagabonds*. Oxford Historical and Literary Studies, Vol. 1 (Oxford: Clarendon, 1913).

Aylward, J.D. *The English Master of Arms from the Twelfth to the Twentieth Century* (London: Routledge & Kegan Paul, 1956).

Baales, Michael, Susanne Birker, and Frank

Mucha. "Hafting with Beeswax in the Final Palaeolithic: A Barbed Point from Bergkemen." *Antiquity* 91, no. 359 (October 2017): 1155–1170.

Bain, Robert Nisbet, *The Pupils of Peter the Great: A History of the Russian Court and Empire from 1697 to 1740* (Westminster, UK: A. Constable, 1897).

Baker, J.H. *An Introduction to English Legal History* (London: Butterworths, 1990).

Baker, J.H., ed. *The Reports of Sir John Spelman* (London: Selden Society, 1978).

Baker, John. *The Oxford History of the Laws of England (1483–1558)*. Vol. 6 (Oxford, 2003).

Baker, Juliet R.V. *The Tournament in England, 1100–1400* (Bury St. Edmunds, UK: Boydell, 1986).

Baldwin, Frances Elizabeth. *Sumptuary Legislation and Personal Regulation in England* (Baltimore: Johns Hopkins University Press, 1926).

Baret, John. *An Alvearie or Triple Dictionarie* (London: Henry Denham, 1574).

Bartlett, Robert. *Trial by Fire and Water: The Medieval Judicial Ordeal* (Oxford: Clarendon, 1986).

Baugh, Albert C., and Thomas Cable. *The History of the English Language*. 5th ed. (Upper Saddle River, NJ: Prentice-Hall, 2002 [1935]).

Bellamy, John. *Crime and Public Order in England in the Later Middle Ages* (London: Routledge & Kegan Paul, 1973).

Bellamy, John G. *Criminal Law and Society in Late Medieval and Tudor England* (Gloucester and New York: Alan Sutton, 1984).

Bellamy, John G. *The Law of Treason in England in the Late Middle Ages* (Cambridge: Cambridge University Press, 1970).

"Bernardine of Siena, St." *New Catholic Encyclopedia*. 2nd ed., Vol. 2 (Detroit: Thomson Gale, 2002), 320–321.

Berry, Herbert. *The Noble Science: A Study and Transcription of Sloane Ms. 2530. Papers of the Masters of Defence of London, Temp. Henry VIII to 1590* (Newark: University of Delaware Press, 1991).

Binder, Richard L. "The Consent Defense: Sports, Violence, and Criminal Law." *American Criminal Law Review* 13 (1975).

Birley, Derek. *Sport and the Making of Britain* (Manchester: Manchester University Press, 1993).

Black, Joseph, ed. *The Martin Marprelate Tracts: A Modernized and Annotated Edition* (Cambridge: Cambridge University Press, 2008).

Blackstone, William. *Commentaries on the Laws of England in Four Books*. Book 4: *Of Public Wrongs*. Ed. Ruth Paley (Oxford: Oxford Edition of Blackstone, 2016).

Blakemore, Evans G., and J.J.M. Tobin, eds. *The Riverside Shakespeare*. 2nd ed. (Boston and New York: Houghton Mifflin, 1997).

Bonfante, Larissa. "Nudity as a Costume in Classical Art." *American Journal of Archaeology* 93 (1989): 543–570.

"Boniface of Savoy (Bishop)." *Wikipedia*. Seen September 18, 2017.

Bosworth, Joseph, and T. Northcote Toller, eds. *An Anglo-Saxon Dictionary* (Oxford: Oxford University Press, 1964 [1898]).

Bowers, Fredson, ed. *The Dramatic Works in the Beaumont and Fletcher Canon*. multiple vols. (Cambridge: Cambridge University Press, 1989–1994).

"Boxer's Fracture." *WebMD*. https://www.webmd.com/a-to-z-guides/boxers-fracture#1-1.

"Boxing." *Encyclopedia Britannica*. 11th ed., Vol. 6 (1910–1911), 350.

Brandt, Francis Frederick, *Habet! A Short Treatise on the Law of the Land as It Affects Pugilism* (London: Robert Hardwicke, 1857).

Brenner, Reuven. "Legal Gambling Can Be Good for Sports—and Even for Opera." *Wall Street Journal*. August 4–5, 2018, A11.

Brindley, Noel C. *Sir Gawain and the Green Knight: A Study of Hautdesert, Wilderness and Purlieus*. http://hautdesertpurlieu.wordpress.com. Seen March 27, 2017.

Brook, G.L., and R.F. Leslie, eds. *Layamon: Brut*. Early English Text Series (EETS) 2, Original Series, no. 250 (London, 1978): 594–595.

Broughton, Bradford B. *The Legends of King Richard I Coeur de Lion: A Study of Sources and Variations to the year 1600* (The Hague and Paris: Mouton, 1966).

Broughton's Rules (1743), cyberboxingzone.com/boxing/1743.htm.

Brown, Terry. *English Martial Arts* (Hockwold-cum-Wilton, UK: Anglo-Saxon, 1997).

Brown, William. "Trial by Combat." *York-*

shire *Archaeological Journal* 23 (1914): 300–307.

Browne, Thomas. "Enquiries into Vulgar and Common Errors." *Pseudodoxia Epidemica*. Book 4, ed. Geoffrey Keynes (Chicago: University of Chicago Press, 1964).

Brundage, James A. *Medieval Canon Law and the Crusader* (Madison: University of Wisconsin Press, 1969).

Burgh, J. *Political Disquisitions*. Vol. 1 (Philadelphia: Robert Bell and William Woodhouse, 1775).

Burnley, David. *The History of the English Language: A Source Book*. 2nd ed. (Harlow, UK: Pearson Education, 2000 [1992]).

By the King. A Proclamation Against Fighting of Duells. (London: John Bill and Christopher Baker, 1660).

Byock, Jesse. "Holmganga." *Medieval Scandinavia: An Encyclopedia*. Ed. Philip Pulsiano (New York and London, 1993), 289–290.

Canetti, Elias. *Crowds and Power* (New York: Viking, 1966 [1960]).

Carew, Richard of Antony. *The Survey of Cornwall*. Ed. F.E. Halliday (London: Andrew Melrose, 1953 [1602]).

Carson, Ciaran. *The Tain* (London: Penguin Classics, 2007).

Castle, Egerton. *Schools and Masters of Fencing from the Middle Ages to the Eighteenth Century* (Mineola, New York: Dover, 2003 [1885]).

Chaucer, Geoffrey. *The Works of Geoffrey Chaucer*. Ed. F.N. Robinson, 2nd ed. (Boston: Houghton Mifflin, 1957).

Chew, Helena and Martin Weinbaum, eds. *The London Eyre of 1244* (London: London Record Society, 1970).

Chrimes, S.B., and A.L. Brown, eds. *Select Documents of English Constitutional History, 1307–1485* (London: Adam and Charles Black, 1961).

Christesen, Paul. "On the Meaning of *gymnazo*." *Nikephoros* 15 (2002): 7–37.

Churchyard, Thomas. *Churchyards Challenge: A Discourse of True Manhood* (London: John Wolfe, 1593).

Ciklamini, Marlene. "The Old Icelandic Duel." *Scandinavian Studies* 35, no. 3 (August 1963): 175–194.

Clanchy, M.T. *From Memory to Written Record: England 1066–1307* (Oxford: Blackwell, 1993 [1979]).

Clanchy, M.T. "Highway Robbery and Trial by Battle in the Hampshire Eyre of 1249." *Medieval Legal Records edited in Memory of C.A.F. Meekings* (London: Her Majesty's Stationery Office, 1978), 26–61.

Clayton, Sarah. "Yorke, Rowland (d. 1588)." *Oxford Dictionary of National Biography* Vol. 60 (Oxford: Oxford University Press, 2004), 855–856.

Cockburn, John. *The History and Examination of Duels* (London: G. Straken, etc., 1720).

Cohn, Norman. *The Pursuit of the Millennium: Revolutionary Messianism in Medieval and Reformation Europe and Its bearing on Modern Totalitarian Movements* (New York: Harper and Brothers, 1961 [1957]).

Collinson, Patrick. "Antipuritanism." In *The Cambridge Companion to Puritanism*. Ed. John Coffey and Paul C.H. Lim (Cambridge: Cambridge University Press, 2008), 19–20.

Colón Semenza, Gregory M. *Sport, Politics, and Literature in the English Renaissance* (Newark: University of Delaware Press, 2003).

Cooper, Thomas. "Admonition to the People of England" (1589) in Joseph Black. "The Rhetoric of Reaction: The Martin Marprelate Tracts (1588–1589), Anti-Martinism, and the Uses of Print in Early Modern England." *Sixteenth Century Journal* 28, no. 3 (1997): 707–725.

Coss, Peter. *The Knight in Medieval England, 1000–1400* (Phoenix Mill, UK: Alan Sutton, 1993).

Coss, Peter. *The Origins of the English Gentry* (Cambridge: Cambridge University Press, 2003).

Cox, Monte, personal correspondence, February 2, 2015.

Craig, Stephen, *Sports and Games of the Ancients* (Westport, CT: Greenwood, 2002).

Cram, David, Jeffrey L. Forgeng and Dorothy Johnston, eds. *Francis Willughby's Book of Games: A Seventeenth-Century Treatise on Sports, Games and Pastimes* (Aldershot, UK: Ashgate, 2003).

"Crime and Disorder in the Localities, Edward Hext to Lord Burghley, Reporting on Somerset, 25 September 1596." *English Historical Documents (1558–1603)*, ed. Ian

W. Archer and F. Douglas Price, Vol. 5a (London and New York: Routledge, 2011).

Cross, Tom Peete, and Clark Harris Slover. *Ancient Irish Tales* (New York: Henry Holt, 1936).

Crouch, David. *Tournament* (London and New York: Hambledon and London, 2006).

Crowther, Nigel B. *Sports in Ancient Times* (Westport, CT: Praeger, 2007).

Cunliffe, Barry. *The Ancient Celts* (London: Penguin, 1999 [1997]).

Daniels, Bruce C. *Puritans at Play: Leisure and Recreation in Colonial New England* (New York: St. Martin's, 1996 [1995]).

Davidson, A.B. "Covenant." *A Dictionary of the Bible*. Ed. James Hastings, Vol. 1 (Peabody, MA: Hendrickson, 1988 [1898–1904]), 509.

Davidson, Hilda Ellis, *The Sword in Anglo-Saxon England* (Woodbridge, UK: Boydell, 1994).

Davis, J.F., and E.G. Kraus. "Dominant Rats are Natural Risk-Takers and Display Increased Motivation for Food Reward." *Neuroscience* 162, no. 1 (August 4, 2009): 23–30.

Davis, Robert C. *War of the Fists: Popular Culture and Public Violence in Late Renaissance Venice* (New York and Oxford: Oxford University Press, 1994).

Day, Robert, *The Last Cattle Drive* (Lawrence: University of Kansas Press, 1987 [1977]).

Dempsey, Jack, *Championship Fighting: Explosive Punching and Aggressive Defence* (New York: Simon & Schuster, 1978 [1950]).

de Neergaard, Margrethe. "The Use of Knives, Shears, Scissors and Scabbards." *Medieval Finds from Excavations in London*. Vol. 1: *Knives and Scabbards*. ed. J. Cowgill, M. de Neergaard and N. Griffiths (Woodbridge, UK: Boydell, 2011 [1987]).

Denholm-Young, N. "The Tournament in the Thirteenth Century." *Studies in Medieval History Presented to Frederick Maurice Powicke* (Oxford: Clarendon, 1948), 257–263.

Denny, William. "Encomiastick To His worthy Friend Mr. Robert Dover, on his Famous Annual Assemblies at Cotswold." *Annalia Dvbrensia: Vpon the yeerely celebration of Mr. Robert Dovers Olimpick Games vpon Cotswold-Hills* (London: Robert Raworth, for Mathewe Walbancke, 1636).

de Quevedo, Jr., Francisco. *The town adventurer. A discourse of masquerades, playes, &c.* (London, 1675), quoted in Markku Peltonen, *The Duel in Early Modern England: Civility, Politeness and Honour* (Cambridge: Cambridge University Press, 2003).

de Saussure, César. *A Foreign View of England in the Reigns of George I & George II: The Letters of Monsieur Céesar de Saussure to his Family*. Trans. and ed. Madame Van Muyden (London: J. Murray, 1902).

Dictionary of Medieval Latin from British Sources. Vol. 13 (Oxford: Oxford University Press, 2010).

Di Grassi, Giacomo, *Art of Defence*. trans. L.G. Gentleman (London: Temple Barre at the Signe of the Hand and Starre, 1594 [1570]).

Dobson, R.B., and J. Taylor. *Rymes of Robyn Hood: An Introduction to the English Outlaw* (Phoenix Mill, UK: Alan Sutton, 1997 [1976]).

Dr. Johnson's Table Talk: or, Conversations of the late Samuel Johnson, L.L.D. (London: G.G.J. and J. Robinson, 1785).

Domestick Intelligence: Or News both from City and Country impartially related. numb. 64. December 29, [1681] to January 2 [1682], 1.

Domestick Intelligence: Or News both from City and Country impartially related. numb. 140. September 1 to September 25, 1682, 1.

Donkin, R.A. "Changes in the Early Middle Ages." *A New Historical Geography of England*. ed. H.C. Darby (Cambridge: Cambridge University Press, 1973), 75–135.

Dougall, Alistair. *The Devil's Book: Charles I, The Book of Sports and Puritanism in Tudor and Early Stuart England* (Exeter, UK: University of Exeter Press, 2011).

Douglas, David C., and George W. Greenway, eds. "The Assize of Arms, 1181." *English Historical Documents, 1042–1189*. 2nd ed., Vol. 2 (London: Eyre Methuen, 1981), 449–451.

Dowling, V.G. *Fistiana or the Oracle of the Ring* (London: Wm. Clement, Jr., 1841).

Drayton, Michael. "The Poly-Olbion." (1613), in Richard Carew of Antony, *The Survey of Cornwall*. ed. F.E. Halliday (London: Andrew Melrose, 1953 [1602]).

Durston, Gregory. *Crime and Justice in Early Modern England: 1500–1750* (Chichester, UK: Barry Rose Law Publishers, 2004).

Earle, Peter. "The Middling Sort in London." *The Middling Sort of People: Culture, Society and Politics in England, 1550-1800.* ed. Jonathan Barry and Christopher Brooks (New York: St. Martin's, 1994), 141-158.

East, Edward Hyde. *A Treatise of the Pleas of the Crown.* Vol. 1 (Clark, NJ: Lawbook Exchange, 2004 [1803]).

Ebert, J. "Zur neuen Bronzeplatte mit Siegerinschriften aus Olympia." *Nikephoros* 10 (1997): 217-233.

Egan, Pierce. *Boxiana* (Vol. 1); *or Sketches of Ancient and Modern Pugilism, from the Days of the Renowned Broughton and Slack to the Championship of Cribb* (Brighton, MA: Elibron Classics, 2006 [1811-1830]).

Egan, Pierce. *Boxiana* (Vol. 2); *or Sketches of Modern Pugilism from the Championship of Cribb to the Present Time* (London: Sherwood Jones, 1824).

Elema, Ariella. "Trial by Battle in France and England." (Ph.D. diss., University of Toronto, 2012).

Eliade, Mircea, ed. *The Encyclopedia of Religion.* Vol. 12 (New York and London: Macmillan, 1987).

Elias, Norbert. "An Essay on Sport and Violence." Elias, Norbert, and Eric Dunning, *The Collected Works of Norbert Elias. Vol 7: Quest for Excitement: Sport and Leisure in the Civilizing Process,* ed. Eric Dunning (Dublin: University College Dublin Press, 2008 [Oxford: Basil Blackwell, 1986]), 154-155.

Erasmus, Desiderius. *The Colloquies of Erasmus.* Trans. Craig R. Thompson (Chicago and London: University of Chicago Press, 1965).

Evans-Wentz, W.Y. *The Fairy-Faith in Celtic Countries* (N.p.: University Books, 1966 [1911]).

Farquhar, George. *The Constant Couple (Or a Trip to the Jubilee).* Ed. Simon Trussler (London: Methuen, 1988).

Farrago. Containing essays, moral, philosophical, political, and historical: On Shakespeare, truth, boxing, kings ... 2 vols. (Twekesbury, UK: Dyde and Son, 1792).

Ferne, John. *The Blazon of Gentrie* (London: J. Windet for T. Cook, 1586).

Fewtrell, Thomas. *Boxing Reviewed: Or the Science of Manual Defence* (London, 1790).

Fisher, John H. *The Emergence of Standard English* (Lexington: University Press of Kentucky, 1996).

Fleischer, Nat, and Sam Andre. *An Illustrated History of Boxing.* 6th rev. updated ed. (New York: Citadel, 2001 [1959]).

Flenley, Ralph, ed. *Six Town Chronicles of England* (Oxford: Clarendon, 1911).

Ford, John. *Prizefighting: The Age of Regency Boximania* (Newton Abbot, UK: David and Charles, 1971).

"Form for Keeping the Peace, 1242." Harry Rothwell, ed., *English Historical Documents, 1189-1327.* Vol. 3 (1975) no. 33, 357-359.

Forshall, Josiah, and Frederic Madden, eds. *The New Testament in English According to the Version of John Wycliffe about A.D. 1380 and Revised by John Purvey about A.D. 1388* (Oxford: Clarendon, 1879).

Forsyth, Joseph. *Remarks on Antiquities, Arts, and Letters during an Excursion in Italy in the Years 1802 and 1803* (Newark: University of Delaware Press, 2001).

Foster, Michael. *A Report of some of the Proceedings on the Commission for the Trial of the Rebels in the year 1746, ... and other Crown Cases to which are added Discourses upon a few branches of the Crown Law.* 3rd ed. (London: E. and R. Brooke, 1792).

Fraser, Angus. *The Gypsies* (Oxford: Blackwell, 1992).

Frazer, James George. *The Golden Bough: A Study in Magic and Religion.* abridged ed. (New York: Macmillan, 1956).

Freeth, John. *The political songster, or a touch on the times, on various subjects and adapted to common tunes, the sixth edition, with additions* (Birmingham, 1790).

Friedman, Matthew, Ames C. Grawert and James Cullen, eds. "Crime in 2016: A Preliminary Analysis." (New York: Brennan Center for Justice, New York University School of Law, 2016).

Fuller, Thomas. *The History of the Worthies of England.* New ed. by P. Austin Nuttall, Vol. 2 (London: Thomas Tegg, 1840 [1662]).

Gairdner, James, ed. *The Historical Collections of A Citizen of London in the Fifteenth Century* (London: Camden Society, 1876).

Gairdner, James, ed. *Three Fifteenth-Century*

Chronicles, with Historical Memoranda by John Stowe, the Antiquary (London: Camden Society, 1880).

Galbraith, V.H. "The Death of a Champion (1287)." *Studies in Medieval History Presented to Frederick Maurice Powicke* (Oxford: Clarendon, 1948).

Gee, Tony. "Figg, James." *Oxford Dictionary of National Biography.* Vol. 19 (Oxford: Oxford University Press, 2004), 534–536.

Gee, Tony. "Stokes, Elizabeth." *Oxford Dictionary of National Biography.* Vol. 52 (Oxford: Oxford University Press, 2004), 857–858.

Gee, Tony. *Up to Scratch: Bareknuckle Fighting and Heroes of the Prize-Ring* (Mackerye End, UK: Queen Anne, 2001 [1998]).

Genin, F., ed. *Lesclarissement de la langue francoyse par Jean Palsgrave, suivi de la grammaire de Giles du Guez, publies pour la permiere fois en France,* in *Collection de documents inedits sur l'histoire de France Deuxieme serie. Histoire des letteres et des sciences* (Paris: Imprimerie nationale, 1852).

Gerald of Wales. *The History and Topography of Ireland.* Trans. John J. O'Meara (London: Penguin, 1982 [1951]).

Given, James Buchanan. *Society and Homicide in Thirteenth-Century England* (Stanford, CA: Stanford University Press, 1977).

Glanvill, Ranulf. *The Treatise on the Laws and Customs of the Realm of England Commonly Called Glanvill* (c. 1187–1189), ed. and trans. G.D.G. Hall (London: Thomas Nelson and Sons, 1965).

Glare, P.G.W., ed. *Oxford Latin Dictionary* (Oxford: Clarendon, 1982).

Glaser, Joseph, trans. and notes. *Sir Gawain and the Green Knight* (Indianapolis and Cambridge: Hackett, 2011).

Godefroy, Frederic. *Dictionnaire de l'Ancienne Langue Francais et de touts ses Dialectes du IXe au XVe Siecle.* Vol. 1 (repr. Vaduz: Kraus Reprint, 1965 [Paris, 1880]).

Godfrey, John. *A Treatise Upon the Useful Science of Defence* (Repr. No location: Andesite Press, 2017 [London, 1747]).

Golden, Mark. *Sport in the Ancient World from A to Z* (New York: Routledge, 2004).

Goodwin, Thomas. *Romanae historiae anthologia* (Oxford: Joseph Barnes, 1614).

Goodwin, Thomas. *Romanae historiae anthologia* (Oxford: Leonard Lichfield for Henry Crypps, 1638).

Gorn, Elliott J. "'Gouge and Bite, Pull Hair and Scratch': The Social Significance of Fighting in the Southern Backcountry." *American Historical Review* 90, no. 1 (February 1985): 18–43.

Grammatici, Saxonis [Saxo Grammaticus]. *Gesta Danorvm.* ed. Alfred Holder (Strassburg, France: Verlag von Karl J. Trubner, 1886).

Grammaticus, Saxo. *The History of The Danes.* Books 1–9, ed. and comm. Hilda Ellis Davidson, trans. Peter Fisher (Cambridge: D.S. Brewer, 2008 [1979–1980]).

The Great Roll of the Pipe for the Eleventh Year of the Reign of King Henry the Second (A.D. 1164–1165) (London: Publications of the Pipe Roll Society, 1887).

Greimas, A.J. *Dictionnaire de l'ancien francais jusqu'au milieu du XIVe siecle* (Paris: Librarie Larousse, 1968).

Grew, F.O., et al. *Medieval Finds from Excavations in London 1: Knives and Scabbards.* ed. J. Cowgill, M. de Neergaard and N. Griffiths (Woodbridge, UK and Rochester, NY: Boydell, 2011 [1987]).

Gross, Charles, ed. *Select Cases Concerning the Law Merchant (AD 1270–1638).* Vol. 1, *Local Courts.* Selden Society 23 (London: Bernard Quaritch, 1908), 29–30.

Gunn, Michael, and David Ormerod. "Despite the Law: Prize-Fighting and Professional Boxing." *Law and Sport in Contemporary Society.* ed. Steve Greenfield and Guy Osborn (London: Frank Cass, 2000), 21–50.

Haddon, Celia. *The First Ever English Olimpick Games* (London: Hodder & Stoughton, 2004).

Hahn, Thomas. "The Turk and Sir Gawain." *Sir Gawain: Eleven Romances and Tales* (Kalamazoo, MI: Medieval Institute Publications, 1995), 337–358.

Hailwood, Mark. *Alehouses and Good Fellowship in Early Modern England* (Woodbridge, UK: Boydell, 2014).

Hall, Edward. "The Triumphant Reigne of Kyng Henry the VIII." [Edward Hall], *The Vnion of the Two Noble and Illustre Famelies of Lancastre & Yorke. Beginning at the Tyme of Kyng Henry the Fowerth, the first aucthor of this deuision, and so successiuely proceadyng to the reigne of the high and prudent prince Kyng Henry the Eight, the vndubiate flower and very heire of both the said linages* (London,1548). Otherwise known as Hall, Edward, *Hall's Chronicle* (London: J. Johnson et al., 1809).

Hall, G.D.G., ed. *The Treatise on the Laws and Customs of the Realm of England Commonly Called Glanvill* (Holmes Beach, FL: Wm. W. Gaunt and Sons, 1983 [1965]).

Hanawalt, Barbara A. *Crime and Conflict in English Communities, 1300–1348* (Cambridge, MA: Harvard University Press, 1979).

Harman, Thomas. *A Caveat or Warning for Common Cursitors Vulgarly Called Vagabonds* (1566), reprinted in Gamini Salgado, ed., *Cony-Catchers and Bawdy Baskets: An Anthology of Elizabethan Low Life* (Hammondsworth, UK: Penguin, 1972).

[Harvey, Richard]. *Plaine Percevall the Peace-Maker of England, Sweetly Indevoring with his blunt persuasions to botch vp a Reconciliation between Mar-Ton and Mar-tother* ([London]: Printed in Broad-Streete at the signe of the Pack-staffe, [1590]).

Haskins, Charles Homer. *The Renaissance of the Twelfth Century* (New York: World Publishing, 1967 [1927]).

Hassall, W.O. "Plays at Clerkenwell." *Modern Language Review* 33, no. 4 (October 1938): 564–567.

Hatmaker, Mark. *Boxer's Bible of Counterpunching: The Killer Response to Any Attack* (San Diego, CA: Tracks, 2012).

Heaney, Seamus. *Beowulf: A New Verse Translation* (London: W.W. Norton, 2000).

Heath, Robert. *A Natural and Historical Account of the Islands of Scilly and a General Account of Cornwall* (London: R. Manby and H.S. Cox, 1750).

Heinz, W.C., and Nathan Ward. *The Book of Boxing* (Kingston, NY: Total Sports Illustrated Classics, 1999).

Helmholz, R.H., ed. *Select Cases on Defamation to 1600*. Selden Society 101 (London, 1985).

Henderson, Robert W. *Ball, Bat and Bishop* (Urbana and Chicago: University of Illinois Press, 2001 [1947]).

Henricks, Thomas S. *Disputed Pleasures: Sport and Society in Preindustrial England* (New York: Greenwood, 1991).

Hentzner, Paul. *Travels in England during the Reign of Queen Elizabeth*. Ed. and trans. Horace, late Earl of Oxford (London: Edward Jeffrey, 1797).

Hernandez, Manuel, et al. "Boxer's Fracture." emedicinehealth.com/boxers_fracture/page2_em.htm. Seen January 26, 2017.

Herzman, Ronald B., Graham Drake and Eve Salisbury, eds. *Four Romances of England: King Horn, Havelok the Dane, Bevis of Hampton, Athelston*. The Consortium for the Teaching of the Middle Ages (TEAMS) Middle English Texts Series (Kalamazoo: Western Michigan University, 1999).

"High Court Voids Ban on Sports Gambling." *Wall Street Journal*. May 15, 2018, A1.

Hiller, Delbert R. "Covenant." *The Encyclopedia of Religion*. Ed. Mircea Eliade, Vol. 4 (New York: Macmillan, 1987), 133–137.

Hindley, A., F.W. Langley, and B. Levy. *Old French–English Dictionary* (Cambridge: Cambridge University Press, 2000).

Holden, A.J., ed. *History of William Marshal* (c. 1219–1226). Occasional Publication Series 1, no. 4 (London: Anglo-Norman Text Society, 2002).

Horder, Jeremy. "The Duel and the English Law of Homicide." *Oxford Journal of Legal Studies* 12, no. 3 (Autumn 1992): 419–430.

Horman, William. *Vulgaria* (London: [Richard Pinion], 1519).

Hughes, Paul L., and James F. Larkin, eds. *Tudor Royal Proclamations*. Vol. 1: *Early Tudors (1485–1553)* (London: Yale University Press, 1964).

Huizinga, Johan. *Homo Ludens: A Study of the Play-Element in Culture* (Boston: Beacon, 1955 [1950]).

Huizinga, Johan. *The Waning of the Middle Ages* (Mineola, NY: Dover, 1999 [1924]).

"Hunt v. Bell." *The English Reports* 130, Common Pleas, Vol. 8, (Edinburgh: William Green & Sons, 1912), 1–3.

Hurnard, Naomi. *The King's Pardon for Homicide before 1307* (Oxford: Clarendon, 1969).

J.K.L. "Osborne, Peregrine 2nd Duke of Leeds (1658–1729)." *The Dictionary of National Biography*. Vol. 14 (Oxford: Oxford University Press, 1964).

Jackson, James L. *Three Elizabethan Fencing Manuals, Facsimile Reproductions with an Iintroduction* (Delmar, NY: Scholars Facsimiles & Reprints, 1972).

Jackson, Kenneth H. *The Oldest Irish Tradition: A Window on the Iron Age* (Cambridge: Cambridge University Press, 1964).

Jaouen, Guy, and Matthew Bennett Nichols. *Celtic Wrestling: The Jacket Styles* (St. Thonan, France: Federation Internationale des Luttes Associees, 2007).

Judges, A.V. *The Elizabethan Underworld* (New York: E.P. Dutton, 1930).

Kappauf, Catherine. "The Early Development of the Petty Jury." (Ph.D. diss., University of Illinois, 1973).

Kaye, J.M. "The Early History of Murder and Manslaughter." *Law Quarterly Review* 83, no. 43 (October 1967).

Keen, Maurice. *The Origins of the English Gentleman: Heraldry, Chivalry and Gentility in Medieval England (c. 1300–c. 1500)* (Stroud, UK: Tempus, 2002).

Kelso, Ruth. *The Doctrine of the English Gentleman in the Sixteenth Century* (Urbana: University of Illinois Press, 1929).

Kiernan, V.G. *The Duel in European History: Honour and the Reign of Aristocracy* (Oxford: Oxford University Press, 1988).

Kinsella, Thomas. *The Tain* (Oxford: Oxford University Press, 1969).

Kittredge, George Lyman. *A Study of Gawain and the Green Knight* (Gloucester, MA: Peter Smith, 1960 [1916]).

Knight, Stephen. "The Tale of Gamelyn." *Medieval Outlaws: Ten Tales in Modern English.* ed. Thomas H. Ohlgren (Phoenix Mills, UK: Sutton, 1998).

Knight, Stephen, and Thomas Ohlgren, eds. *Robin Hood and Other Outlaw Tales.* TEAMS Middle English Texts Series (Kalamazoo: Western Michigan University, 1997).

Koch, H.W. *Medieval Warfare* (New York: Crescent, 1983 [1978]).

Kolbing, Eugen, ed. *The Romance of Sir Beues of Hamtoun.* EETS, Extra Series (ES), multiple vols. (London, 1885–1894).

Krishna, Valerie, ed. *The Alliterative Morte Arthure: A Critical Edition* (New York: Burt Franklin, 1976).

Kurath, Hans, and Sherman M. Kuhn, eds. *Middle English Dictionary* (Ann Arbor: University of Michigan Press, 1957).

Lake, Peter. *Anglicans and Puritans? Presbyterianism and English Conformist Thought from Whitgift to Hooker* (London: Unwin Hyman, 1988).

Larkin, James F., and Paul L. Hughes, eds. *Stuart Royal Proclamations.* Vol. 1: *Royal Proclamations of King James I, 1603–1625* (Oxford: Clarendon, 1973).

Larkin, Peter, ed. *Richard Coer de Lyon.* TEAMS Middle English Texts Series (Kalamazoo: Medieval Institute Publications, Western Michigan University, 2015).

Lea, Henry C. *The Duel and the Oath* (Philadelphia: University of Pennsylvania Press, 1974 [1866]).

Lea, Henry C. *Superstition and Force* (New York: Greenwood, 1968 [1892]).

le Blanc, L'Abbe [Jean Bernard]. "Letter to the Chevalier de B [...]." *Letters on the English and French Nations.* Vol. 2 (London: J. Brindley, 1747).

Lee, Hugh M. "The *caestus* in the Sixteenth Century: Brant, Raphael, Mercuriale, and Ligorio." *Nikephoros* 18 (2005): 207–217.

Le Guin, Ursula K. *A Wizard of Earthsea* (Berkeley, CA: Parnassus, 1968).

Levins, Peter. *Manipulus Vocabulorum: A Rhyming Dictionary of the English Language*, ed. Henry B. Wheatley (London: Early English Text Society, 1867 [1570]).

Lewis, Charlton T., and Charles Short. *A Latin Dictionary* (Oxford: Clarendon, 1962 [1879]).

Lewis, Marjorie Dunlavy. "Shakespeare's Uses of the Duelling Code for Comic and Satiric Effect." (Ph.D. diss., University of Kansas, 1967).

Lindholm, David, and Ulf Karlsson. *The Bare-Knuckle Boxer's Companion: Learning How to Hit Hard and Train Tough from the Early Boxing Masters* (Boulder, CO: Paladin, 2009).

London Journal. January 16, 1725.

Loomis, Roger Sherman. *Celtic Myth and Arthurian Romance* (New York: Columbia University Press, 1927).

L.S. "Osborne, Sir Thomas, Duke of Leeds (1631–1712)." *The Dictionary of National Biography.* Vol. 14 (Oxford: Oxford University Press, 1964).

Lucas, Theophilus. *Memoirs of the Lives, Intrigues, and Comical Adventures of the most Famous Gamesters and Celebrated Shapers in the Reigns of Charles II, James II, William III and Queen Anne, wherein is Contained the Secret History of Gaming.* (London: James Brown and Ferdinando Burleigh, 1714).

Lydgate, John. *Fabula duorum mercantorum and Guy of Warwyk.* Ed. Pamela Farvolden,

TEAMS Middle English Texts Series (Kalamazoo, MI: Medieval Institute Publications, 2016).
Lyly, John. *The Complete Works of John Lyly.* Collected by R. Warwick Bond (Oxford: Clarendon, 1902).
Lyly, John. *Pap with an Hatchet: An Annotated Modern-Spelling Edition.* Ed. Leah Scragg (Manchester, UK: Manchester University Press, 2015).
Macaulay, G.C., ed. *The English Works of John Gower.* Vol. 1: *Confessio Amantis,* EETS, ES (London, 1900).
Macaulay, Thomas Babington. *Macaulay's History of England.* Vol. 1, Everyman's Library (London: J.M. Dent and Sons, 1957 [1848]).
Magraken, Eric. "Prize Fighting persecutions Prosecutions and Combat Sports in Canada." *Combat Sports Law,* http://combatsportslaw.com/2013/07/29/combat-sports-in-canada-and-prize-fighting-criminal-code-prosecutions/.
Magriel, Paul. *A Bibliography of Boxing: A Chronological Check List of Books in English Printed before 1900* (Mansfield Center, CT: Martino, 2002).
Maitland, Frederic W., ed. *Select Pleas of the Crown.* Vol. 1: *AD 1200–1225,* Selden Society 192 (London: Bernard Quaritch, 1888).
Maitland, Frederic W., and Francis C. Montague. *A Sketch of English Legal History.* Ed. and with notes by James F. Colby (London: G.P. Putnam's and Sons, 1915).
Malcolm, James Peller. *Anecdotes of the Manners and Customs of London during the Eighteenth Century.* Vol. 1 (London: Longman, Hurst, Rees and Orme, 1810).
Malcolmson, Robert W. *Popular Recreations in English Society, 1700–1850* (Cambridge: Cambridge University Press, 1973).
The Malefactor's Register, or, the Newgate and Tyburn Calendar (London: Alexander Hogg, [1778]).
Marciano, Rocky. "How It Feels to be Champ." *The Book of Boxing.* Ed. W.C. Heinz and Nathan Ward (Kingston, NY: Total Sports Illustrated Classics, 1999), 218–225.
Marples, Morris. *A History of Football* (London: Secker & Warburg, 1954).
Matson, Garfield. "Holmgang: Its Use, Abuse, and Fictionalization." stavacademy.co.uk. Seen August 30, 2016.

Maxwell, Baldwin. *Studies in Beaumont, Fletcher, and Massinger* (Chapel Hill: University of North Carolina Press, 1939).
Mayhew, A.L., ed. *The Promptorium Parvulorum. The First English-Latin Dictionary,* c. A.D. 1440, EETS, ES (London, 1908).
McCollum, Linda. "Rocco Bonetti." *Fight Master: The Journal of the Society of American Fight Directors* 9 (May 1986): 13–17.
McCoy, Allison N., and Michael L. Platt. "Risk-Sensitive Neurons in Macaque Posterior Cingulated Cortex." *Nature Neuroscience* 8 (2005): 1220–1227.
McEvedy, Colin, and Richard Jones. *Atlas of World Population History* (Hammondsworth, UK: Penguin, 1978).
McKerrow, Ronald B., ed. *The Works of Thomas Nashe* (Oxford: Basil Blackwell, 1966).
Mee, Bob. *Bare Fists: A History of Bare-Knuckle Prize-Fighting* (New York: Overlook, 2001).
Mercvrialis, Hieronymus. *De Arte Gymnastica, Libri Sex* (Venice: Apud Ivntas, 1601).
Michell, E.B. "Boxing and Sparring." Walter H. Pollock et al. *Fencing, Boxing and Wrestling.* Badminton Library of Sports and Pastimes (London: Longman, Green, 1902).
Mihm, Madelyn Timmel, ed. *The Songe d'Enfer of Raoul de Houdenc: An Edition Based on all the Extant Manuscripts* (Tübingen, Germany: Max Niemeyer, 1984).
Miles, Henry Downes. *Pugilistica: The History of British Boxing.* 3 vols. (Edinburgh: John Grant, 1906).
Million, Elmer. "The Enforceability of Prize Fight Statutes." *Kentucky Law Journal* 27, no. 2 (January 1939): 152–168.
Million, Elmer. "History of the Texas Prize Fight Statute." *Texas Law Journal* 17, no. 2 (February 1939): 152–159.
Mills, Maldwyn, ed. *Horn Childe and Maiden Rimnild* (Heidelberg, Germany: Carl Winter, Universitätsverlag, 1988).
Misson, M. [Henri]. *Memoirs and Observations in his Travels over England with some account of Scotland and Ireland.* trans. Mr. Ozell (London: D. Brown, etc., 1719).
[Moelmuiri mac Mic Cuinn Na M-Bocht]. *Fled Bricrend: The Feast of Bricriu.* Ed. George Henderson, Vol. 2 (London: Irish Texts Society, 1899).

More, Thomas. *Utopia*. Trans. and ed. H.V.S. Ogden (New York: Appleton-Century-Crofts, 1949 [1516]).

Morgan, Michael H., and David R. Carrier. "Protective Buttressing of the Human Fist and the Evolution of Hominin Hands." *Journal of Experimental Biology* 215 (2013): 236–244.

Morley, Henry. *Memoirs of Bartholomew's Fair* (Detroit, Michigan: Singing Tree, 1968 [London: Chatto and Windus, 1880]).

Mouratidis, John. "The Origin of Nudity in Greek Athletics." *Journal of Sport History* 12, no. 3 (Winter 1985): 213–232.

Mulcaster, Richard. *Positions Concerning the Training Up of Children*. Ed. William Barker (Toronto: University of Toronto Press, 1994 [1581]).

"The Names of God." *The Interpreter's Bible in Twelve Volumes*. George Arthur Buttrick, ed., Vol. 1 (New York and Nashville: Abingdon, 1952).

Nashe, Thomas [?], *A Countercuffe given to Martin Junior: by the venturous, hardie, and renowned Pasquill of England, Cavaliero*. In *The Works of Thomas Nashe*. Ed. Ronald B. McKerrow, multiple vols. (Oxford: Basil Blackwell, 1966).

Neilson, George. *Trial by Combat* (Clark, NJ: Lawbook Exchange, 2009 [1890]).

Niermeyer, J.R. *Mediae Latinitatis Lexicon Minus* (Leiden, The Netherlands: E.J. Brill, 1984).

Noble, Mark. *Memoirs of the Protectorate-House of Cromwell*. Vol. 1 (Birmingham, UK: Pearson and Rollason, 1784).

North, Sally. "The Ideal Knight as Presented in Some French Narrative Poems, c. 1090–c. 1240: An Outline Sketch." *The Ideals and Practice of Medieval Knighthood*. ed. Christopher Harper-Bill and Ruth Harvey (Dover, NH: Boydell, 1986).

Oliver, Lisi. "Legal Documentation and the Practice of English Law." *The Cambridge History of Early Medieval English Literature*. Ed. Clare A. Lees (Cambridge: Cambridge University Press, 2013), 499–500.

Opler, Morris Edward. *Myths and Tales of the Jicarilla Apache Indians*. Memoirs of the American Folklore Society 31 (New York: American Folk-Lore Society, G.E. Stechert, 1938), 128–136.

Page, William, ed. *Three Early Assize Rolls for the County of Northumberland, Saec. XIII*. Publications of the Surtees Society, Vol. 88 (Durham, UK: Andrews, 1891).

Palsgrave, John. *L'eclarissement de la langue francaise (1530)*. Ed. Susan Baddeley, *Textes de la Renaissence: Serie Traites sur la langue francaise*. no. 69 (Paris: Honore Champion, 2003).

Pallante v. Stadiums Pty Ltd (No.1), Victorian Reports 331.

Paris, Matthew. *The Illustrated Chronicles of Matthew Paris: Observations of Thirteenth-Century Life*. Trans. and ed. Richard Vaughn (Corpus Christi College, Cambridge: Alan Sutton, 1993).

Parkyns, Thomas of Bunny. *The Inn-Play or Cornish-Hugg* (1727), transcribed by Ken Pfrenger and Shannon Pfrenger, http://neohemas.wordpress.com/library/The-Inn-Play-or-Cornish-Hugg-Wrestler-by-Sir-Thomas-Parkyns-of-Bunny-Baronet/. Seen October 10, 2017.

Parpworth, Neil. "Boxing and Prize Fighting: The Indistinguishable Distinguished?" *Sport and the Law Journal* 2 (Spring 1994): 5–8.

Peacham, Henry. *The Complete Gentleman, The Truth of Our Times*. and *The Art of Living in London*, ed. Virgil B. Heltzel (Ithaca, NY: Published for the Folger Shakespearian Library by Cornell University Press, 1962 [1622]).

Pearce, Roger. "When Were the Olympic Games Abolished?" http://www.roger-pearce.com/weblog/2012/08/04/when-were-the-olympic-games-abolished.

Pellegrini, Anthony D. "Rough and Tumble Play from Childhood through Adolescence: Development and Possible Functions." *Blackwell Handbook of Childhood Social Development*. Ed. Peter K. Smith and Craig H. Hart (Oxford: Blackwell, 2002), 438–453.

Peltonen, Markku. *The Duel in Early Modern England: Civility, Politeness and Honour* (Cambridge: Cambridge University Press, 2003).

Pepys, Samuel. *The Diary of Samuel Pepys*. ed. Robert Latham and William Matthews, 11 vols. (London: G. Bell and Sons, 1970–1983).

Perlin, Stephen. *A Description of England and Scotland* (1558), in James Beeverell, *The Pleasures of London*, trans. and ed. W.H. Quarrell (London: Witherby, 1940).

Plunkitt, George Washington. "Honest Graft and Dishonest Graft." (1905), panarchy.org/plunkitt/graft.1905.html.
Poliakoff, Michael B. *Combat Sports in the Ancient World: Competition, Violence and Culture* (New Haven and London: Yale University Press, 1987).
"Prize." *Halsbury's Statutes of England and Wales.* Vol. 34, 4th ed. (London: LexisNexis UK, 2004), 1125–1157.
Pruetz, J.D., et al. "New Evidence on the Tool-Assisted Hunting Exhibited by Chimpanzees (*Pan troglodytes verus*) in a Savannah Habitat at Fongoli, Senegal." *Royal Society Open Science* (2015): 2.
"*Regina v. Coney.*" *Ohio Law Journal* 3 (1882).
Rennie, John. "Evolved Fists or the Best Weapons at Hand." blogs.plos.org/retort/ 2013/02/26/evolved-fists-or-the-best-weapons-at-hand/.
Revised Statutes of Canada, 1985, Vol. 3, Criminal Code, part 2, C-46, sect. 83.
Rex v. Billingham, Savage, and Skinner, The English Reports 172 (Nisi Prius) Vol. 3 106 ([Edinburgh]: Carswell, 1928).
Rex v. Higginson (1762). The English Reports 92 (King's Bench Division) Vol. 26 (Edinburgh and London: Wm. Green and Sons, 1909), 806.
Rex v. Perkins and Others, The English Reports 172 (Nisi Prius) Vol. 3 ([Edinburgh]: Carswell, 1928), 814–815.
Rey, Alain. *Dictionnaire historique de la langue Francaise* (Paris: Dictionnaire Le Robert, 1993).
"Richard Harvey." *Oxford Dictionary of National Biography.* Vol. 25 (Oxford: Oxford University Press, 2004), 674–676.
Riess, Steven A. "Only the Ring was Square: Frankie Carbo and the Underworld Control of American Boxing." *International Journal of the History of Sport* 5, no. 1 (1988): 29–52.
Riley, Henry Thomas, ed. and trans. *Memorials of London and London Life in the XIIIth, XIVth, and XVth Centuries, being a series of extracts from the Early Archives of the City of London* (London: Longmans, Green, 1868).
Riley, Henry Thomas, ed. *Munimenta Gildhalle Londoniensis; Liber Albus, Liber Custumarum, et Liber Horn, Liber Albus.* Roll Series, *Rerum Britannicarum Medii Aevi Scriptores*, multiple vols. (London: Longman, Brown, Green, Longmans, and Roberts, 1859).
Roberts, Randy. "Eighteenth Century Boxing." *Journal of Sport History* 4, no. 3 (Fall 1977): 246–259.
Robinson, F.N., ed. *The Works of Geoffrey Chaucer.* 2nd ed. (Boston: Houghton Mifflin, 1957).
Rogers, James. "Ancient Roman Boxing Gloves Discovered Near Hadrian's Wall." *Fox News*, February 21, 2018, foxnews.com/ science/2018/02/21/ancient-roman-boxing-gloves-discovered-near-hadrians-wall.html.
Role, Raymond E. "The War Games of Central Italy." *History Today.* June 6, 1999, historytoday.com/raymond-e-role/war-games-central-italy/. Seen December 3, 2017.
"Roman Boxing Gloves." archaeology.org/ news/6389-180220-roman-boxing-gloves.
"Roman Boxing Gloves Unearthed by Vindolandia Dig." *BBC News.* February 20 2018, bbc.com/news/uk-england-tyne-43120942.
Romance of the Turk and Sir Gawaine (circa 1500).
Rosenbaum, Stacy, personal correspondence, June 25, 2018.
Rosenbaum, Stacy, et al. "Observations of Severe and Lethal Coalitionary Attacks in Wild Mountain Gorillas." *Scientific Reports* 6, 37018 (2016), 1–8, doi: 10.1038/ srep 37018.
Rosenthal, Joel T. *Nobles and the Noble Life: 1295–1500* (London: George Allen & Unwin, 1976).
Rothwell, Harold, ed. "Form for Keeping the Peace, 1242." *English Historical Documents, 1189–1327* 3, no. 3 (New York: Oxford University Press, 1975), 357–359.
Russell, M.J. "Hired Champions." *American Journal of Legal History* 3, no. 3 (July 1959): 242–259.
Ruzicki, Tim. "From BareKnuckles to Modern Boxing: How Gloves Have Changed the Art of Pugilism." savateaustralia.com.
Ruzicki, Tim. Personal correspondence, December 20, 2006.
Rye, William B. *England as Seen by Foreigners in the Days of Elizabeth and James the First* (New York: Benjamin Blom, 1967 [1865]).
Rymer, Thomas. *Foedera.* 2nd ed. (London: J. Tonson, 1727).

Salgado, Gamini. *Cony-Catchers and Bawdy Baskets: An Anthology of Elizabethan Low Life* (Hammondsworth, UK: Penguin, 1972).

Salgado, Gamini. *The Elizabethan Underworld* (Phoenix Mill, UK: Sutton, 2005 [1977]).

Saviolo, Vincentio. *Vincentio Saviolo, His Practice. In two Bookes* (London: [John Wolfe] 1595 [1594]), in *Three Elizabethan Fencing Manuals*, intro. and ed. James L. Jackson (Delmar, NY: Scholars Facsimiles & Reprints, 1972).

Sayles, G.O., ed. *Select Cases in the Court of the King's Bench under Richard II, Henry IV and Henry V.* Selden Society, multiple vols. (London: Bernard Quaritch, 1971).

Schmidt, Herbert. *The Book of the Buckler* ([Derby?], UK: Wyvern Media, 2015).

Schwartz, David G. *Roll the Bones: The History of Gambling* (New York: Gotham, 2006).

Schwartz, Richard B. *Daily Life in Johnson's London* (Madison: University of Wisconsin Press, 1983).

Scott, Eric, and Jaak Penksepp. "Rough-and-Tumble Play in Human Children." *Aggressive Behavior* 29 (2003): 539–551.

Shakespeare, William. *As You Like It* (1603).

Shakespeare, William. *Henry IV* (1598).

Shakespeare, William. *Measure for Measure* (1604).

Shakespeare, William. *Merchant of Venice* (1596–1597).

Sharpe, J.A. *Crime in Early Modern England 1550–1750* (New York: Longman, 1984).

Shaw, William A. *The Knights of England.* Vol. 1 (Baltimore: Genealogical Publishing Company, 1971).

Sheard, Kenneth G. "Aspects of Boxing in the Western 'Civilizing Process.'" *International Review of Sociology of Sport* 32 (March 1997): 31–57.

Shubin, Daniel H. *A History of Russian Christianity.* Vol. 1 (New York: Algora, 2004).

Silver, George. "A Briefe Note of Three Italian Teachers of Offence." (London: Edward Blount, 1599). Reprinted in *Three Elizabethan Fencing Manuals*. Ed. and intro., James J. Jackson (Delmar, NY: Scholars Facsimiles and Reprints, 1972).

Silver, George. *Paradoxes of Defence* (London: Edward Blount, 1599). Reprinted in *Three Elizabethan Fencing Manuals*. ed. and intro James J. Jackson (Delmar, NY: Scholars Facsimiles and Reprints, 1972).

Simpson, J.A., and E.S.C. Weiner. *The Oxford English Dictionary.* 2nd ed. (Oxford: Clarendon, 1989).

Smith, Peter K., Rebecca Smees, and Anthony D. Pellegrini. "Play Fighting and Real Fighting: Using Video Playback Methodology with Young Children." *Aggressive Behavior* 30 (2004): 164–173.

Sorbiere, [Samuel]. *A Voyage to England Containing many Things relating to the State of Learning, Religion, and other Curiosities of that Kingdom* (London: J. Woodward 1709 [1664]).

Speck, W.A. "William Augustus, Prince, Duke of Cumberland (1721–1765)." *Oxford Dictionary of National Biography.* Vol. 59 (Oxford: Oxford University Press, 2004), 105–113.

Spenser, Edmund. *The Fairie Queen.* ed. George Armstrong Wauchope (New York: Macmillan, 1922).

"Sports." *Wall Street Journal.* Tuesday, May 15, 2018, A12.

Squibb, G.D. *The High Court of Chivalry: A Study in the Civil Law of England* (Oxford: Clarendon, 1959).

"States Eager to Bank on Sports Betting." *Wall Street Journal.* April 9, 2018, A3.

"Statute of Winchester (1285)." *English Historical Documents, 1189–1327.* Ed. Harry Rothwell, Vol. 3 (1975), no. 33, 357–359 and no. 59, 460–462.

Statutes at Large, from the Magna Charta to the end of the tenth year of George III inclusive (London: Mark Baskett, 1769–1771).

Statutes of the Realm, multiple vols. (London: Printed by command of His Majesty King George the Third, 1810–1824).

Stephen, James Fitzjames. *A History of the Criminal Law of England.* 3 vols. (London: Macmillan, 1883).

Stephen, William Fitz. *Norman London* (New York: Italica, 1990).

Stimming, A., ed. *Der Anglonormannische Boeve de Haumtone.* In *Bibliotheca Normannica.* Vol. 7 (Halle, Germany: Niemeyer, 1899).

Stokvis, Ruud. "Sports and Civilization: Is Violence the Central Problem?" *Sport and Leisure in the Civilizing Process: Critique and Counter-Critique.* Ed. Eric Dunning and Chris Rojek (Toronto and Buffalo:

University of Toronto Press, 1992), 123–136.
Stone, Lawrence. *The Crisis of the Aristocracy, 1558–1641*. Orig. ed. (Oxford: Clarendon Press, 1965), abridged ed. (London: Oxford University Press, 1967).
Stone, Louise W., and William Rothwell. *Anglo-Norman Dictionary* (London: Modern Humanities Research Association, 1977).
Stow, John. *The Annales of England ... from the first inhabitation vntil this present yeere 1592* (London, [1592]).
Stow, John. *A Survey of London (1603)* (Oxford: Clarendon, 1908 [1603]).
Struna, Nancy. "Puritans and Sport: The Irretrievable Tide of Change." *Journal of Sport History* 4, no. 1 (Spring 1977): 1–21.
Strutt, Joseph. *The Sports and Pastimes of the English People*, ed. and enlarged by J. Charles Cox (London: Methuen, 1903 [1801]).
Stubbs, William, ed. *Select Charters and Other Illustrations of English Constitutional History*. 8th ed. (Oxford: Clarendon, 1905).
Studley, John. *The fourth and most ruthful tragedy of L. Annaeus Seneca entituled Hyppolytus* (London: Thomas Marsh, 1581).
Summerskill, Edith. *The Ignoble Art* (London: William Heinemann, 1956).
Swanton, Michael, trans. "*Gesta Herewardi* (The Deeds of Hereward)." *Medieval Outlaws: Ten Tales in Modern English*. Ed. Thomas H. Ohlgren (Phoenix Mills, UK: Sutton, 1998).
Thomas, A.H., ed. *Calendar of Plea and Memoranda Rolls of the Corporation of the City of London at the Guildhall, 1364–1381* (Cambridge: Cambridge University Press, 1926).
Thomas, Hugh M. "The *Gesta Herwardi*, the English, and their Conquerors." *Anglo-Norman Studies* 21, ed. Christopher Harper-Bill (1998): 213–232.
Thorne, Samuel E., and J.H. Baker, eds. *Readings and Moots at the Inns of Court in the Fifteenth Century*. Multiple vols. (London: Selden Society, 1990).
Thuillier, Jean Paul. "La nudite athletique, le pagne et les Etrusques." *Nikephoros* 17 (2004): 171–180.
Tolkien, J.R.R., and E.V. Gordon, ed. *Sir Gawain and the Green Knight*. 2nd ed., revised by Norman Davis (Oxford: Clarendon, 1967).
Toller, T. Northcote, ed. *An Anglo-Saxon Dictionary Supplement* (London: Oxford University Press, 1966 [1921]).
Trench, Charles Chenevix. *The Poacher and the Squire: A History of Poaching and Game Preservation in England* (London: Longmans and Green, 1967).
True Protestant Mercury: or Occurrences Foreign and Domestick. No. 103, December 28–December 31, 1681, 2.
Turner, Craig, and Tony Soper. *Methods and Practice of Elizabethan Swordplay* (Carbondale: Southern Illinois University Press, 1990).
Twiss, Travers, ed. *Monumenta Juridica. The Black Book of the Admiralty*. Appendix, part 2, Roll Series. *Rerum Britannicarum Medii Aevi Scriptores*. Vol. 55 (London: Kraus Reprint, 1965).
Underwood, Marion K. "Sticks and Stones and Social Exclusion: Aggression among Girls and Boys." *Blackwood Handbook*, 533–548.
Underwood, Richard. *Anglo-Saxon Weapons and Warfare* (Stroud, UK: Tempus, 1999).
United Nations Office on Drugs and Crime. *Global Study on Homicide Report*. (Vienna: United Nations Office on Drugs and Crime).
Unterharnscheidt, Frederich, and Julia TaylorUnterharnscheidt. *Boxing: Medical Aspects* (London: Academic Press, 2003).
Urbanski, Charity, *Writing History for the King: Henry II and the Politics of Vernacular Historiography* (Ithaca, NY: Cornell University Press, 2013).
Valavanis, Panos. *Great Moments in Greek Archaeology* (Los Angeles: J. Paul Getty Museum, 2007).
Veblen, Thorstein, *The Theory of the Leisure Class: An Economic Study of Institutions* (New York: Mentor, 1953 [1899]).
von Uffenbach, Zacharias Conrad. *London in 1710: From the Travels of Zacharias Conrad von Uffenbach*. ed. W.H. Quarrell and Margaret Mare (London: Faber & Faber, 1934).
Wacquant, Loic J.D. "The Pugilistic Point of View: How Boxers Think and Feel about Their Trade." *Theory and Society* 24, no. 4 (August 1995): 489–535.
Ward, Estelle Frances. *Christopher Monck,*

Duke of Albermarle (London: John Murray, 1915).

Warner, George, ed. *Queen Mary's Psalter: Miniatures and Drawings by an English Artist of the 14th Century, Reproduced from Royal MS. 2 B.VII in the British Museum* (London: British Museum, 1912).

Watson, Alan, trans. *The Digest of Justinian*. Vol. 1 (Philadelphia: University of Pennsylvania Press, 1998 [1985]).

Weinbaum, Martin, ed. *The London Eyre of 1276* (London: London Record Society, 1976).

Whitfield, Christopher, ed. *Robert Dover and the Cotswold Games: Annalia Dubrensia* (London: Henry Sotheran, 1962).

Wiggins, Alison, ed. *Stanzaic Guy of Warwick*. TEAMS Middle English Text Series (Kalamazoo, MI: Medieval Institute Publications, 2004).

Wilkes, G.A., ed. *The Complete Plays of Ben Jonson* (Oxford: Clarendon, 1981).

"William Ward, Killing: Murder, 3rd June, 1789." *The Proceedings of the Old Bailey, 1674–1913*. Ref. t17890603-17, oldbaileyonline.org.

Williams, C.H. *Yearbooks of Henry VI: 1 Henry VI (AD 1422)*. Selden Society 50 (London: Quaritch, 1933).

Woodbine, George E., ed. *Bracton, De legibus et consuetudinibus Angliae*. Trans. Samuel E. Thorne, 4 vols. (Cambridge, MA: Belknap Press of Harvard University Press, 1968).

Woody, Christopher, *Business Insider*. November 1, 2016.

"Wrestling." *The Victoria History of the Countries of England: Lancashire*. Vol. 2 (London: Institute of Historical Research, University of London, 1966 [1908]), 499–500.

Wright, A.R. *British Calendar Customs: England*. Multiple vols. (London: Folk-Lore Society, 1936–1938).

Wright, William Aldis, ed. *The Metrical Chronicle of Robert of Gloucester* (London: Eyre and Spottiswoode, 1887).

Wright, William Aldis. "The Squire Papers." *English Historical Review* 1 (1886): 311–348.

Wriothesley, Charles. *A Chronicle of England during the Reigns of the Tudors, from AD 1485 to 1559*. Ed. William Douglas Hamilton, Camden Society (Westminster, 1877).

Wu, Bin, Xingdong Li, and Yu Gongbao. *Essentials of Chinese Wushu* (Beijing: Foreign Languages Press, 1992).

Wulfing, Ernst J., ed. *The Laud Troy Book* (London: EETS and Kegan Paul, Trench, Tubner, 1902 [c. 1400]).

Yong, Ed. "Scientific Punch Up over Idea That Our Hands Evolved to Fight." *National Geographic*. December 19, 2012.

Yonick, A. "Covenant (in the Bible)." *The New Catholic Encyclopedia*. Vol. 4, 2nd ed. (Detroit: Thomson Gale, 2003), 324–328.

Zupitza, Julius, ed., *The Romance of Guy of Warwick*. EETS, ES 59 (London, 1891), 528.

Zupitza, Julius, ed. *The Romance of Guy of Warwick*. EETS, ES 42 (London, 1883), Auchinleck Ms.

Index

Alehouse 70, 100
Anglo-Saxon culture 20-21, 26-27, 29, 50-51, 95

Belt-wrestling (West Country) 4
Beowulf 6, 20, 95-96, 105
Blackstone, William 132-133, 136, 141, 148
Bonetti, Rocco 64, 75, 96
Boxing rules 1, 9-13, 16, 23, 24, 26, 42, 46-50, 63, 80, 100, 107, 114, 116-117, 119, 120-121, 123, 125, 126, 129, 142, 145, 152
Bramble, Bartholomew 65-66, 143
Broughton, John 63, 86, 116, 183
Broughton's rules 126, 127
Buffet, history of 11, 12, 13, 16, 17, 19, 20, 23-24, 26, 35-36, 38, 40-45, 48, 67-68, 72, 83, 84, 92; pluck buffet 153-155

Caestus fighting in England 155-159
Challenge 11, 14, 16, 19, 37, 46, 69, 72, 82, 85, 104, 136-138
Champions 14, 54, 56, 57, 58, 79, 116, 117
Chaucer, Geoffrey 22, 28-29, 134
Code of Courtesy 25, 72, 77-78, 85
Cotswold Olympics 108, 111, 112, 113
Covenant, religious 12-19, 23, 94-95, 153, 155
Cromwell, Oliver 160-161
Crowd 8-9, 15, 43-45, 46-47, 49, 63, 64, 71, 79, 80-81, 96, 100, 107, 116, 120-121, 125-127, 129-130, 137, 139, 147-148

Dover, Robert 108, 112, 113
Duel of Honor 25, 46, 72, 79-81, 85, 96, 101, 104, 130, 143

Ear Cloute 26

Egan, Pierce 50, 63, 101, 103-104, 106, 127-128, 143

Fair Play 64, 88, 92-107, 121, 138
"The "Fancy" 115, 116, 121, 127, 128, 131
The Feast of Bricriu (c. 875-1106) 14, 15, 16, 23, 94
Fencing history 43, 45, 51, 52, 53, 54-55, 58, 59, 65-67, 74-76, 85-86, 106, 130-136, 144, 175-177, 182-183
Figg, James 81, 105, 117-119, 139.144, 147, 183
Fist-fighting, history of 6, 7, 11, 23-24, 25, 26-27, 31, 32, 35-36, 39, 45, 49, 50, 51, 53, 62, 63, 71, 72-73, 75, 79, 83, 84, 86, 88, 92, 105, 112, 149, 156
Fisticuffs 100, 103, 108, 112-113, 116, 158, 160

Gambling 46, 63, 110, 117, 121, 122, 123-131, 142
Geoffrey of Monmouth 21, 96
Gesta Herewardi (c. 1109-1174) 21, 26, 36, 39, 95
Godfrey, Captain John 7-8, 118-119, 140-141, 144
Grammaticus, Saxo 15, 23, 24, 25

Harvey, Richard 66-67, 70, 71, 92-94, 107
Holmganga 13, 15-16, 46
Honor 12, 13, 15-16, 46, 63, 72, 77-87, 96, 98-99, 101, 104, 105, 119, 130, 133, 134, 136, 143, 155
Horman, William 24, 35, 38, 68
Hunt v. Bell 132, 149, 150, 174, 182

Judge, independent 14, 60-63, 77, 80, 84, 116, 149, 171, 176, 177, 180

Judicial Duel 15, 54, 60, 63, 78–80

Languages of England 20–22, 36, 40, 44, 45, 88, 93, 114, 137
Layaman's *Brut* (1199-1225) 27
Lyly, John 90, 91–93

Marprelate, Martin 66, 70, 88, 89–93, 105, 107, 108, 115
Masters of Defence 46, 58, 63, 64, 74–76, 80–81, 96, 100, 105, 126, 127, 135–137, 140, 143
Misson, Henri 64, 101, 103, 104, 105, 115–116, 120, 143

Norman history 20–21

Palsgrave, John 40, 50
Perrot, John 64
Personal weapons, use 28
Piers Plowman (1370-1390) 22
Plaine Percevall 66, 93
Presbyterian history 89–90, 110
Prizefighting, definition, history 67–68, 87, 121, 131, 132–161, 173, 177
Pugil 45, 51–59, 63, 69, 70, 74, 77, 108, 135–136, 143
Puritan history 82, 89, 107–110, 112, 161

Referee 80, 127
Regina v. Coney 148, 180
Rex v. Billingham 177
Rex v. Perkins 178–179, 182
Richard Coer de Lyon (c. 1325) 11, 13, 22, 23, 151, 155
Ring 15, 44, 46–49, 68–69, 80, 86, 94, 104, 116, 120, 127, 130, 142, 144, 147, 179

Rogues 50, 58, 63, 69–70, 84
Romance of Guy of Warwick (c. 1300-1330) 28, 96, 97, 134
The Romance of Sir Beues of Hamtoun (c. 1327) 28, 37
Ruffian 58–63, 70, 71, 103

Saviolo, Vincentio 63, 65–66, 75, 76, 99
Seconds 80, 84, 100–101, 137, 138, 148
Shadow boxing 66, 67
Shakespeare, William 24–25, 38, 40, 67–68, 71, 72, 98, 99, 103, 135, 140
Shaved Heads of Champions 79
Sir Gawain and the Green Knight (1350-1400) 13, 16–19, 22, 95, 155
Smithfield 42–45, 58, 59, 60, 93
Stripping for battle 8, 9, 48, 118
Sword and Buckler 41, 43, 44, 52, 54, 59, 63, 73, 75, 137, 140, 144
Sword-playing 64, 74, 132, 136, 144

Tudor history 34, 70, 73, 75, 88, 137
Turk and Sir Gawain 19, 24, 36, 72

Umpires 80, 126–127, 138

Ward, William legal case 87, 161–174
Wrestling 1, 3–5, 6, 8, 9, 10, 26, 36, 41, 43–45, 46, 47, 48, 49, 50, 51, 59, 61, 62, 68, 69, 73, 76, 80, 95–96, 100, 101, 105, 107, 108, 109, 112, 113, 120, 125, 126, 134, 135, 140, 142, 146, 157, 181, 182, 183

Yorke, Rowland 59, 75

www.ingramcontent.com/pod-product-compliance
Lightning Source LLC
Chambersburg PA
CBHW032038300426
44117CB00009B/1107